# MANAGERIAL DECISION MAKING

# MANAGERIAL DECISION MAKING

## A Guide to Successful Business Decisions

### *Alan J. Rowe*

University of Southern California

### *James D. Boulgarides*

California State University at Los Angeles

**Macmillan Publishing Company**
New York

**Maxwell Macmillan Canada**
Toronto

**Maxwell Macmillan International**
New York Oxford Singapore Sydney

Editor: Charles Stewart
Production Supervisor: Ann-Marie WongSam
Production Manager: Nick Sklitsis
Text Designer: Eileen Burke
Cover Designer: Robert Freese

This book was set in Times Roman by Publication Services
and was printed and bound by R. R. Donnelly & Sons.
The cover was printed by Phoenix Color Corp.

Macmillan Publishing Company
866 Third Avenue, New York, New York 10022

Macmillan Publishing Company is part of the Maxwell Communication Group of Companies.

Maxwell Macmillan Canada, Inc.
1200 Eglinton Avenue East
Suite 200
Don Mills, Ontario M3C 3N1

**Library of Congress Cataloging-in-Publication Data**

Rowe, Alan J.
    Managerial decision making : a guide to successful business
decisions / Alan J. Rowe, James D. Boulgarides.
        p.      cm.
    Includes index.
    ISBN 0-02-404111-4 (paper)
    1. Decision-making. I. Boulgarides, James D., 1923–
II. Title
HD30.23.R687 1992
658.4′03—dc20          91-30640
                    CIP

Printing :   2 3 4 5 6 7     Year :     4 5 6 7 8

# PREFACE

▲ ▲ ▲ ▲ ▲ ▲ ▲ ▲ ▲ ▲ ▲ ▲ ▲ ▲ ▲ ▲ ▲ ▲ ▲ ▲ ▲ ▲ ▲ ▲ ▲

Why do decisions that on the surface seem the same, work in one organization but fail miserably in another? Although decisions may appear similar, the environment in which the decision is made, the style of management, the timing of the decision, and the kind of decision that is being made may, in fact, be different. The combined effect of all factors relevant to the decision determines whether or not it will be successfully implemented. The decision itself is only one of the many factors that need to be considered in order to work within the context of an organization. Because of the breadth of the subject, the focus of this book is on the decision maker in an organizational context. However, technical as well as behavioral considerations are covered.

Decisions involve choice. The choices managers make, however, are different because of differences in ability to perceive and process information. This is covered in Chapters 3 and 4 on decision styles. Individuals also have blind spots because of their biases and values. Some individuals have impeccable integrity, whereas others do not. Some individuals can think quickly, and others are slow or methodical and thorough. There are creative thinkers and ones who would rather be doing things than thinking about them. Decision style may be used to identify these different types of decision makers. The power of decision style is that knowing how an individual thinks about situations, processes information, and makes decisions enables us to predict outcomes in terms of decision behavior.

To illustrate the complexity facing managers, consider the case of the spotted owl in Glendale, Oregon. Gregory Forest Products may be living on borrowed time because environmentalists have won a federal court decision to protect the spotted owl, which lives in the huge Douglas firs and Ponderosa pines near Glendale (Levine, 1989). Saving the bird is an environmental concern, but the decision could also endanger the Northwest lumber industry. What decision should Gregory Forest Products, Glendale's largest employer, make in the light of this problem? The answer is not simply related to economics, but people's livelihood—and even the existence of Gregory Forest Products—is at stake. This kind of problem is indicative of the complexity confronting today's decision makers. There frequently is no simple technical answer, and political and organizational considerations can be overwhelming.

Another example of the kind of problem that confronts decision makers is the suggested shifting of automobiles from gasoline to methanol in order to clean up the environment (Kupler, 1989). What should the petroleum industry do in response to these pressures? Washington is looking at a number of alternative fuels that will minimize the emissions polluting our environment and lessen our dependence on foreign oil. Some oil companies have decided to respond with a mixture of ethanol and gasoline, which they hope will prevent an economic disaster for them.

The insurance industry has a different set of concerns. Faced with problems of sagging sales that are confronting a number of the companies, the industry has decided to introduce new types of insurance policies as a means of taking them out of the doldrums (Prare, 1989). These decisions are merely illustrative of the complexity facing decision makers who must increasingly cope with environmental, political, social, and economic issues.

Another consideration is that decisions only affect the future. After the fact, decisions can only be corrected and often cannot be remade, just as all the king's horses and all the king's men could not put Humpty Dumpty (an egg) back together again. Thus, managers need approaches to help them anticipate how to deal with the constant stream of problems they face. This book proposes to answer the question, "How can managers be more effective in the way they make decisions?"

Decision makers sometimes overlook critical problems, which may fall by the wayside because of too much attention paid to simple problems. This may give the impression of good decision making, whereas in reality the manager may be avoiding the difficult problems because of an unwillingness to take risks. Although decisions are an everyday activity for all of us, the manner in which managers actually make decisions in an organizational context is emphasized. Decision makers need to understand how to use decision-aiding methodology. In addition, they need to understand the behavior of individuals in the organization in order to ensure effective performance. Effective performance is meeting the goals of the organization at the least possible total cost—in human and economic terms.

Numerous examples of business failure highlight the critical importance of effective decision making. Ford's losses on its Edsel car in the 1950s, the bankruptcy of Continental Airlines, the discontinuation of home computers by Texas Instruments—all are indicative of the kind of problems that confront decision makers. In some cases, decisions are based on erroneous assumptions or have overlooked some critical factors. The effectiveness of a decision must be viewed in its totality from the initial idea, the assumptions made, the methods used for analysis, the basis for choice, the gaining of acceptance of the solution, and the implementation and evaluation of results. Acceptance is both internal as well as external to the organization. Internally, it refers to the acceptance by members of the organization who are committed to meeting the goals. Externally, it represents acceptance by the consumers of the products and services produced by the organization.

Strategic decisions are ones that cover a long span of time and whose consequences are not known until long after the decision was made. Effective decision makers can act to reduce the organization's uncertainty in dealing with future outcomes. Environmental uncertainty must be recognized as a given because it is not possible to control all of the factors that have an impact on an organization. Constant change is a part of the reality that confronts the decision maker; judgment must be involved to determine how to use organizational resources.

The decision maker's role as a manager has changed radically because of the impact of technology and computers. When applied properly, computers allow the manager to spend more time interacting with members of the organization, properly acquiring and allocating scarce resources, and maintaining control of operations. The availability of the computer, however, should not be used by the manager as an excuse for avoiding the critical responsibility of interacting with subordinates.

Decision makers do not all act in the same manner with respect to their level of interaction, use of information, and maintaining control. First, with respect to the level of interaction, some decision makers have a greater need for interaction and will actively seek others before making a decision; other managers prefer a minimum of interaction before making a decision. Second, individuals vary greatly in the amount of information they need or will use prior to making a decision. The analytic individual needs large amounts of information, is quite cautious, and makes decisions only after a thorough analysis. The conceptual individual is able to see many possibilities but does not use information exhaustively. The directive individual is very quick in making decisions and uses limited information or interaction. The behavioral individual does not use much information but needs support from others before making a decision, relying more on reinforcement than personal judgment. Third, decision makers also vary in the amount of control they apply. Some individuals use very tight controls, requiring frequent reports, whereas others use loose control and are more laissez-faire. Because requirements vary with the situation, decision makers will vary in their approaches.

Many decisions involve understanding people's behavior and use of judgment because there are few absolutes in the pragmatic world of organizations. Judgment was required in the spotted owl and the methane–gasoline mixture cases. Because individuals differ in their needs, judgment must also be used to answer questions such as how much control should be used? When should reviews be conducted? What information should be considered? As this book describes, approaches vary with each individual and often depend on the context in which a decision is made.

Many managers use intuition in their decisions. This often is useful; however, decision support tools and quantitative approaches can also be helpful in finding solutions to problems. For example, when building a new plant, the product life cycle and the level of customer demand need to be considered in determining the appropriate capacity. Polaroid made the mistake of expanding its facilities in the United States and Europe in 1979, spending $135 million in anticipation of sales of the new SX-70 camera that did not meet expectations. The result was that Polaroid had to curtail production and laid off 2,500 people (Bernstein, 1980).

The value of a systematic approach to decision making has been described by Kepner and Tregoe (1965) in their book *The Rational Manager*. However, a purely rational basis for decision making does not take into account the realities that exist in complex organizations. As mentioned earlier, to be effective, the decision maker must deal with both the behavioral and the technical aspects of a problem. For example, if a decision does not take into consideration the technical aspects of a problem, it cannot be corrected by a good behavioral approach. Conversely, there are many excellent technical decisions that are not implemented because they ignored the behavioral or motivational considerations.

An important task of a manager is focusing on "critical issues." The organizations that have been most successful have been able to identify what factors in their business contribute to meeting goals and objectives. These can include improved employee performance, increased creativity, and greater risk taking. McDonald's emphasizes quality, value, service, and cleanliness as the basis for success. Organizations that can consistently achieve the proper balance among the factors that are critical for success will most likely survive and be profitable. This requires a constant stream of decisions made throughout an organization by a multitude of managers, all having their own strengths and weaknesses. These managers guide the organization along the tortuous path that confronts almost every organization. It is the decision maker, in the final analysis, who determines the organization's ability to perform smoothly by knowing how to make effective decisions and how to motivate members of the organization to ensure implementation of the decisions.

In an increasingly complex environment, it is no wonder that decision making is a difficult task that often determines the success or failure of an enterprise. Experience or intuition when used alone is seldom sufficient to deal with many of the problems confronting managers. Rather, it is the combination of managerial skills and workable approaches (including computers and quantitative methods) that can ensure making the most effective decisions. With this in mind, this book provides guidelines, concepts, and approaches that can be used to achieve effective organizational performance.

Most decisions are arrived at after going through a number of stages, called the decision process. We view the decision process from the perspective of how the individual manager reacts to various stimuli, and the way in which he or she senses or perceives information. Information perceived also depends on an individual's cognitive ability. The evaluation and choice of response to stimuli and the actual execution of the decision that is chosen often are a political process and can involve considerable negotiation to gain acceptance.

In addition to understanding how an individual makes decisions, specific aspects of how to improve decision making are emphasized. For example, we describe the use of "decision-aiding tools" such as problem-solving methods, heuristics, computer-based information systems, and the use of appropriate models.

A number of other aspects of decision making also are dealt with, such as career choices, organizational structure, measurement of decision styles, factors that contribute to successful decisions, predicting the outcome of a decision, importance of organizational change and adaptation, the role of leadership, the effect of organization life cycle, and the environment in which the organization finds itself. In addition, a number of case studies are included to illustrate the concepts presented.

Effective decision makers are distinguished by their ability to recognize the critical factors in a situation and to translate them into operational requirements that the organization can convert into a reality. They also are able to look at broad issues and anticipate future possibilities in the external environment. These managers recognize that an organization's culture creates an internal environment in which individuals are able to perform. Organization culture reflects the shared values, beliefs, traditions, norms, and expectations within an organization. It is the factor that provides cohesiveness and a sense of belonging to its members. Shared values produce a feeling of oneness among members of an organization, and a unity of purpose that helps eliminate conflict. The energies of the organization with a positive or harmonious culture are not wasted, but rather are focused on a common vision and purpose. Individual needs in such a situation are subordinated for the good of the whole, even if this means self-sacrifice. What results is a coherent system of organization. If the organization culture cannot respond to the requirements of the external environment, the results can be disruptive. This can lead to uncertainty in the organization with a resulting decline in performance.

One reason for the success of the Japanese is an organization culture of *wa* that reflects harmony or consistency between the organization and its members. Individuals subordinate their own needs to the common good. On the other hand, American workers exhibit a sense of independence and typically an unwillingness to "conform" to the requirements of an organization. The American work system is often fragmented and the rights and the responsibilities of the individual to the group or organization are deemphasized. Ours has become a situation of extremes, where such great concern has been expressed for the individual that we have sacrificed or overlooked the need for a common goal both for individuals within the organization and in a larger sense for society as a whole. In order to deal with this situation changes in approaches to management such as "high involvement," "empowerment," or "the team approach," in which organizational members derive "ownership" and "commitment" to the requirements for effective performance, have been initiated in many organizations.

Because decisions in an organization involve behavioral considerations, this book deals with the understanding of what leads to greater acceptance of decisions. Individual decision styles and leadership styles, along with values, communication, and culture of an organization, are covered. Group processes are discussed, as well as considerations relevant to motivation, satisfaction, belonging, and sentiments within the group and between managers and the group. Thus, the manager increasingly assumes the role of an integrator in contrast to that of a controller.

## ▲ Summary

The purpose of this book is to provide the reader with an understanding of decision-making approaches that can be used to improve a manager's decision making. We examine how decisions are made and how the process can be improved. A number of topics related to the decision maker and the context of the decision-making process are addressed. Topics that relate to the individual decision maker include perception, motivation, and decision-making styles. Other topics that are discussed include such techniques as simulation, quantitative approaches, creative problem solving, and decision making under risk and uncertainty. These topics are described in terms of how they contribute to making better decisions.

As the central theme of this book, we study the decision maker, starting with his or her decision style, the organization in which decisions are made, the external environmental considerations, and the tools available to aid the decision maker. The chapters are organized along these lines.

*Part I*
Chapter 1 introduces the subject of decision making.
Chapter 2 describes the decision maker and decision styles.
Chapter 3 discusses managerial decision style application.
Chapter 4 covers the elements of decision style.

*Part II*
Chapter 5 introduces decision making in an organizational context.
Chapter 6 relates decision making to the organization's culture.
Chapter 7 covers implementation, motivation, and control.

*Part III*
Chapter 8 focuses on creative problem solving.
Chapter 9 covers decision-aiding tools.

*Part IV*
Chapter 10 explores the strategic implications of globalization of decisions.
Chapter 11 examines the impact of environmental changes on decision making.

## ▲ Acknowledgments

We want to acknowledge the many individuals and organizations who have contributed to the ideas contained in this book and to thank them. Those who have had a significant impact on the book and provided a better understanding of decision making have our profound gratitude. These include: John Basch, Doug Basil, Warren Bennis, Arvind Bhambri, Mark Carlson, John Carlson, Marjorie Chan, Fran Chandler, George Chilingar, Dimitris Chorafas, Ross Clayton, Pat Connor, Ted Cooke, Jesse Cox, Clifford Craft, Bernie Denburg, Karl Dickel, Dorothy Dologite, Michael J. Driver, Joann Edmond, Lance Eliot, George W. England, Fred J. Evans, Mary A. Fischer, John Fleming, David J. Fritzsohe, Josie Gazzeny, Elizabeth Gjelten, Solomon Golomb, Leon Goure, David Granick, Al Greenfield, Larry E. Greiner, Harry Grossman, Edward Z. Hane, Murdoch Heideman, Phil Hunsacker, George Jacobson, John Jaeger, David Jamieson, Barbara Joans, Richard Kao, Laurie L. Larwood, Margaret Longenecker, Donald Malcolm, Rich B. Mann, Ronald O. Mason, Michael R. McGrath, Robert Mockler, Robert Myrtle, Dan O'Leary, Jim Paisley, Alan Patz, Barry Posner, Richard K. Quan, Kathleen Reardon, Marsha Rebney, Eberhart Rectin, James Rosenzweig, Clifford Rowe, Vince San Filippo, Warren Schmidt, William C. Schutz, Marcus Schwaninger, Herold Sherman, Norman Sigband, Ivan Somers, John F. Steiner, Howard Tagomori, John Thompson, Efraim Turban, William Waddell, Paul Watkins, Stanley R. Weingart, Fred Weintraub, David White, Nancy Wise, and David Wolfe. We also want to thank the following reviewers who provided helpful suggestions for improving the manuscript: Craig C. Lundberg, Cornell University; Richard O. Mason, Southern Methodist University; Terrence C. Sebora, University of Wisconsin–Oshkosh; Barbara A. Spencer, Mississippi State University; and Charles N. Toftoy, George Washington University. Most important are the unsung heroines, who through their conscientious and dedicated administrative support made this book possible: Janet Andrews, Charlene Sanky, Rosemary E. Sostarich, Marj Tamaki, and Pat Tom. We would also like to thank the staff at Macmillan for bringing this text to fruition: Charles Stewart, Barbara Newman, Ann-Marie WongSam, and Nick Sklitsis.

To our wives, Helen Rowe and Wanda Boulgarides, we dedicate this book and want to express our utmost thanks and appreciation for their understanding and support.

## ▲ References

Bernstein, Peter W. "Polaroid Struggles to Get Back in Focus." *Fortune* (April 7, 1980).

Kepner, Charles H., and Tregoe, Benjamin B. *The Rational Manager.* New York: McGraw-Hill, 1965.

Kupler, Andrew. "The Methanol Car in Your Future." *Fortune* (September 25, 1989), pp. 71–82.

Levine, Jonathan B. "The Spotted Owl Could Wipe Us Out." *Business Week* (September 18, 1989), pp. 94–99.

Prare, Terrence. "A Primer on New Wrinkles in an Old Standby Life Insurance." *Fortune* (September 25, 1989), pp. 25–26.

# CONTENTS

▲ ▲ ▲ ▲ ▲ ▲ ▲ ▲ ▲ ▲ ▲ ▲ ▲ ▲ ▲ ▲ ▲ ▲ ▲ ▲ ▲ ▲

# Part I

# THE DECISION MAKER

# 1 Nature of Decision Making

▲ ▲ ▲ ▲ ▲ ▲ ▲ ▲ ▲ ▲ ▲ ▲ ▲ ▲ ▲ ▲ ▲ ▲ ▲ ▲ ▲

In the early 1980s, Edward Cooley, chairman of Precision Cast Parts, made a major decision that could have ruined his company (Beauchamp, 1989). He invested heavily in new plants and new technology at exactly the time that the recession was wreaking havoc with the airline industry, Precision's principal customer. Today, airlines are furiously trying to expand their fleets and are installing many new engines. The result is that Precision has quadrupled sales since 1980 and profits are almost seven times their previous high. By taking the highly dangerous risk, Cooley made the right decision, which resulted in a high payoff.

Other managers have not been as astute. Dr. An Wang built a $3 billion company after having survived Chinese revolutions, the Japanese invasions, American racism, and IBM harassment (Queenan, 1989, p. 48). He was brought down by the one fatal decision he made: turning the business over to Wang Junior, who posted a $424 million loss in 1986. Wang's stock price is now down to 5 3/8 from a high of 42 1/2. Why was Cooley right and Wang wrong in the critical decision each made? Wang Junior may have been the wrong choice to replace his father, or Wang Junior may have inherited his father's mistakes. Was the problem one of nepotism, or a historic mistake of the past?

These cases illustrate one of the major difficulties in evaluating the quality of decisions—the lag time between when the decision is made and when the results are observed. During the interval of time between making a decision and observing the results, conditions surrounding the decision may have changed and could be beyond the control of the decision maker. An effective decision maker, however, anticipates possible changes that can impact the decision and provides contingencies that will minimize the impact of adverse conditions.

In reality, decisions are never ends in themselves, but are the basis for achieving a desired goal. Thus, making what seems to be the "right" decision may not lead to achieving stated objectives. To meet the organization's objectives, managers need to continuously modify what has to be done, how it will be done and the expected results, as well as gain the organization's acceptance of these decisions. Decision making thus is a "process" rather than simply a choice from among possible alternatives. Furthermore, the way in which decisions are carried out often determines the final outcome. A reasonable plan well executed is far superior to an excellent plan poorly carried out.

Because final results are observed only after the original decision has been made, managers must be able to "predict" what course of action to take. Because decision making affects "future outcomes," concepts such as cost control and quality control need to be viewed differently. Once an action has been taken it cannot be retracted. For example, a poorly fabricated product is poor quality. A manager may take actions to correct a wrong situation, such as poor quality, with an associated loss in time and cost; but (like water that is over the dam) it simply cannot be brought back again. Decision making always involves risk and uncertainty whether or not the manager explicitly takes this into account. Although our focus is on the decision maker, the decision process, and organizational considerations, it is equally important to recognize that uncertainty accompanies every aspect of decision making. An effective decision maker needs to provide a margin of safety for critical situations that may develop. These can be in the form of early warning systems for timely notification that things are going wrong, or contingency plans for changing a course of action.

## ▲ ROLE OF THE MANAGER

Decision makers are critical to ensuring that results are achieved. However, achieving results also requires the involvement of the organization so that decisions are properly implemented. The decision maker starts by first identifying the goals and objectives. He or she may involve others in this initial phase. Resources that are needed must be available, and the decision maker must plan the actions needed to reach desired goals.

Many examples abound to illustrate these requirements. Lee Iacocca took a moribund Chrysler Corporation and created a vital entity. He wanted to build a new assembly plant in Ontario, California, to build mini-vans. Estimates were that it would take 18 months to complete. He refused to wait. He insisted that it be done in 18 weeks, and it was done! Situations that confront executives such as Iacocca require a dominant, directive decision maker who focuses on rapid action and results. As can be seen, the decision maker often is central to the process of defining objectives. But he or she must also gain the organization's acceptance that the objectives are achievable.

## ▲ FOUR FORCE MODEL

As a starting point for understanding the decision maker, we start with the basic assumption that managers work with others in achieving desired results. In an organizational context, each manager reacts to four basic driving forces, shown in Figure 1.1. These forces are

1. Environmental forces.
2. Organizational forces.
3. Task demands.
4. Personal needs.

Each of these forces is discussed next.

### Environmental Forces

Starting with environmental forces, we observe that at every level in an organization there is interaction with the external environment. This interaction is not the same for every organization or every individual. In retailing and banking, customer contact occurs at the most basic level of the organization—the sales clerk or teller. In large, technical organizations, the marketing personnel have direct customer contact; and production, engineering, and administrative personnel interact with colleagues or others in the internal environment. At the upper executive levels of organizations, executives may have contact with many stakeholders

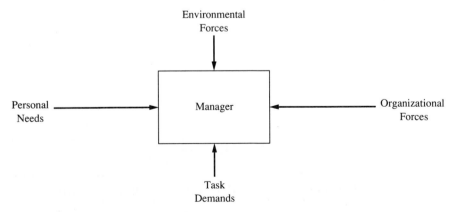

Figure 1.1  ▲  Basic Four Force Model

including government officials, the media, and financial institutions. It is important that appropriate individuals have contact with the external environment. Thus, a bank teller is the goodwill ambassador of the bank. Organizations need to prepare people in those positions to project a positive image to the customer.

Individuals are also the sensors of the organization, detecting how the environmental forces impact the organization. These environmental forces include the government, the economy, competition, customers, consumer groups, or the public at large. Although an organization may be able to influence environmental forces somewhat, it generally does not control them and must be capable of responding to them.

Two examples illustrate how organizations can have impact on the environmental forces. First, IBM is a massive economic force with sales in 1990 of $44 billion, which directly affects the stock market. It is said that as IBM goes, so goes the market. Second, during the period 1990–91 there was a major debacle in the savings and loan (S&L) industry. One of the largest failures was Lincoln Savings Bank headed by Charles Keating. Keating's influence was so great by virtue of his political contributions that five senators interceded in his behalf to hold off federal regulators from taking over the ailing S&L. Needless to say, this caused considerable financial injury to the public.

## Organizational Forces

Organizational forces consist of the interpersonal interactions that occur while working with others in an organization. This describes the way in which people deal with one another as well as pressures from the group in which they work. Managers' interpersonal skills and personality determine how well they deal with the organizational forces. Cohesiveness, anxiety, commitment, and performance are all dependent on the managers' ability to interact effectively.

## Task Demands

Task demands represent the skill requirements, expertise, knowledge, and technical competence that are needed to perform effectively. All individuals in an organization are expected to carry out a given task or function. Task demands represent the technical content of the manager's job. Managerial functions typically are described as a set of activities related to a specific function.

## Personal Needs

Personal needs represent the psychological or emotional pressures on an individual. They reflect personality, values, and beliefs, and have a direct effect on the decisions and choices that an individual manager makes. Just as organizations depend on resources such as funds, physical facilities, and people to carry out their activities, individuals also have needs that must be met in order to perform effectively.

The four "driving forces" of environment, organization, task demands, and personal needs influence the thinking, behavior, and decisions managers make. Each of these forces is examined in greater detail in later chapters of the book.

## ▲ UNDERSTANDING MANAGERIAL DECISION MAKING

Managers can use case analysis to understand how to effectively handle problems they face. As an illustration, consider the clash at Transworld Corporation and what happened to its president, Charles Bradshaw. Using a case analysis, the decisions that were made can more readily be understood. Two methods of analysis are used: the four force model and a linear decision analysis that views the organization as a system. Both of these approaches can help summarize the critical factors in a case. The Linear Decision Analysis is used as the first step in determining the problem at Transworld.

## Starting with the Critical Issues

Effective decision makers focus on the critical issues. This is a skill that can be learned from experience. Critical issues threaten the survival or well-being of an organization. A crippling strike, poor product quality, inappropriate strategies, and poor management are examples of critical issues one might identify when analyzing a case. Generally, the critical issues are apparent and require attention in order to correct an unsatisfactory situation.

## ▲ ▲ ▲ ▲ ▲ The Bradshaw Case: Power in the Board Room—The Miscast Entrepreneur

Transworld Corporation was formed by Transworld Airlines to expand and diversify beyond the airline industry. Edwin Smart was appointed chairman of Transworld to achieve that objective. In the course of the diversification, Transworld bought out Charles Bradshaw's Spartan Food Systems, a chain of 250 steak houses, in 1979. Bradshaw was kept on and allowed to remain in Spartanburg, South Carolina where he continued to expand the chain of steak houses, doubling the size of the chain in five years.

As an entrepreneur and co-founder and builder of Spartan Food Systems, Bradshaw, 50, was not happy simply running an organization. Bradshaw needed new challenges and planned to leave Transworld Corporation in 1984. When Edwin Smart, 62, learned of Bradshaw's plans, he became concerned because he did not want to lose his best operating manager. Smart offered Bradshaw the position of president at Transworld Corporation in anticipation that Bradshaw would be the next chairman of the board when he retired in 1988. However, Smart sowed the seeds for disaster by having as a second backup his senior vice president of finance, Nicholas Salizzoni, whom he appointed vice chairman of the board.

After Bradshaw joined Transworld as C.E.O., he began his search for new acquisitions. He became frustrated when each of his recommendations for acquisition—such as Denny's and Carl Jr.'s—was rejected. Bradshaw and Smart each had a different vision of where Transworld should be heading. Bradshaw's aggressive style collided with Smart's more cautious approach. In some cases, opportunities were lost due to Smart's inability or unwillingness to make a decision. Also, being a born and bred Southerner, Bradshaw never felt comfortable at Transworld headquarters in New York City. He still kept his family home in Spartanburg while renting an apartment in New York City.

The critical issue arose in 1986 when Salizzoni recommended that Transworld acquire American Medical Services which ran a chain of nursing homes. Bradshaw was unable to "go along" with what he knew to be a poor decision and was unable to play the corporate game. Bradshaw felt so strongly that this would be wrong for Transworld that he decided to confront the recommendation at the next board meeting. After the meeting started, it soon became obvious that it had been contrived to thwart Bradshaw. Not only did Salizzoni take charge of the meeting, but the Board's position against Bradshaw led him to believe that he would have to leave Transworld.

He tried to argue that the potential profit for the nursing home chain could not compare with that in the hotel or restaurant field. Nonetheless, he was outvoted 5 to 1. After the meeting, he directly submitted his resignation to Smart and simply walked out.

It did not take him very long to pack his belongings and be on his way back to Spartanburg where he could productively use his portion of the $80 million that Transworld had paid to buy out Spartan Food Systems. It appeared very clear that he really wanted to be an entrepreneur and not a corporate executive in a gray pin-striped suit.  ▲

# ▲  APPLYING LINEAR DECISION ANALYSIS TO THE BRADSHAW CASE

Linear decision analysis is a method for systematically addressing the issues in a complex problem situation. Approaching a complex situation in an orderly manner helps avoid serious omissions that might jeopardize the decisions needed. Using the following outline for the linear decision analysis in Figure 1.2, we can now fill in the information from the case.

## Stimulus

The first question to be answered is, What was the stimulus that started things going wrong? There are several possibilities, but one of the pressing issues is Bradshaw's continuously being rebuffed on his suggestions regarding potential acquisitions.

## Critical Issues

The next item deals with the critical issues. There were a number of issues in the case, including Bradshaw's rebuffs, but the current critical issue was the meeting of the board with Smart, the chairman of Transworld, and Salizzoni, the vice-chairman, where a decision was to be made regarding acquiring a nursing home. Bradshaw felt confident that he was well prepared but found to his dismay that it was Salizzoni who stole the show.

## Organizational Response

After the first six months, the typical honeymoon period for a new employee, Bradshaw became increasingly frustrated when his suggestions were turned down. He also never felt part of the organization, nor did he like the New York City environment.

## Manager's Response

Smart, as chairman, is considered the one in the management role. He initially saw Bradshaw as a person who could be his replacement, but he soon became disenchanted when he recog-

1. Stimulus—why the problem arose
2. Critical issues—threatening problems
3. Organizational response—how the organization dealt with the problems
4. Manager's response—how the manager dealt with the problems
5. Individual performer's reaction—what the individual did
6. Work environment—the context of the situation
7. Result or consequence—the outcome or consequence of actions taken

Figure 1.2  ▲  Linear Decision Analysis

nized that Bradshaw did not share his vision for Transworld. Here is an instance where the manager did not really understand the needs of his subordinate and thus created a situation that was irreconcilable.

### Individual Performer's Reaction

As the individual performer, Bradshaw tried hard to satisfy the needs of Transworld from his perspective of an executive who had been eminently successful and who continued his entrepreneurial behavior. Unfortunately, this did not match Smart's style or perspective, and conflict was therefore inevitable.

### Work Environment

The work environment was cordial but obviously very political. Bradshaw never felt at home, never made friends, and didn't sell his Spartanburg home.

### Results or Consequences

The final phase of the linear decision analysis is the outcome. This is what might be expected—Bradshaw resigned and vowed never again to work for someone else. The stock price for Transworld also dropped 2¼ points. Graphically, the linear decision analysis is shown in Figure 1.3.

## ▲ FOUR FORCE ANALYSIS

The second method of analysis examines the Bradshaw case using the four force model, shown in Figure 1.4. There were two agendas at work, Bradshaw's and the organization's, and they were at variance with each other.

### Environmental Forces

Environmental forces at work here are (1) keen competition in the fast-food industry and (2) other opportunities such as nursing homes.

### Organizational Forces

Bradshaw failed to perceive Smart's needs. Smart did not want Bradshaw's analysis or recommendation; he wanted support for his decision. Obviously, the decision to acquire the nursing homes had already been made prior to the board meeting and the vote was merely a formality. The Board meeting also represented a power play by Salizzoni, who wanted to succeed Smart.

The board of directors of a corporation seldom, if ever, becomes involved in the technical evaluation of a management decision. The board is usually hand selected by top management of an organization and is a rubber stamp for that management. The board is often presold on decisions it must make. Bradshaw was naive to think that he could convince the Board to reverse a decision that his company had made and was bringing to the board for confirmation.

**Stimulus**
Bradshaw's constant rebuff.

**Critical
Issues**
Bradshaw's recommendations rejected. Bradshaw
and Salizzoni input. Board voted against
Bradshaw.

**Organizational
Response**
Brought Bradshaw to New York but created a hostile
environment for Bradshaw.

**Manager's
Response**
Smart saw Bradshaw as his replacement.
However, Bradshaw increasingly became
disenchanted.

**Individual Performer's
Reaction**
Bradshaw made numerous suggestions that were
turned down. The result was frustration for
Bradshaw.

**Work Environment**
New York office was cordial and plush,
but Bradshaw never felt at home.

**Result or Consequence**
Bradshaw really wants to be an entrepreneur. He
blows up at board meeting. Bradshaw resigns
and stock drops.

**Figure 1.3 ▲ Linear Decision Analysis**

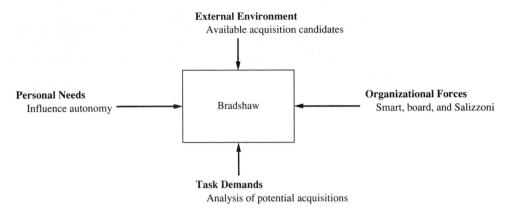

**Figure 1.4** ▲ **Bradshaw's Four Force Analysis**

In the final analysis, the acquisition proved to be a poor decision from a technical point of view. The market perceived it that way, with the resultant drop in Transworld's stock price. However, a valuable employee was lost, and eventually Transworld was acquired by Karl Icahn.

## Task Demands

As president of Transworld, Bradshaw had two major responsibilities. First was to gain knowledge about the organization, its goals and culture, and so forth. Second was to recommend acquisitions that fit the current mission of Transworld.

## Personal Needs

Bradshaw had a strong need to achieve and to lead. Smart, on the other hand, had a need for order, stability, respect, to be liked, and to maintain his image. Salizzoni had a need for power. The board members had a need for their fee and to remain friendly to company management in order to keep their seats on the board.

Having gone through an analysis of the problem, we are now in a position to evaluate what happened and why the decisions that were made resulted in the outcome observed. From the outset, Bradshaw probably should not have joined Transworld. If he had known more about his own personality, he would have realized that working for a large bureaucratic organization eventually would be stifling. He was not a yes man. Smart also should have realized that one can't place limits on an entrepreneur. Smart was trying to fill the post of chairman that he would vacate and lost sight of behavioral considerations when he brought Bradshaw in as president. He could have employed Bradshaw—not in the role of president of Transworld, but rather as president of a separate division where Bradshaw could have employed his talents unfettered by corporate constraints.

The reality of the situation is that fast food has become a highly profitable industry, whereas medical care has suffered severely. The urbane Smart, acting out the role of senior statesmen and mentor to Bradshaw, expected respect and deference to his position. But Bradshaw did not behave the way Smart expected. Bradshaw, the entrepreneur, was results- and task-oriented. He saw the fallacy of the proposed acquisition based on his vision and perceptive ability. Unfortunately, he did not have the patience to play the bureaucratic and political game. To him, the battle and the war were one. He refused to go along with a bad decision. The board of directors were not well informed about the acquisition and thus could not judge whether it was good or bad, although they have a fiduciary responsibility to protect stockholder assets. It appears that their concern was in retaining their membership on the board and receiving their compensation. Bradshaw was playing against a stacked deck and obviously lost.

This is a good illustration of a case where neither the technical nor the behavioral factors were taken into account. The result was the loss of a valuable employee and what appears to be a wrong acquisition decision by Smart. The unfortunate thing here is that Smart was not willing to apply rigorous financial and technical analysis to the acquisition decision. The decision itself also shows that there was no clearly spelled out response to the question, What is your business?

## ▲ DECISION-MAKING PROCESS

A third approach to analyzing decision problems is a simplified decision-making process, which can also be applied to the Bradshaw case. The decision-making process shown in Figure 1.5 describes one way decisions are made. However, in real life decisions are rarely made in this "precise" sequence because in actual situations there are many interactions, feedback, negotiations, and compromises. Figure 1.5 shows the elements that normally go into the making of a decision rather than the exact flow. Specific circumstances will dictate the actual way in which a decision is made.

The decision maker is, in fact, involved in all phases of the decision process depending on his or her area of expertise, style of management, and time available. It is important to recognize that the decision process shown in Figure 1.5 is a static representation of what is in reality a dynamic process. What we learn from experience is that an effective manager will become involved whenever there is a problem to be solved, whether it is only to the extent of an inquiry or active participation. We next examine the decision process in greater detail.

### Stimulus

The stimulus represents an external force that is the causal basis for the problem. For example, a conflict that exists in an organization may give rise to a situation where an employee

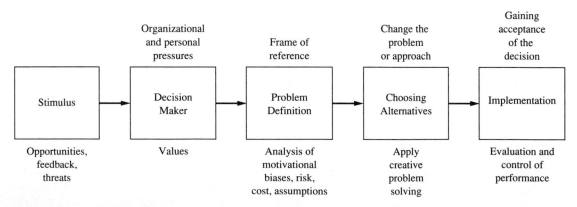

Figure 1.5 ▲ Decision Process

deliberately sabotages an operation in a factory. It is also the same as the stimulus or driving force in a stimulus/response situation.

The stimulus, which represents the imperative for having to make a decision, is followed by the decision maker, who is responsible for making a decision. Next is the problem definition, where the decision maker's perception and cognition play an important role in defining the problem at hand. Analysis techniques such as the linear decision analysis can assist in proper formulation. As we will see later in our discussion on perception, it is possible that the decision maker may fail to recognize the real problem that exists. This may account for the high incidence of crisis management in many organizations. Failure to act in a timely manner leads to reactive as opposed to proactive managerial decision making.

The choice that is made is generally a very complex process, so showing it as a single box is a gross simplification. It involves finding alternatives, negotiating acceptance, and even modifying the problem when needed. Once a decision is made, the next challenge is how to make it come to fruition. This requires implementation, which involves carrying out the steps needed to make the decision a reality.

## The Decision Maker

Because we cannot probe the mind-set of a manager, it is difficult to determine his or her true motives. It is therefore important to recognize that behavioral factors can be critical in the problem-definition phase of the decision process.

## Problem Definition

The initial definition of a problem may need to be changed, modified, or even discarded, depending on circumstances. Organizational considerations, resource requirements, and the personal values of the decision maker are among the many factors that lead to a change in the initial problem statement.

The critical decision in the Bradshaw case was whether to make the acquisition of the nursing homes. Bradshaw may have acted in an immature manner, by quitting because he did not get his way. He certainly demonstrated a lack of flexibility and teamwork, which are often the attributes of an entrepreneur. Such was the case of Steve Jobs at Apple Computer where Jobs, the entrepreneur, wanted to do it his way and had to be eased out by John Scully, who eventually took over the reins.

At Transworld, the apparent (or short-term) decision was whether to make the acquisition. The more significant, long-term decision was whether Bradshaw fit into the corporate culture of the organization where decisions were based more on corporate politics than on merit. In the final analysis, this was not a technical but rather a political issue.

After an initial statement of the problem, identifying the real problem is undoubtedly a critical aspect of decision making. Often it is asking the right questions that determines the course to be followed. It has been suggested that looking at opportunities, not problems, is a better approach to finding meaningful solutions. Problems do exist, however, and they require that action be taken to correct an undesirable situation when one exists. This phase of the decision process has been considered by many managers as the most critical and most difficult.

## Choosing Alternatives

To analyze alternative solutions, quantitative methods are often suggested. However, inadequate data might hamper the manager's ability to analyze a problem. An important question is how to choose from the alternatives available. At this point judgment, intuition, and experience play a significant if not overriding role in choosing from among alternatives. It is painfully obvious that in many complex situations, the human mind cannot examine all the alternatives or even understand all that apply.

## Implementation

Once an alternative is chosen, the organizational aspect of the decision process is set into motion. Gaining acceptance, negotiating, satisfying those in power, and developing a plan of action all must be concluded before anything can be accomplished. The questions of strategy, policy, organizational structure, and resources all impinge on the way in which the decision is carried out. Decisions do not come into existence automatically, and results are not achieved without considerable effort, time, and resources.

The implementation phase of a decision recently has received increased attention. This is the phase that determines what will, in fact, be accomplished. How often have best-laid plans gone wrong? Interpersonal dynamics, organizational behavior, political maneuvering, operating methods, technology, organizational structure, leadership style or the lack of strong leadership, culture, communication, and understanding all influence the actual outcome of a decision. There are no panaceas, and they can't substitute for the reality that exists in organizations. Levels of distrust, lack of confidence in superiors, political considerations, or organizational roles and structure can convert an excellent decision into a failure when the personal needs and expectations of individuals are overlooked.

## Control

During the implementation phase of the decision process, changes inevitably arise. It is rare that the plan for carrying out the decision or the many behavioral considerations can all be predetermined with total precision. Rather, during this phase, the decision is converted from an idea to reality. Managers' attempts to "control" the implementation phase using accounting reports, budgets, performance appraisal, computer outputs, or cost analyses have been less than a resounding success. Achieving desired results can be thwarted when the behavioral impacts of control are overlooked and the implementation process is poorly understood.

## Evaluation

Evaluation is the final phase in the complex process of converting the right decision into effective results. In a rapidly changing environment, evaluation is a continuous process. There must be a balance between the amount of information generated and the degree of control. The benefits to be derived from the availability of detailed information must be balanced against the risk of interfering with subordinates or with operations. Successful organizations, according to Peters and Waterman (1982), have a propensity for taking action and doing their evaluating later.

# ▲ PERFORMANCE AND DECISION EFFECTIVENESS

Both overall performance and individual productivity are key elements of effectiveness. To assure desired results, the following questions should be asked:

1. Has the right problem been identified? (How often is the right solution found for the wrong problem?) Have objectives and priorities been clearly defined and the consequences of carrying out the decision understood?

2.  Are trade-offs known; is there an awareness of the risks involved and the payoffs? Is there a balance of factors such as timing, information, and resources required?
3.  Is there acceptance of the decision? Will the persons involved carry out the decision as it has been communicated? Is there consideration of the values and political factors involved, and is there participation in the decision?
4.  Is there a plan of action? Does implementation take into account the unknowns, and is there a contingent plan of action?

## Decision Consequences

Another concern in the decision process is that decision evaluation depends on both implementation and results achieved or consequences. Every decision has indirect consequences and effects that occur at a later time. Dropping a pebble into a pool of water causes both an initial splash and the ripples that follow. The effect of the ripples may be as important as that of the splash. For example, if a critical decision is made by a narrow 3–2 vote, future consequences may be residual hostility and resentment on the part of the minority, with the intent of getting revenge on the majority in the future or sabotaging implementation of the decision. Another possibility is that the composition of the group may change—and by the change of one vote the decision may be reversed, with serious organizational cost and performance consequences.

To illustrate this situation, consider the case of a California police department. In 1975, the police chief of a California city was fired for failure to perform his duties in a satisfactory manner. A research survey of the police department was conducted by a management professor from the University of Southern California. The study revealed that the police department was divided between loyalty to the chief and loyalty to the city council. The chief was protected by civil service rules from any summary firing, and he had many loyal supporters in the community. The decision to remove the police chief was made by a consensus vote of the city council in a vote of 5–0. The chief was offered an opportunity to resign, which he refused to do.

After the city council acted on the decision and the police chief was removed, there was a storm of protest from some community leaders who were friendly to the chief. The city council had to listen to the protests in public meetings, but held firm. In 1976 there was an election and two new members joined the city council, replacing two of the members who had been part of the vote to remove the police chief. Those two members, new to the council and not part of the original decision, were sensitive to the public pressure and were willing to reconsider the removal of the police chief. The remaining three members of the city council, who had been part of the original decision, resisted this pressure and the original decision prevailed.

If the original decision had not been made unanimously by the city council in 1975—if it had been less than a 5–0 vote—then the 1976 election could very well have resulted in a reversal of that decision. Split votes produce marginal situations that can be quite volatile. It may be better to postpone a critical decision until a consensus can be achieved. Anything less than a full commitment by participants in the decision may prove to be very costly and catastrophic.

## External Factors

In the results phase of the decision process, the emphasis shifts from internal to external considerations. Investors expect to receive an appropriate return. Competitors react to the organization in terms of both product and price. Unions expect increasing participation in the decisions made by management. Government imposes more taxes and regulations. The community, in turn, expects a socially responsible organization.

As an illustration of the vagaries introduced by external forces one must ask, could managers have anticipated currency devaluation, or natural disasters, or extreme emergencies? Regardless, these external forces are important when attempting to find answers to internal problems. Making a decision is only the first step in a continuing series of decisions that align the organization to new and changing external conditions. In the case of Wang Laboratories, mentioned earlier, the results of decisions made were devastating; for Precision Cast Parts the outcome was excellent. Thus, the quality of a decision cannot be measured until all the results are in.

## ▲ TYPES OF DECISIONS MANAGERS MAKE

There have been many approaches to describing the kinds of decisions managers make. One distinction is the rational versus the behavioral decision, where *rational* refers to reasoning applied to the problem and *behavioral* refers to emotions or feelings used as the basis for deciding. Drucker (1954) focused on the external environment and said there are no irrational customers, just stupid product decisions. Simon (1957), in his book *Models of Man,* described decisions as programmed or nonprogrammed to cover routine versus complex decisions. He also introduced the concepts of satisficing and bounded rationality to explain why decision makers choose simplified models of reality in order to find a reasonable or satisfactory solution or choice using limited search.

There are many ways to view decision making. Barnard (1938) suggested that decisions cannot be dictated by management, but depend on personal or psychological factors and require interaction and communication. We can think of decisions as being one of the following types:

1. *Routine decisions:* In order to carry out an organization's goals, prescribed policies or rules are followed. These are considered programmed decisions.
2. *Creative decisions:* New or novel approaches are needed to handle more complex problems. These and negotiated decisions are considered nonprogrammed.
3. *Negotiated decisions:* These are situations where conflict in goals or approaches to problem solving need to be resolved by involving participants.

Gore (1964) used comparable categories to describe the way organizations deal with bringing about change in operations, in contrast to maintaining the "status quo." He claimed that nonprogrammed decisions require innovation and negotiation to obtain group consensus or accommodation.

A research study (Rowe, 1974) showed some of the ways in which decision making is approached.

1. A prominent professor in the field of decision making remarked, "Participation by subordinates in decision making is a myth, and there is too much emphasis placed on achieving results or ends."
2. The manager of a computer department succinctly stated his view as "Every new manager brings a new organization and a new decision style."
3. The president of a large food company said, "My best decisions are made without the help of consultants. My worst decision was based on a very large and detailed study which researched the wrong conclusion."
4. When asked about computer applications, an Army general had this to say: "Top managers don't have the time needed to understand all the details. At best, all they can do is respond to data provided by subordinates."

Although this last statement is generally true, managers can develop means of determining the general validity of the information presented without having to check all the details. Checking the "reasonableness" of data can be determined by asking a few "key questions," or by comparison with other data. Another approach used is to ask counterpart managers in other organizations for their opinions.

# ▲ NUMBER OF FACTORS CONSIDERED IN DECISION MAKING

A useful way of understanding decision problems is to consider the number of factors involved. Problems can be approached as having one, two, four, or "n" factors. (See Table 1.1) These numbers relate to how solutions are approached.

## The One-Factor Approach

The one-factor category typifies a decision maker who focuses on a specific or limited aspect of a problem. This is comparable to Simon's satisficing approach. The one-factor approach often results in "suboptimizing," because the focus is on results, not thought. For example, in a tight financial situation, managers often "cut cost." However, this might be the poorest solution because cutting cost also reduces capability and could increase losses. In almost any decision situation where only one factor is used, there generally will be a poor solution. That is, performance could be expected to be less than the best or optimum. In most situations trade-offs exist. Thus, if only one aspect of a problem is considered, at least one other is ignored, which generally leads to less-than-desired results.

## The Two-Factor Approach

The two-factor approach balances cause-and-effect relations that exist in many situations. Cost-benefit analysis has been used by the government in the procurement of major systems to trade off value received for the cost expended. Methods such as queuing theory involve balancing service capacity with the demand for the service. One of the most widely used applications of the two-factor approach has been in inventory control to balance carrying cost with ordering cost. In an organization, managers balance technical with behavioral factors. The concept of trade-offs is often sufficient to provide a useful framework for making decisions.

## The Four-Factor Approach

The four-factor approach is an extension of the two-factor approach and is used when the problem involves equilibrium. An example of this is shown in Figure 1.6, where the organization is viewed as a system that balances internal tension and demands with external forces, along with resource requirements and organizational pressures.

Table 1.1  ▲  **Number of Factors in Managerial Problems**

| Number of Factors | Typical Application |
|---|---|
| One factor | Cost, profit, growth |
| Two factors | Trade-offs, cost/benefit |
| Four factors | Equilibrium, dual trade-offs |
| Multiple factors | Complex systems, organizational problems |

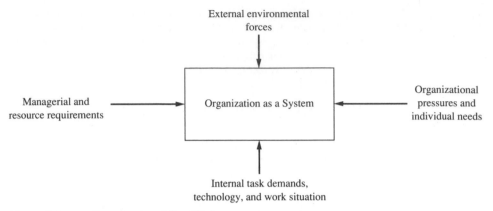

**Figure 1.6　▲　Organizational Equilibrium**

The concept of organizational equilibrium was described by Gore (1964), who said, "Disequilibrium and its consequent stress became the price for attempting to meet clientele demands without sacrificing internal organizational goals oriented toward need satisfaction. To maintain a balance between the streams of behavior, decision making has evolved. Equilibrium is the pivotal concept." Gore recognized that an organization is, at best, in a state of quasi-equilibrium and that decision making is not rational but rather a "twisted, unshapely, halting flow of interactions between people, interactions that shift constantly from a rational to a heuristic mode" (p. 149).

Gore described decision making in organizations where "every decision studied involved both persuasion and negotiation and concessions as a means of achieving external sanction or acceptance. We do not have one case history that shows the executive making the decision through a formal mechanism. Our data suggest that the process through which hard choices are really made are not at all distinct and independent from the full stream of organizational behavior. Stress in the form of tension, anxiety, fear, worry, or strain is a continual drain on the energies of an organization" (p. 133). It quickly becomes obvious why the multiple-factor approach fits decision making in organizations. This approach can be used to deal with the complexities in organizations and the realities of the context in which decisions have to be carried out.

## The Multiple-Factor Approach

The multiple-factor approach can be characterized as a broad "systems" approach that considers the many factors that affect a situation, such as information flow, technological processes, and behavior of individuals. Managers who have a high tolerance for ambiguity can deal readily with multiple factors, whereas other managers tend to avoid complexity and look for simple, direct solutions. These latter managers prefer the single-factor approach such as focusing on "not exceeding the budget," "not missing a schedule," or "not meeting sales targets." However, as was described earlier, the one-factor approach ignores balancing or trade-offs and often leads to suboptimization.

Although it is unrealistic to expect all managers to be equally proficient at all tasks in an organization, it is reasonable to expect that managers can learn which factors are relevant in a given situation and whether they feel capable of dealing with the problem at hand. From a managerial perspective, decisions are often associated with the manager's level in the organization. Senior managers are typically concerned with strategic decisions. Middle managers are concerned with planning decisions, and supervisors with operational decisions.

Performance reviews evaluate the results achieved in an organization. They are sometimes referred to as *managerial control,* and emphasize reports, management by objectives, financial evaluation, and computer analysis. With the changing emphasis regarding empowerment, participation, and self-commitment, the performance reviews take on a different meaning. Rather than absolute standards, results are compared on measures such as flexibility, adaptability, and response to internal and external pressures. These considerations are covered in Chapter 7.

Another way to look at the multiple-factor approach is to compare operational and strategic decisions. Operational decisions have been studied for many years by persons in organizational behavior: from early Western Electric studies on the impact of level of illumination on productivity to more recent studies on teamwork, performance analysis, reward systems, psychological considerations, and so forth. Operational decisions have in the past focused on efficiency and are now emphasizing acceptance, commitment, empowerment, and self-control.

Strategic decisions are those having far-reaching and long-term effects on organizational performance. Strategic decisions require an interdisciplinary perspective, drawing on all disciplines in dealing with both the internal environment of the organization and the external environment of the market. Thinking in global terms, the strategic decisions focus on opportunities and challenges and are not limited to the United States. Other countries as markets and suppliers represent different cultures and customs and thus influence decisions. Strategic decisions also are concerned with organizational structure, mission, goals, and objectives as well as overall organizational effectiveness.

## ▲ Summary

The objective of this chapter has been to introduce the subject of decision making by showing examples and a sample case study. Three approaches to analysis were shown: the linear decision analysis, which assists in formulating a problem; the four force model, which focuses on the driving forces that impel the manager to respond in a manner contingent on the forces; and the decision process model, which examines the flow throughout the situation. The decision process and decision types are used to show the kinds of decisions managers make and the stages through which the process proceeds from the stimulus or need for a decision to the outcome based on the choice made and implementation.

## ▲ Bradshaw Case Questions

1. What goal was Transworld trying to reach?
2. What was wrong about miscasting Bradshaw, an entrepreneur, in a bureaucratic role?
3. What could Bradshaw have done to strengthen his case?
4. Describe decision making at Transworld.

## ▲ Study Questions

1. What is a major problem in evaluating the quality of decisions?
2. Why does decision making always involve risk?
3. What is the role of the manager in decision making?
4. What are the four primary driving forces?

5. How does a linear decision analysis assist in case analysis?
6. Why is decision making considered a process?
7. What phase of the decision process deals with performance?
8. What are the principal types of decisions?

## ▲ References

Barnard, C. I. *The Functions of the Executive*. Cambridge, MA: Harvard University Press, 1938.

Baum, Laurie. "The Day Charlie Bradshaw Kissed off Transworld." *Business Week* (September 29, 1986), pp. 67–68.

Beauchamp, Marc. "Smooth Flying." *Forbes* (September 19, 1989), pp. 94–96.

Drucker, Peter F. *The Practice of Management*. New York: Harper and Brothers, 1954.

Gore, William J. *Administrative Decision-Making: A Heuristic Model*. New York: Wiley, 1964.

Peters, Thomas J., and Waterman, Robert H. Jr. *In Search Of Excellence: Lessons from America's Best-run Companies*. New York: Harper & Row, 1982.

Queenan, Joe. "Remedial Reading." *Forbes* (September 18, 1989), p. 48.

Rowe, Alan J. "A Comparative Analysis of Management Decision Making." *Management Development* No. 6 (December 1974), pp. 6–9.

Simon, H. A. *Models of Man*. New York: Wiley, 1957.

"Transworld President, Operating Chief Quits over Buying Strategy." *Wall Street Journal* (September 2, 1986), p. 12.

"Transworld Resignation." *New York Times* (August 30, 1986), p. 43.

# 2  The Decision Maker

▲ ▲ ▲    ▲ ▲ ▲ ▲ ▲ ▲ ▲ ▲ ▲ ▲ ▲ ▲ ▲ ▲ ▲

This chapter introduces the decision maker as the focal point of the decision process. In the final analysis, it is individuals who make decisions. It is therefore important to understand the individual decision maker in terms of capability, characteristics, and personal preference in order to understand the decisions that are made. Each decision maker has talents that may not have been utilized effectively. At the very least, knowledge regarding decision makers may make it possible for organizations to avoid catastrophic mistakes. Even when in groups, individuals decide for themselves what their level of participation will be. All individuals are not the same in terms of their intellectual ability, commitment, drive, strength of personality, level of ambition, need to dominate, concern for others, level of interest, need for achievement, or need for recognition. There are always differences among the members of an organization. To treat all individuals as homogeneous entities is simplistic.

Understanding and utilizing a person's capabilities are based on the premise that individual differences are the keys to effective decision making. A decision style inventory is described in this chapter; it allows us to measure these individual differences and to understand how to utilize them. Each individual acts in accordance with his or her decision style because that style reflects the person's mental construct. Ultimately, it is that mental construct, combined with the person's value system, that dictates one's behavior as a decision maker.

## ▲   DECISION MAKERS

The individual's decision styles form the backbone of effective decision making. As Drucker (1966) stated, "Effective executives do not make a great many decisions. They concentrate on what is important. They try to make the few important decisions on the highest level of understanding. They try to find the constants in a situation, to think through what is strategic and generic rather than to solve problems." The idea of one best style has been replaced with the idea of style flexibility. Because a flexible style can be modified to suit a specific situation, it can improve effectiveness.

Fortunately, most executives have decision styles that fit their jobs. Some, such as tycoon Charles Wohlstetter, whom Wall Street considered rare, managed to survive the 1929 crash because of the decisions he made. He was a precocious student who at 18 graduated from City College of New York with a degree in English and history. His first job was in a stock brokerage house prior to the 1929 crash, where he saw the impending crisis and advised his boss to sell short. The boss' response was, "Go away and manage your $50,000 stake." With keen insight, he outsmarted the market, and after the crash was the only one with any capital left. Because of that experience, Wohlstetter decided to open his own brokerage firm and brought in a partner.

Wohlstetter's style is typical of a person who is willing to try new things (the conceptual, who has vision). He is described as willing to change his mind if needed. However, his critics claim that he has a tendency to overpay for whatever he buys. (They obviously don't have the same vision of true value.) For example, the price he paid for Contel's cellular telephone licenses was considered by many experts as being too high. When he first met Craig McCaw, he foresaw that Craig would need cash to cover his bid for Lin Broadcasting. Relying on data from his staff, who had analyzed McCaw properties, Wohlstetter spent four days of "almost nonstop negotiations." He completed Contel's largest deal, paying $1.3 billion for 6.1 million potential cellular subscribers. Although the $205 price per customer may seem high, Wohlstetter is convinced that people will "marvel at how cheaply he made the deal." Here is a case of an executive with vision who was willing to risk huge amounts of money on what he believed was right. His understanding and perception concerning events fit him for the role that he pursues (Meeks, 1990, p. 98).

Style also is often a key determinant in the success of an acquisition or merger. Although most mergers do not work out well, the Hewlett-Packard's acquisition of Sanborn Co., a small manufacturer of medical technology, in 1961 was the right move. William Hewlett's father was a doctor who helped him see that HP's measurement products could be extended to the field of medicine. He sensed that medical instrumentation would ultimately need electronics. Because of William Hewlett's persistence, Hewlett-Packard is now considered a leader in medical instrumentation. Hewlett's vision made possible the significant increase in HP's growth, which has now reached $12 billion. Similar to Wohlstetter, Hewlett had the vision and the drive to make medical instrumentation a reality. His management style fit the requirements of the job (Wiegner, 1990, p. 182).

Studying managers at work, Mintzberg (1990) found that they go at an unrelenting pace, and their activities are characterized by brevity, variety, and discontinuity. He also found that they are action-oriented and dislike reflective activities. In addition, he found that managerial work involves performing rituals, ceremonies, negotiations, and all the soft information that ties the organization to its environment.

Although observing decision makers provides valuable information, it does not explain *why* decisions are made the way they are. There are too many unknowns involved that are not visible. By examining the primary driving forces impinging on the decision maker, we can explain emergent decision behavior. Several models are introduced in this chapter to show how decision-making behavior can be explained. Studies of the characteristics of executives such as Mintzberg's provide insights into typical work patterns and some of the clues to understanding the decision maker.

Three approaches are used to examine how decisions are made. First is the individual four force model described in Chapter 1. It focuses on the individual and helps determine what actions are most likely to be taken. Second is examining the situation which includes the organization structure. The third approach uses both the individual's response to situational forces and the definition of the organizational context.

To start, we examine what managers feel are important considerations when they make decisions. Over 450 managers were asked how they would rank the following:

1. *Perception:* Awareness of problems and understanding data.
2. *Tolerance:* Ability to handle stress and ambiguity.
3. *Rationality:* Acting in a deliberate, careful manner and using analytic techniques.
4. *Integrity:* Consistent behavior that builds confidence and credibility.
5. *Commitment:* Willingness and energy to follow through on decisions.
6. *Innovation:* Being creative and seeing opportunities, or finding alternatives.
7. *Compulsive:* Achieving results or closure at any cost.
8. *Openness:* Maintaining communication and group involvement, providing feedback.
9. *Leadership:* Able to influence others and be an effective change agent.
10. *Risk taking:* Willing to deal with future uncertainties; able to forecast implications of decisions.

Responses were obtained from both junior and senior managers in the United States and Europe. The results showed that perception was ranked first, commitment second, and for all individuals integrity was third. Senior managers, on the other hand, ranked leadership third. The single most important factor was the manager's ability to correctly perceive and understand problems. Given the wide range of levels of management and the cultures represented, the level of consensus was significant, indicating what managers felt was important in their decision making.

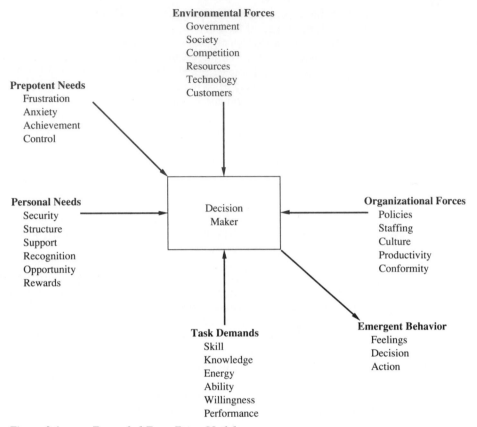

**Environmental Forces**
Government
Society
Competition
Resources
Technology
Customers

**Prepotent Needs**
Frustration
Anxiety
Achievement
Control

**Personal Needs**
Security
Structure
Support
Recognition
Opportunity
Rewards

Decision
Maker

**Organizational Forces**
Policies
Staffing
Culture
Productivity
Conformity

**Task Demands**
Skill
Knowledge
Energy
Ability
Willingness
Performance

**Emergent Behavior**
Feelings
Decision
Action

Figure 2.1   ▲   Expanded Four-Force Model

## ▲   THE EXPANDED FOUR FORCE MODEL

Starting with the four force model introduced in Chapter 1, the expanded model provides an understanding of decision makers' behavior. The four basic driving forces shown in Figure 2.1 are environmental forces, organizational forces, task demands, and personal needs. Prepotent need, which includes both positive and negative elements, is another driving force that influences the behavior of the decision maker. Emergent behavior or the decision maker's response to these forces is directly related to experience, skills, knowledge, energy, and ability to perform.

Using a contingency approach, Tosi and Hamner (1977) have another perspective of the four forces as determinants of behavior. They asked the following questions:

1.   Was the external environment stable or turbulent?
2.   Was the organizational system mechanistic or organic?
3.   Was the organization work system directive or supportive?
4.   What were individual and group attitudes, perceptions, motivation, interpersonal attraction, and past reinforcing experiences?

They considered that individual behavior was contingent on changes in the environment, organizational design, organizational development, and group behavior. Once relevant contingencies are identified, appropriate actions can be taken.

## Environmental Forces

Environmental forces that impact the organization require a response from decision makers. These forces include new technology, government regulations, and competitive pressure, as well as the public at large. In addition, all the stakeholders who have an interest in the activities of the organization must be considered, such as workers, stockholders, and customers.

An example of how the external environment impacts an organization is the *Valdez* oil spill, where the public outcry against Exxon became a dominant force. Similarly, in the Bhopal tragedy, the environmental impact and loss of human life laid a heavy onus on Union Carbide and its management. There was little time for these companies to develop a reasonable and rational solution to the problem. They were times of crisis that called for quick and responsive action, but the public was unhappy with the rate of response. Johnson & Johnson, on the other hand, immediately withdrew Tylenol from the shelves when people died after taking cyanide-tainted capsules.

## Organizational Forces

Group pressure reflecting interaction with other members of the organization is another driving force. This interaction occurs at three levels: with superiors, with peers, and with subordinates. Organizations have committees, task forces, or temporary organizational structures that also contribute to interaction effects. In addition, there are informal relations that provide another form of interaction. Because interactions occur in many ways and at different levels, group pressure covers all interactions.

Groups can exercise differing pressure depending on the cohesiveness and coordination required. Fiedler (1967) described three types of groups based on their interdependence.

1. An *interacting* group: each individual's ability to perform depends on another's doing his or her share of the task.
2. A *co-acting* group: each member acts reasonably independently.
3. A *counteracting* group: members work together to reconcile conflict.

The coordination required among group members and a sharing of goals are highest in the interacting group, whereas aggression and competition among group members is highest in the counteracting group. Thus, the pressures and degree of interaction are a function of interdependencies in the group.

## Task Demands

The next force is the decision maker's response to task demands. This force deals with the decision maker's technical competence, including skills, knowledge, energy, and ability to perform the task. Willingness to perform, on the other hand, generally is influenced by the level of satisfaction. Task demands represent the requirements of the job that need to be met. Jobs that are too difficult can lead to failure, or be demotivating.

Expectancy theory indicates that the "willingness" to perform is influenced by the level of rewards expected and satisfaction achieved. However, a highly motivated, "unskilled" worker would have difficulty in meeting task demands that require a high level of competence. Task demands should provide challenge but be consistent with style and not be excessive to the point of inducing failure. On the other hand, task demands that are too easy and provide no challenge can lead to boredom and loss of interest. Tasks that are attainable generally lead to success and rewards, thus providing satisfaction on the job.

Mowday, Porter, and Steers (1982) have cited a number of models that are used to describe task demands and reactions by individuals. These include:

1. The two-factor theory (hygiene and motivator factors): These lead to either neutral or high motivation.
2. The requisite task attributes model: Meeting requisite task attributes can lead to satisfaction.
3. The socio-technical model: Properly designed psychological requirements of tasks can lead to high performance.
4. The activation theory: Job characteristics activate performance responses.
5. The achievement motivation theory: Enriched jobs can lead to either high performance and satisfaction or low performance and frustration.

Based on this list, there are two outcomes resulting from task demands—the level of performance of the individual and the satisfaction achieved.

## Personal Needs

The fourth force, personal needs, is the one most often overlooked. Personal needs are exhibited in many ways, as reported by Levinson (1973), who described a study of 400 European executives; 61 percent indicated that their primary problem was personnel and almost all had some form of leadership problem. Nadler and Lawler (1983) found that organizations can relieve employee discontent by paying attention to the employees' needs. When needs are not met, it is small wonder that employee satisfaction and commitment do not meet expectations. Viewed from a decision-making perspective, satisfying personal needs is, perhaps, one of the key elements of improving performance.

## Response to the Four Forces

The individual decision maker attempts to maintain a state of equilibrium in the face of the four driving forces. The consequences of the failure to balance the four forces may result in breakdown or failure. Any one of the four forces can be overpowering at any point in time. How the decision maker responds to each of the four forces depends on his or her ability in each of the following areas.

| Force | Positive Response | Negative Response |
|---|---|---|
| Environmental forces | Awareness of the situation | Lacks response |
| Organizational forces | High interpersonal confidence | Little interpersonal confidence |
| Task demands | High technical competence | Lacks technical competence |
| Personal needs | Postive self-image | Poor self-image |

As can be seen, response to the four forces influences the effectiveness of the decision maker. Because the four force model focuses on the individual, it can be used to examine decision making in various situations. The model is *not* a stimulus–response model where the decision maker reacts automatically to the pressures imposed. Rather, because perception filters the stimuli and cognition permits understanding and evokes a "choice" of response, the decision maker "reacts" to situations consonant with cognitive complexity, personal needs, personal values, and organizational goals.

Interestingly, each of the four forces has been approached differently by various disciplines. Personal needs traditionally have been the domain of the psychologist; organizational considerations have been the field of study for behavioral scientists and sociologists. Environmental factors traditionally have been covered in business policy and strategy or by economists; industrial engineers and industrial psychologists have concerned themselves with the task component of the work environment.

## ▲ THE IMPORTANCE OF VALUES

Personal values are an integral part of every individual's life and thought. As such, values are a key factor in determining a manager's decision style. Values are treated in depth in Chapter 4, but they are introduced here to set a framework for understanding why individuals have different styles.

Individuals' values are typically acquired very early in life from parents, teachers, and others who are in a position to influence them. An individual's basic values typically are ingrained by experiences up to the age of seven. Reinforcement determines which values are considered to be good or bad. Values reflect the desirability of a situation and are used as criteria for preference or justification. Values remain strong and are a commitment to an ideal or abstract standards. Values often are considered the normative standards that influence people's choice among alternatives (Ebert and Mitchell, 1975). They provide a relatively permanent perceptual framework that influences a person's learning and behavior.

Rokeach (1973) defined values as "abstract ideals, positive or negative, not tied to any specific object or situation, representing a person's beliefs about modes of conduct and ideal terminal modes." Values reflect global beliefs that guide actions, judgments, and desirable end-states, or future conditions. Decision behavior also reflects basic values and related attitudes.

## ▲ PERCEPTION

Perception is another key element in decision making because information that is obtained about problems involves biases that convert facts to match one's own reality. Managers tend to perceive a situation in relationship to their goals. Managers often deal with preconceived notions based on an individual's "frame of reference." This frame determines a person's psychological structuring and way of responding to stimuli, and decision makers perceive new information consistent with preexisting views.

Organizational realities to a large extent determine a manager's perceptual response to information. A manager's decisions are constrained by perceptual biases that enter into the interpretation and reaction to various situations. A decision maker's perceptual bias is the cumulative effect of subjective perception, unique frame of reference, personal goals, values, beliefs, basic drives, motives, and situational demands. Managers gain insight from past experience and use this as a frame of reference. These considerations are important when determining a manager's decision style.

## ▲ DECISION STYLE

Decision style builds on the two key elements of values and perception. Decision style describes the way a manager makes decisions; it depends on a number of factors, including the context in which a decision is made, the decision maker's way of perceiving and understanding cues, and what the decision maker values or judges as important. Decision style thus reflects the manner in which a decision maker reacts to a given situation—how he or she interprets and understands cues, what he or she believes is important, and how he or she responds to the many demands and forces.

An obvious question is: Can decision style be measured? It can be measured, and we use a test instrument called the decision style inventory to do this. The questions on the inventory are shown at the end of the chapter. They probe the psychological structure of one's mind. Perhaps one of the most important considerations in decision styles is that it clearly shows that each individual thinks differently depending on his or her perception and values. Thus, decisions are made within the unique frame of reference or psychological set of each individual, and reflect the decision maker's subjective reality.

The questions are based on the four driving forces and the situation confronting the decision maker. The scores on the inventory categorize decision makers into combinations of four basic decision styles. Knowing an individual's decision style pattern (combination of basic styles), we can predict how he or she will react to various situations.

In an absolute sense, then, decision styles are the scores one receives after answering the questions on the decision style inventory. In a relative sense, decision style is the "way" in which style is used in decision-making situations. Effective decision makers generally are those individuals whose style matches the requirements of the decision situation. Decision style has also been described as the way in which a manager perceives information and mentally processes that information to arrive at decisions.

## Measuring Decision Style

The decision style inventory instrument has been tested with many groups over a number of years, and it has a very high face validity and reliability. Respondents almost invariably agreed with their decision styles as shown on the test instrument. They agreed that the styles were a correct description of themselves and how they made decisions.

The decision style inventory measures the relative intensity of each of the four decision style categories. The inventory is not used to measure absolute values but rather determines an individual's relative scores compared with the population as a whole. As an example, a group of 26 young corporate presidents given the decision style inventory instrument had "average" scores in all four categories. The implication is that young presidents have considerable flexibility and find little difficulty in changing from one style to another as the situation warrants. Thus, we might expect to observe multiple styles for an individual rather than the stereotype of a single category, although a dominant style would be the one observed most frequently.

At this point, it would be useful for the reader to try the decision style inventory on pages 38–39 of this chapter.

## ▲ SCORING THE DECISION STYLE INVENTORY

The results on the decision style inventory reflect a person's cognitive complexity and values. As can be seen in Figure 2.2, the decision style model has two components: cognitive complexity and values orientation. The lower half of Figure 2.2 shows that the directive and behavioral styles prefer structure, whereas the upper half prefer complexity. The cognitive complexity dimension separates the upper and lower half, and distinguishes managers from leaders as described by Zaleznick (1970).

The values dimension separates the left and right halves and covers the task/people dimension. The left half of Figure 2.2 shows that the analytic and directive styles prefer task whereas the right half prefer people. Decision styles also describe the individual's personal-

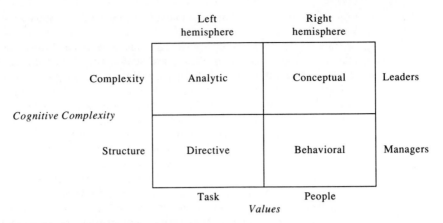

**Figure 2.2  ▲  Decision Style Model**

ity, self-competence, interpersonal competence, situational awareness, and problem-solving capability. A more complete description of the decision style model is shown in Figure 2.3. The description of each of the four styles follows.

1.  *Directive*

This individual has a low tolerance for ambiguity and low cognitive complexity. The focus is on technical decisions, and this style is often autocratic and has a high need for power. Because of the use of little information and few alternatives, speed and satisfac-

|  | Left hemisphere (logical) | Right hemisphere (relational) |  |
|---|---|---|---|
| Tolerance for ambiguity | **Analytical**<br>Enjoys problem solving<br>Wants best answer<br>Wants control<br>Uses considerable data<br>Enjoys variety<br>Is innovative<br>Uses careful analysis<br><br>N-ACH, needs challenges | **Conceptual**<br>Is achievement-oriented<br>Has a broad outlook<br>Is creative<br>Is humanistic/artistic<br>Initiates new ideas<br>Is future-oriented<br><br>N-ACH, is independent<br>and wants recognition | Thinking (ideas) |
| Need for structure | **Directive**<br>Expects results<br>Is aggressive<br>Acts rapidly<br>Uses rules<br>Uses intuition<br>Is verbal<br><br>N-POW, needs power | **Behavioral**<br>Is supportive<br>Uses persuasion<br>Is empathetic<br>Communicates easily<br>Prefers meetings<br>Uses limited data<br><br>N-AFF, needs affiliation | Doing (action) |

*Cognitive Complexity*

Task/technical          People/social

*Values Orientation*

**Figure 2.3  ▲  Complete Decision-Style Model**

tory solutions are typical of these individuals. Generally they prefer structure and specific information, which is given verbally. They are focused and often are aggressive. Their orientation is internal to the organization and short range, with tight controls. Although they are efficient, they need security and status. They have the drive required to achieve results, but they also want to dominate others.

2. *Analytic*

This individual has a much greater tolerance for ambiguity than the directive style manager and also has a more cognitively complex personality that leads to the desire for more information and consideration of many alternatives. Because of the focus on technical decisions and the need for control, there is an autocratic bent. The analytic style is typified by the ability to cope with new situations. As a result, this style enjoys problem solving and strives for the maximum that can be achieved in a given situation. Position and ego are important characteristics, and these individuals often reach top posts in a company or start their own. They are not rapid in their decision making; they enjoy variety and prefer written reports. They enjoy challenges and examine every detail in a situation.

3. *Conceptual*

Having both high cognitive complexity and a people orientation, this style tends to use data from multiple sources and considers many alternatives. Similar to the behavioral style, there is trust and openness in relations and shared goals with subordinates. These individuals tend to be idealists who may emphasize ethics and values. They generally are creative and can readily understand complex relationships. Their focus is long range with high organizational commitment. They are achievement-oriented and value praise, recognition, and independence. They prefer loose control to power and will frequently use participation. They typically are thinkers rather than doers.

4. *Behavioral*

Although low on the cognitive complexity scale, this manager has a deep concern for the organization and development of people. Behavioral style managers tend to be supportive and are concerned with subordinates' well being. They provide counseling, are receptive to suggestions, communicate easily, show warmth, are empathetic, are persuasive, and are willing to compromise and accept loose control. With low data input, this style tends toward short-range focus and uses meetings for communicating. These managers avoid conflict, seek acceptance, and are very people-oriented, but sometimes are insecure.

McClelland (1962) described learned needs in terms of economic achievement and feelings. His terms were:

N-ACH, need for achievement.
N-AFF, need for affiliation.
N-POW, need for power.

As shown in Figure 2.3, these needs precisely fit the categories for decision styles. They also help to define the needs that each style exhibits. For example, an Analytic N-ACH needs challenges whereas a Conceptual N-ACH needs recognition.

The amount that each of the four styles is used can be determined from the score on the decision style inventory. There are four levels of intensity for each category.

1. *Least preferred:* This level of intensity shows that the individual will rarely use the style, but when required could do so. For example, under stress, a high analytic shifts to a directive style.

2. *Back-up:* This level of intensity shows that the individual will use the style occasionally and reflects the typical score on the decision style inventory.

3. *Dominant:* This intensity indicates that the individual will frequently use this style in preference to the other styles. However, individuals can have more than one dominant style and thus can readily switch from one to another.

4. *Very dominant:* This is the highest level of intensity and describes a compulsive use of a given style. This intensity becomes the focus of the individual and will override other styles that have less intensity. In occasional cases, individuals do have more than one very dominant style.

The level of intensity is useful for interpreting what the scores on the decision style inventory mean. Table 2.1 can be used to determine the level of intensity for each person's style based on the scores attained on the decision style inventory. For example, a person with a score of directive = 55, analytic = 95, conceptual = 80, and behavioral = 70 would have the following levels of intensity:

Directive (55): Least preferred
Analytic (95): Back-up
Conceptual (80): Back-up
Behavioral (70): Dominant

Based on the complexity of human beings, one would not expect managers to neatly fit into only one category. Rather, the typical manager has at least one dominant style with at least one, and often two, back-up styles. As noted earlier, a group of young presidents given the decision style inventory had average scores in all four categories of the inventory. The implication is that these people have considerable flexibility and are able to change from one situation to another with little difficulty. Thus, we rarely would observe a decision maker with only a single style category.

Table 2.2 describes the decision style scores for a diverse sample of managers. None of the groups had an "average" score that was dominant for the directive style. On the other hand, top executives and senior military officers, on the average, have a dominant conceptual score in common.

Table 2.2 shows that Group I, middle and upper managers, is most representative of what one might expect in industry. The chief executives in Group II had a dominant conceptual style; military officers, who typically are viewed as domineering decision types, had a combination of conceptual and analytic styles. Given the complexity of today's military services, it is small wonder that a rigid, authoritarian approach does not succeed. In Group IV, the foreign managers show the importance of culture and demand for results. As might be expected, in Group V, students showed a dominant behavioral score that typically indicates the need for affiliation and developing of their self-confidence.

Although these categories appear to be distinct and nonoverlapping, in fact most managers have characteristics that fall into more than one style category. Managers generally have dominant as well as back-up styles. Managers also fit several categories, termed *style*

Table 2.1 ▲ Decision Style Intensity Levels

| Style | Intensity | | | |
|---|---|---|---|---|
| | **Least Preferred** | **Back-up** | **Dominant** | **Very Dominant** |
| **Directive** | Below 68 | 68 to 82 | 83 to 90 | Over 90 |
| **Analytic** | Below 83 | 83 to 97 | 98 to 104 | Over 104 |
| **Conceptual** | Below 73 | 73 to 87 | 88 to 94 | Over 94 |
| **Behavioral** | Below 48 | 48 to 62 | 63 to 70 | Over 70 |

Table 2.2 ▲ Decision-Style Scores

| | | Directive | Analytic | Conceptual | Behavioral |
|---|---|---|---|---|---|
| I. Managers | | | | | |
| Male | (n = 194) | 74 (B) | 89 (B) | 83 (B) | 54 (B) |
| Male—Technical | (n = 54) | 71 (B) | 94 (B) | 74 (B) | 61 (B) |
| Female | (n = 93) | 74 (B) | 88 (B) | 74 (B) | 64 (D) |
| II. Executives | | | | | |
| Chief | (n = 80) | 70 (B) | 90 (B) | 93 (D) | 47 (L) |
| III. Military | | | | | |
| Admirals | (n = 6) | 59 (L) | 102 (D) | 92 (D) | 47 (L) |
| IV. Foreign | | | | | |
| Executives | (n = 110) | 73 (B) | 87 (B) | 85 (B) | 55 (B) |
| V. Students | | | | | |
| Male and Female | (n = 138) | 70 (B) | 87 (B) | 81 (B) | 62 (B) |

L = least preferred     D = dominant
B = back-up             V = very dominant

*patterns.* Although any decision style categorization is approximate, knowing an individual's dominant or very dominant style provides useful information. If one identifies the dominant styles or style patterns for an individual, then decision-making behavior can be better understood.

## ▲ BRAIN-SIDEDNESS AND STYLE

The left half and right half of the decision style model correspond to differences in the left and right hemispheres of the brain. The left hemisphere controls logical thought, is analytic, and processes information serially. It handles speech, pointing, and smiling as well as the abstract logic needed for mathematics and verbal thinking. The right hemisphere is the more creative and perceives things as a whole, has a comprehensive sense of timing, and can encompass many thoughts at the same time using parallel processing of information. The right hemisphere appreciates space, imagery, fantasy, and music. Right-brain thinkers are also more artistic, and dreams seem to be predominately right-brain functions. The right brain exhibits intuition, in contrast to the left brain, which is more rational. Doktor and Hamilton (1973) conclude that decision makers who apply the more logical analytic mode over intuitive synthesis may be limiting the potential for finding good solutions.

Mintzberg (1976) in his article "Planning on the Left and Managing on the Right," explains why some people can master certain mental activities and yet are incapable of handling others. Issues such as why a scientist cannot handle people or why there is a discrepancy in the use of planning and analysis techniques are based on his observations that executives strongly favor verbal media, do not disseminate information freely, enjoy ambiguity and action, delegate handling of organizational crises, and rely on judgment rather than analysis as the basis for making decisions.

## ▲ STYLE–SITUATION INTERACTION

To illustrate the importance of style–situation interaction, Figure 2.4 shows where conflicts between superior and subordinate can occur depending on their respective decision styles. Generally, conflict arises when expectations are significantly different between individuals.

|  | Subordinate Style | | | |
|---|---|---|---|---|
| **Manager Style** | Directive | Analytic | Conceptual | Behavioral |
| Directive | No | Min | Con | Con |
| Analytic | Min | No | Min | Con |
| Conceptual | Con | Min | Min | No |
| Behavioral | Con | Con | No | Min |

Con = potential conflict.
Min = minimal conflict.
No = no conflict.

**Figure 2.4  ▲  Manager - Subordinate Style Conflicts**

The directive and behavioral styles are the ones most likely to encounter conflict. In part, cognitive complexity and personal needs account for this. The directive's need for power goes counter to the behavioral's need for affiliation or the conceptual's need for independence. Because of their high tolerance for ambiguity, both the analytic and the conceptual styles have fewer potential conflicts with subordinates.

In the reverse situation, the analytic manager would tend to criticize a directive subordinate for incomplete work and not "doing his or her homework." The analytic manager has the greatest difficulty with a behavioral counterpart because of a lack of understanding of why feelings are used as the basis for decisions rather than the rational, analytic approach. On the other hand, by understanding style differences, managers are in a better position to resolve conflict or improve communications.

## ▲ COMPATIBILITY AMONG STYLES IN AN ORGANIZATION

How one's style relates to another's can be viewed as a person-to-person relationship or a manager-to-a-group relationship. The manager's relationship with others often is referred to as *leadership*. The relationships between individuals can be synergistic when they have similar styles. There is little question that people with similar styles understand one another more easily than they understand someone with a different style. This is especially true in individuals with high cognitive complexity (analytical and conceptual), who cannot readily communicate with persons who prefer structure and who reject complexity. Conversely, the less complex individual dislikes lengthy explanations used by those with high cognitive complexity. The action-oriented individual has little tolerance for the thinker, whereas the thinker tends to be inept in action-oriented tasks and generally is uninterested in situations that require action.

Understanding someone else's style can be valuable in forming relationships. When working with a partner who is analytic, for example, it is helpful to know that the person's focus will be on the technical aspects of a task and he or she will use logic in thinking about possibilities; this person is very cerebral. A behavioral partner demands much more personal attention. Behaviorals prefer to share feelings directly without much intellectualizing. They listen, participate, and express concern for the well-being of their friends and colleagues. A directive, on the other hand, will approach a relationship in a much more impersonal way. He or she prefers order, status, power, and control in a relationship and often will be the initiator of activities.

A conceptual partner tends to express his or her feelings about relationships viewing them from a longer time perspective. Details are not important, except perhaps as they are related to some broader concern. For example, a conceptual is likely to tolerate an unpleasant condition for a long time and then blow up over a minor detail, such as how one's desk is organized. This quickly escalates into a broad and abstract complaint of dissatisfaction.

Neither the directive nor the behavioral acts that way. Their need for structure and concreteness expresses itself in a concern about specific events in a relationship. The behavioral complains that some event hurt his or her feelings which results in a sense of rejection, whereas the directive complains that an event caused anxiety and a sense of lost control.

The analytic and, to some extent, the conceptual will complain about events that are mundane and boring. The conceptual is opposed to events in a relationship that restrict his or her freedom. The analytic is opposed to the routine events in a relationship that lack intellectual challenge or that conflict with his or her sense of logic.

Knowing the personality attributes of others in an organization can help smooth relationships. For example, the president of a small consulting firm had her office space in a building where the manager constantly yelled at her about minor details. When the president realized that the office manager was a high directive, she knew that the office manager yelled at everyone, not just at her.

The behavioral person who has a high affiliation need wants to be liked and be a part of a group; this person does not make a good manager in situations requiring assertiveness. There is a tendency to make excuses rather than decisions, and havoc can be created by not following rules. This disregard for procedures causes confusion, is seen as being inconsistent, and leaves subordinates in a weak position because they cannot always be sure of what to expect.

On the other hand, the directive style focuses on the task and has been shown to create an effective work environment where structure is important. The directive manager gets results by focusing on worker performance. However, subordinates generally prefer the democratic or supporting style. Directive managers do not necessarily try to make their subordinates feel weak; rather, they exercise the power they have. These individuals feel responsible for building their organizations, find satisfaction in work accomplished, will sacrifice self-interest for results, and use tangible incentives to reward performance.

Whereas the directive manager has a high need for power and typically is very direct, the behavioral manager tends to be concerned with people's needs. One can conclude that the most effective manager is one who has a dominant directive style and has a strong behavioral back-up style. The participative supportive manager who does not achieve results would be considered ineffective.

The conclusion that a purely behavioral manager may not be effective in achieving results must be tempered with several considerations. First, a behavioral manager can often obtain greater productivity where subordinates have freedom to operate as they see fit. Thus, the purely directive-style, power-oriented manager does not achieve results in all situations and in all organizations.

It is important to recognize that the directive and behavioral styles are action-oriented, and these people operate as first-line managers in contrast to the requirements needed at the upper levels of management.

## ▲ USING DECISION STYLES TO PREDICT BEHAVIOR

The manner in which each style reacts to stress, motivation, problem solving, and thinking provides another basis for understanding decision makers' response behavior. The reactions of each style are shown in Table 2.3. Relating decision making to personality,

Table 2.3 ▲ Style Reactions

| Basic Style | Under Stress | Motivated by: | Solves Problems by: | Manner of Thinking |
|---|---|---|---|---|
| Directive | Explodes | Power, Status | Rules and Policies | Focused |
| Analytic | Follows Rules | Challenge | Analysis and Insight | Logical |
| Conceptual | Is Erratic | Recognition | Intuition and Judgment | Creative |
| Behavioral | Avoids | Acceptance | Feeling and Instinct | Emotional |

Holland (1968) examined the causes of errors in administrative decisions. He concluded that insufficient or incorrect facts bearing on a problem were used and that many mistakes resulted from personality and interpersonal factors. He considered mistakes resulting from pesonality-related errors as the most important of four basic behaviors:

1. Impulsive behavior: Results in taking action without due regard for all of the consequences involved because the decision maker is incapable either mentally or emotionally.
2. Obsessive–compulsive behavior: Leads to unwelcome, and sometimes morbid, ideas and a tendency to engage in senseless or meaningless acts. Errors result from a decision maker who applies standards of work and perfection that are not normal for all people.
3. Masochistic–sadistic behavior: Is a desire to hurt oneself expressed in self-belittling—a feeling of inadequacy—and dependency on others. Decisions are made based on maintaining relationships based on approval.
4. Inferiority–superiority behavior: This is typical of a decision maker who is a perfectionist with superiority traits but who feels alone, inferior, and somewhat helpless. Decisions are independent only when approval is certain.

The four behaviors just noted reflect repression of anxieties caused by the conflict of the id, ego, and superego. In addition, personality problems arise due to the repression of strivings for power, jealousies, fears, anger, and the general feeling of helplessness, or of being alone.

Decision style provides the decision maker with a basis for understanding behavior and being able to deal with that behavior. For example, Levinson describes an abrasive personality as the single most frequent cause for the failure of bright persons in executive ranks. This kind of person "like the proverbial porcupine seems to have a natural knack for jabbing others in an irritating and sometimes painful way—unconsciously undermines his success and is usually either fired by an exasperated boss or stuck permanently at the lower levels of his company" (1973, pp. 70–76).

## ▲ STYLE AND FLEXIBILITY

At the outset, two important issues need to be treated. First is the question, Is there one best style? and second, How flexible can one's style be? For many years management theory prescribed the one "best way" to make decisions. However, no single style is always more effective than another because it depends on a style's appropriateness to the situation in which it is used. Boulgarides (1973) conducted research in which he compared decision styles with leadership flexibility. He found that the extremes of being too flexible or too rigid are least effective. Rather than a single best style, a flexible style that can be used to match a given situation appears more appropriate.

Are managers sufficiently flexible to be able to change their styles, or can they be trained to be flexible if they are not? A comparison of individuals having low flexibility (rigidity) with

Table 2.4 ▲ Style Flexibility

| | Flexibility | |
|---|---|---|
| | Low | High |
| Tolerance for ambiguity | low | high |
| Structures the environment | structured | unstructured |
| Power needs | high | low |
| Control orientation | high | low |
| Belief system | firm | open |
| Person orientation | inner | other |
| Concern for people | self | others |

those having high flexibility is shown in Table 2.4. Here flexibility is equated with high or low cognitive complexity.

The rigid, fixed style is less able to adapt compared with managers whose style is flexible and who can adapt readily to most situations. Fiedler (1967) suggests that it is easier to change almost anything than to change a manager's personality or style. Maddi (1972) describes the rigidly controlled, compulsive individual as one who does not change, whereas other personality types can change dramatically.

## ▲  OTHER APPROACHES TO STYLE

One of the early approaches to measuring style was the Myers–Briggs Type Indicator Test (1962). It determined personality types that were described by Swiss psychiatrist Carl Jung (1959). Jung's approach assumed that people use different ways to perceive things and use different judgments in arriving at conclusions concerning what has been perceived. The Myers–Briggs (1962) instrument has been widely used to determine personalities. It has been applied to many situations and has been used to determine suitable types of occupations for each personality type.

Jung defined two ways of perceiving and two ways of judging as follows: perceiving by sensing things directly or by intuition based on unconscious associations; judging by logical, impersonal processes or by the use of feeling or subjective values.

In this approach, four combinations are possible: The sensing individual (ST) relies mainly on facts and makes decisions using impersonal analysis based on a logical process of reasoning. The feeling person (SF) relies on his or her senses for perceiving but prefers feelings as the basis for judging. Feeling persons are warm and are more interested in facts about people than in things. The thinking individual (NT) uses intuition for perception, but focuses on technical, impersonal analysis. Finally, the intuitive individual (NF) uses unconscious associations and focuses on new possibilities. Such people exhibit warmth and commitment and communicate easily.

In addition to the four basic categories, Killman and Mitroff (1978) discuss other factors. The first was the introvert–extrovert dichotomy, where perception and judgment focus on either concepts or ideas rather than people and things. The second is termed the shadow side, which can be construed either as a back-up style or behavior under stress because of suppression of conscious thinking. Diagrammatically, the Jungian model is shown in Figure 2.5.

In this model the ST category matches the directive style of the cognitive contingency model. SF matches the behavioral category. The NT individual corresponds to the analytic category. Finally, the NF category is comparable to the conceptual style in the decision

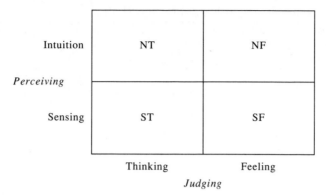

**Figure 2.5 ▲ Jungian Type Model**

style model. The correspondence between the two models offers further support for the cognitive approach in understanding decision styles.

The introversion–extroversion preference is an overlay that can apply to any of the four basic styles. Because the introvert works best with ideas and reflects on the inner world of concepts, this individual is best suited for work demanding the organization of facts, whereas the extrovert is action-oriented and is the person who gets things done.

Jung indicated that the primary thinking process dominates the individual's performance and, in turn, behavior. The auxiliary process can be considered the back-up or balancing of the dominant preference with the other personality attributes. However, people may be too complex to be described either by a dominant or a combination dominant and auxiliary process. As shown in the decision style inventory, patterns of behavior are quite varied, change with time, relate to learning, and are situationally dependent. The basic model proposed by Jung is a framework on which to incorporate contextual and time-dependent variables. As described by users, its primary purpose is to explain personality differences rather than accept random variation as the basis for differences.

## ▲ Decision Style Inventory Instructions

1. Use *only* the following numbers to answer each question:
   **8** when the question is *most* like you.
   **4** when the question is *moderately* like you.
   **2** when the question is *slightly* like you.
   **1** when the question is *least* like you.
2. Each of the numbers must be inserted in the box following the answers to each question.
3. You may only use the 8, 4, 2, and 1 *once* for each question.
4. For example, the numbers you might use to answer a given question could look as follows: **8 1 4 2**
5. Notice that each number has been used only once in the answers for a given question.
6. In answering the questions, think of how you *normally* act in a situation.
7. Choose the *first* response that comes to your mind when answering the questions.
8. There is no time limit in answering the questions, and there are no right or wrong answers. You can change your mind.
9. Your responses reflect how you *feel* about the response to the questions and what you *prefer* to do, *not* what you think is the right thing to do.

## Decision Style Inventory III–Copyright A.J. Rowe 6/6/81, Rev. 9/15/85

Please score the following questions based on the instructions given. Your score reflects how *you see yourself,* not what you believe is correct or desirable, as related to *your work situation.* It covers *typical* decisions that you make in your work environment.

| | | I | | II | | III | | IV |
|---|---|---|---|---|---|---|---|---|
| 1. | My prime objective is to: | have a position with status | | be the best in my field | | achieve recognition for my work | | feel secure in my job | |
| 2. | I enjoy jobs that: | are technical and well defined | | have considerable variety | | allow independent action | | involve people | |
| 3. | I expect people working for me to be: | productive and fast | | highly capable | | committed and responsive | | receptive to suggestions | |
| 4. | In my job, I look for: | practical results | | the best solutions | | new approaches or ideas | | good working environment | |
| 5. | I communicate best with others: | in a direct one-to-one basis | | in writing | | by having a group discussion | | in a formal meeting | |
| 6. | In my planning, I emphasize: | current problems | | meeting objectives | | future goals | | developing people's careers | |
| 7. | When faced with solving a problem, I: | rely on proven approaches | | apply careful analysis | | look for creative approaches | | rely on my feelings | |
| 8. | When using information, I prefer: | specific facts | | accurate and complete data | | broad coverage of many options | | limited data which is easily understood | |
| 9. | When I am not sure about what to do, I: | rely on intuition | | search for facts | | look for a possible compromise | | wait before making a decision | |
| 10. | Whenever possible, I avoid: | long debates | | incomplete work | | using numbers or formulas | | conflict with others | |
| 11. | I am especially good at: | remembering dates & facts | | solving difficult problems | | seeing many possibilities | | interacting with others | |
| 12. | When time is important, I: | decide and act quickly | | follow plans and priorities | | refuse to be pressured | | seek guidance or support | |
| 13. | In social settings, I generally: | speak with others | | think about what is being said | | observe what is going on | | listen to the conversation | |
| 14. | I am good at remembering: | people's names | | places we met | | people's faces | | people's personality | |
| 15. | The work I do provides me: | the power to influence others | | challenging assignments | | achieving my personal goals | | acceptance by the group | |
| 16. | I work well with those who are: | energetic and ambitious | | self-confident | | open minded | | polite and trusting | |

*(Continued)*

| 17. | When under stress, I: | become anxious | | concentrate on the problem | | become frustrated | | am forgetful | |
|-----|-----------------------|----------------|--|----------------------------|--|-------------------|--|--------------|--|
| 18. | Others consider me: | aggressive | | disciplined | | imaginative | | supportive | |
| 19. | My decisions typically are: | realistic and direct | | systematic or abstract | | broad and flexible | | sensitive to the needs of others | |
| 20. | I dislike: | losing control | | boring work | | following rules | | being rejected | |
| | | | | | | | | | |

## ▲  How to Score the Decision Style Inventory

1. Total the points in each of the four columns—I, II, III, IV.
2. Total the sum of these four numbers. The sum of the four columns should be 300 points. If your sum does not equal 300 points, check your addition and that you have not repeated any numbers for a given question.
3. Place your scores in the appropriate box—I, II, III, IV in Figure 2.6.

| Analytic<br>II | Conceptual<br>III |
|:---:|:---:|
| Directive<br>I | Behavioral<br>IV |

Individual Scoring Matrix

**Figure 2.6  ▲  Jungian Type Model**

## ▲ ▲ ▲ ▲ ▲  THE SCHOELLHORN CASE

The board of directors fired Robert Schoellhorn, CEO of Abbott Laboratories, but he refused to leave. He was accused of getting rid of the chief operating officer and of abusing his position. Schoellhorn had threatened to leave if the chief operating officer wasn't fired; however, the real issue seemed to be the complaints about Schoellhorn's autocratic management style. He, in turn, sued Abbott, alleging that their lawyers were threatening him with "severe personal humiliation and drastic economic sanctions" if he didn't change his mind (Schwartz and McCormick, 1990).

Part of the difficulty was that Schoellhorn was accused of being an absentee manager who was constantly flying around in the corporate jet rather than paying attention to his job. In retaliation, the board stripped him of all his perks and removed him as CEO and chairman. They felt that Schoellhorn's autocratic style and his cutting R&D money, which he spent on himself, made him wrong for the job.

How often is this story repeated where capable, hard-driving executives no longer fit the organization? This chapter explores how to recognize and use decision style to avoid the Abbott-type problem.

The lack of restraints at the top of the corporate ladder creates a tempting situation. The increased power can lead to a grandiose self-image. In the case of Schoellhorn, "he felt the company owed him so much because it was so successful." He began to indulge himself. He refused to allow anyone to challenge him and ousted three heirs-apparent over a nine-year period because they were not "yes-men," which is what he demanded. He was sacrificing the future of Abbott by cutting R&D budgets in order to maintain a yearly earnings growth rate of 15 percent. According to a current Abbott top executive, Schoellhorn's primary agenda "was preserving his own power and eliminating his competition." Decision makers cannot afford to lose touch with their organization by isolating themselves, insulating themselves, or having prolonged absences. Outside activities kept Schoellhorn on the road an estimated 70 to 80 percent of the time. His colleagues viewed him as an absentee manager. He lost his ability to lead Abbott "because he lost the respect of its executives."

The Abbott–Schoellhorn type of conflict develops when executives realize what got them to their positions of responsibility. At that point they stop doing the little things that made them so successful and instead begin indulging themselves. In sharp contrast to Schoellhorn's performance, Allen F. Jacobson, CEO of 3M, paid attention to the smallest of details and fostered a creative zeal to the point that few companies can boast of having the innovative culture of 3M. The results are impressive, with a doubling of net income between 1985 and 1990 and with 30 percent of 3M's $13 billion 1990 revenues resulting from new products introduced during that five-year period (Kelly, 1991).

## ▲ Exercise

---

### Characteristics of Decision Making
Which factors do you feel are needed at the top management level for effective decision making?

| Factors | May be Needed | Often Useful | Usually Needed | Very Important |
|---|---|---|---|---|
| **Perception:** Awareness of problems, understanding of data, intuitive insight | | | | |
| **Tolerance:** Handle stress and ambiguity easily | | | | |
| **Rational:** Act in careful manner and use analytic techniques | | | | |
| **Integrity:** Consistent in behavior, build confidence and credibility | | | | |

**Commitment:**
Willingness and
energy to follow
through on deci-
sions and reach a
final conclusion

**Innovative:**
Creative, see oppor-
tunities, find many
alternatives

**Compulsive:**
Achieve results or
closure at any cost

**Openness:**
Maintain commu-
nication and group
involvement; pro-
vide feedback

**Leadership:**
Able to influence
others by convinc-
ing; an effective
change agent

**Risk taking:**
Willing to deal with
future uncertain-
ties; able to fore-
cast implications of
decisions

## ▲ Summary

An important aspect of managerial decision making is the identification of decision styles. Early work on decision making focused on how individuals actually used information—the amount of data used and the number of ideas perceived. These and the concern for people are incorporated in the current decision style model presented in this chapter.

Individuals have combinations of the four decision styles—directive, analytic, conceptual, and behavioral. One or more styles may be dominant for an individual, with possibly one or more back-up styles. Individuals can be relatively "fixed" or flexible in decision making depending on their decision styles. The decision style inventory has had wide acceptance and has been applied to many situations and groups.

Although drive and ambition lead a decision maker to the top of a corporation, the excessive use of drive can lead to problems. Zaleznik (1970) refers to this as "unhealthy narcissism." Decision makers, as with all individuals, strive to fill "an inner, ego-related need." According to Flamholtz (1979), the inner agenda centers on an executive's needs for self-esteem and control over people and events. "While these needs are healthy in moderation, they cause problems if they get out of hand."

Decision styles are an important but not the only aspect of a managerial decision situation. It would be unrealistic to expect that styles alone could provide the total basis for more effective decision making. Rather, when considered in an organizational context as one facet of the decision process, decision styles provide a valuable insight into understanding the decision maker, for explaining actions taken, and as the basis for relating the individual to the task requirements.

## ▲ Study Questions

1. What are the characteristics of decision makers?
2. What factors are important in decision style?
3. What is the effect of values on style?
4. What are the characteristics of the four decision styles?
5. What is meant by a dominant decision style?
6. How is a flexible decision style determined?
7. Why are decision styles important in decision making?
8. What is the typical style of an executive?

## ▲ References

Boulgarides, J. D. "Decision style, values and biographical factors in relation to satisfaction and performance of supervisors in a governmental agency." (MDAC paper WD 2040). Unpublished doctoral dissertation, University of Southern California, Los Angeles, June 1973.

Doktor, Robert H., and Hamilton, William F. "Cognitive Style and the Acceptance of Management Science Recommendations." *Management Science* (April 1973), pp. 400–405.

Drucker, Peter F. *The Effective Executive*. New York: Harper & Row, 1966.

Ebert, Ronald J., and Mitchell, Terence R. *Organizational Decision Processes*. New York: Crane, Russak, 1975.

Fiedler, F. E. *A Theory of Leadership Effectiveness*. New York: McGraw-Hill, 1967.

Flamholtz, Eric. "Organizational Control Systems as a Managerial Tool." *California Management Review* (Winter 1979), p. 55.

Holland, Howard K. "Decision Making and Personality." *Personnel Administration* (May–June 1968), pp. 24–29.

Jung, C. G. *Psychological Types*. New York: Pantheon Books, 1959.

Kelly, Kevin, "3M Run Scared? Forget About It." *Business Week* (September 16, 1991), pp. 59–62.

Killman, R. W., and Mitroff, I. J. *Methodological Approaches to Social Science*. San Francisco: Jossey-Bass, 1978.

Kotler, Philip. *Market Management: Analysis of Planning and Control*. 6th ed. Englewood Cliffs, NJ: Prentice Hall, 1988.

Levinson, H. "Asinine Attitudes Toward Motivation." *Harvard Business Review* (January–February 1973), pp. 70–76.

Maddi, Salvatore R. *Personalty Theories*. Homewood, IL: Dorsey Press, 1972.

McClelland, David C. "Business Drive And National Achievement." *Harvard Business Review* (July–August 1962), pp. 99–112.

Meeks, Fleming. "Fail Is Not a Four-Letter Word." *Forbes* (April 30, 1990), p. 98.

Mintzberg, H. "Planning on the Left and Managing on the Right." *Harvard Business Review*, Vol. 54, No. 4 (1976), pp. 49–58.

Mintzberg, H. "The Manager's Job: Folklore and Fact." *Harvard Business Review* (March–April 1990), pp. 164ff.

Mowday, R. T., Porter, L. W., and Steers, R. M. *Employee-Organization Linkages*. New York: Academic Press, 1982.

Myers, I. B. "Manual For The Myers-Briggs Type Indicator." Princeton, NJ: Educational Testing Services, 1962.

Nadler, David A., and Lawler, Edward E. III. "Quality of Work Life: Perspective and Directions." *Organizational Dynamics* (Winter 1983), pp. 20–30.

Rokeach, Milton. *The Nature Of Human Values*. New York: Free Press, 1973.

Schwartz, John and McCormick, John. "The CEO Who Won't Go." *Newsweek* (May 7, 1990), pp. 46–47.

Tosi, Henry L., and Hamner, W. Clay. *Organizational Behavior and Management*. Columbus, OH: Grid Publishing, Inc., 1985.

Wiegner, Kathleen. "A Doctor's Son Had a Vision." *Forbes* (April 30, 1990), p. 182.

Zaleznick, A. "Power and Politics in Organizational Life." *Harvard Business Review* (May–June 1970), pp. 101–109.

# *3* Applying Decision Styles

▲ ▲ ▲   ▲ ▲ ▲ ▲ ▲ ▲ ▲ ▲ ▲ ▲ ▲ ▲ ▲ ▲ ▲ ▲

Decision styles can be applied in many ways to assist the decision maker in solving problems confronting the organization. Decision styles have been applied successfully in training; organization design; selection, retention, and promotion of employees; career counseling and planning; explaining behavior; predicting performance based on matching style to job; developing an individual's self-confidence; and facilitating problem-solving sessions. Styles become invaluable tools for any situation involving human interaction, predicting behavior, defining job requirements, and creative problem solving. Style serves as a window into the minds of managers, employees, customers, and so forth. The ability to communicate, negotiate, reinforce behavior, improve performance, and increase decision effectiveness are all derived from the correct application of decision styles. Because the range of applications is large, this chapter concentrates on work in organizations. Thus, emphasis is on what style is expected of executives, how style is related to job content, the role of style in an organization, and choosing meaningful careers based on style. One of the places that style has had a significant impact is on women managers. The role of women in management is treated as a critical element of finding qualified managers and executives.

This chapter shows how the knowledge of decision styles can improve one's performance by matching style to the job. The relationship of style to choice of careers, women as managers, and the organizational impact of style are covered.

Irwin Mautner, chairman of Programming and Systems, started his company because, as he stated, "I hated being an accountant." His ambition drove him to start the computer training company that he has made so successful by fanatical attention to details and efficiency. He had always wanted to be an entrepreneur. Halfway through a programming course while at Paine-Webber, he came to the realization that there are many people who needed that kind of training. With $3,000 of working capital, he and a partner started their company (Chitelen, 1990).

## ▲ SUCCESS IN MANAGEMENT

What does it take to succeed as a manager? Boyden Associates (1980) found that Americans prefer managers who are strong problem solvers and who can develop imaginative solutions. This typically is a combination of the analytical and conceptual styles. Europeans, on the other hand, want managers who are good at communicating and who have good interpersonal skills. This is a combination of the conceptual and behavioral styles. Interestingly, administrative ability (a combination of the analytical and directive styles) was ranked lowest on both sides of the ocean.

What this points up is that the manager's style needs to fit the context in order to be effective. If we translate these differences into the workaday world of the manager, we can see that who is hired, promoted, or transferred in an organization reflects how well the individual can accommodate to the organizational environment. What this also means is that the careers one pursues often determine how effective he or she will be and the level of satisfaction that can be expected in the work performed.

Style can be applied to identifying who would perform best in given jobs. For example, Union Bank of Los Angeles found that the most successful loan brokers were analytical. The bank tested 20 of its very top brokers and found that 19 of them had dominant analytical styles. The twentieth broker had a very high behavioral score, and relied on empathy for people as his strength in making loans.

## ▲ STYLE AND THE EXECUTIVE

Because environmental factors directly influence the long-term survival of an organization, it is important to have an executive whose style fits the demanding requirement of understanding that environment. Social change, competition, technology, and so forth are all part of changes in the external environment in which an organization needs to adapt to ensure continued growth and profitability.

The bald eagle's journey from the brink of extinction and back, very much like the spotted owl's, is an example of how the external environment can impact on organizations. The eagle is the symbol of America as well as of "all that is wild and beautiful and free." Its brush with death is also a symbol of the survival of our environment. The combination of ranchers' using strychnine to poison wolves and coyotes and chemical companies' producing enormous amounts of DDT produced a colossal assault on our environment and affected the food chain of the eagles. The chemicals not only killed the birds, but made the eggshells too thin to hatch.

Because the government made the decision to cope with our environment, the eagle has made a spectacular recovery. The government's position is that organizations should change their human folly and greed so that we can save nature. This is another example of how environmental factors directly affect decisions executives make (Budiansky, 1990).

Fortunately, most executives have styles that do fit their jobs. Some, such as tycoon Charles Wohlstetter (see Chapter 2), have managed to survive catastrophe because of the decisions they make. Wohlstetter's style—conceptual—is typical of a person who is willing to try new things and who has vision. He was willing to change his mind, if needed. Wohlstetter relied on data from his staff, who analyzed properties for him. As we noted in Chapter 2, Wohlstetter is an example of an executive with vision who was willing to risk huge fortunes on what he believed was right. His understanding and perception concerning events fit him for his role.

## ▲ CHOOSING MEANINGFUL CAREERS

In attempting to identify why executives suffer from burnout, Levinson (1990) found that they had chronic fatigue; anger at those making demands; self-criticism for putting up with demands; cynicism, negativism, and irritability; a sense of being besieged; and hair-trigger display of emotions. How often do people complain about their job or about not wanting to come to work each day? The chances are they are in a career that does not match their style or in a career that was chosen for them. According to Boulgarides, "Not knowing what job to take is a universal problem." A person needs to know himself or herself in order to find work that is meaningful. Although there are no simple answers as to what job one should choose, it is possible to narrow the field by looking for the ones that are best suited to one's personality (Grant, 1985).

In a research study on job design, Steers and Mowday found that there was a need to identify a wider range of individual factors that potentially influence the way employees do their jobs (1977, p. 656). When designing jobs, it is helpful to understand individual differences along with organizational factors that influence job characteristics and in turn affect work outcomes (O'Connor, Rudolf, and Peters, 1980).

## ▲ MATCHING NEW EMPLOYEES TO JOBS

The other side of the career question is how companies hire people. The right hiring decision often means the difference between success and failure for new employees. To ensure that employees can perform effectively, management needs to ascertain their physical stamina as well as the requisite knowledge, skills, and personality (style) to fit a given job. It is surprising how many companies do not try to determine new employees' style. Style, knowledge, and experience often can be used to predict an applicant's behavior and performance. In many instances, intelligence is not as important as attitude on the job. If managers match a new employee's personality to the job, it is more likely that performance will meet expectations (Weiss, 1988).

Many managers assume that the more experience an applicant has, the more likely that person will perform well. However, if a candidate's personality characteristics do not match a particular position, there is a reasonable chance that the individual will not perform well. For example, Wall Street is not sure that Gerald Greenwald, 54, who left his job as vice-chairman of Chrysler, can spearhead the effort by three airline unions to buy United Airlines. He was the financial manager who obtained the funds that kept Chrysler from bankruptcy. Even though faced with severe competition, he managed to develop a new strategy for the 1990s. Although there were many problems at Chrysler, more may await him at UAL Corp. This will be a challenge for his new career. Greenwald needs to find $4 billion in order to have a viable deal (Labich, 1990).

In an attempt to compete in a global economy, many organizations have gone through a restructuring by selling off assets and cutting staff. As one part of a company shrinks or disappears, another may be expanding or may need new talent to fill the changed positions. As new divisions are formed, proper hiring can ensure keeping costs down. However, because the cost of hiring the wrong people can be excessive, this becomes a critical consideration. An employee who fails in a job and leaves after a short period can cost a company anywhere from $5,000 for an hourly worker to $75,000 for a manager in terms of lost productivity and money spent on training and other hiring costs (for example, relocation and housing). The cost may be even greater if the wrong person stays on. He or she makes mistakes and may sabotage morale. It is helpful to make a careful list of what the position covers rather than a typical job description. The list can be brief, but it should be specific about what is expected of the new employee and what characteristics lead to success for a given position (Greenberg and Greenberg, 1980).

An imaginative approach to hiring new employees was developed by American Employment Registry (AER). If an employer needs to find the right worker for a job and there is an employee looking for that exact job, the system developed by AER using a computerized list of job candidates provides a database from which to choose. A prospective employee pays $25 for an electronic resume to be entered into the database. Companies that use the service pay a $2,000 annual fee plus $5 for each resume examined as well as $2 per minute when they are connected to the computer. It's a simple concept that is relatively inexpensive and produces results. When a company needs an employee, time is worth money because lack of a worker could cause a major crisis ("Computer Service Helps," 1985).

Many companies have developed their own system for identifying potentially good managers from among their current employees. NCR Corporation's approach is to continuously look for high flyers by trying to spot promising young employees who have the potential to become executives. NCR uses questionnaires and other techniques to find approximately 24 high-potential employees from their 900 top performers. The objective is to find people very early who have strong potential. Spotting these superstars is not limited to NCR. Finding new executives is an ongoing task for any company that is growing and has to replace retired managers or staff new divisions (Wysocki, 1981).

## ▲ MATCHING STYLE WITH CHANGES IN THE ORGANIZATION

Why is the introduction of organizational change such a difficult task? Every executive knows that organizations must continuously adapt to new external environmental demands. Although many executives recognize the need to deal more effectively with the change process, it is still extremely difficult to achieve.

As most executives know, the introduction of change creates anxiety and fear. When a major adjustment is required because of some newly proposed reorganization, it can cause high levels of "fight," "flight," or "freeze." A good illustration is a *Los Angeles Times* business headline that read, "Wells Fargo Is Ready to Crack the Whip at Crocker." Wells Fargo chairman Carl Reichardt is known for his relentless drive to cut costs. When Wells Fargo announced that it would pay $1.08 billion to buy Crocker Bank from British Midland Bank, it was estimated that only 10 out of the 50 top Crocker officers would remain and that as many as 100 of the combined 626 offices would be eliminated. It was felt that the Crocker people would be "very upset" (Broder, 1986, p. 1–2). Managers will be confronted more and more with situations similar to the one at Crocker Bank. In situations such as this, style provides guidelines for alternative careers and clues as to whether there would be compatibility with the new owners. The trauma of organizational change can be minimized when style is used to understand the situation.

In order to introduce a change effectively, executives need to recognize that there is more to take into account than the technical factors. Four key elements can be used that together determine the potential for successful change (Rowe and Mann, 1986). These four elements are (1) the executive who is the change agent; (2) the corporate culture, which reflects the change environment; (3) the values and beliefs of the individual performers that affect the change process; and (4) the match, or fit, between the values of the individual performers and the corporate culture. When the change agent introduces a change, it is critical that the organization be ready to follow and lend support. Although the need for change may be recognized at the top level, it does not follow that the organization is ready to pursue the change agent's goals.

The match often determines whether the change is acceptable, how easy the change will be, and whether change will take place at all or become distorted or blocked. Howard Schwartz, a vice-president at Management Analysis Corporation, is actively involved with organizations dealing with changing culture. He has observed that if the chief executive is to be an effective change agent, any new direction should be identified in the context of the organization's core values and guiding beliefs (Rowe and Mason, 1987).

As an organization changes, executives determine whether they can cope effectively with the new requirements. There are constantly changing requirements as technology changes, as new competitors impact the organization, and as economic and social conditions dictate new demands. It is precisely because of the increasing complexity of decisions in organizations and the increasing desire for involvement and commitment on the part of subordinates that managers have been turning to participative or collaborative decision making as a means of sharing power. As with any approach, participative management has benefits and shortcomings. The theory rests on the assumptions that employees at all levels of an organization are capable of contributing to the decision process and that, in general, this willingness and capability have not been used. Often, when subordinates are involved in decision making, because of a sense of ownership there is a positive effect on how decisions are carried out. A natural question is, Why is participation not used more widely? Perhaps sharing of power is not really feasible if managers are held accountable for results. Or it may be unreasonable to expect a subordinate who does not have information or experience to have the same perspective that the manager has. Most important, employees have to be "willing" to assume responsibility. For example, there is evidence that workers' councils, which have existed in Europe for many years, are rather apathetic toward decisions that do not directly involve their own work or expertise. The contrast, of course, is the Japanese worker, who feels at home with involvement. Participation is viewed as "contributing" to the general well-being of the organization.

## ▲ WOMEN'S MANAGEMENT STYLES

One of the more interesting applications has been to show that women managers, based on their decision style, are indeed capable of performing as well as male managers in comparable positions. Why then are women considered differently than men as far as management is concerned? Studies claim that there are significant differences in mental functioning between men and women—despite a nagging doubt about their validity. In these studies, men were described as excelling in numerical reasoning and spatial judgment, whereas women were considered superior in verbal fluency and rote memory. Social, cultural, and environmental influences were discounted, and differences between men and women were attributed to their levels of androgens (male hormones), which are generally associated with aggressive or assertive behavior. The studies claimed that females with high levels of androgens were more likely to excel in math and to be as aggressive as men are supposed to be. A research study by Gary Powell (1990) shows that there are few differences in needs, values, or leadership styles between male and female managers. He also questions the findings in laboratory studies and claims that field studies do not bear them out. His findings are consistent with the studies done by Boulgarides, described in this chapter.

Where then does the truth lie? Do physiological factors account for differences? Or is it perhaps that personality factors, such as being assertive or having interpersonal skills, account for the way in which women think, perceive, behave, and react to their jobs? Research has shown that decision styles appear to play a dominant, if not overriding, role in determining how individuals respond to stimuli, solve problems, interact with others, and make decisions. For example, women in technically oriented occupations were compared with women in socially oriented work. There was a significant difference between the decision styles of the two groups. However, we found there was no real difference in style between men and women in the same field. Supporting this finding was a study of women engineers that showed that their values were closer to those of male engineers than to the values of women who were not in engineering.

Women architects are more thinking- than action-oriented, and they show a predominant upper-half orientation that demonstrates high cognitive complexity. A comparison of the decision styles of women architects with women and male managers is shown in Table 3.1.

The decision styles of the women architects are close to the decision styles of male managers in the conceptual and behavioral categories. The strength of the women architects is in their analytic and conceptual styles, with behavioral as a back-up. This certainly reflects a high level of intellectual competence in analysis and creativity. In terms of decision style, women architects are left-brain, which indicates they are logical, are adept at problem solving, and are more oriented toward task than most people. The women architects are also top-half, capable of dealing with complexity and having a strong propensity for thinking.

Table 3.1 ▲ Comparison of Decision Styles of Women Architects with Women and Male Managers

| Decision Style | Women Architects (N = 452) | Women Managers (N = 93) | Male Managers (N = 194) |
|---|---|---|---|
| Directive | 69 | 74 | 74 |
| Analytic | 95 | 88 | 89 |
| Conceptual | 82 | 74 | 83 |
| Behavioral | 54 | 64 | 54 |
| | 300 | 300 | 300 |

A rather clear and unique profile of the women architects emerged from this study. The size of the sample population ($N$ = 452), and the national coverage, adds to the validity of the results. Professionally, architecture appears to be a rewarding career area for women who have an affinity for architectural work and are less concerned with salary or status (Boulgarides, 1985).

It is clear that many women have decision styles, personalities, and values that are closer to those of their male counterparts than to the stereotype of the female population. Are male–female differences simply fascinating, or are they relevant to women managers? Factors such as aggressive behavior and numerical reasoning are not being dismissed, however, they are not always the competencies considered relevant for managerial effectiveness. Consider, for example, Wynetka Ann Reynolds, who as head of the California State University System was never really comfortable in the job that she took in 1982 and that she won on a split vote. The real problem for discontent was described as the manner in which she interacted with trustees and university presidents, who said "her manner was imperious and her administration weak." When she was at Ohio State she was given the nickname "Queen Ann" because of her abrupt and insensitive management style. Her style was exemplified by the blistering session with Richard Butwell, president of Cal State Domingues Hills. He had a heart attack two weeks after "she blamed him for problems on the campus and told him to find another job" (Banks, 1990).

As a hard-driving, bright, and energetic executive, Reynolds did improve the university system in a number of areas. Some people even found her charming and warm, but her style was "icy and cutting" at times. She publicly criticized subordinates, and personally could not take criticism. At 52, Reynolds felt she should turn over her job to "another energetic person." Most sources felt the resignation was a way to avoid conflict between herself and the trustees. Here is another instance of a person's personality not matching the job because of the way she interacted with subordinates and trustees (Banks, 1990).

## ▲ WOMEN MANAGERS

In many cases, women are being recognized and accepted as equals in the world of business. However, to cope with discrimination, 200 women executives have formed the Committee of 200 to respond to the exclusively male Business Round Table. Moreover, women in many business schools represent more than one-half of all the MBA students and often are among the top performers. At Columbia University's Graduate School of Business, for example, female enrollment has increased from 5 percent to 40 percent, and these women are doing superbly well. In other bastions of management education, it is conceded that female competence equals or exceeds that of their male counterparts. Robin Burns, who at 37 is the president of Estee Lauder, USA, earns an estimated $1.5 million per year. The attitude that helped bring her to the top was to love the job she was in and always find a way to "play the hand you are dealt." Too often, people simply give in or give up and wonder why they don't succeed. Burns learned as a child to develop an emotional attachment to whatever job she was in, and thus was able to give it her all (Duffy, 1990).

One of the striking aspects of the careers that women pursue is that it may be years between promotions. Managers are in their jobs longer regardless of age or skills, because flatter organizations limit the number of openings. Susan Doten, 31, director of marketing in Quaker Oats' pet food division, has had six jobs in nine years. But, she says, "I will hang out at this level for a lot longer than I hung out at the lower levels" (Konrad, 1990).

Anne Pol, 42, of Pitney Bowes has the same message. She spent five years in human resources. She left a senior position at Pitney to be a plant manager making parts for mailing machines. As a potential candidate for the company's top jobs, she wanted solid operating experience. She returned to a top personnel job and was on Pitney Bowes' corporate management committee. She insisted that she could go back to operations later. She returned to the company as vice-president for manufacturing operations. Her conclusion: "It's very obvious that lateral moves are necessary if you want to progress up the corporate ladder." Pol says that personal fulfillment and flexibility goals are "the key issue for people to get satisfaction in their work and feel they were making a contribution." Many people are more willing to exchange these feelings for job security (Konrad, 1990).

Career women often face a "glass ceiling" in corporate advancement. However, experts believe that women's careers will be more satisfactory in the future corporate environment. Neil Yeager, 37, who recently wrote "Career Map: What You Want, Getting It, and Keeping It," says, "Women know how to network in a less politicized way. They know how to nurture relationships and empower other people. They manage better than men. And they have a greater appreciation of motivations other than money." These may be what companies will need to succeed in the 1990s (Kirkpatrick, 1990).

There are woman-friendly companies such as U.S. West or Pitney Bowes where CEO George B. Harvey recognized that "women were putting in more time than the men—and more consistently beating their sales quotas." He decided to boost the top female ranks. "If I'm going to get the best talent, I've got to look at the entire population." By Harvey's directive, women get 35 percent of new management jobs or promotions, and a growing number of women at Pitney are building impressive careers. Unfortunately, competence doesn't mean acceptance. Women have complained that they often are ignored. For example, during a leadership conference at Du Pont Co., Marcia Coleman, a laboratory director, told Vice-President Anthony J. Cardinal, "Did you notice what happened in the meeting whenever a woman offered a thought? Pay attention tomorrow," she challenged. Cardinal noticed she was right that whenever a woman brought up an idea, it was ignored. "I had never appreciated the problem before. I started to get an inkling of what women go through every day," Cardinal says (Konrad, 1990).

On the other hand, women have clearly demonstrated their ability to perform effectively in business. Lore Harp, chief executive of Vector Graphic, talked in a soft voice about the transition from an entrepreneurial enterprise to a sophisticated corporation that is managed aggressively and pursuing a $30–$50 million expansion. Moya Lear, fondly known as Queen Lear, took over the reins of the Lear Jet after Bill Lear died in 1978 and started a new firm, LearAvia, in Reno. According to its boosters, what Moya did with the Lear fan jet could well reshape general aviation technology. Navy Captain Grace Hopper has been a living legend in the computer world. She created the COBOL (Common Business Oriented Language) compiler used to translate computer instructions into programs. She is a self-styled maverick who is known for having clocks that run backwards: "Who said a clock has to run clockwise?"

These women are hardly isolated examples of success in the business world. In a survey of 43 companies chosen for their preeminence by *Business Week,* 7 included women in top management positions. This survey, however, clearly shows that there's still considerable room for expansion of women's role in management (Rowe, Bennis, and Boulgarides, 1984). In *Fortune*'s proxy statements of companies on its list of the 1,000 largest U.S. industrial and service companies, it was found that of 4,012 listed officers and directors, only 19 were women.

Progress has been limited and slow. "Corporate males still don't know how to deal with women. They are afraid to yell at them or give them negative feedback. It's as though they think they are yelling at their mothers or their wives. Men often worry that women will run from the room in tears or, worse yet, yell back. They're not really sure the women will come through for them. They just don't trust them as much as the guys with whom they talk football." One explanation given for why women don't get top positions is that they leave jobs more often than men. Women seem more willing to act on their desires (Fierman, 1990).

An intriguing example of a successful woman executive is Sandra Kurtzig. In 1972, at the age of 24, she left the software firm of ASK Computer Systems, which she had founded but couldn't stand to see deteriorate. Thirteen years later, she returned to take over the reins once again. "We coasted," Kurtzig says. "For a long time, we were coasting very well." Because of her frustration, Kurtzig resigned again in February 1989. She perceived that there was lethargy on the part of Ronald Braniff, the president, and members of the board. "There were opportunities that the company was not seizing. There wasn't a sense of urgency."

Investment banker Thomas Unterberg in desperation asked Kurtzig to rejoin the company. Braniff resigned for reasons unknown shortly thereafter. In describing her predecessor, Kurtzig said, "He didn't do anything wrong. In all fairness the only mistake he made was that he wasn't a visionary." The change that took place in ASK was immediate. "Sandy has no sense of organizational structure. She has no qualms about going to people directly, bypassing the hierarchy of managers. Hands-on doesn't even describe it." Kurtzig's style can "sometimes be a problem," but she has boosted morale. She sees herself as a compulsive worker and a leader rather than a hands-on manager (Pitta, 1990).

## ▲ STYLE AND COMMUNICATION

Another very important application of style is in communication. Periodically, research is done on what contributes most to effective management and invariably communication heads the list. Although there is no doubt about the importance of communication, the role of style has not been explored until recently. Even the term *communication* is not well understood. Acker (1990) describes communication as the sender's desire to influence the receiver's behavior. He then describes barriers to communication that result from words that are used, ability to understand meaning, and ambiguity. In addition to the words used, the following barriers cause problems of communication in organizations:

1. *Time pressure:* Managers use this as an excuse for not communicating.
2. *Filtering:* This reflects the sender's biased information.
3. *Premature evaluation:* The receiver's evaluation that is based on excessive or insufficient input.
4. *Failure to listen:* For any number of reasons, the listener fails to pay attention.
5. *Psychological distance:* This is where communications relies on unwarranted status symbols.

These barriers are indicative of the problems confronting managers who are attempting to achieve meaningful communication in their organizations. An example of how this can occur was described by Julie Pitta (1990). Kaypro, a successful computer company that was an outgrowth of Non-Linear Systems, was started by Andrew Kay, a brilliant scientist who graduated from MIT. He invented the digital voltmeter that Non-Linear Systems sold to the aerospace industry. Kaypro's employees were avid surfers and often would hold staff meetings at the beach. Communication was described as open and friendly, and they would often talk while waiting for the next wave. Employees had a free health bar where they could get freshly squeezed orange, carrot, and apple juice.

A number of the Kay family members were involved in the company. However, problems began to arise because of family squabbles that got in the way of running the business. For example, David Kay found it impossible to convince his father, Andrew, that inventories were out of control. As time went on, the squabbles increased and it seemed that after a while every decision became a fight between the two men. Questions were interpreted as threats, and Kaypro had a serious communications problem. The result was an empty parking lot and offices that looked like a ghost town as Andrew tried to rescue his ailing company.

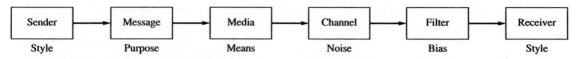

**Figure 3.1** ▲ **Communication Process**

## ▲ MEASURING COMMUNICATION STYLE

A companion test instrument to the decision style inventory has been developed, called the communication style inventory (CSI), (Rowe, Housel, and Skopek, 1989). This inventory is based on viewing communication as a process. This is shown in Figure 3.1.

Associated with each block of the diagram are style implications. For example, the sender uses a given style of communicating based on his or her decision style, has a purpose in sending the message, and uses given media that is subject to various levels of noise or interference; finally, the message is received by the intended person, but it is subject to that individual's style which acts as a filter or biases the information received. Thus, communication is closely related to the perception and cognition of decision style. Knowing a person's communication style, we can predict both the kind of messages he or she would be prone to send and the preferred media for sending those messages. For example, a high director in communication style tends to use short messages that convey control or power. The media used most likely is impersonal, such as using a telephone or memo, and the message tends to be cryptic.

A description of the four communication styles is shown in Figure 3.2. Effective communication in business is critical in order to be successful in an increasingly competitive environ-

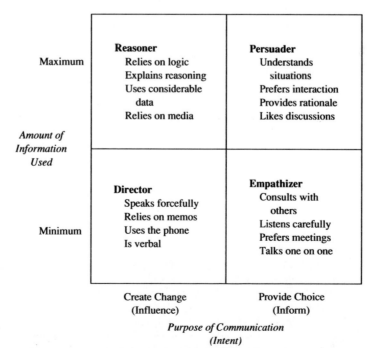

**Figure 3.2** ▲ **Communication Style Inventory**

ment. However, little attention has been given to the importance of individual differences in preferred communication style and the impact this has on communication effectiveness. The communication style inventory (CSI) can help one to understand these individual differences by identifying the communication styles of each individual. The ability to identify those characteristics that can make people more open and responsive to communications potentially can improve performance. The CSI is proving to be an effective instrument that can be used to identify a communicator's preferred communication style. The inventory identifies people's preferred and back-up communication styles. Like the decision style inventory, it is a 20-question instrument. People revert to their back-up styles in situations where it is clear that their preferred styles will not be effective. The CSI therefore allows one to strategize—to adjust stylistic approaches that will work best depending on the receiver.

Each communication style has strengths and weaknesses. Knowing which will work and which will fail—and what styles are available—gives the communicator flexibility and a greater likelihood of effectiveness. The style used often depends on the context and is manifested differently depending on the situation. Some communication styles require, for example, considerable detail, other styles rely on discussions, memos, meetings, or the broad array of communication options available.

Because it reveals individual differences, the CSI also can be applied as a motivational tool. Individual differences are a key element in motivation theory and practice; understanding how a person communicates is closely related to deciding what forms of motivation will work best. In this sense, use of the CSI helps avoid stereotyping because people are seen as unique and different. In doing so, managers are able to select the style that will best get across motivational messages.

## ▲ DESCRIPTION OF COMMUNICATION STYLES

There are four communication styles: director, reasoner, persuader, and empathizer. The "director" avoids spending time on long, drawn-out communications because of his or her perceived rapid recognition of critical issues. Being forceful speakers, these individuals use direct statements and are concise. At times, they may appear abrupt. They use short, pointed memos and are inclined to use the telephone as the fastest and most effective communication tool.

The "reasoner" is a manager who relies on logic and who would prefer to spend time being thorough in his or her communication. The reasoner is not likely to make his or her position known until every minute detail of a situation has been analyzed. The reasoner may tend to overpower listeners with the "logic" and "facts" of a situation and consequently is perceived as a poor listener. Reasoners use considerable information from published sources, and available data to support and explain their position. Because of their reliance on detail and analysis, reasoners may tend to send lengthy written messages in which the crucial points generally are not highlighted.

The "persuader" believes that understanding of situations provides the rationale needed to discuss things with people. The persuader is open to others' viewpoints and will try to convince them that his or her point is the correct one. Persuaders tend to "sell" others rather than "tell" them. Persuaders are good at seeing all points of an issue, and because of this may be perceived as good listeners. Persuaders are as likely to rely on emotional arguments as on logical arguments. The persuader style puts a premium on interaction in groups.

The "empathizer" is the most "people"-oriented of the four types and is a good listener. This style likes people and listens to their point of view. The empathizer also enjoys meetings in groups or "one on one." He or she attempts to understand others rather than speaking "at" them, and gains information using open statements or questions. The empathizer tries to understand others' feelings as well as the substance of their messages. Empathizers may spend more time communicating about social issues than task issues.

It would be unusual to find a manager who exhibited only one of the four communication styles, although such persons do exist. Most often, however, individuals are comfortable using multiple styles. Which style is used is often determined by the requirements of the communication context and the speaker's communication skills.

The most effective basis for communicating our thoughts, speech style, and content is when they are tailored to each situation. Knowing other people's preferences, we can relate them to our own communication style, and by doing so can become more effective communicators. This is a significant means for improving managerial effectiveness.

## ▲ HOW TO COMMUNICATE WITH STYLE

One of the ways to be successful when communicating is to know the comfort zones of others. "Everybody has a particular style of communication that they rely on," says Betsy Gilbert, a presentation consultant whose company, The Corporate Image, is headquartered in Great Neck, New York. According to Gilbert, "the way people talk and like to be talked to is determined by their personality. There are three basic personality molds: the detail-oriented type, the action-oriented type, and the creative-oriented type. Each person fits into one of these three basic molds. But, the thing you have to be aware of is that there is no way to manipulate or intimidate another person into being comfortable with dealing with you if you're coming at each other using different communication styles." She says that managers need to make others feel a sense of trust because they can't change someone else's style. "Adapting your communication style to the other person's is a fundamental technique to successfully getting your points across and of being persuasive" (Smith and Ross, 1989).

Even though every individual has communication style preferences, it is possible to become skillful in the use of other styles. What is required is a willingness to change and to take the risks required in approaching communication requirements with unfamiliar styles.

## ▲ THE COMMUNICATION STYLE INVENTORY

The CSI that follows was developed after careful testing and validation of the results obtained. The principal basis for this validation was the correlation with the decision style inventory covered in Chapter 2. The CSI is scored in the same way as the decision style inventory. The first column represents the directors, the second the reasoners, the third the persuaders, and the fourth the empathizers. To score the CSI instrument, one adds all the numbers in each column to find the total score. For example, column 1 might total 85. What this means is that the person taking the inventory has a dominant preference for the director style. The scoring for each style is shown in Table 3.2 and Table 3.3.

A study done by Eric Skopek, one of the co-authors of the inventory, found the following scores for people in a major internationally focused company.

Table 3.2 ▲ Communication Style Scores

|  | Director | Reasoner | Persuader | Empathizer |
|---|---|---|---|---|
| 1. Customer support teams | 70–Occ | 69–Occ | 83–Occ | 78–Freq |
| 2. Senior managers | 82–Occ | 75–Occ | 82–Occ | 61–Sel |
| 3. Plant managers | 71–Occ | 77–Occ | 73–Occ | 79–Freq |

Sel = seldom used.    Occ = occasionally used.    Freq = frequently used.

## Communication Style Inventory

INSTRUCTIONS

Place an 8, 4, 2, or 1 after each response to the 20 questions. The numbers *cannot* be repeated. 8 is used for the response that is most like you. 4 is one that is somewhat less. 2 is for the response that is a little like you, and 1 is for the response that is least like you. There is no time limit, so please respond carefully.

| | | | | | | | | |
|---|---|---|---|---|---|---|---|---|
| 1. I prefer to communicate: | by phone | | in writing | | in a group | | one-on-one | |
| 2. In social gatherings, I: | talk to others | | listen to what is said | | discuss many things | | enjoy the conversation | |
| 3. I explain things based on: | experience | | factual data | | broad knowledge | | my feelings | |
| 4. I express my ideas best: | orally | | on paper | | graphically | | in conversation | |
| 5. To convince others I'm right, I: | speak forcefully | | use logical arguments | | explain my reasoning | | speak gently | |
| 6. When confronted by others, I: | become defensive | | answer them back | | try to smooth things out | | avoid arguing | |
| 7. I describe others: | objectively | | using details | | using comparisons | | favorably | |
| 8. People say I speak: | assertively | | carefully | | thoughtfully | | patiently | |
| 9. When making a suggestion, I: | tell others what I think | | am very careful | | point out consequences | | try to be helpful | |
| 10. When I'm not sure what to say, I: | rely on my experience | | search for information | | consider how to say it | | ask for advice | |
| 11. When I reject a request, I: | am firm | | rely on policies | | show concern | | try to be pleasant | |
| 12. I always try to: | get results | | solve problems | | explore new ideas | | talk with others | |
| 13. When under stress, I: | talk rapidly | | become cautious | | look for options | | ask for help | |
| 14. If I am late, I: | speak first | | look for an excuse | | apologize | | avoid the subject | |
| 15. When talking to others, I: | am direct | | cover many details | | discuss my ideas | | talk about friends | |
| 16. When I write, I: | am brief | | am factual | | use anecdotes | | describe others | |
| 17. I enjoy reading: | adventure stories | | technical books | | historical novels | | biographies | |
| 18. In business meetings, I: | speak my mind | | observe what's happening | | respects others' opinions | | listen to what is said | |
| 19. I learn best when given: | examples of what to do | | supporting theory | | explanations | | when it has relevance | |
| 20. When questioning others, I: | come directly to the point | | expect complete answers | | explain what I want | | consider their feelings | |

Alan J. Rowe, Tom J. Housel, Eric Skopek (c) 2/22/88, Rev. 2/2/89

Table 3.3  ▲  Communication Style Intensity Levels

|  | *Seldom Uses* | *Occasionally Uses* | *Frequently Uses* | *Always Uses* |
|---|---|---|---|---|
| Directors (Column 1) | Below 68 | 68–82 | 83–90 | Above 90 |
| Reasoners (Column 2) | Below 68 | 68–82 | 83–90 | Above 90 |
| Persuaders (Column 3) | Below 73 | 73–87 | 88–95 | Above 95 |
| Empathizers (Column 4) | Below 63 | 63–77 | 73–85 | Above 85 |

One can see that the customer support team frequently use the empathizer style. Senior managers, on the other hand, seldom use the empathizer style. Plant managers who are directly responsible for performance and working with people almost always use the empathizer style and occasionally use the other three styles. This example illustrates differences for each occupation. Within each of these groups, however, we still find individual differences, such as one of the plant managers who always used the reasoner style and seldom used the persuader or empathizer style. Perhaps that individual would be more effective by at least trying to use the empathizer style.

## ▲ ▲ ▲ ▲ ▲  Air Handlers Case

The phone rang off the hook, sounding like an alarm as if in anticipation of what was to follow. "Why can't I ever get my packages delivered on time?" bellowed Jim Jarden of Speedy Printing. "This is the third package that you've delivered late. Don't you know how to run a delivery business!"

Lisa, the branch manager, could tell instinctively by the tone of Jim's voice that she was in trouble. She hesitated slightly before answering, worried that she might say the wrong thing or respond too emotionally to the barrage she had just encountered. It was Monday morning, and the plane bringing the Air Handler packages was late again.

### The Start of a Bad Day

Cautiously, she said, "Mr. Jarden, although I could say it wasn't our fault, that doesn't solve your problem. But, let me assure you that we will have a messenger deliver the package to you immediately." Having calmed Jarden temporarily, Lisa now had to decide who should deliver the package to Mr. Jarden. He would certainly sound off at anyone from Air Handlers, so she had to find someone who could handle that situation. Her head was swirling as she thought about what was happening.

As she was thinking about the problem, in walked Charlie. "I've had enough of this rotten job," he announced, "I'm leaving." All Lisa could say was, "But, but . . ." and he was gone. What a way to start the day! She could feel herself becoming tense. She could barely think about which problem to tackle first. After a few moments, she calmed down enough to think straight about things. Lisa felt it would be best to let Charlie cool down before talking to him. More importantly, she had an irritated customer waiting for his late package.

### Finding a Solution

He first impulse was to ask David to make the delivery. He was always so reliable and really good at delivering packages to difficult people. She asked herself if David would be best. He was a good problem solver and responded well to a challenge, but would this win Jarden over?

After thinking about it for awhile, Lisa decided that Jarden was one of those people who sound off whenever something goes wrong. They demand immediate results and won't tolerate mistakes such as a late delivery. She then thought about Anne. Could she handle this? She would certainly understand Jarden's dilemma and would even be creative in explaining how he could correct the situation. But her approach would be too general to deal with Jarden's specific need. Then Lisa thought about Betty. She would empathize with Jarden and would understand him as a person, not just as a problem. "That's it." A smile came to Lisa's face. She was sure that Betty was the right person to handle the job.

But now came the hard part. How could she convince Betty to do the job? Betty always seemed willing to help when needed. Lisa recalled that Betty had delivered a package to Jarden just last month that also was late. Lisa walked into Betty's office and asked her, "Do you remember the package you delivered to Jarden last month? We were proud of how well you handled the situation, and how you were able to deal with Mr. Jarden. You were sympathetic and understood why he was angry, and that helped to calm the situation. You have never refused to handle these difficult cases. It is important to all of us here at Air Handlers to help solve the problem."

### Still Another Impossible Situation

Lisa remembered that Betty wanted to be considered "part of the family" and would feel good about doing something that was needed. Lisa knew she had made the right decision about the Jarden problem. However, just as Lisa was patting herself on the back, Roger, the district manager, walked in. He was a stickler for details who often "barked" orders rather than talked and who was considered very aggressive in dealing with subordinates. Roger's first words were, "Well, things seems to be all messed up around here—as usual!"

You can imagine Lisa's feelings. After finding an answer to the Jarden problem, she still had to deal with Charlie's threat to quit, and now she had to deal with her boss. She was almost in tears. Her mind went blank for a moment. The stress of dealing with an irritated customer, a problematic subordinate, and a difficult manager who simply did not understand people created a crisis for her.

Lisa knew that Roger disliked confrontation. She reflected for a moment about what to do now. If she talked back to Roger, he would back off for now. But, because he needed absolute control, he would get back at her later.

At this point, Lisa felt that she couldn't handle any more harassment from Roger. She would have to take a stand although she knew full well that there would be repercussions. "If you used a more reliable airline," Lisa blurted out, "we would have fewer problems around here. Air Handlers will have to decide whether it wants to be the cheapest operator in the business, with all the related problems, or whether it is willing to face up to the need for a change." Visibly upset, Roger merely grunted some unintelligible sounds as he slowly walked out of Lisa's office. What had she done? Did she handle the situation in the right way, or had she merely opened Pandora's Box?

### *Taking Action*

Lisa felt totally wrung out. At this point, she decided to take a long lunch before tackling Charlie. With all that had happened, she was not sure that she even wanted to stay at Air Handlers. She mused to herself about how well she was able to handle some problems yet seemed inept at others. In a flash of insight, she realized that although she was successful at her job, she was not always able to deal effectively with the demands placed on her.

She quickly returned to her office and decided to write a letter to the president of Air Handlers, outlining what she thought was needed. She suggested that more training was necessary to cope with the demands of a company whose strategy is to be a low-cost service provider. She had to deal with lost and late packages, with personnel who were underpaid and disgruntled, and with managers who did not understand people, without mentioning Roger by name.

Lisa felt better after writing the letter. But before mailing it she hesitated. Had she thought about the president's reaction to getting this letter from someone in her position? She realized that she hardly knew him. But then she remembered what had been written about him in the company newspaper. She reconsidered her letter and decided to add a closing paragraph that stated there was considerable growth potential for the company if it would be willing to hire appropriate personnel and change its image to that of a quality handler of packages rather than the lowest-priced handler.

### *What about Charlie?*

On reflection, Lisa decided not to try to convince Charlie to stay at Air Handlers. From the day he was hired, he had talked about wanting to be a musician but that he could not afford to do it. He was really not cut out for delivering packages or confronting irritable customers. He had come to the right conclusion that he should leave.

The following week Lisa received a letter from the president asking her to make an appointment to meet with him to discuss her ideas. He said that there were very few people who would speak up and that he admired her courage and concern for the welfare of Air Handlers.

Lisa had obviously learned that business involves a series of interpersonal relationships and that each individual has a characteristic way of thinking and of making decisions. Each has a different need for structure in his or her world and is guided by different orientations in values and different basic motivations. Each also responds differently under stress. And as a supervisor, Lisa had to be able to deal effectively with each of these different situations (Rowe and Mason, 1988).  ▲

## ▲ Summary

Decision style has proven to be one of the more effective tools to guide managers through the maze of problems confronting them. It has applications ranging from determining an individual's decision style to training, organizing, career choice, and problem solving. An important application is to evaluate new employees to more effectively match them with a position that increases the chance of good performance. This is a win–win solution because both the organization and the individual gain from this situation.

Decision styles have been useful in demonstrating that women can contribute significantly in the role of manager and executive. The decision style inventory provides unequivocal data to support the proposition that women in professional occupations perform as well as, if not better than, their male counterparts. Women represent a valuable resource and are beginning to be appreciated for their technical as well as behavioral contributions. Recognizing that women's decision style does not differ significantly from men's, organizations can improve decision making and effectiveness by allowing women to assume responsible positions.

Recognition of the value of women's role as managers shows the importance of planning for new hires and also career planning. Potential for growth and promotion should be based on examining the match of style to a proposed career track.

Finally, style affects every major aspect of managerial decision making, from recognizing or formulating problems correctly to finding solutions and then ensuring the acceptance and implementation of those solutions. Throughout the process, communication plays a vital role. Any phase of the process could break down if communications are inappropriately applied. Because communication is so important to decision making, this is included in the applications of style. A review of the communication process clearly reveals the relevance of the style in knowing the way the sender communicates and the receiver listens.

## ▲ Study Questions

1. What are important applications of decision style?
2. Why do executives experience burn-out?
3. How does style help in choosing a career?
4. Why do women have a difficult time in being hired as managers?
5. What is the relation of women's style in social and technical occupations?
6. Why is communications considered so important?
7. When should one use the communication style inventory?

## ▲ References

Acker, David D. "Skill in Communication: Something Every Manager Should Possess." *Program Manager* (May-June 1990), p. 2.

Banks, Sandy. "Reynolds Legacy: Advances Amid Controversy." *Los Angeles Times* (April 21, 1990), p. A22.

Boulgarides, James D. "Decision Styles, Values and Characteristics of Women Architects in the U.S." *Equal Opportunities International* Volume 4, No. 3 (1985), p. 118.

Boyden Associates. *Management Alert* (1980), Internal document.

Broder, John M. "Wells Fargo Is Ready to Crack The Whip at Crocker." *Los Angeles Times* (February 16, 1986), Part 4, p. 1.

Budiansky, Stephen. "More Environmental Than Thou." *U.S. News and World Report* (March 26, 1990), p. 10–11.

Chitelen, Ignatius. "I Hated Being an Accountant." *Forbes* (September 3, 1990), p. 91.

"Computer Service Helps Match Right Worker with Perfect Job." *The Seattle Times* (July 9, 1985), p. C2.

Darnton, Nina. "Mommy vs. Mommy." *Newsweek* (June 4, 1990), p. 64.

Duffy, Martha. "Take this Job and Love It." *Time* (August 6, 1990), pp. 70–72.

Fierman, Jaclyn. "Why Women Still Don't Hit the Top." *Fortune* (July 30, 1990), pp. 40 ff.

Grant, Jana. "Author (Boulgarides) Wants You to Get Out of the Rut." *West Hawaii Today* (July 1, 1985), p. 2.

Greenberg, Herbert M., and Greenberg, Jeanne. "Job Matching for Better Sales Performance." *Harvard Business Review* (September-October 1980), p. 128.

Kirkpatrick, David. "Is Your Career on Track?" *Fortune* (July 2, 1990), pp. 39 ff.

Konrad, Walecia. "Welcome to The Woman-Friendly Company Where Talent Is Valued and Rewarded." *Business Week* (August 6, 1990), pp. 52 ff.

Labich, Kenneth. "The United Job Is History Making." *Fortune* (July 2, 1990), pp. 53–57.

Levinson, Harry. "When Executives Burn Out." *Harvard Business Review Retrospect* (March-April 1990), p. 72.

Meeks, Fleming. "Fail Is Not a Four-Letter Word." *Forbes* (April 30, 1990), p. 98.

Mintzberg, Henry. "The Manager's Job: Folklore and Fact." *Harvard Business Review* (March-April 1990), pp. 164–167 ff.

O'Connor, Edward J., Rudolf, Cathy J., and Peters, Lawrence H. "Individual Differences and Job Design Reconsidered: Where Do We Go From Here?" *Academy of Management Review* Vol. 5, No. 2 (1980), p. 253.

Pitta, Julie. "Mommy Track, Revised." *Forbes* (March 19, 1990), p. 158.

Pitta, Julie. "We Had a Communication Problem." *Forbes* (May 28, 1990), pp. 344–346.

Powell, Gary. "One More Time: Do Female and Male Managers Differ?" *Academy of Management Executive* Vol. 4, No. 3 (1990), pp. 68–75.

Rowe, Alan J. and Mann, Richard B. "The Key to Unlocking Decision Making Effectiveness." Unpublished papers (April 1986).

Rowe, Alan J. and Mason, Richard O. "A Case of Alignment: Tying Decision Styles to Job Demands." *Management Solutions* (April 1988), pp. 15–21.

Rowe, Alan J. and Mason, Richard O. *Managing with Style*. San Francisco, CA: Jossey-Bass, 1987, pp. 83–84, 106–107.

Rowe, Alan J., Bennis, Warren, and Boulgarides, James D. "Desexing Decision Styles." *American Management Association* (1984), pp. 43–45.

Rowe, Alan J., Housel, Thomas J., and Skopek, Eric. "Communication Style Inventory." Copyright, February 2, 1989.

Smith, Rich, and Ross, Rachel. "Learning to Be a Great Communicator." *Apartment Association, Greater Los Angeles* (April 1989), p. 59–60.

Steers, Richard M., and Mowday, R. T. "The Motivational Properties of Tasks." *Academy of Management Review* (October 1977), p. 645–58.

Weiss, Alan. "Hire from Strength." *Success* (January-February 1988), p. 24.

Wiegner, Kathleen, "A Doctor's Son Had a Vision." *Forbes* (April 30, 1990), p. 182.

Wysocki, Bernard. "More Companies Try to Spot Leaders Early - Guide to the Top." *Wall Street Journal* (February 1981).

# 4 Elements of Decision Styles

▲ ▲ ▲   ▲ ▲ ▲ ▲ ▲ ▲ ▲ ▲ ▲ ▲ ▲ ▲ ▲ ▲ ▲ ▲ ▲

This chapter explores the basic foundations of decision styles. It builds on a cognitive model of decision making that includes perception, cognition, and volition. The brain and reasoning are related to style and decision making. Cognition is related to judgment and style. Basic values are discussed, and the Rowe–Boulgarides values inventory is explained. Application and validation of the values inventory are covered along with the relation of values to style.

## ▲ A COGNITIVE DECISION MODEL

Several years ago, Richard R. Green was the head of the Minneapolis school system where there were 40 percent minority students. The quality of education was very low. After only a short period, Green firmly put the Minneapolis system in shape.

He started by shutting down 18 schools that were underused. He also imposed a uniform curriculum for the whole city as well as achievement tests. Any student who failed was held back, including kindergarten students. Green was very successful in obtaining corporate gifts to aid the system. A key aspect of his program was to break segregation. He used busing, magnet schools, and continuous monitoring of how the racial balance was maintained. One of his major goals was to "halt white flight." He convinced real estate agents that turned-around schools were desirable. Minneapolis is now rated one of the best in the nation. While Green had been described as "arrogant and closed-minded," the community came to admire him and to respect his views (Bowen, 1988).

To help you understand decision makers such as Green, this chapter examines a cognitive model of decision making. This model is shown in Figure 4.1, where the focus is on the perceptual and cognitive aspects of decision making. The model is based on the individual's cognitive complexity and values, just as in the decision style model. The process starts with a stimulus or need to which the decision maker responds. The information taken in depends on the individual's perception. A tentative choice is made after the manager examines the implications of a decision (cognition). Next, the decision maker maneuvers for position to accommodate power centers. At the last phase, leadership, a generic process, is crucial to gaining acceptance of a decision. The cognitive decision model thus covers:

1.  *Perception/Cognitive process:* All aspects of reasoning, understanding, and problem solving. Also included as part of the cognitive process are perception, frame of reference, and rationality.
2.  *Personality:* Those attributes that affect the manner of interaction with others, attitudes, needs, values, beliefs, and drives.
3.  *Leadership:* The manager's vision and ability to influence others, ability to assert power, and ability to share power in order to achieve significant goals. Just as managers have different decision styles, each individual has different leadership styles that are needed to achieve goals.

Starting with the stimulus, the decision maker uses a frame of reference in reacting to the information perceived, which is a function of experience and cognitive complexity. Perception acts as the filter, allowing only certain information or cues to be taken in. Perceptual attitude structure is described by Schroder, Driver, and Streufert (1967) as the way people respond to situations. Managers who exhibit rigid attitudes are described as authoritarian and can be described as having a concrete attitude structure that is insensitive to changes in the situation or to new and subtle information. This helps explain the persistence of bias in managers' decisions despite the fact that there is conflicting information. At the other extreme are individuals who have a highly abstract attitude structure that helps them relate to varied perceptual constructs. These individuals are willing to consult with others and to search for

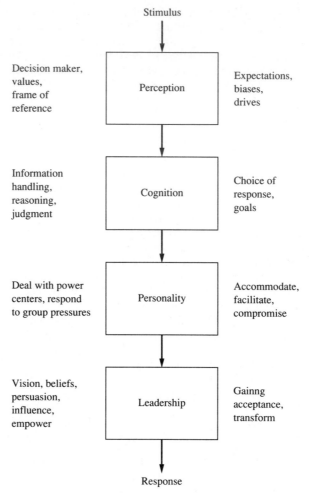

Stimulus

| Decision maker, values, frame of reference | Perception | Expectations, biases, drives |
| Information handling, reasoning, judgment | Cognition | Choice of response, goals |
| Deal with power centers, respond to group pressures | Personality | Accommodate, facilitate, compromise |
| Vision, beliefs, persuasion, influence, empower | Leadership | Gainng acceptance, transform |

Response

**Figure 4.1** ▲ **Cognitive Decision Model**

information. They can handle highly complex structures and are also able to resolve conflicting perceptions. The difference in attitude structures helps to explain an individual's degree of tolerance for ambiguity, which in turn affects decision making.

Perception also can be described as a continuum, as shown in Figure 4.2. Instinct is shown at one extreme and describes the limited use of information. Intuition is used when individuals rely on information based on experience. Insight, on the other hand, involves analysis of available information. At the other extreme, judgment involves cognitive complexity and is used to weigh the relative worth of various alternatives. Judgment also is used to examine complex problems where there is limited information.

| Instinct | Intuition | Reasoning | Judgment |

**Figure 4.2** ▲ **Perceptual Continuum**

# ▲ THE PERCEPTUAL PROCESS

The perceptual process includes cognition, as shown in Figure 4.3. The process starts with response to stimuli or pressures encountered. These stimuli are modified by the individual's past exposure to different situations. Perception is influenced by past inputs as modified by the individual's frame of reference. Perception depends on motivation, learning, personality, and social development. The needs, tensions, values, defenses, and emotions of the individual directly influence perception.

Starting with perception, problems are viewed from each person's frame of reference. Because of this, feelings may be confused with the factual content of a situation or problem. Roadblocks to decision making are often a result of our perceptual limitations. Elbing (1978) suggests that roadblocks can be described as:

1.  The tendency to jump to conclusions rather than questioning.
2.  Using available solutions rather than analysis.
3.  Using single goals rather than relationships.
4.  Relying on referent group's values.
5.  Dealing with symptoms rather than real problems.
6.  Responding automatically rather than inquiring systematically.

An interesting illustration of how people respond to problems and their blind spots is the case of Eastern Airlines. Charles E. Bryan, president of Eastern Airlines' machinists' union, was naive in thinking that he could gain favor with the new owners when Eastern was sold to Texas Air. Bryan sent a warm telegram to Frank Lorenzo. He said he looked forward to a cooperative relationship. Lorenzo never responded to the telegram. Bryan did not read Lorenzo's "silent message" correctly. As chairman of Eastern, Lorenzo was more interested in making sweeping changes. It was clear that his intention was "to slash the wages of the union members. He vowed to gain control by changing work rules." Lorenzo believed that work rules inhibited the union's productivity. He started by attacking Bryan's members. In response, the union would not reopen its contract; the salaries of pilots and flight attendants were cut 20 percent. The union's position on part-time mechanics was a thorn in Lorenzo's side. He felt that paying baggage handlers and janitors $16 an hour was outlandish considering that this was twice what he paid at Continental. Not being satisfied with those cuts, he wanted to cut the wages of Eastern's pilots even though their contract had not expired (Engardio and Norman, 1986).

## Cognition

The second phase of perception, cognition, is the way we understand information perceived. Values, risk propensity, rationality, and bias all influence the way an individual reasons about problems. Reasoning describes the manner in which the brain deals with stimuli, and depends on the individual's ability to handle complexity of cues received. A more intuitive individual, for example, tends to respond quickly and, in a sense, bypasses reasoning as a conscious act. Chase and Simon (1973), describing skill in chess, concluded that players seldom consider more than two or three possible moves per position rather than thinking through the total situation.

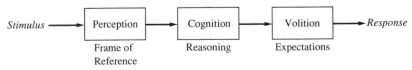

Figure 4.3 ▲ The Perceptual Process

Our minds work both at the conscious and subconscious levels. At the conscious level we are aware of what we think. At the subconscious level, physical or emotional influences can affect our thought processes. For example, in a study done by Mihalasky (1969), he found that some executives have more precognitive ability than others, which allows them to anticipate the future intuitively rather than logically, and when they do not have adequate data, they can still make good decisions. He also found that the higher the level in the organization, the more complex the executive's decisions and the more intuition was used in making decisions.

Considerable effort has been spent in trying to understand how the mind operates and how cognition influences perception. As an example, if a teacher attributes a student's poor performance to a lack of motivation, he or she is more likely to express open disappointment rather than consider the performance to be due to a lack of ability. Similarly, a supervisor's appreciation of a subordinate is dependent on the supervisor's feeling toward that individual and reflects prior notions as to which characteristics and behaviors are considered acceptable.

## Volition

Volition, the third phase of the process, reflects the choice that a manager makes. Volition incorporates feelings and needs, in addition to analysis, and reflects the manager's expectations. A choice depends on the individual's personality, drives, and feeling of security. Choice thus involves multiple factors and is intertwined with problem solving and reasoning. For example, Simon (1983) describes bounded rationality as a psychological phenomenon labeled cognitive strain. This is a breakdown of the decision maker's cognitive processes when subjected to information overload. Janis and Mann (1977) quoted President John F. Kennedy as saying, "How could I have been so stupid?" He realized that the miscalculation of approving the Bay of Pigs invasion reflected an error in judgment. Many ill-conceived or poorly implemented decisions are a result of conflict and stress generated by "agonizingly difficult choices." One cannot overlook the effect of information overload, group pressures, blinding prejudice, organizational constraints, or bureaucratic politics on decision choices.

## Response

The final phase of the process is the response to stimuli based on the mind's information processing, reasoning, problem solving, and the individual goal-seeking behavior and expectations. The response may be very rapid, where little reasoning is needed. However, more complex problems require more cognitive processing and typically are slower. Also, creative solutions often require insight and time for incubation as well as understanding in contrast to speed.

The human mind is indeed a paradox. Perception and cognition are complex, and in many respects can be considered the foundation of decision making. The manager who does not respond appropriately to stimuli, who does not perceive problems properly, who does not instinctively and intuitively know how to respond, who cannot handle the analytic techniques required, who lacks appropriate judgment, and whose personality traits either prevent or interfere with the process will inevitably be less than effective. It becomes increasingly obvious that perception and cognition are critical elements of effective decision making.

## ▲　JUDGMENT AND REASONING

During the U.S. Civil War, President Lincoln asked one of his generals, "How many legs does a cow have if you count the tail as one of the legs?" Bewildered, the general replied,

"Five." "No," answered Lincoln. "Calling a tail a leg doesn't make it one." Likewise, calling a computer program intelligent does not necessarily make it so (Hertz, 1988). Obviously, Lincoln's reasoning process was different from the general's.

Managers often require judgment in order to cope with the myriad problems they face. Examples abound where there are conflicting judgments from experts in a given field who are expected to know the answers to problems. For example, should President Bush have negotiated for release of the hostages in Iraq? Some experts argued that there should be no negotiations, others advised discreet negotiations, and still others suggested that the goal of releasing hostages transcends any position taken about how to deal with the captors. Treatment of cancer is another example where there is considerable uncertainty and where quality of life is often balanced with possible treatment. How does one determine which is better? What we can deduce is that a "correct action" solves a current problem but also considers future consequences. Concern for balancing current solutions with possible future outcomes is important and is governed by value-laden judgment. Wisdom is required to arrive at an appropriate balance. The balancing of assumptions, beliefs, and consequences leads to a wise decision.

In attempting to understand how managers think, we often make assumptions regarding how facts are perceived, how judgments are made, and how preferences affect decisions. Penrose (1989), in his book *The Emperor's New Mind*, deals with the issue of consciousness, showing that human minds are constantly coming up with questions for which there are no general answers. In a strict sense, intuition, imagination, emotion, common sense, and judgment are all part of what we call thinking. Intuition, although not an obvious part of thinking, nonetheless is often the basis for creative problem solving. Successful managers learn how to adapt to unknown situations by "creating" meaningful solutions to complex problems. Cognition helps to explain how the mind perceives cues and creates constructs that are used for solving complex problems.

Cognition also involves the manner in which the brain uses information to understand and reason about problems. As shown in Figure 4.4, there are four styles of reasoning that can be related to decision styles. The cognitive model of reasoning illustrates the different ways in which managers exercise reasoning and judgment.

The four types of reasoning can also be related to the structure of the brain. There are four primary lobes. The frontal lobe is often considered to be where reasoning and analysis are done. This lobe provides the capacity for foresight and planning. The temporal lobe is where action is relevant. It acts as the hearing center and may be where long-term memory is

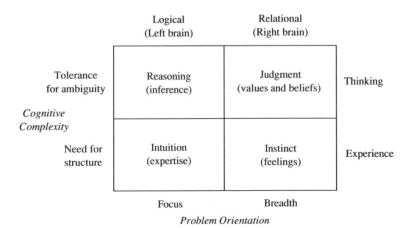

Figure 4.4 ▲ Cognitive Model of Reasoning

stored. The occipital lobe is considered the instinctive or emotional center. The parietal lobe receives sensations of touch and spatial information and monitors broad events. This is the lobe where judgment would most likely take place. Wisdom might be considered as residing in the cerebral cortex, the brain's outer layer, which controls all higher mental functions, and would support the exercise of wisdom (Begley and Springen, 1986).

When we examine the anatomy of the brain, we find that it differs for each individual. The pattern of convolutions, the tissue in the major areas of the brain, and the corpus callosum connecting the two hemispheres of the brain with 200 million nerve fibers are all different. Variations in the intracell interaction create different nerve functions. Also, the conductivity of electrical impulses and the time it takes to cross synapses appear to be determined genetically.

McGeer (1971) describes the chemistry of the mind as a means of understanding our thought processes. The cells of the brain that are involved in conscious activity, awareness, or emotion, and all the functions we associate with the mind, are different from any other living cells. The brain uses amine pathways that are thought to have a great deal to do with setting the level of activities of brain cells and in guiding them toward goal-oriented tasks.

One of the salient differences between the brain and computers (Penrose, 1989) is a phenomenon called brain plasticity that allows the interconnections (synaptic junctions) between neurons to change. One method for neurons to communicate is at junctions of dendritic spines. These are protuberances on the dendrites where contact is made with synaptic knobs. It is felt that the changes in neuron contacts determine how long term memory is stored. Learning is a result of reinforcement of a connection called the Hebb synapse that links two neurons. If the synapse is fired it is presumed to be strengthened, and if it is not fired then it becomes weakened. Earlier research also showed that reinforcement was a means to improve retention of material learned.

Although synapse formation may be preprogrammed, specific experiences "select" which synapse will be strengthened. Major connections are genetically determined; however, the environment is a major factor that influences human behavior and decisions. What is most intriguing is that long-term memory is related to the permanent structural changes in the synaptic connections (Lavigne, 1983). In *The Mind's New Science*, Gardner (1986) describes certain universal modes of cognition as sets of "mental representations" called a natural "language of thought." These determine the symbols, rules, and images of mental operations, and include how these representations are contrasted, joined, or transformed.

Another significant difference between the brain and computers, according to Penrose (1989), is the ability to judge truth from falsity. He describes consciousness as a key element of the difference because "knowing" is "nonalgorithmic"; and beliefs, values, and instinct are too difficult to set up in algorithmic form. Computers also lack inspiration, insight, ingenuity, and originality, which are properties of the brain. It cannot yet be explained why some ideas come in a "flash" while others require careful analysis.

A current effort at using computers that work like the brain is called neural networks, which are quite unlike conventional computers. They have no central processors that act on all the data at once, and the system's memory is spread throughout the network. When faced with the new power of transistors, the semiconductor industry is pleading conceptual poverty. The only thing missing in these "superchips" is imagination. "When you have a billion transistors on a chip . . . all kinds of chips—even memory chips—will have central processing units on them," says John Moussouris, a co-founder of MIPS. MIPS stands for millions of instructions per second and shows how fast computers can function compared with the human brain.

Although our neurons may be considered sluggish (roughly 100,000 times slower than a typical computer), they make it up in size or capacity. A typical brain has from 10 billion to a trillion neurons, with each neuron connected to anywhere from 1,000 to 100,000 other neurons (Kelves, 1986), and the mind can store an estimated 100 trillion bits of information (Begley et al., 1983).

But the physical structure of the brain alone is not sufficient to understand thinking. For example, emotions are considered as the base for many long-term memories, affecting access and retrieval. Thus, fear, happiness, and love are all part of the mind's machinery. Fear, anger, love, and sadness are complicated mixtures of feeling and physical response and are labeled emotions. Recent research shows that the experience of emotion depends on the complicated circuitry that interconnects them as well as the patterns of nerve impulses (Begley and Springen, 1986).

When the power of the computer is contrasted with the genius of humans, we have another picture of how the brain functions. In describing Cray, the father of the supercomputer, Russell (1990) relates, "That spartan desk speaks volumes about Cray, a man of simple tastes and the concentration of a laser beam. These days the 64-year-old Cray is scrambling to finish his most far reaching and risky creation, the CRAY-3. At peak speeds, it should blast through at a mind bending 16 billion calculations a second—eight times as fast as any computer like it. For thirty years, his ideas have dominated the super computer field. While Cray is shy and soft spoken, his mind is possessed with the singular ambition to build ever faster computers that will attack ever-more challenging problems" (1990, pp. 81–88)

## ▲ COGNITION AND JUDGMENT

Because the cognitive process involves understanding and evaluating information, judgment represents a very critical aspect of decision making and often determines the quality of decisions. Clough (1984) describes judgment and inference by examining the way in which cognition directly influences choices. He describes these as:

1. Judgment depends more on preconceptions than relevant new information.
2. Intuitive judgments can be misleading.
3. Availability describes intuitive judgment about the frequency of events and proportion of objects.
4. Representation attempts to classify concepts and can be illusive.
5. Judgmental fixation describes the anchoring of an individual's thinking regarding consequences.

The above varies with individuals because of their cognitive complexity. Although judgments may be reasonable, they can produce bias or fixation regarding a particular event or object.

Because judgment is often a result of conditioning of an individual's behavior, positive or negative reinforcement can affect an individual's ability to correctly perceive information. Conditioning, in turn, can affect the ability to correctly encode or represent knowledge, as described by Wickelgren (1977). He also describes learning and memory associated with access to data that affects judgment and inferences.

Judgment depends on an individual's recall ability and the recognition of events. Where retrieval is complex, it can be considered as a sequence of elementary recognition and recall stages. It is postulated that recall and recognition require the brain to utilize associative memory. Cognitive complexity considers associative memory as the ability to deal with higher levels of complexity to be able to relate perceived cues to known patterns in memory.

Vividness describes how information is represented in a person's mind; people apply different importance to the information depending on its vividness. Vividness also reflects the emotional interest of information, as well as the sensory aspects of the information.

Value judgments determine how managers make selections from among alternatives. Nisbett and Ross (1980) suggest that preconception strongly influences intuitive judgments because people often search selectively for data that support their existing beliefs and give little weight to new evidence that opposes existing beliefs. England (1967), who did basic research on values, found large differences with respect to the number and kinds of values held by individuals. He indicated that personal values tend to be stable and not subject to change.

Value judgments also describe how a person's values influence information search and processing. Harrison (1987) regards value judgments as the "capacity to make reasonable decisions and as essential to the process of reaching a correct decision." Judgment reflects evaluation and prediction of consequences. It is virtually impossible to separate an individual's values from judgments, especially in complex, ill-structured decisions. Judgment thus combines both factual data and individual values. Furthermore, because many decision situations involve uncertainty, value judgments remain important for evaluating, classifying, and selecting from among possible choices that can be made.

Another way we can explore how the mind operates on new subject matter is to examine heuristic reasoning. Clough (1984) introduced a concept called the *representativeness heuristic*, which deals with similarity or resemblance. That is, an object can be represented by a collection of features; similarity is described as a feature-matching process. Typically, only salient features are captured—and these are used for feature matching and categorization. Judgment is used to determine into which category an object belongs and to project general features from sample features. Judgments are made about events based on prior experiences, and predictions are also based on prior events.

The representativeness heuristic depends on the individual's cognitive complexity and judgments to determine salient features. Individuals also make judgments intuitively based on their recall of objects in a given category. These judgments may be reasonable, but they can produce bias. Tversky and Kahneman (1973) referred to judgmental fixations and anchoring to describe how people make estimates given some prior information. Individuals tend to be remarkably resistant to new or further information even where the new data show that previous conclusions were wrong. Thus, initial choices have a disproportionate impact on judgment.

Analogical reasoning is another way decision makers solve problems using prior experience or similar problems. Eliot (1986) suggests that the analogical process makes use of learning by example or by being told specifics about some events. Glass, Holyoak, and Santa (1979) examined the memory codes that humans use to represent analogies. For example, a map is essentially an analog representation of a given area. Humans represent analogies in memory by examining the size of common objects (such as a car). The memory code visualizes what a car looks like. Encoding can be abstract and relate knowledge about the object to its properties (e.g., temperature with a thermometer or cold with snow). Thus, analogs are stimuli that the mind uses to visualize representations of a given object.

Judgment is a critical element when searching for solutions to problems (Keeney and Winterfeldt, 1989). Initially, judgment is required to determine whether a problem should be explored. Next, judgment is needed to understand the dimensions of the problem and how to proceed with the solution to the problem. Decisions have to be made concerning what alternative to explore, what data to collect, what models to employ, how to analyze the data, and estimates of the probable outcome as well as time and cost. Managers can exercise these judgments because of prior experience or knowledge related to the subject.

## ▲ COGNITION AND STYLE

There is a growing recognition of the importance of conscious goal setting as an important aspect of understanding individual behavior and decision making. A number of studies have examined the effect of goals, intentions, desires, and purposes on task performance. The basic premise is that an individual's expectations affect what he or she does.

Cognition describes the process by which people think, evaluate information, and understand meaning. In discussing the need for a new approach to understanding behavior, Locke (1968) claimed, "Psychologists have become dissatisfied with the limitations placed upon research and theory by behaviorist dogma. A growing number of investigators have begun to study conscious goals, intentions, desires and purposes on task performance. The basic premise of this research is that man's conscious ideas affect what he does, i.e., that one of the (biological) functions is the regulation of action." Because of the intimate interaction of motivation and action, this facet of conscious thought assumes a critical role in decision making and decision styles. Thus, a manager's decision style is dependent on cognitive complexity, which helps explain individual differences in thinking, understanding, and perceiving. The cognitive process describes how people's minds use information to conceptualize ideas and how they respond to pressure.

Schroder, Driver, and Streufert (1967) describe an individual's capacity to distinguish among cues as stimuli discrimination. The highly cognitively complex individual is capable of perceiving more complex structures, and can make judgments based on a larger number of stimuli. These individuals have a broad perspective and are open to change.

Early work in the field of decision styles focused on how individuals actually used information and how they derived meaning from data. A person who used minimal data sacrificed completeness in exchange for saving time. At the other extreme, individuals who used a maximum amount of data to achieve the best possible solutions showed little concern for the time involved. In addition, some individuals would consider a single solution, whereas others saw many meanings in the data.

Benbassat and Taylor (1978) attempted to find out what influences decision strategies and what were the characteristics of users and problems. They considered cognitive complexity as the ability to differentiate a number of dimensions that were extracted from data. Some individuals could separate data from the background, but others could not. Highly analytical individuals readily perceive patterns of data interrelatedness; individuals with low cognitive complexity tend to perceive the environment in terms of rigid rules. The highly cognitively complex individual can easily tolerate ambiguity and can use contradictory cues.

## ▲  VALUES AND DECISION MAKING

Values have a significant impact on the decision process, according to Ebert and Mitchell (1975). Values may be understood as "the normative standards by which human beings are influenced in their choices among alternative courses of action." They provide a stable perceptual framework that influences the person's behavior. Human values fuse with organizational values and determine the "value judgments" in a given situation. Value judgments are most important when comparing alternatives and assigning priorities based on the decision maker's assessment of the acceptability. This evaluation is determined by the individual's values as biases reflected in his or her preconceptions, stereotypes, convictions, and beliefs about right and wrong behavior.

Rokeach (1973), a major figure in the study of values, maintains that values constitute stable beliefs concerning what is personally and socially preferable. Rokeach noted the similarity of values with other belief systems, which include thought, emotion, and behavior. Values guide the decision maker to:

1. Take particular positions on social issues.
2. Favor one particular political or religious ideology over another.

3. Determine how one presents himself or herself to others.
4. Evaluate and judge; to give praise and fix blame on self and others.
5. Permit comparative assessments of morality and competence in relation to others.
6. Persuade and influence others.
7. Permit rationalization of beliefs, attitudes, and actions to bolster personal feelings of morality and competence.
8. Maintain and enhance self-esteem.

England (1967) commented on the function of values in managerial decision making when he noted that values affect:

1. Perception of situations and problems.
2. The process of choice.
3. Interpersonal relationships.
4. Perception of individual and organizational achievement and success.
5. Limits for "ethical" behavior.
6. The acceptance of or resistance to organizational pressures and goals.

He suggested that values are acquired principles used to assist the decision maker to choose among alternatives, resolve conflicts, and make decisions, and may be modified based upon believed utility. He noted that values can also be used to predict career success within certain organizational settings, and that such values are both measurable and predictive.

Maslow (1970) was one of the early proponents of equating values to needs. He claimed that the individual's behavior is motivated by physiological, safety, social, self-esteem, and, finally, self-actualization needs. He defined this final need as "realizing the potentialities of the person . . . becoming fully human, everything that the person can become." According to Maslow, as each lower level need (value) was filled, an individual would move to the next higher level of need (value).

Based on Maslow's hierarchy of needs, Porter (1968) developed a hierarchy of values for managers. He considered that managers' physiological needs were already satisfied and could be replaced by a higher-order need. Porter's system of values was studied by Boulgarides (1973), who found that the five levels postulated by Porter could be reduced to fewer than four. A comparison of the Maslow and Porter value systems is shown in Table 4.1.

Schmidt and Posner's (1983) study of 1,500 executives and managers concluded that the shared values between an individual and the organization are a major source of both personal and organizational effectiveness. Based on responses to their shared values scale, they divided respondents into high sharers, moderate sharers, and low sharers, and noted significant differences among the groups. High sharers, tend to have:

1. Greater feelings of personal success.
2. Stronger feelings of organizational commitment and loyalty.
3. Clearer perspectives on ethical dilemmas.

**Table 4.1 ▲ Maslow–Porter Values Comparison**

| Maslow | Porter |
| --- | --- |
| Self-actualization | Self-actualization |
| Esteem | Autonomy |
| Social | Esteem |
| Safety | Social |
| Physiological | Safety |

4. Lower levels of work or home stress.
5. Better understanding of others' values.
6. Greater commitment to organizational goals.
7. Higher regard in general for other organizational stakeholders.
8. Different perceptions of important personal qualities.

Moderate and low sharers did not have particularly strong feelings with respect to the factors in the study.

A manager's personal values are linked to organizational values acquired from experience in the managerial role, according to Ebert and Mitchell (1975). The evidence indicates that where there is conflict between personal and organizational values, the latter will take precedence. They assert that a manager often will adapt his or her personal value system to the purposes of the organization in order to promote self-interest.

## ▲  THE ROWE–BOULGARIDES VALUES INVENTORY

The German philosopher Eduard Spranger (1928) was one of the first to propose a system of six values: theoretical, economic, aesthetic, social, political, and religious. Spranger's classification system was standardized by Allport et al. (1951). "For years, Allport's scale was the only standardized instrument that claimed to measure personal values" (Harrison, 1987). The study of values measures the relative strength among the six values. A strong orientation to one value is obtained through a reduced interest in one or more of the other values. The Allport study of values has been used in a variety of settings and has demonstrated high reliability and validity. Guth and Tagiuri (1965) studied 653 industrial managers, 178 research managers, and 157 scientists using the values categories developed by Spranger and by Allport et al. The industrial managers, both in self-ratings and in ratings expected from others, showed strong pragmatic, economic, and political values, with theoretical concern following close behind.

A major influence on the development of the Rowe–Boulgarides values inventory (VI) was the Allport study of values. After years of experience with the Allport values test, it was felt that a more efficient design could be achieved. Over the years, the Allport test had become dated, was male-oriented, and, in one major study of women architects, was judged to be chauvinistic (Boulgarides, 1985). However, not to be overlooked is the tremendous benefit of the Allport values as a baseline and reference point since it was well validated and universally recognized. A comparison of the Allport values test and the VI is shown in Table 4.2. As can be seen, the Rowe–Boulgarides values categories relate directly to the six Allport categories. The four categories of the VI are generic values and in effect capture the fuller Allport categories.

Table 4.2  ▲  Comparison of VI and Allport Values

| Allport | Values Inventory |
| --- | --- |
| Economic<br>Political | Pragmatist |
| Theoretic | Theorist |
| Aesthetic | Idealist |
| Social<br>Religious | Humanist |

## ▲ THE VALUES INVENTORY MODEL

The values inventory (VI) is based on two key factors. The vertical axis represents personal (or internal) focus, whether self-oriented or others-oriented. The horizontal axis represents the external focus, whether technical or social. Thus, each axis covers either the inner- or outer-directed values. The descriptions in the model incorporate significant factors identified by philosophers such as Spranger and Singer and researchers Allport et al. and England, among others. The complete Rowe–Boulgarides Values Inventory Model is shown in Figure 4.5.

Similar to the decision style inventory, an individual will not fit only one of the four values—pragmatist, theorist, idealist, or humanist. Rather, he or she will have combinations among the four. The scores for the four types identify an individual's relative strength among the four values. Different professions or industries will have unique value profiles, as will different cultures. On the individual level, the individual's value profile is compared with the general population norm. It can also be compared with the norm of his or her peer or professional group. The VI values categories can be described as follows:

*Pragmatist:* This individual is a composite of the Allport economic and political values. They are interested in power, material things, success, and wealth. This type is typical of the American business person.

*Theorist:* This individual is similar to the Allport theoretic person. An abstract thinker, he or she depends on knowledge for influence. The theorist has a need for position and status from which he or she derives a feeling of self-esteem. Typical of technical professions such as engineering.

*Idealist:* This value is similar to the Allport aesthetic. The idealist values autonomy and independence of thought, and may be a utopian. Sometimes unrealistic, but not as materialistic as the pragmatist or theorist. The idealist tends to search

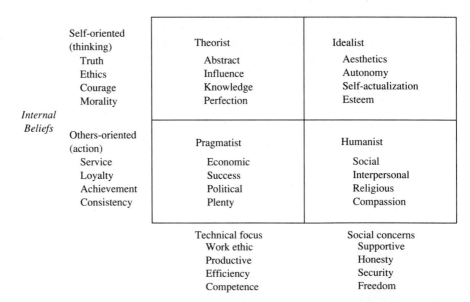

*External Concerns*

**Figure 4.5** ▲ **Rowe–Boulgarides Values Inventory Model**

for self-actualization as described by Maslow. Shows concern for others and appreciates art.

*Humanist:*  This value combines the qualities of the Allport social and religious. Very concerned about society as a whole with compassion for the less fortunate. Not materialistic, willing to work and share, and a loyal individual.

## ▲ VALIDATION OF THE ROWE–BOULGARIDES VALUES INVENTORY

The Allport values test is well validated and has been accepted by the professional community for many years. To validate the VI, it was correlated with the Allport test. In a major study of women architects ($N = 404$), both the Allport values and the decision style inventory (DSI) were administered. Boulgarides (1983) found the results shown in Figure 4.6.

The direction of the correlations in all cases were as expected. The detailed correlations are shown in Appendix A. The DSI's directive style is positively correlated with Allport's economic and political values, which indicate materialism, interest in results, and power. The directive style is negatively correlated with aesthetic and religious values. This would indicate a lack of artistic sensitivity and spiritual values. The directive individual is results- and task-oriented.

The analytic style is positively correlated with Allport's theoretic value, which relates to theory and problem solving. The analytic is negatively correlated with economic and social values. The analytic person is a theoretical individual who is not involved with results or social issues.

The conceptual style is negatively correlated with economic, aesthetic, and social values. Often, the creative thinker is conceptual and is not always very practical.

The behavioral style is positively correlated with social and religious values, indicating strong social concerns, caring, and spiritual interest. The behavioral style is negatively correlated with theoretic and political values, indicating lack of interest in abstract issues or in having power over others.

Next, the correlation between the VI and the DSI was examined. Two tests were run. The first sample was for a police department ($N = 65$) and the second was a sample of women managers ($N = 71$). The results are shown in Figure 4.7. In both cases the results were as expected, and the details are shown in Appendixes B and C. Having obtained the results expected, this supports the assumption of consistency between the VI and the Allport values test.

|  | *Allport Values* | |
|---|---|---|
| *Decision Style* | Political Economic Theoretic | Aesthetic Social Religious |
| Directive/ Analytic | Positive | Negative |
| Conceptual/ Behavioral | Negative | Positive |

**Figure 4.6  ▲  Correlation between Allport and DSI**

_Values Inventory_

|  | Pragmatist/<br>Theorist | Idealist/<br>Humanist |
|---|---|---|
| _Decision_<br>_Style_ | | |
| Directive/<br>Analytic | Positive | Negative |
| Conceptual/<br>Behavioral | Negative | Positive |

**Figure 4.7** ▲ **Correlations between the DSI and VI**

## ▲ APPLICATIONS OF THE VALUES INVENTORY

The values profiles for various professions, occupational groups, and cultures have been reported in Guth and Tagiuri (1965), England (1967), England and Keaveney, (1969), and Posner (1981). One would expect that individuals in widely different professional pursuits would have different values. Boulgarides (1983) reported differences in values between women engineers, women personnel managers, and women managers. The women engineers had theoretic as their highest value, the women personnel managers had aesthetic, and the women managers had economic. Values profiles for these and other groups are shown in Table 4.3.

The dominant value for all the groups is pragmatism, not surprising considering that we live in a very materialistic society. The male population's values are closer to each other, with the women managers being somewhat lower on pragmatism and somewhat higher

**Table 4.3** ▲ **Comparison of Scores on the Values Inventory**

| Population | Pragmatist | Theorist | Idealist | Humanist | Average Age |
|---|---|---|---|---|---|
| Male police (N = 65) | 89 | 82 | 74 | 55 | 33 |
| Women managers (N = 71) | 85 | 82 | 74 | 59 | 37 |
| Male managers (N = 71) | 87 | 84 | 74 | 55 | 39 |
| Women managers (N = 545) | 81 | 81 | 75 | 63 | 38 |
| Male managers (N = 561) | 82 | 81 | 77 | 60 | 40 |
| Male students (N = 134) | 85 | 82 | 75 | 58 | 26 |
| Female students (N = 155) | 81 | 82 | 76 | 61 | 26 |

# Values Inventory

8 = Most like you
4 = Moderately like you
2 = Slightly like you
1 = Least like you

Only use each number for the four responses to each question. Please score the following questions based on the instructions given. Your score reflects how you see yourself, not what you believe is correct or desirable, as related to *your work situation*. It covers the typical values that are related to the current work or organization you are in.

| | | | | | | | | |
|---|---|---|---|---|---|---|---|---|
| 1. Loyal individuals: | Follow orders | | Contribute to the organization | | Meet their obligations | | Assist others to succeed | |
| 2. If stealing is suspected, I would: | Take remedial action | | Evaluate the facts | | Understand the cause | | Discuss the problem | |
| 3. I feel it is important to be: | Strong | | Patient | | Honest | | Caring | |
| 4. In my work I prefer to: | Follow my instincts | | Have complete information | | Act on my own | | Work with others | |
| 5. I feel that people should be: | Dependable | | Intelligent | | Ethical | | Compassionate | |
| 6. When conflict exists, I: | Resolve it | | Look for a solution | | Improve the situation | | Defer to others | |
| 7. I prefer co-workers who: | Have drive | | Are careful | | Have original ideas | | Are supportive | |
| 8. A good worker | Takes responsibility | | Analyzes what needs to be done | | Considers consequences of actions | | Shows concern for people | |
| 9. As a member of society, I want to: | Progress | | Contribute to knowledge | | Make it a better place | | Help those less fortunate | |
| 10. I feel that people should: | Live in the present | | Plan for the future | | Aspire to greatness | | Be receptive to others | |
| 11. My ambition is to: | Be wealthy | | Have advancement | | Be independent | | Have many friends | |
| 12. A true friend: | Supports what I do | | Provides me guidance | | Respects my ideas | | Accepts me as I am | |
| 13. Beauty is: | A natural phenomenon | | An abstract ideal | | Universal | | An emotion | |
| 14. I worry about: | Being demoted | | Making mistakes | | Being restricted | | Feeling helpless | |
| 15. In my organization, I: | Follow through on tasks | | Comply with group norms | | Am committed to group goals | | Accept group values | |
| 16. I would feel distressed about: | Failing in an assignment | | A loss of prestige | | Being embarrassed | | Being rejected | |
| 17. I admire people who are: | Competitive | | Inventive | | Flexible | | Sociable | |

*(Continued)*

| 18. I believe our society needs: | Economic growth | | Technological advances | | Opportunity for individual growth | | Social justice | |
|---|---|---|---|---|---|---|---|---|
| 19. I expect others to have: | Ambition | | Dignity | | Autonomy | | Leisure | |
| 20. I strongly value: | Accomplishment | | Challenge | | Self-respect | | Being loved | |
| | | | | | | | | |

Alan J. Rowe & James D. Boulgarides ©10/29/83; Rev. 1/15/84

on humanism, very slightly lower on theoretic and very slightly higher on idealism. We would expect to see different value profiles for different professions, and possibly even at different levels in an organization.

The profiles in Table 4.3 typify managerial values. If the pragmatic value was low and the humanistic value was high, it would be difficult to manage in our current economic-oriented business culture. The development of these profiles provides a baseline for other comparisons. The simplicity of the values inventory should make it an appealing tool for management. When combined with the DSI, the VI provides a significant dimension for understanding and managing an organization more effectively. Ultimately, what people value determines the kinds of decisions they will make.

A manager's personal values are often contingent on his or her experience in the managerial role. Managers rely on the normative standards they use in their decision making. Values thus become a relatively permanent perceptual framework that influences the manager's choices.

## ▲ ▲ ▲ ▲ ▲ CASE: "MONEY FOR NOTHING"

On any given day about 1 million American workers don't show up for work. Some are sick, some are on vacation—but the ones who do the real damage are the ones who don't show because they just don't feel like it. Managements have tried every form of carrot-and-stick incentive imaginable, but still the problem continues, in 1987 draining between $30 billion and $40 billion from the nation's already overburdened economy (Greene, 1988).

Few companies have it tougher on this score than General Motors, which routinely loses 9 percent of employee payroll hours—at a cost of $1 billion a year—to unjustified absenteeism, the highest rate of the big three automobile companies. In the fall of 1987 the company had to close operations at the Pontiac East assembly plant in Michigan for two days at the start of the hunting season, when much of the workforce disappeared, rifles in hand, into the woods of the Upper Peninsula.

GM has been fighting this battle for more than a decade. Now the company plans to go ahead and begin firing people. Under the new UAW contract, which took effect in January 1988, any worker who consistently stays out more than 20 percent of the time can be fired after four unacceptable absences. General Motors had wanted to fire workers who were out more than 15 percent of the time, but the UAW resisted and negotiations led to a 20 percent rate, which was reduced to 16 percent in 1990.

What's an unacceptable absence? GM and the union agreed to be tough on absentees. Truly disabling problems such as heart attacks or broken limbs won't get a worker fired. But taking a day off for a headache, runny nose, or backache may. "All doctors' slips are not acceptable," said Henderson Slaughter, the UAW assistant co-director for the attendance program. The new plan was a return to the kind of punitive efforts that

GM had success with in the early 1980s. Then, to get people to turn up for work, GM simply penalized workers who were absent more than 20 percent of the time by cutting benefits such as profit sharing and vacation time by a percentage equal to the number of days they were absent.

In 1985 GM told the *Wall Street Journal* that this plan succeeded in getting its controllable absences down from 11 percent to about 9 percent. But although the plan continued, there the gains stopped. So, in early 1985, GM decided to try another tack. For every quarter in which a worker did not miss any days of work, he or she got $50. If a worker came in every day for a year, he or she got an additional $300, for a potential payoff of $500.

Unfortunately, the bonus plan, which as of early 1988 had cost GM about $400 million, did not cut absenteeism one bit. Why?                                         ▲

## ▲ Summary

This chapter covered the underlying foundation that was used as the basis for developing decision styles and contributing to understanding why and how managers make decisions. Cognition and values are the two key factors used for the decision style model discussed in Chapter 2. The discussion of cognition started with perception, which is the means for taking in information from the environment. Our personal frame of reference forms the background for the information input. Cognitive complexity affects the amount of information we can take in and the way we envision various cues.

Cognition is often equated with understanding but obviously is intimately linked with perception. Cognitive complexity refers to the mind's ability to handle complex cues and the level of tolerance for ambiguity. Where cognitive complexity is low, the individual tends to have a high need for structure, concreteness, or simplicity in viewing and understanding information input. Cognitive complexity overlaps with values when dealing with the decision maker's ability to exercise judgment. Value judgments refer to the way in which decision makers view new information or how they compare or categorize objects.

Because cognition deals with the mind and how we reason, this material has been included here to elaborate on our understanding of brain functions and their influence on decision making. Reasoning also overlaps value judgments because the way in which the mind reasons is directly related to cognitive complexity and decision styles.

The material on values has dealt in considerable depth on the background and development of the values inventory. The values inventory test is scored in a similar way to the decision style inventory. When taken together, the two instruments provide powerful measuring tools to better understand the decision maker and to better predict the behavior and decisions he or she will make.

## ▲ Study Questions

1.  What are the two fundamental factors in decision styles?
2.  What is the difference between perception and cognition?
3.  What does volition refer to?
4.  How is reasoning related to decision styles?
5.  Why is judgment important in decision making?
6.  Who is considered the founder of values theory?
7.  How is the Rowe–Boulgarides values inventory related to Allport?
8.  What are some of the applications of values?
9.  How do values affect decision making?
10. What is meant by value judgment?

## Appendix A
## Significant Correlations—Allport Values and
## Decision Styles, Women Architects (N = 404)

| Allport Values | Decision Styles | | | |
| --- | --- | --- | --- | --- |
| | Directive | Analytic | Conceptual | Behavioral |
| Theoretic | | +.1759<br>.003 | | −.2995<br>.001 |
| Economic | +.1953<br>.001 | −.1063<br>.046 | −.2101<br>.001 | |
| Aesthetic | −.2045<br>.001 | | −.2462<br>.001 | |
| Social | | −.0995<br>.058 | −.0920<br>.073 | +.2768<br>.001 |
| Political | +.1793<br>.002 | | | −.1551<br>.007 |
| Religious | −.0991<br>.059 | | | +.1200<br>.029 |

## Appendix B
## VI–DSI Correlations
## Police Department (N = 65)

| Allport Values | Decision Styles | | | |
| --- | --- | --- | --- | --- |
| | Directive | Analytic | Conceptual | Behavioral |
| Pragmatist | +.5485<br>.001 | +.1870<br>.068 | −.2868<br>.010 | −.4909<br>.001 |
| Theorist | +.0683<br>.294 | +.4030<br>.001 | −.1939<br>.061 | −.2418<br>.026 |
| Idealist | −.4589<br>.001 | −.1854<br>.070 | +.4534<br>.001 | +.2314<br>.032 |
| Humanist | −.3132<br>.006 | −.3563<br>.002 | +.0761<br>.274 | +.5813<br>.001 |

## Appendix C
## VI–DSI Correlations
## Women Managers (N = 71)

| VI | Decision Styles | | | |
| --- | --- | --- | --- | --- |
| | Directive | Analytic | Conceptual | Behavioral |
| Pragmatist | +.5820<br>.001 | | −.5143<br>.001 | −.2036<br>.044 |
| Theorist | | +.4675<br>.001 | −.2193<br>.033 | −.3524<br>.001 |
| Idealist | −.3981<br>.001 | −.1367<br>.128 | +.5058<br>.001 | |
| Humanist | −.3819<br>.001 | −.4185<br>.001 | +.3234<br>.003 | +.5088<br>.001 |

## ▲ References

Allport, G. W., Bernon, P. E., and Lindzey, G. *A Study of Values: A Scale for Measuring the Dominant Interests in Personality*. (rev. ed.) Boston, MA: Houghton Mifflin, 1951.

Begley, S., Carey, J. and Sawhill, R. "How the Brain Works." *Newsweek* (February 7, 1983), pp. 40–47.

Begley, S., and Springen, K. "Memory." *Newsweek* (September, 1986), pp. 48–49.

Benbassat, I., and Taylor, R. N. "The Impact of Cognitive Styles on Information System Design." *MIS Quarterly* (June 1978), pp. 43–54.

Boulgarides, James. "Decision style, values and biographical factors in relation to satisfaction and performance of supervisors in a governmental agency." (MDAC paper WD 2040). Unpublished doctoral dissertation, University of Southern California, Los Angeles, June 1973.

Boulgarides, James D. "Decision Styles, Values and Characteristics of Women Architects in the U.S." *Equal Opportunities International* Vol. 4, No. 3 (1985), pp. 1–18.

Boulgarides, James D. "On applying the Decision Style Inventory." Paper presented at the annual meeting of the Academy of Management, Western Division, Santa Barbara, CA, March 1983.

Bowen, Ezra. "Tough Guy for a Tough Town." *Time* (January 18, 1988).

Chase, W. G., and Simon, H. A., "The Mind's Eye in Chess," in *Carnegie Symposium on Cognition*, W. G. Chase, ed. Orlando: Academic Press, 1973.

Clough, D. J., *Decisions in Public and Private Sectors*. Englewood Cliffs, NJ: Prentice-Hall, 1984.

Ebert, Ronald J., and Mitchell, Terence R. *Organizational Decision Processes*. New York: Crane, Russak & Company, Inc., 1975.

Elbing, Alvar. *Behavioral Decisions in Organizations*. Dallas, TX: Scott, Foresman & Co., 1978.

Eliot, Lance B. "Analogical Problem Solving and Expert Systems." *IEEE Expert* (1986).

Engardio, Pete, and Norman, James R. "Frank Lorenzo Starts to Strafe Eastern's Unions." *Business Week* (November 10, 1986).

England, G. W. "Personal Value Systems of American Managers." *Academy of Management Journal* Vol. 10 (1967), pp. 53–68.

England, G. W., and Keaveny, T. J. "The Relationship of Managerial Values and Administrative Behavior." *Manpower And Applied Psychology* Vol. 3, Nos. 1–2 (Winter 1969), pp. 63–75.

Gardner, H. "The Mind's New Science: A History of the Cognitive Revolution." *The New Republic* (February, 1986), p. 38.

Glass, A. L., Holyoak, K. J., and Santa, L. J. *Cognition*. Reading, MA: Addison-Wesley, 1979.

Greene, Richard. "Money for Nothing." *Forbes* (January 25, 1988).

Guth, W. D., and Tagiuri, R. "Personal Values and Corporate Strategy." *Harvard Business Review* (September-October 1965), pp. 124–125.

Harrison, Frank E. *The Managerial Decision Making Process*. Boston, MA: Houghton Mifflin, 1987.

Hertz, D. B. *The Expert Executive*. New York: John Wiley & Sons, 1988.

Janis, I., and Mann, L. *Decision Making*. New York: Free Press, 1977.

Keeney, Ralph L., and Winterfeldt, Detlof Von. "On The Uses of Expert Judgement on Complex Technical Problems." *IEEE Transactions* Vol. 36, No. 2 (May 1989), pp. 83–94.

Kelves, D. J. *The Mind's New Science*. New York: Howard Gardner, Basic Books, 1986.

Lavigne, M. "The Secret Mind of the Brain." *Columbia Magazine* (December 1983), p. 16.

Locke, E. A. "Toward a Theory of Task Motivation and Incentive." *Organizational Behavior and Human Performance* Vol. 3 (1968), pp. 157–189.

March, James G., and Simon, Herbert A. *Organizations*. New York: Wiley, 1958, p. 11.

Maslow, Abraham H., *Motivation and Personality*. 2nd ed. New York: Harper & Row, 1970.

McGeer, Patrick J. "The Chemistry of the Mind." *American Scientist*. Vol. 59 (March-April 1971).

Mihalasky, J. "Question: What Do Some Executives Have More of?" *Think* (November-December 1969).

Nisbett, R., and Ross, L. *Human Inference*. Englewood Cliffs, NJ: Prentice-Hall, 1980.

Penrose, R. *The Emperor's New Mind*. New York: Oxford University Press, 1989, pp. 396–418.

Porter, L., and Lawler, E. E. *Managerial Attitudes and Performance*. Homewood, IL: Richard D. Irwin, 1968.

Posner, B. Z., and Munson, J. M. "Gender Differences in Managerial Values." *Psychological Reports* Vol. 4–9 (1981).

Rokeach, Milton. *The Nature of Human Values*. New York: Free Press, 1973.

Rowe, Alan J., and Boulgarides, James D. "Values Inventory Instrument." (rev. ed.) (1984).

Russell, M. "The Genius." *Business Week* (April 30, 1990), pp. 81–88.

Schmidt. W. H., and Posner, B. Z. *Managerial Values in Perspective*. New York: American Management Association, 1983.

Schroder, H. M., Driver, M. J., and Streufert, S. *Human Information Processing*. New York: Holt, Rinehart & Winston, 1967.

Simon, Herbert A. "Search and Reasoning in Problem Solving." *Artificial Intelligence* Vol. 21, Nos. 1–2 (1983), pp. 7–30.

Spranger, E. *Types of Men*. Trans. P. J. W. Pigors. Halle: Hiemeyer, 1928.

Tversky, A., and Kahneman, D. "Availability: A Heuristic for Judging Frequency and Probability." *Cognitive Psychology* Vol. 5 (1973), pp. 207–232.

Wickelgren, Wayne A. *Learning and Memory*. Englewood Cliffs, NJ: Prentice-Hall, 1977.

# Part II

# DECISION MAKING IN ORGANIZATIONS

# 5 Decision Making in Organizations

▲ ▲ ▲   ▲ ▲ ▲ ▲ ▲ ▲ ▲ ▲ ▲ ▲ ▲ ▲ ▲ ▲ ▲

This chapter examines how decisions are made in organizations and how they impact performance. To achieve this objective, the dynamics of the organization with respect to structure, power, participation, values, and culture are covered.

## ▲ DECISION MAKING IN ORGANIZATIONS

To examine decision making in an organizational context, the emphasis shifts from a focus on the individual to an understanding of the individual in an organizational context. Because an organization is, after all, a collective activity, it cannot be understood without examining the behavior of people. Structure, group behavior, politics, power sharing, work demands, and environmental forces all need to be examined to understand organizational decision making.

Robert Dockson, when he was chairman of California Federal Savings and Loan, describes his approach as wanting to get his executives totally involved. He aims at involving people in the total picture—in solving problems and in the decision-making process. Dockson pushes his executives hard, yet most of his staff find working for him challenging because of their involvement in problems. He sits down with his subordinates and together they identify the problems to be worked on. The results seem to justify the approach taken by Dockson, for not only have revenues increased, but earnings rose by almost 25 percent in the first year that he was president.

Decision making in an organizational context has been studied by many authors. Reddin (1970) considers situational analysis to be a critical aspect of effective decision making. Lawrence and Lorsch (1967), using the concepts of integration and differentiation, deal with problems that exist in the organization in terms of conflict resolution, improved coordination, and cooperation among divisions. Gore (1964) has indicated that organizations are constantly in a state of tension, and the best that a manager can hope for is a condition of quasi-equilibrium. Internal stress is, perhaps, as important as dealing with uncertainty in the external environment, and conflict can be good for an organization when it is handled properly. If there is some anxiety and a moderate level of uncertainty, then conflict can be constructive.

An early approach to organizational decision making was studied by Gore. He examined the underlying dynamics that influenced the way decisions were made in organizations. He viewed the organization as a collective activity for handling stress, and he introduced the concept of organizational equilibrium as "the fluid elements that change based on their independent dynamics. The organization can be considered as three streams of behavior (production, resource procurement and individual need satisfaction) which are constantly out of adjustment and seeking equilibrium, yet are never quite in balance with each other in spite of a leader's best efforts" (Gore, 1964, pp. 26–27). He describes disequilibrium that leads to stress as the price managers pay when attempting to meet clientele demands without sacrificing internal goals. These goals focus on meeting the needs of individuals. If internal stress is recognized as a vehicle for change, then the balance described by Gore helps to describe what managers must confront when making organizational decisions.

Another approach to organizational decision making was proposed by Shull, Delbecq, and Cummings (1970). They identified five factors that affect both the kinds of decisions and how they were made:

1. *Group structure:* Describes the relationships among members.
2. *Group roles:* Define the behavior needed to facilitate tasks.
3. *Group processes:* Describe the manner of proceeding toward goals.
4. *Group style:* Relates interpersonal relations with stress, congeniality, and consequences of success or failure.
5. *Group norms:* The shared frame of reference, social pressures, and prescriptions regarding behavior, beliefs, or feelings that are reinforced by sanctions.

Using these five dimensions, they describe three basic decision types, which are:

1. Routine decisions.
2. Creative decisions.
3. Negotiated decisions.

Using these three decisions types, an organization attempts to deal with the five factors previously noted.

# ▲ UNDERSTANDING ORGANIZATIONS

Behavior in organizations can be understood based on the psychological characteristics of individuals as well as organizational influences and characteristics. The current emphasis in organizations is to allow the individual to have greater control because authority is based on individual competence, and work is less structured and changes constantly. This requires greater flexibility; performance is enhanced due to the personal involvement that leads to commitment. In a controlling organization, authority and coordination are formal and impersonal, which leads to demotivation of workers.

Cummings and Molloy's (1977) analysis of sociotechnical systems projects showed that individual worth was the key element. Increased productivity was reported in the large majority of these projects, and well over half reported that worker satisfaction improved. Cummings and Molloy studied which factors contributed most to improved productivity and quality of working life. He identified that the following factors were key to improving worker productivity and satisfaction: pay–reward systems, autonomy of the worker, technical and physical work settings, task variety, and job enlargement.

To be effective, organizational decision making needs to take into account the relationship of individual expectations to performance. Because expectations are difficult to assess, the ability to achieve organizational aims is complicated. Levinson (1972) reasons that motivation often does not work because executives may be fearful of losing control. Furthermore, if managers destroy an individual's sense of worth and accomplishment, they cannot expect to have motivated employees. Explicit recognition of individuals' needs often determines the effectiveness of organizational decisions.

Organizational decision making also relates in part to the question of what makes a good manager. McClelland and Burnham (1976) found that achievement-motivated workers will do things for themselves. A manager therefore is needed where the workers are not self-starters. In those situations, a good manager is one who has a high need for *power* or *control*. These managers are more concerned with using their power to improve productivity than for the individual's benefit.

Over a period of time, even workers who are self-starters will lose their motivation when they feel that management is no longer interested in them. To illustrate the point, we have the case of Ore-Ida, the J. J. Heinz Co. producer of frozen potatoes. There was limited new-product development even though innovation had been a strategic priority for several years. However, the research people at Ore-Ida did not believe that their top management was serious about new product development. When the CEO and top managers held meetings at the R & D facility and shared their thinking or answered questions and established ongoing programs, there were positive results. A million dollars in cost savings was uncovered in one year, and over a three-year period there were numerous new products and product line extensions. This represents a deliberate action on the part of the decision makers to demonstrate sincerity. They did this by paying attention to those responsible for the execution of the decision (Waterman, 1987).

Peters and Waterman (1982) gained notoriety for their prescription of how to achieve high organizational performance. Their prescription was based on their research on the characteristics of high-performing organizations. Interestingly, not all of the companies studied were excellent for the same reasons. Companies identified as excellent do not continue to be so indefinitely. Although they may be considered excellent at some point in time, the external environment and the competition may require changes with which they are unable to cope. Interestingly, the high-performance organizations identified by Peters and Waterman were revisited; a number of them had problems and would no longer be considered excellent ("Who's Excellent Now?" Business Week, 1984). Even the best organizations experience setbacks in performance. These may occur due to either external factors that had not been foreseen and could not be controlled, or internal errors in judgment. The excellently performing organizations will have the ability to adjust their operations so that they minimize the negative impacts of the setbacks they experience.

On April 12, 1991, IBM reported its first-ever quarterly loss, of $1.73 billion. The deficit was attributed to the recession, the Persian Gulf war, and a new method of accounting for retiree benefits. By comparison, first-quarter 1990 profits for IBM had been $1 billion. The one-time charge for retiree benefits was $2.3 billion, which means that the profit without this special charge still would be $468 million below the profit in 1990. Obviously, IBM will survive, but it must also take drastic action to adjust for the change. Among the actions to be taken, IBM planned to trim 10,000 jobs from its worldwide workforce in 1991. A decline in IBM's share of the personal computer market has become a matter of concern. Competition from Apple Computer, AST Research, and other low-cost manufacturers has taken its toll on IBM. Even IBM cannot coast on its past glory in the face of fierce competition.

When viewed from a decision-making perspective, an organization has three distinct levels, as show in Figure 5.1. Each of these levels requires differing responsibilities, authority, and skills. As individuals are promoted, they typically have to change what they were doing in their previous jobs and take on new roles. Unfortunately, this does not always work out because old habits persist. In these situations, one can anticipate the Peter Principle, which states that people are promoted to their level of incompetence (Peter and Hull, 1969).

Traditional, bureaucratic organizations have persisted for many years and are based on a concept called the *chain of command*. In a bureaucratic type of structure, lines of authority are clearly spelled out, but these lead to built-in barriers to communication. To change this situation and improve organizational performance, the direction that now is being taken is a flatter organization structure, with a reduced number of levels that eliminate the barriers. This produces more effective communication leading to organizational teamwork. Effective communication is a characteristic of Japanese organizations, but has not been so in the United States.

Figure 5.1 ▲ Decision Levels in an Organization

## ▲  THE ORGANIZATION LIFE CYCLE

Changes in organizations are often a result of the organization life cycle. Greiner's (1972) work describes the stages through which an organization passes and the related changes in management focus, organization structure, top management style, control system, and reward emphasis. Greiner identifies five factors contributing to change: (1) age of the organization, (2) size of the organization, (3) stages of evolution (defined as growth through creativity, direction, delegation, coordination, and collaboration), (4) stages of revolution (defined as crises of leadership, autonomy, control, red tape, and uncertainty), and (5) growth rate of the industry.

As was described in Chapter 2, decision style can be related to the organization life cycle. At the initial, or entrepreneurial, stage, the manager most often is a combination of the conceptual and directive styles (Figure 5.2). This individual is the entrepreneur who has ideas and the drive to implement them. This combination of styles is conductive to taking the risks associated with starting a new business.

At the start-up phase, the organization is small and under intense pressure because of the possibility of failure, but it often leads to a cohesive culture. The high level of stress and excitement creates a situation where everyone knows what is happening. Communication is face-to-face, and there are few written procedures. This is sometimes referred to as a hip-pocket operation.

Start-up organizations typically have only two levels—one concerned with ideas and the other with operations. Examples are Lockheed's Skunk Works, which produced advanced avionics, and Jobs and Wozniak, who started Apple Computer in a garage. Even Jobs and Wozniak's former employer, Hewlett-Packard, many years earlier had also started in a garage. Many individuals have ideas that they never implement because they do not have the desire, drive, or courage to act on them. This would be the case of the researcher who is conceptual but does not have a directive style and thus does not have the necessary drive. Typically, the conceptual or creative individual is more interested in inventing new ideas than in implementing those ideas. That is, conceptual and directive styles are generally inversely correlated.

Another life cycle is concerned with research and development needed to develop new products. Typically, 60 ideas introduced into R & D produce only one final product. The product in turn must be engineered, fabricated, marketed, and managed. The critical management role occurs when the product has reached saturation. Unless an innovative approach is taken

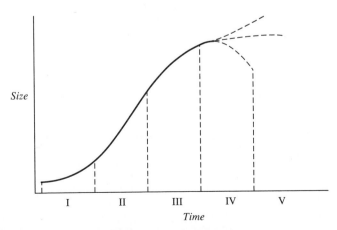

Figure 5.2  ▲  The Organization Life Cycle

again, the product life will decline. As discussed by Scheuble (1964), meaningful overall growth requires continuous new-product development to offset the decline in older products. Similar considerations apply in companies that are project-oriented, for each project also has a life cycle—perhaps not as predictable as consumer products, but nonetheless demanding constant management attention to the changing situation.

After the original idea is proven and the product or service is implemented, the organization begins to grow. At this point, the hip-pocket approach to running the organization is no longer suitable. When Apple Computers began to grow, the fun was gone and Wozniak took his money and left. Jobs, on the other hand, did not want to run a large organization, so he brought in John Sculley, a friend and an organization man from Pepsi Company. The chemistry seemed to be good at the beginning, but eventually power and control became an issue between the two and Jobs was forced out. Apple now can be represented by the classic three-level pyramid diagram of an organization. This reflects Sculley's analytic decision style that he uses to develop systems, procedures, rules, and the discipline essential to continued growth in a large organization.

Although John Sculley may be successful at running a large corporation, he probably could not invent a computer. It takes a conceptual style to invent a new product. On the other hand, "ideas belong to those who buy them." Loosely interpreted, "buys them" refers to whoever is receptive and accepts the idea. During 1990, Sculley "took on the most important inside job: overseeing the development of technology that would eventually replace the Macintosh" (Buell et al., 1990). Although "there was tremendous skepticism among the engineers," according to Larry Tesler, Apple's vice-president of advanced products, Tesler has been surprised at how well his boss has done. Sculley applied his organizational skills to the consolidation of development units, created quarterly operations review, and instituted daily 7:30 A.M. meetings with his chief engineer. As a result, the time for decision making has shortened the development cycle. He accomplished this by improving communication and getting closer to the action. He applied his full attention to the critical issue of development. It takes a courageous leader with great self-confidence to place himself or herself on the firing line in this way. According to Buell et al., "Sculley's long-term aim is to get new products out the door in 9 to 12 months rather than the 12 to 24 months it now takes" (1990, p. 96).

The organization life cycle also provides a perspective for understanding changes in performance. For a number of years, management has recognized and accepted the product life cycle as a meaningful basis for sales and advertising decisions. Table 5.1 shows the five basic phases in the change cycle.

Organizations go through many cycles, and individual departments or divisions might have different cycles than the overall organization. Organizations grow and change as management shifts and matures, as technology changes, as competition changes, and as economic conditions dictate new requirements. Changes in divisions or products or combinations of these also combine to change management and thus affect the overall organization life cycle.

In part, the organization life cycle also includes the career life cycle of managers. Five to seven years after individuals have completed their education, half of what they learned typically is obsolete. Filley (1976) et al. report on a number of studies that suggest that there

Table 5.1 ▲ Changes during the Organization Life Cycle

| Phase | Function | Organization | Control | Crises |
|---|---|---|---|---|
| I | Innovation | Informal | Creative | Leadership |
| II | Transition | Functional | Direction | Autonomy |
| III | Growth | Decentralized | Delegation | Control |
| IV | Consolidation | Groups | Coordination | Red tape |
| V | Adaptation | Teams | Collaboration | Survival |

are regularities in the growth of organizations and that the S-shape curve is a good means for describing the growth of a business.

## Decision Making Related to the Organization Life Cycle

As was seen in Table 5.1, each phase of the life cycle requires a different organizational form and thus a different style of decision making. The initial or start-up phase is generally characterized by considerable freedom and high risk (entrepreneurial). Because of the loose nature of the organization, a crisis in leadership typically arises. Individuals who are suited to start new organizations are not necessarily the same ones who are suited for the transition or growth phase, where more structure is required.

However, once the direction is defined, there is a tendency for management to overcontrol and for the organization to overreact to the direction taken, which then leads to a crisis of autonomy. At the next phase of the life cycle, the reins are loosened again and delegation is used to distribute decision making to decentralized divisions. In most organizations, another crisis arises because of the need for tighter control and direction of the organization. To achieve more control, coordination and more centralization tends to be the answer, which in turn leads to the red tape crises because of another instance of overcontrol. Thus, alternate phases of the organization life cycle represent tight and loose control.

The final phase of the organization life cycle, adaptation, is the most critical. It is often too late to prevent radical change if appropriate action was not taken in Phase IV. The adaptation phase determines whether the organization will survive and enter a new growth cycle or if it will decline and eventually be taken over or go bankrupt. This last phase is sometimes very painful, as evidenced by the kinds of action taken by companies when attempting to consolidate the growth from Phase III. Organizations will undoubtedly move toward adaptive strategies in Phase IV to avoid the trauma that can occur in Phase V. The information requirements for each phase of the organization life cycle are shown in Table 5.2.

Each phase requires a different emphasis to meet the organization requirements. In a start-up situation, cooperation and involvement of personnel are important in order to overcome the many problems encountered. Information requirements at this phase tend to be current due to rapidly changing conditions, and thus have a minimal impact on decision making.

During the transition phase, decision making must be flexible in order to change from a start-up to the steady growth of Phase III. Here again, because there are many changes taking place, only a slight increase in information is warranted. Phase III is what normally is thought of as conventional management. This represents a reasonably steady state, even though there is rapid growth. The analytic manager, using automated information to maintain control over the decentralized operations, is the one who performs effectively.

Phase IV requires an innovative manager who can anticipate the changes required to avoid a decline in Phase V. The information requires a decision support system that can predict future alternatives in contrast to merely keeping operations "under control." If successful, the coordinative style of Phase V facilitates the transition into a new mode of operating. Because

**Table 5.2  ▲  Organization Life Cycle, Management Functions, and Information Requirements**

| Phase | Function | Management | Information Requirements |
|-------|----------|------------|--------------------------|
| I | Innovation | Participative | Status reports |
| II | Transition | Flexible | Demand reports |
| III | Growth | Analytic | Automated, real-time reporting |
| IV | Consolidation | Innovative | Decision support systems |
| V | Adaptation | Coordinative | Network processing |

of the changes taking place, the information requirements shift to being more selective, using critical item analysis, and having a moderate volume of data.

## ▲ EFFECTS OF POWER AND POLITICS ON DECISION MAKING

Merely using the term *power* conjures up an image of managers who are highly authoritarian, arbitrary, and self-serving. However, a constructive rather than political basis for power appears to be emerging. There is also a recognition that power often is needed when making decisions in order to achieve results, and under those circumstances it does not have negative connotations.

Although there are many definitions of power, we consider five factors: power, authority, informal power, influence, and politics. It is difficult to look at power without understanding the situation in which the power is being used and how the manager employs it. Each of these five factors is examined in detail.

1. *Power:* As defined by Max Weber (1947), it is "the possibility of imposing one's will upon the behavior of other people." Heller (1971) defines power as the result of direct or indirect intervention of preferences in the decision process. Thus, power sharing determines whether the manager wants to exercise the power available. Power also reflects how a manager exercises authority.
2. *Authority:* Considered to be the legitimacy the manager has for acts that come under his or her surveillance. This is considered formal authority.
3. *Informal power:* This is a set of relationships that permit the accomplishment of tasks having interdependent activities and requiring cooperative effort. Coalition formation, negotiation, and consensus all are activities that take place in organizations relying on informal power.
4. *Influence:* This can be defined as the result of direct or indirect intervention in which the manager's preferences are the basis for arriving at a decision. In participation, two or more parties influence each other in making decisions. When conditions arise where people are given a semblance of power but little effective influence, possible alienation may occur.
5. *Politics:* As described in Patz and Rowe (1977), "a political process is one that increases certainty in an organization, based on reducing the effect of factors contributing to uncertainty." Politics is often related to negotiations, consensus formation, assertion of influence, or devious practices used to achieve an objective.

Power is a fact of life in most business organizations, and it often has a disruptive effect on managers and on the performance of the organization. Zaleznick (1970) states that when managers purport to make decisions in rationalistic terms, a sense of disbelief occurs because most observers and participants know that personalities and politics play a significant if not overriding role in making decisions. He goes on to question, "Where does the error lie? In the theory which insists that decisions should be rationalistic and nonpersonal or in the practice which treats business organizations as a political structure? Whatever else organizations may be, problem solving instruments, sociotechnical system, reward systems, and so on, they are political structures. This means that organizations operate by distributing authority and setting a stage for the exercise of power. It is no wonder, therefore, that individuals who are highly motivated to secure and use power find a familiar and hospitable environment in business" (Zaleznick, 1970, p. 47).

Zaleznick (1970) identified the four styles of power, which are:

1. *Bureaucratic:* Emphasis on procedures and power to achieve control.
2. *Conversion:* Human relations, participation, and so forth, to convert movement toward a power figure.

3. *Compliance:* Use of power or an authoritarian personality to achieve compliance.
4. *Problem solving:* Relies on organizational structure as the means for negotiation and compromise. It is based on demonstrated leader competence to determine outcomes.

Because change is endemic to an organization, conflict arises between the more powerful members, who have a vested interest, and the less powerful members of the organization. Conflict may be the case of honest disagreement about an issue or a decision under consideration. This type of conflict should be aired in order to resolve the issue in the best way possible. Another type of conflict arises as a result of a struggle for power. If the struggle is not resolved—if the hidden agendas are not brought to light so they can be dealt with—then the conflict remains hidden and represents a future pitfall for the organization.

Power is viewed as personal as well as linked to position. The traditional base of power has been on structure or the job responsibility. This approach is being eroded. Managers must know what to do, as well as have the skill and confidence needed to carry out responsibilities. Thus, power is shifting more toward leadership in that it is used to influence others to follow what the manager wants. Highly directive managers could find themselves unable to influence subordinates using "raw power."

## Power and Authority

Figure 5.3 shows the relationship of kinds of authority and uses of power that management can exert in a variety of situations. Thus, for example, power can be based on formal authority and be applied in an authoritarian manner. At the expert level, legitimacy becomes important. At the informal level, control and politics become the basis for the authoritarian (or manipulative) approach. In a similar vein, rewards or inducements and sanctions are based on motivation and bargaining coalitions, whereas the persuasive (participative) approach utilizes delegation, power sharing, and consensus as the manner in which results are achieved.

On the horizontal axis, the authoritarian manager manipulates people or the situation to achieve results. The reward–punishment manager uses sanctions or inducements to accom-

|  |  |  |  |  |
|---|---|---|---|---|
|  | Informal Group | Control politics | Bargaining coalitions | Consensus |
| *Kinds of Authority* | Expert Referent | Legitimacy roles | Human relations | Power sharing |
|  | Formal Position | Power | Motivation | Delegation |
|  |  | Coercive Authoritarian (Manipulative) | Reward Sanction (Inducements) | Persuade Influence (Participation) |

*Kinds of Power*

Figure 5.3 ▲ **Relationship of Power to Authority**

plish the ends desired. Finally, there is the persuasive manager who attempts to influence subordinates through a more intellectual process rather than brute force.

An examination of Figure 5.3 reveals that, in fact, no single approach to the kinds of authority or uses of power is appropriate. Each approach depends on the situation. In some instances, a more forceful or coercive approach is appropriate, whereas in others it might lead to resentment. Power sharing or participation obviously is only one manner of exercising power or authority, but it is by no means the best way of applying power under all circumstances. When relating power and authority to decision styles, flexibility is considered exceedingly important in making effective decisions.

John Kotter (1982), who has done extensive studies regarding power, stated, "Americans have probably always been suspicious of power. And partly, that may be because of the political processes and distrust of individuals who exploit and corrupt through power." But, as Kotter indicated, the dependence of managers on other people and the need to be skilled at using and acquiring power affect how well they can perform their jobs. Relating power to structure, he claimed that "as organizations have become more complex, it is difficult if not impossible for managers to achieve their ends either independently or through persuasion and formal authority alone. They increasingly need power to influence other people on whom they are dependent. Furthermore, effective managers tend to be very successful at developing four different types of power which they use along with persuasion to influence others. They do so with maturity, great skill, and sensitivity to the obligations and risks involved."

The four ways in which Kotter feels that a successful manager establishes power relationships are:

1.  Create a sense of obligation in others which the manager uses to influence these others.
2.  Build a reputation as an expert in a given field.
3.  Foster others' unconscious identification with the manager or with his or her ideas or what he or she stands for.
4.  Feed others' beliefs that they are dependent on the manager either for help or for not being hurt.

The approach suggested by Kotter covers a number of the relationships of authority to power shown in Figure 5.3.

## ▲ POWER IN ORGANIZATIONS

The political system in the United States was brilliantly set up to have a balance of power among the three branches of government—the legislative, executive, and judicial—in order to achieve checks and balances. For example, the same person cannot collect money and also write checks. Audits are conducted both in the government and in industry as a means of keeping the system honest. Despite these divisions of authority and checks and balances, corruption still exists. Where individuals or agencies have influence, collusion and corruption can exist. Power in the public domain depends on the ability to deliver what constituents want. Money is the life blood of politics. Power in an elected office lies in the ability to deliver votes for a desired cause. This often involves exchanges, compromises, or consensus building. For the manager, power lies in the ability to influence and gain commitment, as opposed to executing decisions by dictum or coercion.

The conventional bureaucratic structure has a built-in power orientation. This generally leads to conflict, empire building, rivalry, frustration, and the kind of environment that may not be conducive to effective performance. For example, Bennis (1966) suggested that the death of bureaucracy may come because of its inability to cope with an increasingly complex and turbulent environment.

This point is seen in those situations where group pressures lead to conformity and dependence on the group for satisfaction. Likert (1967) discussed the manner in which groups made decisions and concluded that when properly used, the group process deals with important issues but that managers are ultimately responsible for making the decision and for the results achieved.

Collins and Guetzkow (1964) have examined the question of power and influence in an organization, and concluded that when subordinates are involved in decision making, superiors have more influence in how decisions are carried out. The distribution of power among individuals in decision-making groups as they move from problem to problem may vary from a concentration within one or two persons to widespread influence among many members of the group. Yet, when one examines the power of individuals vis-à-vis particular issues, there tend to be those who have large amounts of power with respect to particular problems.

Power alone does not provide an adequate explanation for the results observed in organizations. As Zaleznick (1970) explained, there are two dimensions that define an executive's cognitive biases when exercising power. First is the selection of goals, whether only partial or total; second is an orientation toward action. He concluded that the use of power is a function of cognitive styles. Zaleznick contended that most problems involve a conflict of ideas and interests. Organizations that rely on a purely bureaucratic approach do not deal with vital issues that make organizations dynamic. Zaleznick's cognitive style model has four styles: bureaucratic, problem solving, compliance, and conversion.

In Zaleznick's approach, issues are resolved using action versus goals. The action orientation is comparable to cognitive complexity, and goal selection reflects task versus organizational orientation. The bureaucratic style is analogous to the analytic; the problem-solving style is similar to the conceptual; conversion is the behavioral; and compliance reflects the directive, who is the more power-oriented leader. Zaleznick recognized that the organization structure is a product of negotiation and compromise among executives who hold varying power bases. However, the power base of the executive is often a function of demonstrated competence.

While there are many sources of power, it is primarily used when resources are scarce, goals are uncertain, organizational units have discretion, and possible success is not impeded by other parties (McCall, 1979). Power is not universally good or bad but depends on how it is used. Power can be used to achieve results but it can be dysfunctional in terms of attitudes and commitment to performance. Nonetheless, power exists whether we like it or not and the challenge is how to make it productive without incurring negative effects. According to McCall:

1. Power comes from many places and is used in many ways.
2. Power can be contradictory and create tensions.
3. Whether power is good or bad depends on value judgements.
4. Power depends on the situation and the appropriateness of various actions.

It becomes painfully clear that power is a double edged sword that when used properly leads to desirable results but when misused can create alienation and undesirable consequences.

## ▲ PARTICIPATION AND POWER SHARING

Because of the increasing complexity of decisions in organizations and the increasing desire for involvement and commitment on the part of subordinates, managers have been turning to the practice of participative or high-involvement management. As with any approach, participative management has benefits and shortcomings. The theory rests on assumptions that employees at all levels of an organization are capable of contributing usefully to the decision process and that, in general, this willingness and capability have not been used.

Perhaps we can best examine participative management if we define participation as the sharing of power and influence in decision situations. Heller (1971) in his monumental study of participative management (Figure 5.4) showed that senior managers use prior consultation 37 percent of the time, whereas they make decisions on their own only 36 percent of the time, and that delegation is the least frequently used decision style. His research indicated that power is shared between senior managers and their immediate subordinates in nearly 50 percent of all important decisions.

To help define manager–subordinate interaction, Heller used 12 skill factors. He compared the perception of senior levels of management regarding their own job and the next level below. He examined the basis managers used for sharing power. He found that the skills that most affect a senior manager's decision styles are technical ability, decisiveness, and intelligence. Not only did Heller consider the question of how the manager and his or her subordinate viewed their respective capabilities, but he found that subordinates consistently overestimated the power they held. Senior managers and subordinates do not agree on the amount of skill needed for their respective levels of work, except regarding technical specialists.

A basic question that continues to be raised regarding organizational decisions is whether authority is determined by the leader's personality and characteristics, or whether the organization with its power bases and structure is critical. Both of these positions relate to still a third factor, the role of employee participation in the decision-making process. Participation is concerned with power sharing and influence over the final decision rather than the situation where the employee is consulted but has no effect on the decision. A strong proponent of the structure approach, Perrow (1970) stated that "organizations are people, their problems and leadership, not personalities. Leadership depends on the situational demands. The structure of the organization is more critical than effective leadership." Heller considered that the combination of situational, structural, and environmental circumstances explain variations in a leader's style. He further concluded that if a decision is important to the company, little influence is shared; if it is important to the subordinate, considerable influence is possible.

Zaleznik has stated, "Many rituals, such as participation, democratization and the sharing of power are associated with organizational life, yet their real outcome is the consolidation of power around a central figure to whom other individuals make emotional attachments." Fitzgerald (1971), on the other hand, felt that "it is questionable whether participation will

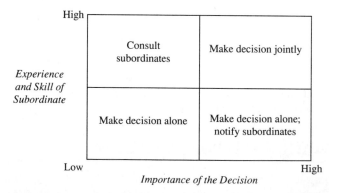

Figure 5.4 ▲ Adapted from Heller's Model of Decision Sharing

correct the pervasive apathy and indifference which exist in workers and provide the unqualified good that is claimed by many so called corporate liberals." Albrook (1967) reported, "One conclusion is that the participative or the group approach doesn't seem to work with all people and in all situations. Research has shown that satisfied, happy workers are sometimes more productive—and sometimes merely happy."

Effective participation requires good communication. It also relies on an understanding of workers as individuals, including their decision styles. Participation involves making decisions by consensus. The Japanese use consensus because of their concern for how decisions impact the organization. The consequences of a decision are studied and discussed before it is made. To the Japanese, consensus decision making is an integral part of their culture. To Americans, this appears to be an unnecessary and time-consuming process. The consensus approach is without question time-consuming; however, it provides the opportunity for understanding the thinking of senior management while providing an opportunity for bright young members to both learn and contribute. The consensus process can contribute to building an esprit de corps in an organization. It is not just the literal message that is communicated, but also the visceral commitment to the execution of a decision. The consensus approach also builds a stronger commitment to decisions in contrast to authoritarian, top-down decision making.

Given the diverse and conflicting positions on participation, what should management do? The answer, in part, is that subordinate response to participative style is dependent on the subordinates' personality and the situational demands. House and Mitchell (1974) performed a number of studies and suggested the following approach to handle conflicting positions on participation:

1. Where subordinates are highly ego-involved in a decision or task and demands are ambiguous, participation will have a positive effect on satisfaction of the subordinate, regardless of the subordinate's predisposition toward self-control, authoritarianism, or need for independence.
2. When subordinates are not ego-involved in their tasks and when demands are clear, those individuals who do not have high needs for independence or self-control and are authoritarian will respond less favorably to participation.

Both of these statements are based on the path–goal approach in which task characteristics and subordinate characteristics interact to determine the effect of leader behavior on satisfaction, expectancy, and performance. There is evidence that participative systems work best in organizations where there is openness and do not work as well in rigid, highly structured organizations.

Participation does not achieve its full potential when:

1. It violates traditional value systems.
2. Managers are not convinced of its worth or feel threatened.
3. Employees quickly perceive management's lack of interest and so resist real participation.
4. Benefits of participation are not visible in short-term results and tend to be limited to long-term benefits.
5. Participative systems imposed from the top become authoritarian and nonparticipative.
6. Power distribution curtails managers' ability to retain authority and leadership functions.
7. Subordinates gain more influence over their jobs and work environment only when it does not oppose management power.

Workers' councils which have existed in Europe for some time are rather apathetic toward decisions that do not directly involve their work or expertise, as described by Mulder (1971) in his study of power equalization through participation. Empirical research on the functioning of Dutch work councils showed that half of the voluntary members of workers' councils were not strongly motivated to participate in decision making; the other half complained about insufficient expertise, even though the workers' councils had been functioning for as long as eight years. This combination of low levels of motivation and expertness has appeared in all the investigations made in Dutch-speaking areas. This is an example of the difference between Western cultures and the Japanese.

Participation, influence, power sharing, job enrichment, and quality of working life continue to be important considerations in managerial decision making. With advances in worker aspiration levels, it seems clear that these issues will become more important, rather than less important. It also appears likely that the application of the decision styles approach in an organizational context can help explain the many conflicts that exist in the work environment and potentially help to resolve these conflicts by changing the worker's position or reporting relationship.

## ▲ STYLE AND MANAGER–SUBORDINATE INTERACTION

What do subordinates expect from their superiors? The expect specific characteristics and do not like a compulsive individual. Hofstede (1984) in the paper on leadership styles in an international survey of almost 20,000 individuals from marketing and service organizations, responded that although subordinates preferred a style that "consults," they did not perceive that this was the behavior, in general, of their managers. Interestingly, a manager who "sells" seemed to be the style that dominated management behavior.

Managers whose dominant style is behavioral have a high need for affiliation and want to be liked and be part of the group. These individuals may have difficulty in situations requiring an assertive manager. They tend to make excuses rather than decisions and can create havoc by not following rules. This disregard for procedures causes confusion, is seen as being inconsistent, and leaves subordinates in a weak position because they cannot always be sure of what to expect. On the other hand, a dominant directive style manager is overly concerned with the job to be done. Nevertheless, he or she can create an effective work environment where structure is important. The directive manager gets results by focusing on the work and on worker performance. Workers, however, generally prefer a supportive manager style. Directive managers do not necessarily try to make their subordinates feel weak; rather, they exercise the power they have. These managers feel responsible for building organizations, find satisfaction in work accomplished, will sacrifice self-interest for results, and use tangible incentives to reward performance.

Whereas the directive manager has a high need for power and typically is very direct, the behavioral style manager may be too concerned with people's needs. One can conclude that the most effective manager is a person who has a dominant directive style and has a strong behavioral back-up style. The conclusion that a purely behavioral manager may not be effective in achieving results must be tempered with several considerations. First, a behavioral manager can often obtain greater productivity when subordinates have freedom to operate as they see fit. Thus, the purely directive style, power-oriented manager does not always achieve results in all situations and in all organizations.

It is important to recognize that the directive and behavioral styles are action-oriented, and they operate as first-line managers in contrast to the requirements needed at the upper levels of management. Thus, power may be important when dealing with operating problems and may be inappropriate when dealing at higher levels in the organization. We cannot ignore Korda's (1977) advice when he says, "Action makes more fortunes than caution. This is a piece of advice worth remembering whenever you are tempted to do nothing." But there are always consequences of acting too rapidly, such as failing. The advantage of taking action even when failure occurs is that time is not lost in delays, something is learned from the failure, and corrective action can be taken. The manager who plays the power game always incurs some risk. However, the use of power must lead to practical decisions or the organization will not achieve desired results.

There appears to be a growing consensus that the strong, one-person rule cannot survive in today's turbulent environment. In a study conducted by Argyris (1973), he claimed, "Directive, controlling executives became strong at the expense of subordinates who became weak. Weak subordinates, in turn, protected themselves from the strong superior by carefully censoring the information they send to the superior, or timing the moment when he would receive it. These subordinates learned that the safest tactic was to censor information or delay its transmission until a correct solution could be shown. All these consequences tended to make the organizations increasingly rigid and sticky." Without the commitment of organization members to a single purpose, much organizational energy is wasted through half-hearted efforts and hedging when uncertainty dictates that individuals protect themselves.

A study of the Kansas City fire department showed that "every decision involved persuasion, negotiation, and concessions. There was not a single instance of an executive's making a decision through a formal mechanism. Rather, the process through which the hard choices were made involved the full stream of organizational behavior" (Gore, 1964). Likert (1967) also concluded that "the group process of decision making improves communication in which important issues are appropriately dealt with. However, the group method of supervision still requires that the superior is accountable for all decisions, including their implementation and results."

The question of moving from consensus to fragmentation is discussed by Bennis (1976). He described persons in positions of authority as having to cope with an avalanche of data that often are counterproductive. Although openness and candor are admirable, the effective manager has to recognize the difference between secrecy and confidentiality, between optimum and maximum openness. The manager needs to create conditions that encourage being truthful about where information can be gathered and that avoid bureaucratic rigidity. When there are limited data, Bennis concluded that groups are more effective in evaluating decisions that have to be made than individuals. Groups act as a security blanket as well as being in a better position to evaluate the consequences of decisions to be made. According to Bennis, few individuals, regardless of whether all the information needed to make a decision was available, would be courageous enough to make it alone.

Of course, the group approach to decision making has had its opponents as well. In an article on group think, Janis (1982) pointed out that there is considerable pressure for social conformity that is brought to bear by the members of a cohesive group whenever a dissident begins to voice his or her objections to the general consensus. Group norms are developed that bolster morale at the expense of critical thinking. Even when policies are obviously bad, the group will persist in carrying out that policy. Another illustration of this phenomenon is seen in the win–lose complex in which every member of the group approaches problems from the point of view of what it means to the individual rather than the organization as a whole.

Managers simply don't trust their subordinates and want to "keep the fun of the game" to themselves rather than share prestige and authority. This position is supported by the findings of Argyris (1973), who indicated that there was considerable distrust and antagonism in a group of 165 top executives whose behavior was observed. Seventy-one percent of the middle managers did not know where they stood with their superiors; 87 percent felt that conflicts were seldom coped with; 65 percent felt that management was unable to help them overcome intergroup rivalries, lack of cooperation, and poor communication; and 82 percent felt that they could not communicate their desire for increased responsibility to management.

When managers are not able to exercise authority because they lack the courage to do so, many decisions are perceived as a risk to their well-being. This becomes especially important in an organization where mistakes in judgment are punished. The results reported by Argyris indicate that managers felt inadequate and most likely would not perform as required. What we have found is that the one indispensable ingredient in successful managers is a sense of self-confidence. When managers feel good themselves, they can also feel good about others. The converse implies that weak or insecure managers will use subordinates as their excuse for lack of performance.

To be effective, managers will have to shift from an orientation that is concerned solely with personal decisions to ones that are organizationally oriented. Managers who are analytic and conceptual are able to deal with the broader problems confronting organizations. In addition, a conceptually oriented decision maker is willing to share power, and because of his or her need for self-achievement and strong self-image, is able to help others achieve.

## ▲ ANALYSIS OF THE ORGANIZATIONAL SYSTEM

One approach to analyzing an organization is the use of a four force model as shown in Figure 5.5. The organization responds to forces from the external environment and in turn exerts forces on the manager to achieve objectives. In turn, the organization affects the manager. First we need to consider the manager's perceptual ability and the values employed. The manager's response is also dependent on the situation. The Merton Effect (Dalton and Lawrence, 1971), relates to an organization's demand for more effective performance. The feedback from the work situation reflects both worker attitude regarding the legitimacy of the demands and how the worker performs in response to the demands. If the demands are considered unreasonable, workers feel alienated and performance deteriorates. This in turn leads to new demands for improved performance because of customer complaints and poor quality. The situation continues until there is an explosive event that leads to total worker discontent and complete deterioration in performance.

A manager's perception depends on the level of ambiguity, stress, threats, pressures, and flexibility. The manager's influence on the workers and the acceptance or rejection of that influence also depend on their perception. The workers, in turn, are influenced by their personality and decision style. Workers prefer managers who facilitate the work, in contrast to managers who use a more authoritarian approach. The work itself depends on structure and technology, which affect the worker's ability to perform. There is also the demand for conformity from peers. Peer pressure is a function of work group size and pressures from external groups. The resulting behavior reflects the feelings of individuals.

The diagram shown in Figure 5.6 can be used to analyze the demands that influence individual workers. Formal organizational demands can be anticipated, but when relationships are informal, social behavior and social bonds become important. The decision maker thus is dependent on structure and the functions or activities needed to accomplish organizational output.

When considering the reaction of an individual to organizational pressures, we can apply the win–lose concept. Organizational demands are contrasted with personal needs. The dotted lines in Figure 5.6 represent the total effort expended. The solid lines show the combined effect of the opposing demands. Thus, individual A tends to be organizationally oriented, whereas individual B tends to behave in a win–lose pattern. That is, if it is good for individual B the organization benefits, but if the two are in conflict the individual will tend to pursue his or her own personal needs; the effect contributed toward organizational goals tends to be minimal in comparison to individual A, who has high organizational goal congruence. An

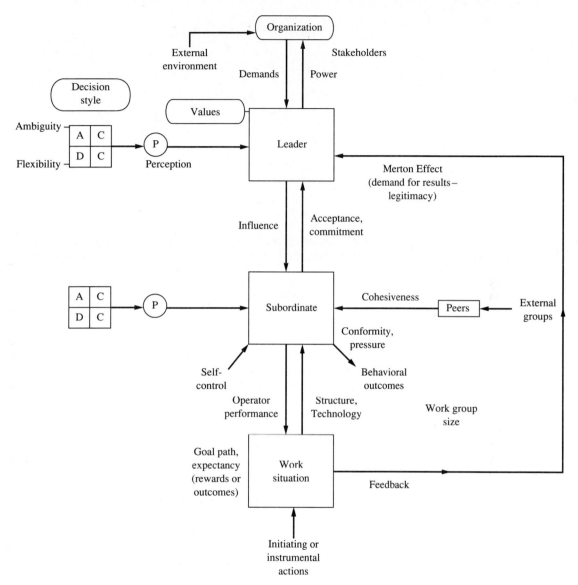

**Figure 5.5**  ▲  **The Organizational System**

important role of management is bringing people to the type A position and helping them to achieve correspondingly improved performance.

Another factor that influences the role and effectiveness of the manager is the levels of cohesiveness in the organization. As shown in Figure 5.7, high levels of cohesiveness exist when there are low levels of anxiety; or conversely, as the anxiety level or tension tends to increase, the organizational cohesiveness tends to disintegrate. In a tense situation, small groups, cliques, and individuals will tend to fend for themselves rather than meeting the organizational demands.

Group cohesiveness and group conflict also bear directly on interaction. Bobbitt et al. (1974) describe group cohesiveness in terms of the degree of power over their members. When

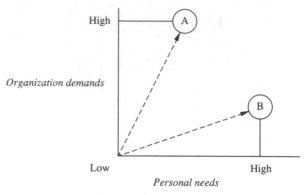

Figure 5.6 ▲ Organization Demands

the group is important to its members or the felt need to stay is strong, greater conformity can be demanded by the group. In turn, the attractiveness of the individual to the group depends on:

1. Needs for affiliation, recognition, or security.
2. Goals, method of operation, or prestige.
3. Expectancy of beneficial or detrimental consequences.

Role definition and status are two additional elements of social relations that are important. Both define the prescriptions for a particular position in a social system. Because of potential conflict and personal emotional states, both role and status are relevant in determining the individual's reactions to group pressures. Once again we refer back to Bradshaw (case in Chapter 1). After six months, he was still not part of the inner circle of decision makers. He had failed to develop strong relationships, which is critical for managers and executives. He was on the outside looking in, as demonstrated in the final board meeting.

Reaction to group pressure occurs in many ways and is described as interpersonal competence. Individuals who listen and communicate well, who can deal with pressure for conformity, who resolve conflict, and who get along have demonstrated a number of attributes of interpersonal competence. Thus, with the addition of personal needs and environmental forces, the four force model provides us with a broader perspective of the decision-making environment.

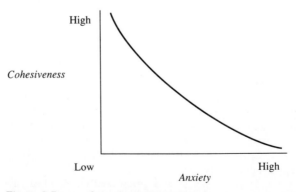

Figure 5.7 ▲ Organizational Cohesiveness

## Homans' Model

A model developed by Homans (1950) provides an understanding of the interactions and sentiments of individuals in a group, as shown in Figure 5.8. Individuals interact with the group and have emergent sentiments. As members of the group, individuals react to company environment and policies by exerting minimal effort. Social influences, both internal and external, affect the group. Reaction to social pressures and organizational requirements results in performance and morale. The interactions described by Homans are helpful when examining the performance expectations of the work group.

Because environmental factors directly influence long-term survival, they have a direct effect on the structure of the organization. There is constant change taking place in the external environment, and organizations must be able to adapt their internal structures in order to survive. The organization not only responds to the pressures of the external environment, but copes with internal forces as well.

Perhaps one of the most important interactions between managers and groups, as well as within groups themselves, is interpersonal communications. People's awareness, self-definition, and understanding depend on the frequency and type of communication utilized. Sigband and Bell (1989) succinctly expressed this: "There is much more to communication than merely the cogent presentation of a message. If the communication is not understood, believed and regarded as having a positive value for its recipients, it will fail in its mission. The overestimation of the effectiveness of communication media employed is one of the greatest sources of managerial error in dealing with customers, personnel, and the public." The significance of communication problems in organizations is highlighted by Jackson (1982), who describes the following as areas of concern:

1. Individuals have powerful forces to communicate with those who assist them or make them secure and away from those who threaten them or may retard their accomplishments.
2. Communications are directed at improving one's position.
3. Effectiveness of managerial communications depend on:
    a. prior feelings and attitudes.
    b. preexisting expectations and motives.
    c. level of satisfaction of superior–subordinate relations.
    d. level of support received by peer group.

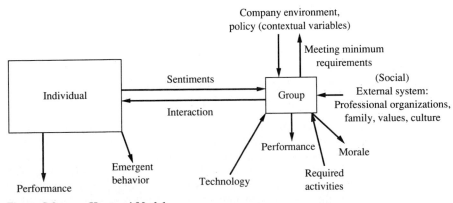

**Figure 5.8 ▲ Homans' Model**

Because all stimuli are perceived in some frame of reference, communications will be filtered to meet individual expectation. Thus, effective communication requires an understanding of the recipient's expectations, values, and aspirations.

## ▲　▲　▲　▲　▲　CRAY RESEARCH CASE

High technology organizations must work to maintain the innovative process as represented by Phase I of the life cycle and avoid becoming bureaucratic and bound by procedures as they grow. An excellent example of this challenge is the case of Cray Research.

There is a tendency for management to overcontrol and for organizations to overreact to changes that lead to a crisis of autonomy. Cray Research illustrates the problems that can occur when there is organizational change (Mitchell, 1990, p. 86). Cray Research had achieved $785 million in sales in 1989; however, its free form culture was being jeopardized by the crawling bureaucracy that had emerged. John Rollwagen, the CEO, asked the president of Cray to step down because of the president's bureaucratic demands for paperwork, reports, and meetings. Morale had noticeably decreased, which caused concern to Rollwagen. The credo at Cray had been very open and trusting and typical of creative employees who resent being told what to do.

Creative individuals thrive in a free-wheeling, unrestricted, and informal atmosphere. The demand for reports produced an atmosphere of fear and distrust, according to CEO Rollwagen. Up to that point, Cray had thrived without strict controls. As the leader in the field of supercomputers, Cray could only compete by taking risks. The conflict between a controlling president and a research oriented organization which depended on loose controls for its existence was inevitable.

Recognizing that he was losing the creativity that had made Cray such an outstanding computer company, Rollwagen opened the flood gates so that ideas could flow again unimpeded by bureaucratic restrictions. Because Cray's supercomputers are unique in their design, they must meet the specific needs of its customers.

From this case we can also see that a manager who is successful in one situation may not be able to function effectively in a different situation. While the retired president had been successful as the head of marketing from 1983 to 1988, during which time sales quadrupled, he proved not able to manage the company effectively.　　　　▲

## ▲　Summary

The management of organizations is an art. The effective executive knows how to inspire personnel and recognizes their needs. While creative tension is a stimulus in organizations, stress is counterproductive. Overstructuring organizations and an overdependence on rules can lead to counterproductive behavior on the part of the workers. Workers thrive and work improves when workers feel they are cared for. It is difficult to motivate workers and it is simple to discourage them.

If organizations are to be successful in the future, they must capitalize on the creativity of workers. This creativity must be nurtured by creating a positive atmosphere in the organization. Communication is the essence of a positive atmosphere. Managers must interact with workers to convey to them a feeling of being needed, appreciated, and belonging. Workers like to be kept informed. When there is an information void, rumors abound.

Changes in effective style occur over the various phases of the organization life-cycle. However, the one constant throughout is that workers need recognition and appreciation.

Politics in an organization can be very counterproductive. If politics replaces meritorious performance as a basis of recognition, reward, and promotion, it can have a very demoralizing effect on the work force.

Power can be used in both a constructive as a well as a destructive manner. The willful, as opposed to reasonable, use of power can have quite negative effects. However, the use of consultative management practices can preclude the need for the use of unreasonable power. Authority can be used in a reasonable manner with proper explanation and be accepted by workers without negative reaction.

## ▲ Study Questions

1. What types of decisions are made at each level of an organization?
2. What are the necessary qualifications of individuals to make those decisions effectively?
3. What are the consequences of poor decisions at the different organization levels?
4. What system of checks and balances can be used to avoid catastrophic decisions in an organization?

## ▲ References

Albrook, Robert C. "Participative Management: Time for a Second Look." *Fortune* (May, 1967).

Argyris, Chris. "The CEO's Behavior: Key to Organizational Development." *Harvard Business Review* Vol. 51, No. 2 (1973), pp. 51–52.

Bennis, Warren. "The Coming Death of Bureaucracy." *Think Magazine* Vol. 32, No. 1 (1966).

Bennis, Warren. "Leadership: A Beleaguered Species." *Organizational Dynamics* Vol. 5, No. 1 (1976), pp. 3–16.

Bobbitt, R. H., Breinholt, R. H., Doktor, R. H., and McNaul, J. P. *Organizational Behavior.* Englewood Cliffs, NJ: Prentice Hall, 1974.

Buell, Barbara, Levine, John, and Gross, Neil. "Apple: New Team, New Strategy." *Business Week* (October 15, 1990), pp. 86–96.

Collins, B. E., and Guetzkow, H., *A Social Psychology of Group Process for Decision Making.* New York: Wiley, 1964.

Cummings, Thomas, and Molloy, E. *Improving Productivity and the Quality of Work Life.* New York: Praeger, 1977.

Dalton, Gene W., and Lawrence, Paul R. *Motivation and Control in Organizations.* Homewood, IL: Richard D. Irwin, 1971.

Filley, Alan C., House, Robert J., and Kerr, Steven. *Managerial Process and Organizational Behavior.* Glenview, IL: Scott Foresman, 1976.

Fitzgerald, Thomas H. "Why Motivation Theory Doesn't Work." *Harvard Business Review* (July-August 1971), pp. 37–44.

Flanigan, James. "IBM Pained by Industry's Speedy Gnats." *Los Angeles Times* (December 6, 1989), p. D1.

Gore, William, J. *Administrative Decision Making: A Heuristic Model.* New York: Wiley, 1964.

Greiner, L. E. "Evolution and Revolution as Organizations Grow." *Harvard Business Review* (July-August 1972).

Heller, Frank A. *Managerial Decision Making.* London: Tavistok, 1971.

Hofstede, Geert. "The Cultural Relativity of the Quality of Life Concept." *Academy of Management Review* Vol. 9, No. 3 (1984), pp. 389–398.

Homans, George C. *The Homan Group*. New York: Harcourt, Brace, 1950.

House, Robert J., and Mitchel, Terrence R. "Path Goal Theory of Leadership." *Journal of Contemporary Business* (Autumn 1974).

Jackson, Victoria. "The Masked Meaning of Nonverbal Messages." *Modern Office Procedures* Vol. 27 (July 1982), p. 44.

Janis, Irving L. *Group Think*. 2nd ed. Boston, MA: Houghton Mifflin, 1982.

Korda, Michael. *Power: How to Get It and How to Use It*. New York: Simon and Schuster, 1977.

Kotter, John P. "Power, Dependence and Effective Management," in *Organizational Behavior and the Practice of Management* by David R. Hampton, Charles E. Summer, and Ross A. Webber. Glenview, IL: Scott Foresman and Co., 1982.

Lawrence, P. R. and Lorsch, J. W. *Organization and Environment*. Boston, MA: Harvard Business School, Division of Research, 1967.

Levinson, Harry. "In Effort Towards Understanding Man at Work." *European Business* (1972), pp. 19–29.

Likert, R. *The Human Organization: Its Management and Value*. New York: McGraw-Hill, 1967.

McCall, Morgan W. Jr. "Power, Authority and Influence" in *Organizational Behavior*. Steven Kerr, ed. Columbus, OH: Grid Publishing Co., 1979, p. 185.

McClelland, D. C., and Burnham, D. "Power Is the Great Motivator." *Harvard Business Review* (March-April, 1976), pp. 100–111.

Mitchell, Russell. "Can Cray Reprogram Itself for Creativity?" *Business Week* (August 20, 1990), p. 86.

Mitchell, Russell. "The Genius." *Business Week* (April 30, 1990), pp. 81–88.

Mulder, Mark. "Power Equalization Through Participation." *Administrative Science Quarterly* (March 1971), p. 31.

Patz, Alan E., and Rowe, Alan J. *Management Control and Decision System*. New York: John Wiley, 1977.

Perrow, C. *Complex Organizations*. Glenview, IL: Scott Foresman, 1970.

Peter, Laurence J., and Hull, Raymond. *The Peter Principle*. New York: Morrow, 1969.

Peters, T. J., and Waterman, R. H., Jr. *In Search of Excellence: Lessons from America's Best-Run Companies*. New York: Harper & Row, 1982.

Reddin, William J. *Managerial Effectiveness*. New York: McGraw-Hill, 1970.

Scheuble, P. A. Jr. "R.O.I. for New Product Planning." *Harvard Business Review* (November-December, 1964), pp. 110–120.

Shull, Fremont A., Delbecq, Andres L., and Cummings, L. L. *Organizational Decision Making*. New York: McGraw-Hill, 1970.

Sigband, Norman B., and Bell, Arthur H. *Communication for Management and Business*. Glenview, IL: Scott Foresman, 1989.

Waterman, Robert. Excerpts from "The Renewal Factor." *Business Week* (September 14, 1987), p. 104.

Weber, Max. *Theory of Social and Economic Organizations*. New York: Free Press, 1947.

"Who's Excellent Now?" *Business Week* (November 5, 1984), pp. 76–86.

Zaleznick, Abraham. "Power and Politics in Organizational Life." *Harvard Business Review* (May-June 1970), pp. 101–109.

# 6 Organization Culture and Group Decision Making

▲ ▲ ▲  ▲ ▲ ▲ ▲ ▲ ▲ ▲ ▲ ▲ ▲ ▲ ▲ ▲ ▲ ▲

This chapter deals with the importance of organization culture and how it affects organizational performance. Many organizations in the United States are still pursuing old and ineffective models of organizational behavior that are largely authoritarian and bureaucratic in character. The rapid decline of the United States in the competitive world market has accelerated the serious study of organization culture and how it impacts on productivity and effectiveness. The search for answers to the dilemma of reduced productivity leads to the need for finding methods used by the most effective and competitive organizations in the United States as well as those used by major competitors in the world arena, such as Japan. Unfortunately, methods used in Japan are not directly transferable to the United States because of basic differences in the national cultures of the respective nations. Other topics covered in this chapter deal with the components within the total organization that are affected by organization culture such as group decision making, intergroup communication, group creativity, and group problem-solving methods. An organization culture instrument is introduced as a means to determine how participants view the culture of their organizations.

# ▲ ORGANIZATION CULTURE

What is now known as organization culture was previously described as organization character (Harrison, 1972), organization climate (Haberstroh and Gerwin, 1972), or organizational norms. These authors helped identify the factors that contribute to effective organizational performance. The culture of an organization represents group interactions and group expectations. A number of the critical factors that have emerged include the norms, beliefs, values, standards, rituals, structure, rewards, climate, and kinds of interactions expected within an organization. Organization culture also reflects the managerial demands on the organization. Thus, it incorporates all of the policies, procedures, goals, strategies, and actions of the management.

Research has shown that culture has a powerful influence on organization life (Sathe, 1983). Culture is described as the often unstated understandings that are commonly accepted by a group. This concept of organization culture emphasizes shared, invisible understandings in the minds of organizational members. The shared understandings include sayings, doings, feelings, beliefs, and values. Many of the underlying premises of organization culture are based on the personality of the organization's founder, which tends to remain outside people's awareness.

In the United States, employees are less willing to follow the top man blindly, and they tend to be more adversarial. Furthermore, culture varies greatly from one company to another, and often within the same company. Thus, executives in America must have broader skills because they cannot rely on shared cultural value systems for legitimacy and support (Lawrence, 1985). An exception to this is the phenomenal success of the Ford Taurus. Ford studied needs, made quality a top priority, and streamlined both operations and the organization. It was a radical departure for Ford. A program management approach was used for the design of new cars where planning, engineering, design, and manufacturing all acted as a team that took final responsibility for the new cars.

# ▲ RELATIONSHIP OF INDIVIDUAL VALUES TO ORGANIZATION CULTURE

An individual's personal values have been related to performance and organization culture. This parallelism is illustrated in Figure 6.1. Organizations attempt to match individual actions and organization behaviors in order to achieve desired performance.

The relationship between culture and values is described by Sathe (1983), who strongly supported the interdependency. "Culture has a powerful influence on organizational behavior

| *Individual Values* | | |
| --- | --- | --- |
| *Values* | *Actions* | *Results* |
| (Needs) | (Individual) | (Outcomes) |
| (Beliefs) | | |
| *Organization Culture* | | |
| *Culture* | *Behaviors* | *Results* |
| (Values) | (Workers) | (Performance) |
| (Norms) | | |

**Figure 6.1  ▲  Comparison of Individual Values and Organization Culture**

because the shared beliefs and values represent basic assumptions and preferences that guide such behavior." Sathe also identified three factors that explain the difference in the extent of culture influence on behavior. "First, cultures with more shared beliefs and values have a stronger influence on behavior because there are more basic assumptions guiding behavior . . . . Second, cultures whose beliefs and values are more widely shared have a more pervasive impact because a larger number of people are guided by them. . . . Finally, cultures whose beliefs and values are more clearly ordered (that is, where the relative importance of the various basic assumptions are well known) have a more profound effect on behavior because there is less ambiguity about which beliefs and values prevail when there is a conflict."

Although organization culture links both the tangible and intangible factors in an organization, it also reflects the shared values of individuals in the organization. These shared values determine the degree of commitment that individuals will have to the goals of the organization and provide the unity of purpose needed to meet the challenge of competition. It is difficult to separate personal from organization goals. Many researchers have found that there are a diverse set of goals in any organization (Drucker, 1954; England, 1967; Gross, 1968; Richards, 1978). These diverse sets of goals lead to a lack of consensus in defining the relationship between the concept of personal values and that of organizational goals. Some researchers have distinguished personal values from organizational goals and found consistency between two of the three organizational goals: organizational efficiency and profit maximization as reported by England (1967) and Posner and Munson (1981). In another study, Harrison (1987) found that "personal and organizational values permeate all decisions." It is clear that there is a strong link between values and culture.

## ▲  IMPORTANCE OF ORGANIZATION CULTURE TO PERFORMANCE

The importance of organizational culture was highlighted by Moos (1974), who noted that most people intuitively believe that culture has a significant impact on any organization. He describes situations in which some people were supportive of others whereas some had a strong need for control. Some organizations were extremely rigid while others emphasized order, clarity, and structure. We can see that decision style influences both the way people make decisions and the way they act in organizations and influence culture.

A corporation's culture influences its employees' attitudes toward customers, competitors, suppliers, and even one another. Often cultural norms are laid down by a strong founder and hardened by success into custom. However, as an article titled "Corporate Culture" (1980) indicates, "a company's culture is so pervasive, changing it becomes one of the most difficult tasks that any chief executive can undertake." A number of books evidence the importance of building an appropriate culture (Ouchi, 1981; Deal and Kennedy, 1982) or organizational conditions (Kanter, 1983), and of identifying goals that challenge and excite (Pascale and Athos, 1981; Peters and Waterman, 1982).

Organization culture often determines the ability to change, or to adapt to new environmental conditions. Because continued survival depends on the ability to change, organizations that are incapable of changing as conditions change will fail to maintain their position in the market and will often fail to survive. Desire for stability can be an obstacle to changing the organization in order to meet the changing needs of the environment.

A study done by Peters and Waterman (1982) identified eight attributes that characterize excellent companies. These companies all

1. Had a bias for action.
2. Stayed close to and understood the customer.
3. Provided autonomy and encouraged entrepreneurship.
4. Recognized that productivity was based on people.
5. Were hands-on, value-driven.
6. Would stick to their knitting.
7. Had a simple form and lean staff.
8. Maintained simultaneous loose–tight controls.

These attributes are indicative of what excellent companies consider when searching for commitment from people. In contrast, bureaucratic organizations have boardrooms where decisions are made based on somber presentations and staff reports. Excellent companies most often are distinguished by the intensity of strongly held beliefs that are "accepted" by members of the organization. In excellent companies, from the leader down, individuals are not afraid to get their hands dirty; there is trust and mutual respect. There is a feeling of intense excitement, of a spirit of being part of an excellent company. Peters and Waterman did a follow-up to their study and found that executives lead by example, not dictum.

Thomas Watson, Sr. recognized the importance of beliefs and their lasting value for any organization. In order for an organization to succeed and survive, a sound set of beliefs are needed to guide its policies. He characterized the basic beliefs needed for an organization to succeed as respect for the dignity and rights of individuals, the best customer service, and finding a superior way to carry out tasks (Thompson and Strickland, 1990). When workers feel secure and respected, there is trust and confidence that the system is fair. Such a situation contributes to the loyalty and commitment of the worker to the organization. This, in part, is the basis for support of organizational goals by the individual.

Emphasis on the customer focuses on the organization's commitment to provide service. Service has been the hallmark of IBM, and customers have responded positively because they know that they can depend on IBM when they have problems. This produces customer loyalty, and price becomes a secondary factor. An organization concerned with customers will be responsive to their needs and will keep moving forward as opposed to becoming stagnant and obsolete. Watson's son, on the other hand, takes a somewhat different position. He claims that a "business is a dictatorship" and "the best way to motivate people is to put them against one another" (Watson and Petre, 1990).

Excellence often is a result of a desire to be a superior performer, to have the best product, or to achieve the highest quality. Customers respect and support excellent products, in part because they are the most economical in the long run. Thus, Watson's key point of starting from within the organization and then working outward has been very successful. Internally the organization's culture produces the conditions wherein workers are willing to devote their energies to the good of the organization. The workers, whose values match the organization's culture, strive for excellence and show concern for the customer, who is the final judge of the organization.

Sony Corporation attributes its success to trust: "True trust, not trust as a tool but as a living concept governing human relationships" (Lyons, 1976). Values and beliefs such as trust, respect for the individual, and respect for the customer reflect an openness and honesty in all personal relationships with a strong commitment to the mission of the organization. Ouchi (1981) extended this to "trust, subtlety and intimacy." The success of one company was ascribed to a core group of managers who shared a common vision of their business, a long-term commitment to one another, and a common managerial culture.

A "culture of pride" has been seen by Kanter (1983) as what distinguishes the innovative company from others in the field. Market success does not necessarily create an internal climate of success; rather, the practices with respect to people are what make them feel important. When employees assume responsibility for solving company problems, there is a greater likelihood of meeting goals. These become overarching goals that form the core purpose of mission of an organization and that contribute to commitment and cohesiveness among group members.

## ▲ HOW TO UNDERSTAND ORGANIZATION CULTURE

There have been many descriptions of an organization's internal environment, which is now identified as organization culture. The concept of organization culture is a recognition that organizations are social as well as economic entities and may lead to conflicting goals. Looking at what they identified as culture gaps, Kilman and Saxton (1983) developed an organization culture model. The four types of culture gaps they defined relate to whether the culture is short or long term versus technically or human-oriented. Quinn and McGrath (1984) also defined four different cultures and their effectiveness as consensual, developmental, hierarchical, and rational. Their approach is based on competing values that determine congruence and encompass information processing, leadership, and organization culture.

An extensive analysis of organization culture was completed by Martin et al. (Martin and Powers, 1983, p. 93; Siehl and Martin, 1983), who summarized their assessment of organizational culture by describing a structural/functional approach in which "first, cultures offer an interpretation of an institution's history that members can use to decipher how they will be expected to behave in the future. Second, cultures can generate commitment to corporate values or management philosophy so that employees feel they are working for something they believe in. Third, cultures serve as organizational control mechanisms, informally approving or prohibiting some patterns of behavior. Finally, there is the possibility . . . that some type of organizational cultures are associated with greater productivity and profitability."

The finding that corporate culture can generate commitment was described in Martin and Powers' study of corporate "war stories." They concluded that these anecdotes lead to a better understanding of commitment in contrast to descriptive statistics. Martin, Feldman, Hatch, and Sitkin (1983) expanded their description of this methodology as they highlighted the basis on which corporations claim uniqueness. They used the following:

| *Concerns* | *How Expressed* |
|---|---|
| Equality versus inequality | What do I do when a higher-status person breaks a rule? Is the big boss human? Can the little person rise to the top? |
| Security versus insecurity | Will I be fired? Will the organization help me if I have to move? How will the boss react to mistakes? |
| Control versus lack of control | How will the organization deal with obstacles? |

Martin and Powers' stories helped explain the discomfort caused by conflicts between organizational difficulties and individual values. Five values that were expressed frequently in interviews, written documents, speeches, and informal conversations with top executives are:

1. Quality of the firm's products.
2. Financial prosperity of the firm.
3. Social responsibility to maintain the environment.
4. Being a good neighbor to the surrounding community.
5. Humanitarian concerns for employees (Siehl and Martin, 1983).

In addition to these values, there were four that were actually used, which were identified by direct observation. These are:

1. The family of an employee is an integral part of the company.
2. The company does not undercut the future by considering only the short-term consequences of decisions.
3. People are clearly the most important asset of the company.
4. We build a unique product and our people are unique also.

Based on Siehl and Martin's findings, expressed values differed significantly from the values-in-use in an unexpected way. The values-in-use proved to be more humanistic than the concern expressed for profitability. The combination of social and business environment forms the single largest influence on corporate culture, as defined by Deal and Kennedy (1983) in "what it takes to succeed in business." From their perspective, organizational culture is determined by:

1. The degree of risk associated with the company's activities.
2. The speed with which companies and employees obtain feedback on the success of their decisions and strategies.

Deal and Kennedy noted that companies with weak cultures have no clear beliefs about how to succeed in business, or they have too many notions and are unable to commit to a single course of action.

"We used to fly airplanes, now we fly people." These words by Jan Carlzon, the president and CEO, reflect the changed attitude and culture that prevails at SAS. In order to recover from the crises in the 1970s, SAS decided to depart from the traditional airline environment. They decided they would become the preferred airline of the frequent traveler. They accomplished this goal by giving their staff the training needed to change and then supplied them with the information they needed to do a responsible job. The result is a group of service-minded people who are innovative and feel appreciated (Carlzon, 1989).

In many organizations it is necessary to differentiate activities and at the same time provide for integration. Both processes have to be considered in dealing with the inevitable conflicts that arise in the process of designing a structure that integrates cultural considerations. Mintzberg (1979) developed a taxonomy of organizational structures, which include:

1. Entrepreneurial structures.
2. Bureaucratic structures.
3. Divisional structures.
4. Matrix structures.

The principal advantages of an entrepreneurial structure are that it (a) permits maximum opportunity for flexibility and innovation, (b) allows rapid response to start-up situations, and (c) permits initiative and informality. The principal disadvantages are that (a) the organization is critically dependent on the president, (b) employees must be very flexible and be willing to assume multiple responsibilities, and (c) nonspecialization may lead to inefficiencies in operation and lack of responsibility.

The principal advantages of the bureaucratic form of organization are that (a) it provides centralized control of policies and procedures, (b) it requires specialized knowledge of each functional manager, and (c) if each functional area is staffed and managed effectively, product opportunities receive more complete analysis. The principal disadvantages are that (a) problems of functional coordination often occur, (b) overspecialization may result, (c) tight control may stifle creativity, and (d) an overload is often forced on the chief executive.

Decentralized, or divisional, organizational structure has the advantages that (a) it permits shared authority and responsibility, (b) it allows more rapid response to changing environmental and market conditions, (c) it allows direct measurement of product or geographical performance, and (d) shared authority and responsibility help develop future management. The principal disadvantages are that (a) a duplication of effort often results, (b) a large staff is needed, and (c) divisions may become too independent.

In recent years, another form of organizational structure, called the matrix organization, has evolved. The matrix form of organization combines the product form with the functional form. The principal advantages of the matrix structure are that (a) it permits major projects to be worked on within the functional structure, (b) it focuses on specific requirements of a given market, product, or project, (c) decisions can be made by project managers with the input and perspective of top management, and (d) management of new projects that do not fit into a current product or functional structure is facilitated. Disadvantages of this structure are that (a) problems may develop from dual command and multiple responsibilities, (b) authority relationships are constantly changing, (c) problems of organizational continuity and conflict of authority may arise, and (d) it is difficult to adequately reward individuals who perform well.

One of the critical factors in the implementation of a decision is having the right people in the right jobs and offering a culture in which they are motivated to achieve the objective. Not only must goals be clearly specified, but they must be communicated clearly, signifying a receptive culture so that the organization accepts the decisions that are made. Recognizing the differences in organizations is critically important to the success of performance. People are not interchangeable; each individual has unique characteristics, and when one individual in a group is changed, the character or culture of the group changes.

The approaches to organization culture are almost as varied as differences that are observed in an organization. What can be concluded is that organization culture is multidimensional, is environmentally dependent, and has a significant influence on behavior and performance in organizations.

## ▲ MEASURING ORGANIZATION CULTURE

Although definitions of organization culture abound, little has been done to measure this organization culture. Much of the work on organization culture has dealt with theories, models, verbal mapping, war stories, and case histories. A test to measure organization culture facilitates the study of culture, and it can be used as a basis of comparison among organizations or to evaluate the relative strengths. In addition to measuring culture, *internal consistency* is determined by comparing an individual's decision style and values with perceived organization culture.

As a basis for validation, the organization culture model has been compared with results from the decision style inventory (DSI). As has been described in earlier chapters, decision style refers to the way in which individuals make decisions in response to information perceived. The DSI is an instrument used to measure cognitive aspects of personality. That inventory has been applied to a large number of different groups to determine what style is characteristic of various occupations (Rowe and Boulgarides, 1983). Because of the extensive testing of the DSI for validity and reliability, the approach to organization culture and the instrument developed to measure organization culture (Rowe and Boulgarides, 1984) were validated using the DSI.

## ▲ DEVELOPMENT OF AN ORGANIZATION CULTURE INSTRUMENT

The development of an instrument test to measure the perceived organization culture (OCI) was begun in 1983, and after a number of revisions was completed in 1984. One objective was to determine relevance of perception to the culture of an organization because individuals respond based on how they see reality. The organization culture instrument was based on the model shown in Figure 6.2. The vertical axis covers values or norms that are shown as performance and control being the short-term goal and achievement and growth the long-term goal. The horizontal axis covers the organization's work orientation. The four categories of culture follow.

Quality: The emphasis is on effectiveness, the importance of planning, and problem solving. The focus in this culture is technical.

Creativity: The emphasis here is on invention, innovation, entrepreneurship, experimentation, and risk taking.

Productivity: The emphasis is on efficiency, consistency, and adherence to procedures. This culture is closest to the classic management concepts of the past.

Cooperation: This culture emphasizes teamwork, interaction, communication, group processes, support, and reinforcement of fellow workers.

In a business setting, the organization may have requirements and expectations ranging from performance and control to achievement and growth. The organization can tend toward a technical focus and be differentiated, or tend more toward a social focus with integration or cooperation as the primary orientation. This combination of values and orientation produces four types of cultural environments within which the organization functions. For example, the *productive* culture concentrates on control and technical problems, whereas the *quality* culture has concern for people, their growth within the organization, their effective planning, and problem solving. The *creative* culture tends to be innovative and entrepreneurial, including risk taking. Most organizations would prefer this type of culture, in which change is most easily made. Organizations often go about trying to make change as though they did have it. But, if they have some other cultural focus, the change is likely to fail. The *supportive* culture produces an environment of teamwork, cooperation, and reinforcement.

In practice, the productivity-oriented organization tends to use many procedures, rules, and very rigid approaches, whereas the approaches of the quality cultural environment are

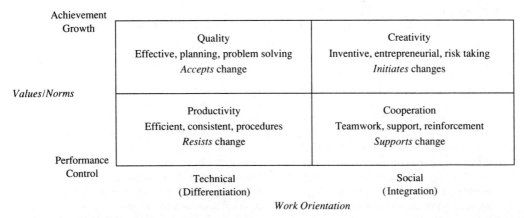

Figure 6.2 ▲ Model of Organization Culture

Table 6.1 ▲ Organization Culture Intensity Levels

|  | Least Preferred | Back-up | Dominant | Very Dominant |
|---|---|---|---|---|
| Productivity | below 68 | 68–82 | 83–90 | above 90 |
| Quality | below 73 | 73–87 | 88–95 | above 95 |
| Creativity | below 78 | 78–92 | 93–100 | above 100 |
| Cooperation | below 53 | 53–67 | 68–75 | above 75 |

more flexible and adaptable. In a creative-innovative culture, there is a great deal of diversity and acceptance of change and innovation. To be effective, change needs the support and implementation prevalent in the supportive-cooperative culture.

Organization culture is a critical element in determining an organization's level of performance and willingness to change. In the past, organization culture has been measured based on anecdotal or other indirect approaches. The instrument shown here is an attempt to obtain a direct measure of the individual's perception of organization culture. Because we generally behave in a manner that is consistent with our beliefs, this approach to measuring culture appears to have strong face validity. In addition, because of the high positive correlation between the OCI and the DSI, we are in a good position to predict the most likely culture that would be consistent with a leader's decision style.

Scores for the organization culture instrument are shown in Table 6.1.

In Japan, a general attitude of consensus and cooperation prevails, which has been called "consensus" management. Although there certainly is much discussion over a long period of time and a great deal of input from all levels, ultimately the top executive makes and is held responsible for decisions. These decisions are generally accepted without question and are supported at all levels. Hisao Tsubouchi is a Japanese boss whose "consensus" is an iron fist. Tsubouchi's tough, autocratic style has earned him a reputation for breaking unions, firing employees, and instilling fear in subordinates. Is he successful? He is the sole owner of Kurushimadork Group, which had revenues of $3.3 billion in 1983. Is Tsubouchi the exception? According to *Nihon Keizai Shimbum*, Japan's leading business newspaper, in their list of excellent companies, numbers 1 and 2 were like military dictatorships ("International Corporation Scoreboard," 1984). Ichiro Isoda, chairman of Sumitomo Bank, says, "You need someone at the top who can change gears fast." The one-man shows are running the most aggressive companies, and they are the pacesetters in their industries (Smith, 1985).

## ▲ CHANGE AND ORGANIZATION CULTURE

How does one teach an elephant to dance? This provocative question comes from a book that James Belasco (1990) wrote on how to bring about culture change. He likens organizations to elephants, which rarely forget and do unlearn old habits. The process starts by defining the company's vision of what it wants to be. This is used to inspire workers and to encourage change and innovation. He claims that the key is to gain the support of the managers. They must be committed to taking action and to "rouse the troops." Although this may sound like a reasonable way to proceed, it does not take into account the basic needs of the people who must make any change work. Individuals' beliefs and values play a dominant role in determining the degree to which a cultural change will be effective.

In order for change to be accepted, there has to be a match between the individual's values and the organization's cultural norms. Ultimately, the likelihood of successful implementation requires that there is a change in a person's outlook. The function of a leader, then, is to blend the individual's values with the cultural norms of the organization and to inspire individuals to accept ownership of the proposed change. In Japan, this is a normal part of the culture–values process. In the United States, it too often is only an afterthought.

A company's successful performance depends on its being able to deploy resources and having a culture that is adaptive to an ever- and rapidly changing external environment (Zakon, 1983). The organization is the only entity that can make a change become a reality. To accomplish successful change, Alan Zakon, past chairman and CEO of the Boston Consulting Group, recommends the following rules that the CEO must follow:

1. Understand current needs and match these to making the organization adaptive so that it can meet new needs.
2. Use information to continuously revise the view of the world.
3. Develop an organization culture that is focused on learning, not doing things the way they are currently being done.
4. Build into the corporate culture a sense of being able to lead as well as to change as requirements dictate.
5. Encourage both administrative effectiveness and creativity.
6. The CEO must be creative and envision the future.
7. He or she must be comfortable with exploring new opportunities.
8. Be willing to take risks when needed.
9. Being able to adapt to new opportunities requires communication and a motivated organization.
10. Most of the opportunities for the future already exist; they merely need to be exploited rather than invented.

In the summer of 1984 EDS was purchased by General Motors for $2.5 billion. The result was a total lack of fit between the cultures of GM and EDS. A clash between H. Ross Perot, the president of EDS, and Roger B. Smith, GM chairman, resulted in the GM board voting to buy out Perot's stake in GM for $700 million in December 1984 (Risen, 1987).

The reason for the short-lived union? A total difference in management styles. According to James P. Buchanan, then EDS Manager of Finance and Administration, "You couldn't find two companies more diverse in management style" (Mason and Brandt, 1985, p. 118).

A few years later, the feisty Perot offered to advise GM on how to revitalize the organization (Perot, 1988). He had a list of items that he felt would change the culture and outlook of General Motors.

1. Call all the top executives of GM together and announce the following:
   a. GM'ers should fight the competitors, not each other.
   b. The power struggle between the financial people and manufacturing would not be tolerated.
   c. The relationship with the United Auto Workers should be teamwork, not adversarial.
   d. The executive offices on the fourteenth floor in Detroit would be closed down.
   e. Words such as *management*, *labor*, *salaried*, and so forth, would no longer be used—everyone is a GM'er and would be treated as an individual.
   f. Stock would substitute for bonuses to provide ownership.
   g. Leadership would be substituted for management; leaders must earn the respect of people working with them.
   h. Most committees would be scrapped and promotion would be based on performance.
2. Organize a training program where the CEO would meet the people.
3. Send executives out into the field to meet dealers, customers, mechanics, stockholders, UAW leaders, and factory employees.
4. Ask dealers to identify customer needs; then design cars to meet those needs.

5. Leadership has to make GM an exciting place to work so that the full potential of the company could be tapped.

Smith, as chairman of GM, replied to Perot by saying that you can't run GM by the seat of your pants, committees only review decisions, dealers are not bashful about telling GM what they want, he personally answered as many customer complaints as he could, finance is crucial to any organization, there is cooperation between management and the union, and the purchase of companies such as EDS and Hughes Aircraft shows that the leadership at GM is forward looking and is concerned about the long haul. While it is obvious that there was a clash of styles between Perot and Smith, who would be best for General Motors is not clear. Perot is action oriented and clearly demonstrated his ability to achieve extraordinary success. However, given the many complex relationships confronting GM, perhaps a conceptual leader with more vision than either Perot or Smith exhibit is what is needed to get GM out of its doldrums.

## ▲ INTRODUCING CHANGE

Why is the introduction of organizational change such a difficult task? Every executive knows that organizations must continuously adapt to new external environmental demands. Many executives recognize the need to deal more effectively with the change process, yet it is still extremely difficult to achieve.

As most executives know, the introduction of change creates anxiety and fear. When a major adjustment is required because of some newly proposed reorganization, it can cause high levels of "fight, flight, or freeze." In order to introduce a change effectively, executives need to recognize that there is more to take into account than the technical factors. Four key elements can be used that together determine the potential for successful change (Rowe and Mann, 1986): (1) the executive who is the change agent; (2) the corporate culture, which reflects the change environment; (3) the values and beliefs of the individual performers who effect the change process; and (4) the match, or fit, between the values of the individual performers and the corporate culture.

The match often determines whether the change is acceptable, how easily change will occur, and whether change will take place at all or will become distorted or blocked. Howard Schwartz, a vice-president at Management Analysis Corporation, is actively involved with organizations dealing with changing culture. He has observed that if the chief executive is to be an effective change agent, any new direction should be identified in the context of the organization's core values and guiding beliefs (Rowe and Mason, 1987, pp. 83–84, 106–107).

When the change agent introduces a change, it is critical that the organization be ready to follow and lend support. Although the need for change may be recognized at the top level, it does not follow that the organization is ready to pursue the change agent's goals. Change, to be effective, requires a match or fit among the factors discussed. Most important, change must be carried out within the culture in an organization. The achievement and self-actualization of individuals leads to the development of a quality culture where technical orientation is strong, and to creativity when there is a more social focus and more integration. When organizational values and norms stress performance, the technical orientation leads to a productivity culture. When there is greater interpersonal competency, the result tends to be the supportive-cooperative culture. In this latter culture, managers stress teamwork, and there are supportive and helpful systems.

The culture change model relates decision styles to organization culture and to values of individual performers. As can be seen in Figure 6.3, the decision maker initiates change

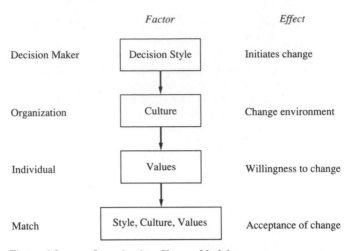

**Figure 6.3** ▲ **Organization Change Model**

based on his or her style. A directive style manager introduces change by announcing it. The culture environment this creates will tend to be rigid. A conceptual style would discuss change, have meetings, and explain why it's needed. This creates a more open, trusting organization culture. Thus, the style of senior managers often determines what the organization focus will be. Values reflect the willingness of individuals to accept change. The acceptance of change requires a match between the culture resulting from a manager's style and the values held by individual performers.

Cultural change and innovation are by no means easily come by. Even where the culture has produced dramatic results, factors such as growth, competition, or environmental change can produce requirements that are hard to fill. Take, for example, Byrne's (1985) description of People Express. Donald Burr, founder and chairman, started the airline with a "humanistic" concept of a company where every employee was an owner-manager. His most important goal was developing people. However, as revenues grew from zero in 1980 to an estimated $1 billion in 1985, Burr was forced to change his mind. Mounting competition required his acquiring Frontier Airlines to meet the demand for a broader geographical system. His new management style of installing a new layer of managers in what was a lean organization jeopardized People's success. Here is an illustration of how match is critical. The new culture at headquarters prevented employees from asking questions, and fear pervaded because of Burr's change from a humane to a one-man style, which caused the ultimate demise of the airline.

Values permeate every level of an organization, and reaction to change more often than not is based on the values held by individuals. For example, the president of National Duplicating considered the social values of employee security, welfare, and happiness as more important than meeting competition by expanding its markets (Guth, 1965). The emphasis was on slow but steady growth of a high-quality product and a refusal to compete on price. Although he was aware of the economic risks, the president chose a strategy that fit his personal values. Unlike the chairman of People Express, the president of National Duplicating chose not to change his basic values.

Other examples of how values influence change include Acoustic Research, which considered high quality at the lowest possible cost to the consumer (Guth, 1965). This policy was maintained in spite of pressure and unfounded claims by competitors. For many years Hewlett-Packard emphasized values that stressed concern, trust, and respect for employees.

During a downturn in business, HP opted to reduce the workweek by 10 percent rather than lay off employees. The result has been an unflinching loyalty and dedication by the employees that has helped maintain HP's technological lead. Tandem Computers is an example of a company whose values were loyalty, hard work, self-esteem, and respect for co-workers. These values are reinforced by rites and rituals such as beer parties, jogging trails, and so forth. Tandem today still has a unique niche in the "nonstop" computing system arena.

As we've illustrated, values are an integral part of strategic change because they reflect the decision maker's beliefs. Likewise, the willingness to accept and support change depends on the values of the individuals who must carry it out. Where these values coincide, there is a natural acceptability of the goals of the organization and the commitment of individuals in the organization. Examples abound where there are crucial differences. Mason and Brandt's (1985) description of how Ross Perot's shock troops ran into flak at GM, or how culture shock shook up the Bell system (Main, 1984), reveals the problem of change. Recognition of the potential differences can help smooth over such transitions and avoid confrontations.

Acceptance takes place when corporate values or culture is characterized by shared values, trust, and concern for people and their individual values (for example, openness) as described in previous examples. When workers who are externally oriented are exposed to this culture, the result is accommodation: They become committed, and there is goal congruence and support for the organization. The more internally focused employee working in a corporate culture of openness closely relates with the organization, and the result is identification with the goals of the organization and collaboration. This is the "secret" of Japanese management style. It works in Japan because of that country's more monolithic culture.

Examples that have led to a changed culture abound. Before the process of divestiture began at AT&T, chairman Charles L. Brown started the process of culture change in a speech where he emphasized that the telephone company had to satisfy customer requirements by utilizing high technology and applying advanced marketing strategies. The new strategy included starting an overseas subsidiary, a joint venture with Phillips, and reorganizing Western Electric and Bell Labs. The major shift was from a profit center orientation to a national line of business profit centers, including reassigning 13,000 corporate staff employees (Tunstall, 1983). The result was what Main (1984) dubbed "Waking Up at AT&T: There's Life after Culture Shock." After 103 years as a regulated monopoly, suddenly the culture was obsolete and lifetime employment, promoting from within, consensus in decisions, and high-quality service were no longer sacred. The new culture is market-oriented, lower cost, and a stream-lined organization. The outcome is wrath and expletives aimed at Bell Labs and Western Electric for not being market-oriented. Time will tell whether the culture has adapted or perhaps been replaced since Archie McGill, a former IBM vice-president, was brought in to establish the new AT&T marketing department.

How did AT&T go about shifting to a changed outlook and a new culture? They started with a changed managerial "mind set." They followed up by creating a new environment by setting an example. This entailed developing a new system of managers who are fully related to the change in corporate "values." Training was then used to create a new "cultural environment" that was consistent with the new strategy. Finally, implementation will ultimately depend on the "acceptance" by employees who will be needed to carry out the new plans.

Other companies have used a similar approach to introduce a new strategy by creating a changed culture. In one organization with which the authors worked, the change was from a low- to a high-technology company. The strategy was set by the CEO in consultation with his executive committee and urged on by outside consultants. The executive's decision style was clearly entrepreneurial—a combination of the conceptual and directive styles. The culture of the company was primarily oriented with cost, delivery, and availability of product being dominant factors. To create a change in the cultural environment, a combination of approaches was used. Training helped identify the new direction needed, and the management systems used to support the strategic change. In addition, a major reorganization was undertaken that shifted individuals to new responsibilities, including hiring technically qualified personnel and establishing an R&D lab. The development of new, higher-technology products required investment of company resources. The payoff? A changed strategic direction and a changed cultural environment where the focus shifted from daily shipments to new product development and bringing in highly qualified people.

# ▲ GROUP DECISION MAKING

"A camel is a racehorse put together by committee." We've all heard expressions such as this to describe various forms of group decision making. How often have we been part of some committee or other group that was charged with making a particular decision and come to a conclusion that agreed with this expression? Executives express concern and condemn group meetings as a waste of time, and tend to encourage individuals to make decisions. Why then do committees and other groups continue to make decisions?

Because information technology has made it feasible for organizations to formulate objectives more explicitly, groups can deal with more complex problems in a more meaningful way. The journal *Organizational Intelligence* suggests that insofar as managers ask the right questions, collect the right data, and communicate the right information, group decisions will be more efficient. Argyris (1977) maintains that the quality and accuracy of information collected depends on the people in an organization. The accuracy of the information and the way it is presented also depend heavily on all levels of the organization. Because computers generate information that is beyond the capability of individuals to understand, groups will be needed to evaluate the information. Groups can also provide a basis for ensuring employee commitment to decisions.

# ▲ WHEN IS GROUP DECISION MAKING APPROPRIATE?

When faced with a particular decision situation, a manager can choose from a variety of alternative ways of "deciding how to decide." These include:

1. Make the decision alone.
2. Make the decision and inform subordinates.
3. Consult subordinates before making the decision.
4. Consult other managers before making the decision.
5. Depend on staff for input to the decision.
6. Make the decision jointly with subordinates.

The choice of which alternative to choose depends on the circumstances surrounding the decision. Given these alternatives, what criteria can a manager use in deciding how to decide? Maier (1963) has suggested that the following factors would prove helpful: the effectiveness of the decision, the quality needed in the decision, the acceptance of the decision, and the time it takes to make the decision. If the quality of the decision is affected by whether the manager makes the decision alone or involves others in the process, then, to some extent, the decision should involve others. If the decision depends on acceptance by those affected, it may need a high level of involvement. The quality and acceptance considerations must be related to the amount of time each takes and how they will affect the effectiveness of the decision.

Vroom and Yetton (1973) have identified five methods that managers could use in various decision situations.

1. The manager makes the decision alone using the information available at that time.
2. The manager obtains necessary information from subordinates, and then decides on solutions to the problem. Subordinates provide the necessary information, rather than evaluate alternative solutions.
3. The manager shares the problem with subordinates, obtaining ideas and suggestions. The manager makes the decision, which may or may not reflect subordinates' influence.
4. The manager shares the problem with subordinates as a group, obtaining their collective ideas and suggestions. The manager makes the decision, which may or may not reflect subordinates' influence.
5. The manager shares the problem with subordinates as a group. Together they generate and evaluate alternatives and attempt to reach agreement (consensus) on a solution.

Vroom and Yetton further suggest that the following factors be considered when determining which decision method to employ:

1. The importance of the quality of the decision.
2. The extent to which the manager possesses the information or expertise to make a high-quality decision.
3. The extent to which subordinates have the necessary information to generate a high-quality decision.
4. The extent to which the problem is structured.
5. The extent to which acceptance or commitment on the part of the subordinates is critical to the effective implementation of the decision.
6. The probability that the manager's decision will be accepted by subordinates.
7. The extent to which subordinates are motivated to achieve the organizational goals.
8. The extent to which subordinates are likely to be in conflict over preferred solutions.

Given these factors, the manager can decide which decision method would work best. An example of these rules is presented in Table 6.2 along with the situational factors used in the model. Under situation 1 ("make decision alone"), the decision to be made is not of great importance; the information and expertise possessed by the leader and subordinates are not critical; and the problem is relatively structured. Acceptance by subordinates is likely if the manager makes the decision alone.

**Table 6.2  ▲  Selecting Decision Approaches**

| Factors | Make Decisions Alone | Obtain Information | Share Problem | Subordinate Influence | Seek Consensus |
|---|---|---|---|---|---|
| 1. Importance high | | ✔ | ✔ | ✔ | |
| 2. Manager expertise | | | | | |
| 3. Subordinate expertise | | ✔ | ✔ | ✔ | ✔ |
| 4. Structure high | ✔ | ✔ | ✔ | | |
| 5. Acceptance critical | | | ✔ | | ✔ |
| 6. Acceptance probable | ✔ | ✔ | | | |
| 7. Subordinate motivation | | | | | ✔ |
| 8. Potential conflict | | | | ✔ | |

Under situation 5 ("seek consensus"), however, the manager does not possess sufficient information or expertise to make a high-quality decision alone. Subordinates collectively possess the necessary information and expertise, and acceptance and commitment are critical to effective implementation. Subordinates would probably not accept a unilateral decision by the manager, and subordinates are motivated to attain the organization objectives in the statement of the problem. Given these factors, the model would suggest that the manager should share the problem with subordinates and that they should work as a group to generate and evaluate alternatives, attempting to reach a consensus.

## ▲　METHODS USED TO IMPROVE GROUP DECISION MAKING

What are some of the problems and pitfalls of the group decision-making process? How can group decision making be improved? We begin with a consideration of the process of group decision making and a discussion of its advantages and disadvantages on page 124.

One of the important characteristics is the way the group structures itself for decision making, that is, how the group actually goes about "attacking" or approaching the given decision problem, how the group structures its interactions. A closely related consideration is the nature of the task or problem. For other decisions it is preferable that group members have face-to-face interaction. Two other characteristics of group processes are the size and composition of the group. Shaw (1959) suggests that as a group's size increases, relatively fewer members actively participate and the potential for conflict increases. Smaller groups are usually considered more positively by members than are larger groups. Also, the larger the group, the more time required for carrying out the task. Group composition also affects performance. When members have similar characteristics, knowledge, attitudes, needs, and interests, in general quality and acceptance of solutions will be higher.

Cohesiveness is another important factor in group decision making. Cohesiveness is the extent to which the group "sticks together." Both size and composition affect group cohesiveness. The larger the group and the more diverse its membership, the more likely that cliques will form, and hence the lower the cohesiveness of the group. Members of highly cohesive groups tend to communicate more with each other than do members of less cohesive groups. However, this tendency can lead to conformity and to "groupthink," which occurs when pressures for conformity become so great that the group is prevented from critically assessing opposing, minority, or unpopular opinions and viewpoints. Hence, the desirability of cohesive decision-making groups must be weighed and balanced against the potentially negative consequences of conforming behavior.

To facilitate interaction and reduce conflict in group decision making, a number of techniques have been employed. These include:

*Brainstorming*:　Brainstorming is a technique that can be used to aid small decision-making groups in their attempts to generate ideas. There are two variations of the technique: group brainstorming and individual brainstorming. Group brainstorming could be applied when a problem has been defined and the group needs to identify alternative solutions. This process requires four basic rules: (1) criticism is prohibited—assessment or judgment of the ideas must await completion of the idea-generation process; (2) free-wheeling is encouraged—the bolder or more radical the idea, the better; (3) quantity is important—the larger the number of ideas, the greater the likelihood of a good one; (4) improvement and combination are pursued—that is, besides thinking up ideas of their own, participants should suggest how several ideas can be combined. The intent of group brainstorming is to force people to think freely by removing the barriers of inhibition, self-criticism, and criticism of others. The technique tends to generate more ideas and increases the chances of success.

Brainstorming can avoid potential inhibitions and fears of others' criticism by having members work as individuals and independently.

*Nominal group technique:* The nominal group technique (NGT) is a process that follows a structured set of problem-solving steps. It intentionally restricts group discussion and interpersonal interaction during various phases of the decision-making process. All group members are present in the same room, but their communications and interactions are structured.

The steps in the process are:

1. There is a silent generation of ideas; that is, problems, criteria, alternatives, and so forth, are formulated in writing.
2. Ideas are recorded without any further discussion.
3. There is discussion for the purpose of clarification of each of the ideas.
4. There is a preliminary vote on the importance of each idea.
5. There is a discussion of the preliminary vote involving inconsistencies in voting patterns and ideas that were perceived as receiving too few or too many votes.
6. A final vote is taken. A group decision is reached by combining individual judgments. This final vote determines the meeting's outcome and closure, gives group members a sense of accomplishment, and documents the group's judgment.

The NGT involves several characteristics that facilitate effective group decision making. It reduces conflict between members and the group leader. It gives members social reinforcement while generating a large number of ideas. In general, meetings end with a sense of accomplishment while still maintaining group members' interest in future phases of the decision problem.

*Automated decision conferencing:* Another approach to group decision making is referred to in a variety of ways, but the most accurate description is automated decision conferencing (ADC). Automated decision "conferences" are intended for use in urgent (or important) and complex decisions in which there are divergent opinions as to the best course of action. These conferences are usually conducted in two- or three-day sessions in which an executive team or group works on a major organizational decision. Aiding the executive team are staff members trained in management science techniques and computer technology as well as in organizational development. When the process is completed, the executive team leaves with a solution that is based on group consensus, and that documents the process used in making the decision.

A typical automated decision conference involves from 6 to 15 group members and 3 staff members. Typically, one staff member aids the group decision-making process, one operates the computer, and one records the decision rationale. All individuals from the organization who are key in the decision process should be present. Typically, participants are not allowed to bring supporting records, files, or written information as these are often more of a distraction than an aid in the conferencing process.

The ADC process usually proceeds as follows:

1. The problem or decision is clearly identified and delineated.
2. The problem or decision is described in detail in written form by the group leader and is simultaneously entered into a microcomputer or other computer support system.
3. Once the problem is fully described, the completed computer output is presented to the group and is subjected to extensive scrutiny and examination as well as to a careful analysis.
4. The solution is refined until all participants are satisfied.

Decision conferencing incorporates the advantages of quantitative techniques and behavioral aids that promote an open group process and help resolve conflict. The process not only assists managers in dealing with complex decisions involving large amounts of information (thanks to computer support), but it also helps reduce conflict and encourages commitment by members of the group to difficult organizational decisions.

## Teleconferencing and Videoconferencing

With people in organizations working at widely scattered locations in a global sense, rapid communication and exchange of information becomes imperative. Travel costs and travel time make frequent or sudden meetings both impractical in terms of dollar costs as well as individual availability. Advanced technology, however, now provides for group on-line communication and two-way communication via teleconferencing and videoconferencing.

Teleconferencing involves telephone linkages with locations throughout the world. Individuals can give and take ideas, ask questions, provide explanations and clarify their ideas. Voice messages can provide some feeling by inflection of voice as to how strong the individual feels about the message. The time to set up such a meeting or conference call is very short with the costs minor in comparison to the costs of traveling to a single meeting site. Individuals can participate in a teleconference while sitting at their own desks with their personal files close at hand for ready reference. When combined with a fax machine, communication of data becomes very rapid. The teleconference is the most flexible way to conduct meetings and group discussions among individuals in widely dispersed locations.

Videoconferencing is more complete because the information provided allows participants to see display charts, data, and items being discussed on a screen. Videoconferencing is less flexible and more costly than teleconferencing because participants must gather in front of the camera at a conference location at a prescribed time to communicate with counterparts at a similarly equipped facility at another location. It is however, a very convenient way to conduct regularly scheduled meetings with staff at remote locations. Metropolitan Life Insurance Company has seven videoconferencing rooms set up in six eastern and midwestern cities. A variety of meetings are conducted, such as vendor presentations, job interviews, award presentations, and personnel training, to name a few. According to Rich Owens, a vice president at Metropolitan Life, "You get a sense of being there and people are much more likely to contribute" (Kozlov, "Hello Out There In Wichita").

## Advantages and Disadvantages of Group Decision Making

In general, a group as a whole tends to make more effective decisions than would any single member of the group. Availability of information in a group tends to be more comprehensive than when a decision maker operates independently. Implementation is more effective if members participated in making the decisions. Also, understanding and acceptance of a decision by those involved in its implementation tend to be more thorough when the individuals are also involved in making the decision. Training and developing subordinates may be a beneficial outcome of participation in the decision-making process. Subordinates' information and skills can be increased if these individuals are included in the decision process.

On the other hand, group decision making usually consumes more time and is more difficult than individual decision making. Occasionally, groups make decisions that are not in accord with the goals of the organization. Members of the organization may come to expect involvement in all decisions. Groups may be unable to reach a decision because of disagreements among members, or because of pressures for conformity. Nonetheless, the group decision-making process has increasingly been used to obtain the potential benefits, while still allowing the manager to choose when to make a decision alone.

## ▲ VALIDATION AND SCORING OF THE ORGANIZATION CULTURE INSTRUMENT

Based on the premise that culture is often the result of an executive's leadership style, the culture test (the OCI) was correlated with the decision style inventory (the DSI). It was expected that a positive relationship would be found between the two instruments. Table 6.3 shows the results for three groups—a police department ($N = 65$), male business managers ($N = 71$), and female business managers ($N = 71$).

Table 6.3 ▲ Correlation for the Organization Culture Instrument

| OCI | DSI | Correlation |
|---|---|---|
| Productivity | Directive | 94–99% |
| Quality | Analytic | 97–99% |
| Creativity | Conceptual | 99% |
| Cooperation | Behavioral | 98–99% |

The consistency of the results in the cases shown in the table gives a high degree of confidence in the "fit" between the DSI and the OCI. Considering the importance of leadership's influence on culture, these results allow us to predict the expected culture based on the style of the executive. Thus, the directive style emphasizes productivity, whereas the analytic style prefers quality. The conceptual style supports creativity, and the behavioral style encourages cooperation. The culture instrument was also validated by testing ten organizations with a total sample of 459 individuals. The results showed that the scores predicted what would be expected for each organization. For example, business organizations were dominantly productivity-oriented, whereas government agencies emphasized people orientation and educational institutions the creative culture.

## ▲ Exercise: Group Decision-Making Checklist

1. Be attentive to the *nature of the task* (the decision problem that is being assigned to the group). The way in which the group structures its activities and interactions will be heavily dependent on the nature of the decision problem.
2. Be sure that the *size* of the decision-making group is appropriate for the decision problem the group will work on. (For most groups, this will be five members.)
3. Be sure the *composition* of the group is appropriate for the decision problem being faced. Include members who possess the needed expertise, skills, abilities, and perspectives.
4. Be alert to the need for *cohesiveness* in small decision-making groups. Try to achieve a balance between cohesiveness as harmony and cohesiveness as negative conformity.

8 = Most
4 = Moderate
2 = Slight
1 = Least

Please score the following questions based on the instructions given. Your score reflects your perception of the culture or climate of your organization. It determines how you feel the organization reacts to you and to others at the present time.

| | | | | | | | | |
|---|---|---|---|---|---|---|---|---|
| 1. | In my organization, a leader: | directs the organization | | establishes objectives | | is open to new ideas | | respects others | |
| 2. | My organization has a: | strong work ethic | | well-defined direction | | creative atmosphere | | cooperative spirit | |
| 3. | In my organization, employees are: | reliable | | truthful | | moral | | helpful | |
| 4. | My commitment is based on: | trust in my superior | | advancement opportunities | | meeting my personal goals | | sharing of sentiments | |
| 5. | My management emphasizes: | meeting schedules | | quality of work | | innovative approaches | | employees' suggestions | |
| 6. | I feel that power is used to: | achieve objectives | | maintain control | | negotiate goals | | gain acceptance of programs | |
| 7. | In my organization, participation: | does not work | | leads to mediocre solutions | | is a desireable process | | is always worthwhile | |
| 8. | My organization: | rewards performance | | provides potential for growth | | has fair policies | | has stable employment | |
| 9. | My work provides me with: | personal status | | challenging assignments | | broad experience | | a friendly atmosphere | |
| 10. | My organization: | rewards my accomplishments | | considers my advancement potential | | is concerned about my career | | considers my feelings | |
| 11. | My co-workers are: | persistent | | competent | | creative | | understanding | |
| 12. | My organization values: | responsible individuals | | technical skills | | independent thinking | | communication skills | |
| 13. | My manager expects me to be: | committed to the job | | able to plan my work | | concerned about the future | | sensitive to others | |
| 14. | I enjoy my work because of: | good incentives | | the latest technical advances | | the open atmosphere | | the accepting group | |
| 15. | My organization is effective because: | results are emphasized | | techical support is provided | | new approaches can be tried | | there is good supervision | |

(*Continued*)

| 16. | Performance improves when | goals are clear | work is challenging | one can contribute freely | personal needs are met | |
|-----|-----|-----|-----|-----|-----|-----|
| 17. | If there is a serious problem, my organization: | expects greater effort | changes procedures | consults with employees | reorganizes | |
| 18. | My organization is: | efficient | good at managing resources | able to handle politics | concerned about worker satisfaction | |
| 19. | My superior is good at: | appraising my performance | planning the work to be done | making needed changes | improving the work environment | |
| 20. | In my organization, priorities are based on: | meeting current requirements | analysis of available options | discussion with key people | people's needs | |
| | | | | | | |

5. Clearly specify and define (as much as possible) the *decision problem* the group is to work on. Make clear whether the group is identifying and defining a problem; identifying and designing alternatives, criteria, and future conditions; choosing an alternative; or some combination of these.

6. Clearly define the decision group's *responsibilities* and the *requirements* that the group must meet. Make clear the group's intermediate and final output or product and exactly when these need to be completed.

7. Be sure that the group is *representative* of those individuals who will be affected by the decision.

8. Make sure all necessary *resources* (information, equipment, support, and so forth) are readily available to the decision group.

Using this list, describe a decision problem you have faced recently. How well did you follow these guidelines? If you did not use them, explain why.

## ▲ ▲ ▲ ▲ ▲ FORD TAURUS CASE

The news that U.S. carmakers can build automobiles that excite the American driver and elicit rave reviews is an encouraging sign for the country's industrial production. The team approach borrowed from the Japanese has made the Ford Taurus a four-star success. How did Ford accomplish this feat?

There were some radical steps taken at Ford. Quality was made the number one priority. Ford invested $3 billion—"an unprecedented amount for a new-car project" (Mitchell, 1986, p. 69.) To make sure that Taurus and its sister Sable would succeed, Ford changed the traditional organization structure and created Team Taurus. Team Taurus, using the program management approach, brought representatives from the various units such as planning, design, engineering, and manufacturing, which had previously worked in isolation, together to work as a group.

As a result, problems were resolved early which proved less costly to fix, saving time and producing higher quality. Ford engineers did some "reverse engineering" by taking a Honda Accord and a Toyota Corolla and dismantling them layer by layer looking for things to copy or to make better. Ford engineers also studied other cars such as the Audi 5000, Toyota Supra, and BMW528e, looking for features best in class. Workers were involved in making recommendations to improve assembly, which the designers adopted. Suppliers were also involved in the development process. The Ford Taurus example illustrates the power of the team approach and worker involvement. This was a strong departure from traditional auto manufacturing in the United States.

Once the original Ford Taurus was introduced, it reflected a major change that was able to capture many small car buyers. The result was increased profits and sales. Since then Ford has spent $600 million to update the car. While dealers praised the improvements that were made, they were disappointed with the small change in the car's exterior.

Ford expressed concern that a radical design change would alienate the current 1.5 million owners of Taurus and decided not to make the change. Unfortunately, Japanese automakers who represent the major competition, change their models more frequently than Ford. Perhaps Ford should have spent the money required for redesign before profits began recently turning down. Without a new design, Ford may find that holding onto its number two slot behind Honda will become increasingly difficult (Treece, 1991, p. 43).

What one can conclude is that Ford was unwilling to continue to invest the large sums of money needed to stay abreast of Japanese competition. Instead, they fell back on the old way of doing things in the U.S. automotive industry by doing a face lift rather than a total redesign of the Taurus. The excuse of not wanting to alienate current owners is not borne out by the market place. Ford will have to bite the bullet and recognize that to stay out front requires continuous innovation and large investment in new design.                                                                    ▲

## ▲ Summary

Culture defines the organizational environment for group decision making. Participation is increasingly being used in organizations to benefit from more worker involvement in improving productivity. The use of groups has become an integral aspect of management decision making. The new information technology has provided new options to managers in their search for effective decision making. Just as management teams were developed to cope with the volume and complexity of information, worker teams dealing with operational issues may be the answer to achieving greater productivity.

Given the options available to managers, whether to act alone or with others depends on the circumstances surrounding the decision to be made. The requirement for quality of a specific decision, expertise available, and time constraints are factors that affect how managers should go about making a decision. The situation strongly influences the method managers employ in reaching decisions.

Group techniques such as brainstorming and the nominal group technique provide good results in group problem solving and decision making. Specific procedures can be followed that maximize the results of group decision making. There are advantages and disadvantages to group decision making that must be kept in mind. Group decision making, when coupled with the abilities of capable managers, ensures that the benefits from both modes of decision making will accrue to the organization.

## ▲ Study Questions

1. What are the manager's alternatives in making a decision?
2. What are the situational factors to consider when choosing which decision method to use?

3. What is brainstorming?
4. What is the nominal group technique?
5. What are the advantages of group decision making?
6. What are the disadvantages of group decision making?
7. How does the culture instrument compare with the decision style inventory?
8. When should one use the culture instrument?

## ▲ References

Argyris, Chris. "Management Information Systems: The Challenge to Rationality and Emotionality." *Management Science* (February 1977), pp. 275–292.

Bartimo, Jim. "At These Shouting Matches, No One Says a Word." *Business Week* (June 11, 1990), p. 78.

Belasco, James. "Teaching the Elephant to Dance." *Success* (July/August 1990), pp. 50–51.

Broder, John M. "Wells Fargo Is Ready to Crack the Whip at Crocker." *Los Angeles Times* (February 16, 1986), Part 4, p. 1.

Byrne, John A. "Up, Up and Away?" *Business Week* (November 25, 1985), p. 80.

Carlzon, Jan, "We Used to Fly Airplanes: Now We Fly People." *Business Forum* (Summer 1989), p. 6.

"Corporate Culture: The Hard-to-Change Values that Spell Success or Failure." *Business Week* (October 27, 1980), pp. 148–160.

Deal, T. E., and Kennedy, A. A. *Corporate Cultures*. Reading, MA: Addison-Wesley, 1982.

Deal, T. E., and Kennedy, A. A. "Corporate Tribes Identifying the Cultures." *Modern Office Procedures* Vol. 23, No. 3 (March 1983) pp. 12–16.

Drucker, P. F. *Management: Task Responsibilities and Practices*. New York: Harper and Row, 1974.

England, G. W. "Personal Value Systems of American Managers." *Academy of Management Journal* No. 10 (1967).

Gross, B. M. *Organization and Their Managing*. New York: Free Press, 1968.

Guth, William D., and Tagiuri, Renato. "Personal Values and Corporate Strategies." *Harvard Business Review* (September-October 1965), pp. 123–132.

Haberstroh, Chadwick J., and Gerwin, Donald. "Climate Factors and the Decision Process." *General Systems* Vol. 17 (1972).

Harrison, E. Frank. *The Managerial Decision-Making Process*. Boston, MA: Houghton-Mifflin, 1987.

Harrison, R. "Understanding Your Organization's Character." *Harvard Business Review* (May–June 1972).

"International Corporation Scoreboard." *Business Week* (July 23, 1984), p. 176.

Kanter, Rosabeth M. *The Change Masters*. New York: Simon and Schuster, 1983.

Kilman, Ralph H., and Saxton, Mary J. *Kilman-Saxton Culture Gap Survey*. Pittsburgh, PA: Organizational Design Consultants, Inc., 1983.

Kozlov, Alex. "Hello Out There in Wichita." *Management Digest*, Special Advertising Section.

Lawrence, John F. "A Company's Culture Shapes Performance." *Los Angeles Times* (January 27, 1985).

Lyons, Nick. *The Sony Vision*. New York: Crown, 1976.

Maier, Norman. *Problem Solving Discussions and Conferences*. New York: McGraw-Hill, 1963.

Main, Jeremy. "Waking Up at AT&T: There's Life After Shock." *Fortune* (December 24, 1984), pp. 66–72.

Martin, J., and Powers, M. *Truth or Corporate Propaganda: The Value of a Good War Story*. In *Organizational Symbolism, Number 1*. L. R. Pondy, P. J. Frost, G. Morgan, and T. C. Dandridge, eds. JAI Press, 1983, pp. 93–107.

Martin, M., Feldman, M. S., Hatch. M. J., and Sitkin, S. B. "The Uniqueness Paradox in Organizational Stories." *Administrative Science Quarterly* 28 (1983), pp. 438–453.

Mason, Todd, and Brandt, Richard. "How Ross Perot's Shock Troops Ran into Flack at G.M." *Business Week* (February 11, 1985), p. 118.

Mintzberg, Henry. *The Structuring of Organizations*. Englewood Cliffs, NJ: Prentice Hall, 1979.

Mitchell, Russell. "Can Cray Reprogram Itself for Creativity?" *Business Week* (August 20, 1990), p. 86.

Mitchell, Russell. "How Ford Hit the Bulls-Eye with Taurus." *Business Week* (June 30, 1986), p. 69.

Moos, R. H. *The Social Climate Scales Consulting*. Palo Alto, CA: Psychologists Press, 1974.

Ouchi, William G. *Theory Z*. Reading, MA: Addison-Wesley, 1981.

Pascale, Richard T., and Athos, Anthony G. *The Art of Japanese Management*. New York: Simon and Schuster, 1981.

Perot, Ross. "How I Would Turn Around G.M." *Fortune* (February 15, 1988), pp. 44–49.

Peters, Thomas J., and Waterman, Robert H. Jr. *In Search of Excellence*. New York: Harper & Row Publishers, 1982.

Posner, B. Z., and Munson, J. M. "Gender Differences in Managerial Values." *Psychological Reports* No. 49 (1981).

Quinn, Robert E., and McGrath, Michael R. "The Transformation of Organizational Cultures: A Competing Values Perspective." Paper presented at the Conference on Organizational Culture and Meaning of Life in the Workplace, Vancouver, British Columbia, April 1984.

Richards, M. D. *Organizational Goal Structures*. St. Paul, MN: West, 1978.

Risen, James. "Perot Sounds Off." *Los Angeles Times* (November 18, 1987), Business Section, p. 1.

Rowe, Alan J., and Boulgarides, James D. "Decision Style—A Perspective." *Leadership and Organization Development Journal* Vol. 4, No. 4 (1983).

Rowe, Alan J., and Boulgarides, James D. "Validation of the Organization Culture Instrument." *DSMC* (Defense Systems Management College) (June 24, 1984).

Rowe, Alan, J., and Mann, Richard B. "The Key To Unlocking Decision Making Effectiveness." Unpublished paper, April 1986.

Rowe, Alan J., and Mason, Richard O. *Managing with Style*. San Francisco, CA: Jossey-Bass, 1987, pp. 83–84, 106–107.

Sathe, Vijay. "Implication of Corporate Culture: A Managers Guide to Action." *Organization Dynamics*, American Management Association (Autumn 1983).

Shaw, Marvin E. "Acceptance of Authority, Group Structure and Effectiveness of Small Groups." *Journal of Personality* 27 (1959), pp. 196–210.

Siehl, C., and Martin, J. *Inside Organizations: Quantitative Studies of Management and Worklife*. In M. O. Jones, M. Moore, and R. Snyder (eds.) in press, 1983.

Smith, Lee. "Japan's Autocratic Managers." *Fortune* (January 7, 1985), p. 56.

Thompson, Arthur A., and Strickland, A. J. *Strategic Management*. Homewood, IL: BPI-Irwin, 1990, p. 48.

Treece, James B. "New Taurus, New Sable, Old Blueprint,"*Business Week* (September 9, 1991), p. 43.

Tunstall, G. "Culture Shock in Shaking the Bell System." *Business Week* (September 26, 1983), p. 112.

Vroom, Victor H., and Yetton, Phillip W. *Leadership and Decision Making*. Pittsburgh, PA: University of Pittsburgh Press, 1973.

Watson, Thomas J. Jr., and Petre, Peter. "Terrible Tommy Watson Tells Almost All." *Business Week* (June 6, 1990), p. 18.

Zakon, Alan. *Strategy and Style*. Boston, MA: Boston Consulting Group, 1983.

# 7

# Implementation, Motivation, and Management Control

▲ ▲ ▲   ▲ ▲ ▲ ▲ ▲ ▲ ▲ ▲ ▲ ▲ ▲ ▲ ▲ ▲ ▲ ▲ ▲ ▲ ▲

An effective decision is one that achieves desired results. This requires that it be goal-oriented. If it is clear what the decision hopes to achieve, then it becomes a matter of picking the path to get there. Implementation is the path for attaining desired results and includes the selection of people, facilities, organizational structure, and external support. Implementation is often equated with management control. However, implementation involves consideration of motivation and the actions required to achieve results, including evaluation of performance, modification of activities when necessary, and measurement of output. The focus of this chapter is on how to integrate motivation and management control to ensure that decisions are appropriately implemented.

## ▲ IMPLEMENTATION AND MANAGEMENT CONTROL

A reasonable plan properly executed is superior to an excellent plan poorly executed. The truth of this statement can be observed almost daily in team sports. The challenge to managers is to pick the right players both in terms of individual ability and in the willingness to play together. The requirements are no different in any other organization.

Because results rather than intentions are what count, implementation of decisions is a key element of decision making. Implementation includes management control, which involves performance evaluation and often utilizes computerized information systems. Effective implementation becomes complex when linked to the motivational requirements of performance. No matter how carefully decisions are made, the results depend on acceptance by the individuals involved. Undoubtedly, many excellent technical solutions are never implemented simply because the organizational considerations have not been incorporated as part of the solution.

Any decision is at best only a guide to what is needed, because as actual conditions change they give rise to new requirements, and thus the exact manner in which the decision is implemented cannot be determined ahead of time. When there is a lack of commitment, or poor definition of objectives, or simply conflict in the organization, the output often does not meet the desired performance. It is precisely because conditions change continuously that any decision must accommodate to new requirements. Management needs to deal with a change process when attempting to reach a meaningful target or goal. If tasks are predictable, an organization can rely on formal procedures. On the other hand, if tasks change continuously and are highly uncertain, then more extensive problem-solving approaches appear appropriate, and self-control and member participation in decision making is far more effective. In this sense, performance has to be related both to the type of decision being made and to the kind of organizational and environmental demands. Because decisions affect the future and involve uncertainty, it is difficult to predict precisely what changes are likely to take place or how people will respond. Decisions have both direct and indirect consequences and are a function of the organizational effectiveness including number of organization levels, centralization, organization structure, and organization cohesiveness.

Implementation utilizes management controls to determine whether goals are being met effectively. There are basically five approaches to management control used for performance evaluation:

1. *Historical control* is based on past performance, historical data, or standard performance measurement.
2. *Real-time control* uses computers to provide information that is as current as possible to measure actual performance.
3. *Adaptive control* is a search to determine how the organization should respond to the changes that are required.

4. *Predictive control* anticipates or develops strategies that minimize the potential deviations or changes in the desired outcome. Predictive controls typically involve computer models, simulation, or other approaches used by management.
5. *Motivational approaches* are the means used to achieve goal congruence, commitment, acceptance of decision, empowerment, and organizational effectiveness.

Management control is multidimensional and involves many organizational factors.

## ▲ MOTIVATIONAL BASIS FOR DECISIONS

Understanding the motivational basis for decision making is critical for effective implementation. It is concerned with the process used to reach decisions rather than finding an optimal technical solution, or "what" decisions should be made. To explore motivation in depth, this section examines a number of approaches.

All management control systems are, in effect, response mechanisms that react to various stimuli and pressures. In an organizational system, behavior must also be considered. The influences on the behavior of individuals and their effect on performance in an organizational context are shown in Figure 7.1. The individual responds to the manager's direct supervision and indirectly to the influence of personal needs. In turn, the satisfaction

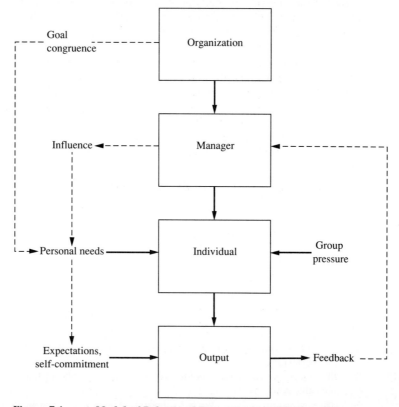

**Figure 7.1** ▲ **Model of Behavioral Determinants of Performance**

of personal needs determines whether the individual's expectations are met and the likelihood of commitment to the performance desired by the organization.

Where there is goal congruence between the individual and the organization the commitment is high and expected performance is high. However, goal congruence is generally a result of an exchange between the manager and the individual, which results from the manager's being able to influence the individual's personal needs. Performance output is measured and the results are reported to the manager. Computer reports are often included in this loop, but taken alone they do not ensure performance. The information presented to the manager may lead to the Merton effect which is the effort by the manager to influence the personal needs of his or her subordinates (Dalton and Lawrence, 1971). (When performance does not meet expectations, the manager demands increased output. If the subordinate does not consider the demands legitimate, there is felt a need to react, which may take the form of resistance or even lower performance. This in turns leads to increasing pressure from the manager until the situation either becomes explosive or is ameliorated.)

The right-hand side of Figure 7.1 corresponds to the classic closed-loop feedback system discussed later in this chapter; the left-hand side deals with behavioral requirements. The dichotomy is obviously artificial and the premise is that both halves form the basis for management control in an organizational context. When we recognize that management controls have traditionally meant keeping things going smoothly although there is constant change in most organizations, the simple concept of correcting deviations and keeping things "under control" is no longer adequate. Furthermore, where the volume of data and the level of complexity increase, management control systems can no longer be the simple, technical ones that have been utilized in the past. What is needed is responsiveness that ensures the organization's ability to meet the continuous stream of new and changing conditions.

Nord (1976) describes four bases that determine why individuals behave in given ways. These include:

1. *Instincts:* These are complex patterns of unlearned behavior contributing to survival.
2. *Drives:* These parallel physiological change in adjusting to sensed environment, such as equilibrium creation; drive reduction away from intense evoked emotional responses.
3. *Growth:* This includes drive seeking, self-actualization, or self-competence and would be considered the opposite of drive-reduction assumptions.
4. *Environment:* This stresses situational factors that influence habitual responses to a particular set of stimuli.

Nord described motivation as both innate and acquired. He also considered internal and external factors that act as drive reducing or tension producing. He considered Skinner's approach of operant conditioning as an important determinant of motivation. He indicated the value of positive reinforcement, especially in job enrichment, and suggested that self-stimulation can itself be reinforcing, especially if there has been deprivation of reinforcement. Tosi and Hamner (1974), on the other hand, define motivation as an inner state of the individual that causes action or energy to be directed at achieving goals. They treat motivation at the cognitive level by suggesting that the path of action is chosen in response to driving forces. They claim that understanding motivation requires an understanding of the meaning and relationships among need states, drives, and goals. Drive is described as a psychological condition that moves individuals toward satisfying needs, and self-actualization is meeting the need of becoming what one is capable of becoming.

Another perspective is offered by Greene and Cralt (1972), who deal with intrinsic and extrinsic rewards. Intrinsic rewards are the individual's felt satisfaction or self-reward such as self-actualization. Extrinsic rewards are "administered" by the organization and tend to satisfy Maslow's lower-level basic needs or higher-level status needs. Greene suggested that rewards are a more direct cause of satisfaction than performance and that current performance is a better predictor of subsequent performance than satisfaction as a causal factor. Deci (1971), who examined the effect of rewards, concluded that intrinsic motivation is affected by the individual's perception of a change either in what is causing the change or in feelings of self-competence and self-actualization. Furthermore, intrinsic motivation depends directly on the feedback received. Negative feedback decreases intrinsic motivation, and positive feedback and interpersonal support increase it. Deci also found that intrinsic motivation decreases when there is dependence on extrinsic rewards of money or avoidance of punishment.

Patz and Rowe (1977) looked at intrinsic motivation in terms of self-consistency; that is, behavior is motivated and action undertaken when it is "consistent" with one's image of one's self-definition. In turn, self-definition is determined by the meaning that individuals attribute to themselves when viewed objectively. However, self-definition continues to change and individuals tend to become what other people think of them.

Satisfaction, whether a result of intrinsic or extrinsic rewards, acts only indirectly in determining performance. Rather, actions are generally directed by one's goals based on personal values, reaction to a given situation, perception, and cognition. Locke (1968) described external incentives that incite or motivate action. He reached a number of conclusions concerning performance.

1. The harder the goal, the higher the level of performance.
2. Individuals who genuinely strive to achieve difficult goals work hard. Those with easy goals work less hard.
3. Instructions only affect behavior if "consciously" accepted and translated into specific goals or intentions.
4. Active goal setting by the individual has a greater effect on performance than merely participating in the goal-setting process.
5. Compared with intentions, money does not act as an incentive.
6. Depending on the goals of the individual, praise and reproof have a variable effect on performance.

Locke's research supports the importance of individual goal setting and intentions in maintaining "self-image." It also provides a basis for establishing performance requirements and the means for ensuring achievement of goals.

## ▲ UNDERSTANDING MOTIVATION BY KNOWING ONE'S PERSONALITY

Personality and personal needs were used as the basis for explaining motivated behavior by Richards and Greenlaw (1972) as shown in Figure 7.2. The relationship of personality structure to motivation can be used to describe both the needs and the cognitive reaction in terms of goal-seeking strategies. The feedback loop from behavior to basic needs can change goal-seeking strategies based on the reaction to the behavioral response. This personality–motivation model provides a useful insight into how individuals react to needs stimuli.

Levinson (1978), in explaining the motivations behind man at work, sees an unfolding and refinement of internal capacities at the emotional and cognitive levels that give rise to feelings, wishes, fantasies, and attitudes. He describes the "ego ideal" as the most powerful motivating force for any human being. This stems from three basic needs of the ego model.

1. *Ministration:* care and support from others
2. *Maturation:* growth and development
3. *Mastery:* control of one's own fate.

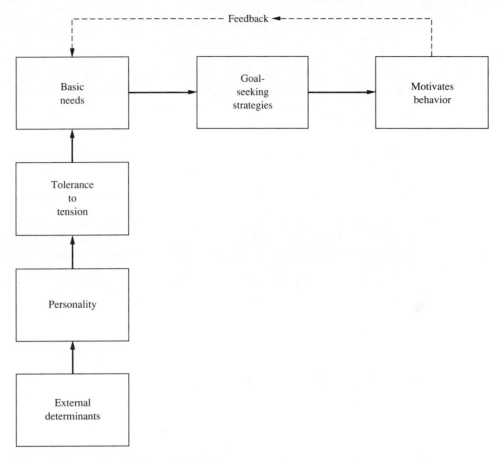

**Figure 7.2**  ▲  **Personality and Motivation**

Levinson also described motivation as related to the individual's self-image in terms of one's ego ideal. The concept of self-image or self-identification is a critical one in terms of decision style. An individual who has a positive self-image based on a knowledge of his or her style is more likely to perform more effectively than one who has a low or negative self-image. The decision style inventory has proven to be a useful tool in helping individuals identify their strengths and thus reinforce their self-image.

## ▲ EXPECTANCY AND MOTIVATION

Expectancy theory as developed by Vroom (1964) is based on the premise that a person's behavior depends on the individual's perceived likelihood that an action will lead to a certain outcome along with the value or attractiveness of the outcome. Vroom defined motivation as a process governing choices made by persons who choose from among alternative forms of voluntary activity. Motivation is the combination of valence (preference) times expectancy, and is the result of actual or perceived rewards received for accomplishing a goal. Vroom described direct (or first-level) outcomes such as productivity and indirect (or second-level)

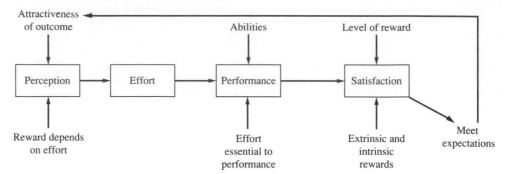

Figure 7.3 ▲ Motivation Model: Adapted from Porter, Lawler, and Hackman.

outcomes such as receiving a promotion. The perceived relationship between these was defined as instrumentality; that is, the individual perceives that productivity will lead to a promotion. He then described valence as the person's preference for a particular outcome, and expectancy was defined as the probability that a specific action will lead to a first-level outcome.

Despite the considerable effort in studying and applying "expectancy," there are questions concerning its consistency. The value of an approach such as expectancy is that it shows the importance of individual goal setting and reinforcement on satisfaction and performance. Porter, Lawler, and Hackman (1975) utilize an approach where individuals are motivated by future expectations based on previously learned experiences. The model shown in Figure 7.3 describes how effort relates to performance and satisfaction. Although managers often assume that satisfaction leads to better performance, the Porter, Lawler, and Hackman model indicates that performance depends on whether rewards meet expectation and thus lead to satisfaction.

It is obvious that the motivational miasma is yet to be resolved. Nonetheless, managers must manage and make decisions that influence the motivation of subordinates. Although motivation is sometimes considered manipulation, it nonetheless is important for a manager to be aware of individual needs, drives, aspirations, values, goals, and expectations in order to predict the outcome of decisions. Motivated behavior is a natural part of organizational life. To the extent that it can be dealt with appropriately, there is a greater likelihood that performance will meet goals and that decision-making effectiveness will be enhanced.

## ▲ CLOSED-LOOP FEEDBACK CONTROL SYSTEMS

For a long time, the closed-loop approach was the basis on which management exercised control. That is, they would look at deviations from standard or budget and would take corrective action to restore the system back to its original objective. When looked at from the perspective of a purely mechanistic base, there are three ways in which a system can be restored to its original position.

1. *Underdamped or hunting approach:* There is no real plan of action. The system is restored by trying a number of approaches, hoping that one will meet the target.
2. *Overdamped approach:* This is being so cautious in restoring the system to its basic position that it never reaches the target in time to achieve the goals or objectives.
3. *Critical damping:* This utilizes information feedback and restores the system precisely to the position desired. However, critical damping is also a slow process and generally would be equated to following rules and procedures, which characterizes the normal bureaucratic organization.

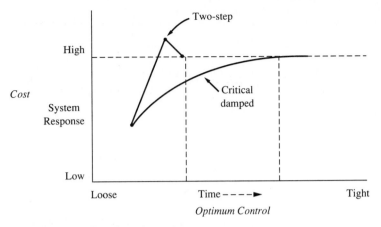

**Figure 7.4** ▲ **Two-Step Control**

To correct a deviation, a two-step or optimum control is used to reach the target. In an organizational sense, the two-step approach typifies the flexibility required of an adaptive system. In effect, this method is a way of approaching the target, realizing that it is not fixed. It basically argues that it is better to get close to an objective and then refine the adjustment than to continuously adjust or correct the system to meet the objective. For example, if sales are lagging, the approach would be to take some corrective action while waiting for market research data and consumer reaction. The second action might differ significantly from the first one, but will mean a smaller correction and thus a faster and more accurate closure on the objective. This approach requires organizational flexibility because it means establishing intermediate objectives that will again change. If an organization has a low tolerance for ambiguity or if the manager's style is a very decisive one, then applying the concept of two-step control may be difficult even though on a technical level it is the correct approach.

Too often, management control has become the mechanism for attempting to achieve efficiency in an organization without any consideration for social costs or human values. Although there may be a sound technical basis for the improvement, the result may be poor implementation, sabotage, or lowered morale. For short periods, it is possible to induce unreasonable controls, but the long-term effects can be devastating. Recognizing that efficiency, when used alone, can be detrimental to the "effective" performance of an organization, management control systems should explicitly balance the effect of proposed technical changes with anticipated behavioral responses. Even purely technical control decisions involve a minimum of two factors. For example, improved delivery performance generally requires increasing production capacity, and the cost of that capacity should balance the benefits from better deliveries. The concept of balancing of factors generally is contrary to the efficiency approach, which tends to focus on a single factor.

## ▲ BEHAVIORALLY ANCHORED MANAGEMENT CONTROL SYSTEMS

Beyond the purely technical closed-loop feedback control systems are behaviorally anchored management control systems. The difference between the two approaches is the recognition that the decision maker should be in the loop and that feedback should be compared with objectives when closing the loop. From this perspective, the management control problem can be viewed as shown in Figure 7.5. It is described in four levels.

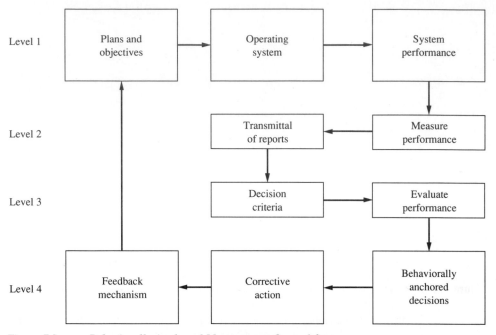

**Figure 7.5** ▲ **Behaviorally Anchored Management Control System**

*Level 1* deals with the system itself—the plans, objectives, strategies, values, goals, and desires of management. These in turn are transformed into a system design such as a production control system. The system then performs based on the design that was developed to meet the objectives.

*Level 2* deals with the information and measurement of performance. These in turn form the basis for reports that are transmitted to managers.

*Level 3* is the evaluation of performance based on established decision criteria, such as performance standards. The objective is to clearly recognize that performance standards should contain explicit behaviorally anchored measures. This level is where motivation and satisfaction determine whether performance will meet goals.

*Level 4* is where corrective action, if needed, is taken based on a behaviorally anchored decision that considers the individuals who are responsible for the performance. Redefinition of the problem, collecting additional information involving the workers, or brainstorming alternatives all facilitate corrective action.

A behaviorally anchored management control system responds to needs based on a meaningful evaluation of performance in contrast to rigid standards. The behavioral approach asks the question, If performance is off, is the variation too large, or is there an explanation for the difference? The behavioral control system reexamines the behavioral content when determining system operation.

## ▲ ADAPTIVE CONTROLS

Considering that the basic strategy of a firm continuously undergoes modification, it is obvious that an effective management control system will likewise have to be able to adapt to the changing environment. The primary concern of adaptive controls is at the operating level and

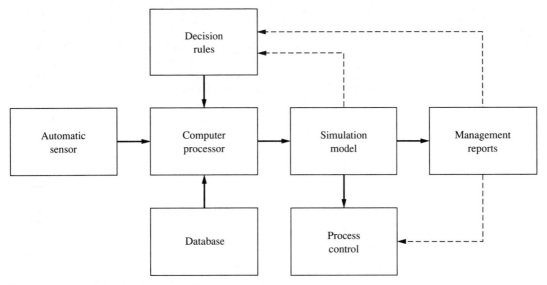

**Figure 7.6 ▲ Adaptive Computer-Based Controls**

the ways of modifying the internal environment to match the changing external forces. An obvious approach is to have "anticipatory" controls that project possible deviations, such as is done in statistical quality control. For example, if an employee plans a trip, the fact that it might exceed the budget should be ascertained ahead of time rather than after the fact.

An adaptive control system permits management to change both the desired objectives and the control process, depending on the response required and the performance expected. An appropriate approach needs to be used to provide a means for adapting the output in an optimum "technical" manner where there is a single target or objective. However, organizations with many products or large and complex projects might require a computer-based system to achieve adaptive controls. Complex systems generally require large amounts of data for purposes of control so that the system can be monitored in order to take appropriate corrective action in time to achieve the desired objectives. Thus, an adaptive computer-based approach requires a real-time system that utilizes large-scale databases and simulation models to forecast the future states of the system. The operation of an adaptive computer-based system is shown in Figure 7.6.

It starts with the gathering of data and sensing of the environment. These data then update master files or a database and produce management reports, or real-time displays and inquiries. An appropriate simulation model is often used to provide "predictive" control. The adaptive feature is represented by the ability of management to modify the specific decision rules or to override the computer control of a process. A pure computer process control system, such as is used in refineries, has adaptive capability based on the decision rules built into the software. Human modification of such systems is more difficult unless that capability is provided in the software. Many companies use computer reports or remote inquiry terminals to respond to customer requests or for control of operations. For example, a carburetor test stand at one of the large automobile manufacturers is linked directly with a computer that monitors the output, and the data are used to accept or reject the unit being processed. Adjustment of the process utilizes the two-step approach to minimize the time required to test the article and, at failure, reset the process.

Adaptive systems by definition are constantly changing to meet new conditions. An important question is, When has the system changed sufficiently to warrant a modification?

Because performance involves randomness and uncertainty, a single target, objective, or budget does not provide a basis for correction; there inevitably will be deviations merely due to chance. To deal with this situation, control limits can be used that are comparable to the ones in statistical quality control. When the process under control is primarily governed by the results of a physical process, then probability limits are most appropriate. However, if the process involves human behavior, then consideration of motivation is needed, and control limits can be a matter of negotiation. Furthermore, since objectives are often based on estimates, there is considerable uncertainty as to the validity of the base itself. Estimates are based on past experience, comparable work, or sometimes an arbitrarily determined standard. In any event, using the estimate as a rigid basis for measuring performance, or adapting the system, appears incongruous with meeting goals. Rather, what appears appropriate is a control limit approach so that deviations do not signal the need for a change in performance when it is not really warranted.

## ▲ LOOSE AND TIGHT CONTROLS

The degree of management control varies with the type of operation being considered. For example, in manufacturing operations, a high level of control is often used to ensure that quality products are produced. Without a consistent level of quality, a company will experience a downgraded reputation and potentially lose its customers which, in turn, could result in reduced profits. This reality has embarrassed American car manufacturers, which have not yet been able to match the quality of Japanese cars. There has been some progress. It has been quoted that "the best of ours is now almost as good as the worst of theirs." This is quite a comedown for a nation that at one time was considered the industrial leader of the world. But the world has caught up with the United States, and now quality products come from everywhere: for example, Japan, Korea, Taiwan, Hong Kong, Singapore, Germany, Italy, and Sweden.

In a research or high-technology organization, controls are generally looser. In a research laboratory, creative people will work around the clock when they are in pursuit of a hot idea. They often sleep in their offices. To expect them to arrive at work on time every day is an inappropriate use of control. To require regular reports from creative individuals is also an inappropriate control imposed by uncreative administrators. The Cray Research case is a stark example of this (see Chapter 5), where Rollwagen had to remove the president, who by requiring reports was having a negative impact on the creative environment of that high-tech organization. Although reports may keep managers amused and happy, they do not stimulate the creative process. A key consideration in determining the degree of control to apply in an organization depends on how creative the organization is.

## ▲ INTERACTION OF PERFORMANCE MEASUREMENT AND CONTROL

An important question in management control is how frequently and in what form performance should be measured. Obviously, historical measures do not adequately deal with the ongoing dynamics of a situation. Frequent interaction and multidimensional measures are needed for determining the effectiveness of performance. Measures such as cohesiveness, responsiveness, adaptability, and effectiveness provide meaningful insight into the organization. This is not to say that conventional measures should be discarded, but rather that they serve a different purpose than what is proposed here for "organization control" in contrast to "technical control."

How best to identify deviations in performance and how to measure them in order to determine the causes of these deviations are crucial aspects of implementation. Because measurement impinges on the information system and organization structure, it is not simple. For example, in a decentralized organization the manager is closer to the decision point, and a different type of control is required than in a highly centralized organization where management receives only summary information regarding what is happening, rather than first-hand details.

A significant concern is how to do performance measurement because when inappropriate performance measurement is used, it can create dysfunctional behavior. McGregor (1957) pointed out that the manner in which control is imposed often induces unintended consequences such as widespread antagonism, successful resistance, noncompliance, unreliable performance, need for close surveillance, and high administrative costs. Ridgway (1956) also showed that there are dysfunctional consequences of performance measurement and that, when a single criterion of performance is used, it leads to undesirable results.

Ridgway reported on a study that showed that public workers who were attempting to improve performance would use easy caseloads in order to make up the quota established for them. Argyris (1967) reported the same tendency for people to use easy jobs as fillers to meet imposed quotas. A study reported by Granick (1960) revealed the same behavior—that there is neglect of repair and maintenance in order to meet unreasonable standards that are based on arbitrary criteria of performance.

To examine the impact of measurement on performance, it is necessary to review the five basic phases: (1) identifying when something has occurred; (2) measuring the event; (3) reporting the information; (4) making a decision based on an evaluation of the deviation; and (5) taking any necessary corrective action. Each phase has an impact on performance. For example, when an occurrence is sensed, some basis for inquiry is needed. Events often are overlooked simply because no one is aware that they should be followed. Having identified that an event has occurred, control is concerned with measurement and the standard or bases for the measurement. Estimates generally form the basis for standards and are most often based on historical data (by definition, after the fact). As a result, the control process is like driving a car using the rearview mirror. This has a number of serious implications.

Furthermore, estimates rarely include any provision for variability; rather, absolute data are used, such as keep equipment busy 100 percent of the time, or meet 100 percent of quotas. However, when there are capacity constraints, the impact of queuing is critical, because 100 percent utilization of capacity leads to an infinite queue. Another measurement problem is the use of averages that tend to hide or eliminate any variations in performance. Arbitrary allocations of expense such as for overhead or general and administrative expenses cause problems because there is little relationship between performance and requirements. It is almost axiomatic that because of the inherent problems in establishing standards, goals, and objectives, and the basis on which measurement is done, there will be dysfunctional consequences. Performance and behavioral effects can be expected as a result of the interaction of measurement with performance.

## ▲ MANAGEMENT CONTROL SYSTEMS FOR EFFECTIVE IMPLEMENTATION

In the design of management control systems, it is necessary to examine the cost of control, which changes depending on whether there is loose or tight control. The cost increases exponentially as tight control systems are used, whereas, on the other hand, the value contributed by tighter control systems reaches a maximum. Thus, the net value is used to define the optimum control point as shown in Figure 7.7.

Controls are never an end in themselves. Rather, they are a means toward an end of achieving some objective such as more effective implementation. For instance, quality control

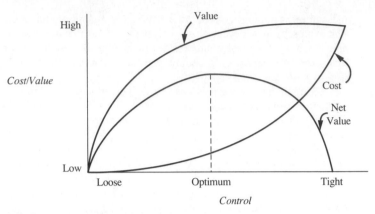

**Figure 7.7** ▲ **Value of Control**

does not build quality into the product, it merely identifies whether the quality is satisfactory, which is useful in knowing when to change the manufacturing process. In a similar manner, if performance does not meet the standard desired, a control system cannot change that performance. Management has to deal with the individuals involved in performing a task. Thus, a fundamental consideration in designing controls is that they are indicators that identify when change is needed and how it might take place.

In order to have controls that facilitate implementation and adapt to new and changing conditions, an understanding of causality is needed. The reason variances occur must be determined so that appropriate corrective action can be taken. In addition, there is a need to forecast the impact of decisions in order to know how the control should be implemented. A basic requirement in the design of a control system, therefore, is determining effectiveness of the output. As was seen in Figure 7.7, the value of control reaches a point of diminishing returns. Loose control can be equated with open systems; tight control can be viewed as a purely technical system that imposes constraints and requirements both on behavior and cost.

Although the effectiveness of a control system is typically judged by how close performance meets a predetermined target, another way to view effectiveness is:

$$\text{Effectiveness} = \frac{\text{Value received}}{\text{Resources used}} \times \text{Control system cost}$$

where the control system cost includes both behavioral and resource costs and is dependent on the "process" or managerial style used to achieve control.

Control effectiveness is considered at three levels, rather than as a single overall measure—individual, managerial, and organizational. Obviously, these three levels interact and thus influence one another, but their separate evaluation is needed to determine the best way to design a management control system. Starting with the individual decision level, effectiveness is concerned with the technical or analytical soundness of the control system. For example, doubling capacity does not increase throughput twofold, where random disturbances are experienced. Thus, using resources in the "hope" of doubling production would not be an effective technical decision, and performance would not reach the level desired without additional costs to the organization in terms of overtime or reduced morale because of the increased pressure and stress to meet an unrealistic goal.

At the managerial level, effectiveness is concerned with the decision process used to carry out the control system. Thus, decision styles, control styles, and the exercise of power all are ingredients of managerial effectiveness. An effective style, then, is one that matches the situational requirements with the manner in which the manager exercises control. This is

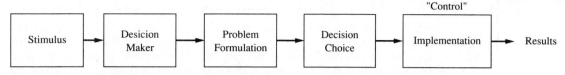

**Figure 7.8** ▲ **Control as a Part of Implementation**

the phase of the decision process called "implementation" (see Figure 7.8). Style, thus, is an integral aspect of the decision process, and provides a significant input to the control process.

Organizational effectiveness is the area most generally associated with performance. Because of its interaction with the other two levels—the individual and the managerial levels— organizational effectiveness really cannot be treated separately. Too often, poor performance is a result of organizational behavior and the technical aspect of the problem. Although managerial controls have not emphasized this aspect of the problem, a sociotechnical approach would incorporate all three levels of control.

Because decision styles are related to an individual's cognitive ability and to organizational situations, there is a relationship between the demands of a given situation and a manager's ability to handle them. For example, directive managers tend to satisfice or settle for satisfactory solutions, whereas the conceptual and analytic styles tend to seek optimum solutions to problems. Because personality is an integral aspect of decision style, conflicts may arise between managers and subordinates and directly influence the manager's ability to achieve control.

One can define control styles as an extension of decision styles, as seen in Figure 7.9. On the bottom axis is shown the manager's orientation. The environmental influence is shown on the left-hand axis. If complexity is included on the environmental axis, control styles are analogous to decision styles. Thus, for example, the directive manager has a high need for control, and the analytic manager tends to be more flexible and oriented to problem solving. Although the conceptual (who is the creative manager) also needs control, he or she is willing to examine options and alternatives, listen to arguments, and even share control with subordinates. The behavioral is the considerate manager who constantly shares control because of a high need for affiliation. The behavioral style does not really exercise control, but rather desires approval from other individuals. The conceptual style is most participative and willing to share control.

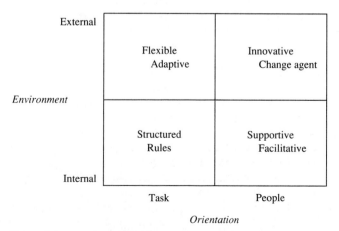

**Figure 7.9** ▲ **Control Styles**

## ▲ ORGANIZATION PERFORMANCE

An important consideration in management control systems is the overall organizational performance in contrast to departmental or divisional performance. Less-than-desired performance nearly always results from dealing with only one division, area, or product at a time. For example, profit centers that have been assigned responsibility as subunits of a firm can cause difficulties if there is a high degree of interdependency or joint sharing of cost among several units. To overcome this problem, interdependencies must be clearly defined and the basis for joint effort established.

A mechanism is required that ensures effective joint action. For example, in many companies Engineering sends blueprints to Manufacturing to produce an end product. Difficulties often arise because of problems in producibility while still trying to meet the design specifications. At Lincoln Electric, all new designs are prepared jointly by Engineering and Manufacturing so that there is no future conflict. Unless the organization is designed to facilitate cooperative effort, the tendency is for subunits to act independently, often to the detriment of other units. In the final analysis, it is the total system performance that determines the outcome.

A number of approaches have been developed to provide for appropriate interaction of subunits. Program evaluation review technique (PERT) has helped define the program relationships for major projects, including schedules, manpower, and cost information. Thus, the program becomes the basis for measuring performance. In a similar vein, both organizational structure and the span of management influence the ability to ensure control. For example, in a highly decentralized company it is difficult to retain central coordination, let alone control. In these instances, control tends to take on the role of budgetary constraints or restrictions on subunit performance. The problem is compounded by requirements for allocation of costs, sharing of bonuses, or reporting of profits. Integrating independent activities while still maintaining coordinated effort and conflict resolution is a difficult control task.

When considering the span of management, a manager who insists on tight control generally has few people reporting to him or her and becomes a bottleneck because no decisions are made without his or her consent. This type of manager is typically the directive style, who is often a dedicated, task-oriented individual.

Figure 7.10 shows that the cost of supervision decreases as more people are supervised by a single manager, but the delays also increase as the span of management increases. It

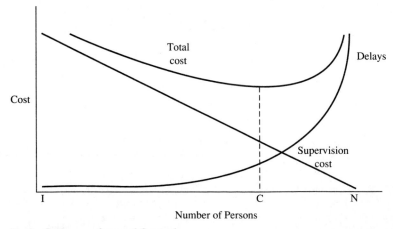

Figure 7.10 ▲ Span of Control

is this latter effect that gives rise to the bottleneck phenomenon. The precise shape of the two curves would obviously depend on the manager's decision style, the kind of work being supervised, and the level of the people being supervised. Although, in a technical sense, it is easy to find an optimum solution, in a behavioral context the exercise of power, the sharing of decision making, and decision styles all influence where the optimum is located.

Finding optimum solutions for control problems involves, at a minimum, some form of joint optimization. That is, most problems confronting management involve at least two factors, such as seen in Figure 7.10. If only one factor is considered, such as delay, the total cost would be higher than when considering both costs together. Furthermore, whenever there is joint optimization, each component operates at less than the individual optimum. That is, minimal delay would occur if only one person was being supervised, but this obviously leads to the highest cost on the supervision curve. This same reasoning applies to unit profit centers. If they are truly operating independently, the chances are that the total system cost is higher than if there is cooperative effort.

Another consideration in finding the optimum organizational performance, from a managerial-control perspective, is the interaction of decision rules and policies on system behavior. People behave and systems function in a manner not intended when controls were set up. In the case of cash flow, a considerable amount of money is tied up to avoid running out of funds. A number of alternatives might be used to reduce the cash balance level. An open line of credit could prove cheaper for the few times there are heavy cash demands, or a probabilistic approach could be used to establish the float required, or a probability model may be used to predict cash receipts. In the latter case, if the receipts were predicted to fall below requirements, corrective action (such as special price concessions) could be taken to induce customers to pay more quickly.

One of the major problems in control system design is the need to avoid inducing undesirable fluctuations into the system behavior. Forrester (1961) has shown that a small amount of variability in the rate of incoming orders can lead to wide fluctuations in production because of delays in the system or wrong forecasts that amplify the expected flows and cause uncontrolled fluctuations. Simulation models have proven especially helpful in identifying such system behavior and for testing decision rules used to control a given process to determine how to provide optimum system performance. Recognizing the impact that controls and decisions have on system behavior and performance, one can readily appreciate that performance standards or other normative approaches often contribute to poor performance rather than controlling it.

Finding appropriate decision rules for use in control systems is a task that requires understanding both the behavior of physical systems and human behavior. Complex systems, policy issues, questions of strategy, and so forth appear to be solved best by heuristic methods and simulation models. The principal advantage of these latter methods is that they are understandable by the manager and thus are more readily accepted. Managers use intuition to find good solutions that are preferable to optimal solutions that are not used because the methods are not understood.

## ▲  THE PARETO LAW AND CONTROL

Perhaps one of the oldest maxims in management is the "exception principle." Essentially, this approach to control was based on a reasonably stable environment and was used only when deviations were significant or there were "exceptions." At that point, management was required to take corrective action. Partly because of the stability and partly because of the volume of data that would have to be handled manually, the exception principle served a

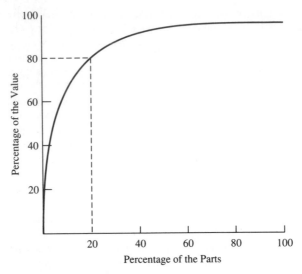

**Figure 7.11** ▲ **Pareto Distribution**

useful purpose. It even provided for some power sharing and participation through delegation of the routine portions of tasks.

With the advent of the computer and the changing approach to controls, the simple yes–no exception principle no longer is an adequate basis for control. Because computer-based data permit continuous monitoring and updating of systems and simulations forecast the future direction of the system, the exception rule should be applied in a different manner. In Figure 7.11, the Pareto Law is shown describing the relative frequency of items that management desires to control.

For example, if management wants to control inventory, then approximately 20 percent of the items typically represent 80 percent of the value of the inventory. Thus, by controlling these 20 percent of the items, the majority of the impact in terms of value is under control. If the computer is used to continuously monitor these 20 percent (the critical items), then the remaining 80 percent of the items (not value) can be handled on an exception basis. In effect, we can separate items into two categories—the relatively important and the unimportant. The two-step approach to control utilizes this principle; that is, the first step only has to achieve 80 percent of the goal and then the remaining 20 percent is readily achieved. Because of its universal applicability, the Pareto Law provides a very powerful basis for control. Not only does 20 percent of the inventory represent 80 percent of the value, but 20 percent of the customers represent the majority of the sales. A small percentage of components of a product are the ones that cause the majority of the problems; a small percentage of the workforce has most of the accidents, and so on. Interestingly, the same approach applies to decision making in that a small percentage of the decisions a manager makes has a significant impact on the organization. The effective executive concentrates his or her effort on those decisions that have the highest payoff. In too many cases, all decisions are given equal weight or priority, and there is no recognition of their relative importance.

As a basis for control, the Pareto Law provides a direct means for partitioning any problem into important and unimportant items. This approach can be used in decision making, distribution of sales effort, budgeting projects based on payoff, or allocating time to activities that must be performed. For example, a data-processing department was changing from one computer to another and was concerned with how best to reprogram while still retaining an efficient operation. By starting with those programs that were used most frequently, they minimized the problems of changeover.

## ▲ APPLYING MANAGEMENT CONTROLS

Management by objectives (MBO) has made a significant contribution to the field of management control, but it also has introduced a number of dysfunctional aspects. In an article by Levinson (1970) titled "Management by Whose Objectives?" he describes some of the concerns. MBO is often viewed as simply a top-down descriptive measure of the requirements to perform rather than achieving a commitment on the part of individuals who are expected to carry out the stated objectives. In order for MBO to be successful, an appropriate organizational climate, including trust and support, is required. In addition, in order to carry out objectives, resources are needed.

Management by objectives has been one of the notable examples of how to obtain personal involvement as the basis for improving the productivity and performance of an organization. An example of how this was done is shown for a large aerospace company in Table 7.1. The five vice-presidents in charge of the major functions listed their key milestones. In each instance, the vice-president in charge was asked what his objectives were for the year in his area of responsibility. Not only is the definition of milestones important, but the specific objective or target a vice-president proposed was required. For example, in the financial area, the objectives included a 5 percent reduction in overhead costs, a 15 percent profit objective,

**Table 7.1  ▲  Key Milestone Plan, 1991**

| Key Milestones for Each Major Functional Area | Plan or Objective | Current Performance | Forecast Performance | Projected Deviation |
|---|---|---|---|---|
| **1. Financial** | | | | |
| a. Reduction in overhead cost | 5% | 2% | 3% | −2% |
| b. Profit objective (on sales) | 15% | 12% | 13% | −2% |
| c. New decentralized controllers | 2 | 1 | 2 | — |
| **2. Marketing** | | | | |
| a. Analysis of new products | 13 | 2 | 10 | −3 |
| b. Increase sales efforts | 20% | 30% | 25% | +5% |
| c. Shift product mix (civilian/military) | 50% | 80% | 75% | +25% |
| d. Sales per employee | $25,000 | $25,000 | $25,000 | −$500 |
| **3. Manpower** | | | | |
| a. Number of key personnel needed | 6 | 1 | 3 | −3 |
| b. Standard of labor efficiency | 88% | 80% | 82% | −6% |
| c. Manpower development program | 400 | 418 | 418 | +18 |
| d. Ratio of indirect to direct cost | 10% | 17% | 15% | +5 |
| **4. Engineering** | | | | |
| a. Recruitment of senior engineers | 25 | 16 | 18 | −7 |
| b. Application of project control systems | 3 | 0 | 1 | −2 |
| c. Increase % R&D per sales | 5% | 6% | 6% | +1% |
| d. New technological programs | 5 | 1 | 2 | −3 |
| **5. Operations** | | | | |
| a. Increase in production capacity | 150% | 110% | 150% | — |
| b. Reduction in labor variance | 10% | 0 | 2% | −8% |
| c. Increase interdivisional sales | $200,000 | $120,000 | $150,000 | −$50,000 |
| d. Application of new computer systems | 15 | 3 | 4 | −11 |

and the hiring of two additional controllers for the decentralized operations. Each of the other vice-presidents had similar plans or targets.

In marketing, the objectives included analyzing 13 new products and increasing sales per employee to $10,500. In the manpower area, the targets included hiring six new key personnel and reducing the ratio of indirect to direct costs to 10 percent. In the case of engineering, not only did the vice-president plan to recruit 25 additional senior engineers, but he also tried to have a minimum of five R&D projects in the area of advanced technology. Operations needed to increase capacity by 150 percent and had as a target increased interdivisional sales of $200,000 a year, as well as installing 15 new computer systems.

As can be seen in the table, each month there was a performance review to compare the current status with the plan. By reviewing the figures, for example, instead of a reduction of 5 percent in overhead, 2 percent was achieved and the forecast was that only 3 percent would be possible by the end of the year, so a net deficit of 2 percent is shown in the column labeled Projected Deviation. Because all aspects of the objectives are defined, including the target, current status, future forecast, and an explanation of why it cannot be achieved, management is in a position to examine the alternative actions needed to meet the desired objectives.

In some instances, the target underestimated the ability to perform. For example, in item 2b, the plan called for a 20 percent increase in sales effort, but 30 percent was actually achieved. However, because this overshot the target, it was going to be reduced to 25 percent, still showing a net 5 percent increase. In the case of product mix, the 50 percent plan was increased to 80 percent current, with a forecast of 75 percent change in product mix — actually exceeding the initial target by 25 percent.

Here again, obviously, some of the targets did not have the degree of precision that one might think was desirable, such as item 3c, manpower development. It was estimated that 400 managers would be sent to various courses. As it turned out, 418 actually went, showing an excess of 18. This, however, should not be construed as being out of control, or necessarily bad. It simply means that the original target of 400 was the estimate on which the plan was based. This is a good illustration of how to apply control limits. Obviously, 400 is only a target or estimate. An allowable variation should be determined so that the variance of plus 18 does not reflect poor performance. One of the most difficult targets to achieve was increased interdivisional sales. The results showed only a $150,000 increase, whereas the target was $200,000. The forecast of $150,000 (a deficit of $50,000) requires the attention of management if performance is to match the desired objective.

The management control approach shown here illustrates how information, properly utilized and properly displayed, can provide management with a tool for achieving more effective performance when it is recognized that both the information and the behavioral aspects of the problems must be jointly considered. That is, the managers themselves set the targets; therefore, they are held accountable on the basis of their own estimates, not something that management had given them and then might use to criticize them if the results are not achieved.

Although MBO has been used extensively by many organizations, research reported by Singular (1975) indicates that fewer than 10 percent of the Fortune 500 companies reported that their programs were successful and only 2 percent considered them "highly" successful. There are more failures than successes, and consulting firms spend more time correcting programs than installing them. The evidence is that MBO is far from a simple process and too often is equated with performance appraisal. The successful programs tend to have three elements in common:

1. Objectives are specific and set jointly with those who will carry out the activities.
2. Feedback is concrete and periodic and includes effective communication.
3. Top management is involved and supports the program.

There are a number of problems in attempting to achieve these three requirements. First, even when subordinates are involved in establishing objectives, they often do not have the information required to contribute meaningfully. Second, feedback can be construed as performance appraisal, which has not enjoyed success on its own. As an alternative, Keeley (1984) proposed a framework for performance evaluation. He suggested that performance expectation factors cover degree of detail, compatibility with one another, stability, and consistency of importance. He recommended consideration of three appraisal techniques:

1. *Behavioral:* Define performance in observable, physical action, such as behaviorally anchored rating scales.
2. *Objective:* Use of procedures that are objective in terms of results, such as MBO.
3. *Judgment:* Use of knowledgeable evaluators or multirater techniques.

Each of these is a function of the given situation, including the individual differences in the job performers. The appropriate evaluation approach is contingent on a combination of worker characteristics and situational determinants. Thus, behaviorally based procedures work best for structured tasks where workers do not desire autonomy. Objective procedures fit moderately structured organizations and moderate desire for autonomy. Finally, judgmental procedures are most appropriate for uncertain tasks where workers have a high desire for autonomy.

The requirement for top management support of MBO, depends on more than interest or even involvement. As Sherwin (1976) pointed out, individuals do not achieve objectives alone, but depend on contributions from others. Further, no one organization structure can meet all objectives; a functional approach works best for routine business operations. Sherwin suggested that "failing to recognize the multifunctional aspect of objectives may explain some of the problems with conventional MBO programs." He recommended a team approach based on an "objectives grid" for accomplishing objectives and for assigning accountability for objectives. Thus, teams of individuals become the basic unit of an organization instead of one division per objective as the basis for organizing.

Another organizational issue is the appropriateness of measures used for MBO. As has been described, individual profit centers suboptimize because each unit is measured on its own performance, does not consider the overall organization. Similarly, overall objectives, such as 15 percent return on investment, may be appropriate for some divisions, but not necessarily for the organization as a whole. Often, the objective itself is inappropriate, such as meeting 95 percent of scheduled commitments, while having an average delay not to exceed 1/2 percent per month. Based on queuing theory, these "conflicting" objectives cannot be met simultaneously. As was described in Chapter 2, measures of effectiveness are multidimensional, are highly interdependent, change with the situation, and depend on the life cycle of the organization. It is small wonder, therefore, that the "objective" measures of MBO do not adequately handle the problem of performance.

An alternative to MBO, called performance management system (PMS), was proposed by Beer and Ruh (1976). It was applied at Corning Glass Works for 3,800 managerial and professional employees. They previously had used MBO but changed because of the shortcomings they experienced. The PMS approach was designed to provide constructive feedback to subordinates on their performance. It emphasizes the manager's role in facilitating meeting organizational goals, and developing and evaluating subordinates. It uses a profile to define the individual's strengths and developmental needs while integrating results achieved with supportive means for achieving performance goals.

The principal difference between PMS and MBO is the "process of arriving at performance standards." MBO starts with agreed-upon objectives using criteria to develop and carry out plans. PMS starts with a description of the subordinate's behavior, showing his or her strengths and weaknesses. Using developmental interviews, the manager and the subordinate jointly identify areas needing improvement. Plans are established to develop the abilities needed for effective performance. Some of the factors considered in developing a performance profile include initiative, setting priorities, accomplishment, accuracy, communication, cooperation, decisiveness, and flexibility. Using the profile as a starting point, a development program is designed for improving attitude, ability, interpersonal skills, or personality. Given this base, evaluation interviews are held covering the subordinate's current performance, potential promotability, and salary increase. At Corning, merely identifying performance dimensions helped organizational effectiveness.

An examination of PMS reveals why purely technical control systems that operate primarily at the task level do not achieve the objective of improved performance or output. Rather, goal congruence—meeting expectations and individual self-commitment—tends to be a function of the influence exerted by the manager in the context of the task and peer relations. When the control system operates entirely on a closed-loop feedback basis, performance tends to meet minimal expectations, and win–lose tends to replace goal congruence. Thus, formal control systems are only adjuncts to the motivational and informal control systems.

In the past, the emphasis has been on a closed-loop feedback approach. However, as Hofstede (1984) pointed out, objectives are often unclear, missing, or changing; accomplishment is difficult to measure in unambiguous, quantitative output standards; and feedback information is often not relevant or usable. Given the complexity of management control, it is small wonder that the emphasis is increasingly being placed on how to "motivate" rather than "control" performance.

## ▲ ORGANIZATION STRUCTURE, MOTIVATION, AND CONTROL

People who are willing to cooperate can make any organization structure work. The converse is also true—unwilling workers can foul up the best system of organization that can be devised. However, there are certain organization structures that work effectively in different situations. Over time, we have come to consider the human element and have revised production methods from the assembly line method of the Ford Model T days to the team production methods used by Volvo in Sweden. Job specialization has yielded to job enrichment. Theory X, the scientific method based on the idea of rationality in human beings, has yielded to theories Y and Z, which are more humanistic and take the social and emotional needs of people into consideration. The authoritarian approach to management has resulted in a turned-off workforce. The team concept—common goals, participation, recognition, and sharing rewards openly and fairly—has worked in the past and is working in the present. Companies such as Lincoln Electric, Nucor, IBM, and Hewlett-Packard have been able to win the support and maintain the loyalty of their employees. Japanese companies have provided what is essentially lifetime employment and housing for their employees. Generally speaking, Japanese companies in the United States also have been able to win the support of American workers. American managers, who are more left-brain or task-oriented (directive-analytic), often are less effective than Japanese managers, who are more right-brain or people-oriented (conceptual-behavioral). These facts seem to defy logic. We would tend to think that task emphasis would be more effective in producing results. The reverse appears to be true. That is, emphasis on people and their needs produces better results. It suggests that if managers take care of their people, the people in turn will take care of the work.

In many organizations it is necessary to differentiate activities and at the same time provide for integration. Both processes have to be considered in dealing with the inevitable conflicts that arise in the process of formulating a strategy and designing a structure to carry it out. One of the most critical factors in the implementation of a decision is having the right people (who are motivated to achieve the objective) in the right jobs. Not only must goals be clearly specified, but they must be communicated clearly to all parts of the organization and must be repeated from time to time. Recognizing the differences in people is critically important to the success of the group. People are not interchangeable; each individual has unique characteristics, and when one individual in a group is changed, the character of the group changes.

## The Team Approach

Because formal organization structures inhibit communication and interaction among personnel, there is a tendency to develop subcultures that protect their turf and are less than effective when implementing decisions. A more recent approach of teamwork removes artificial organizational barriers and encourages a sense of openness. Teams share a common goal and help to focus energy by emphasizing "self-control" on the part of participants. Companies such as Nabisco have solved their labor problems when factory workers and management joined hands to solve high-tech bakery problems (Lord, 1991). Another instance of teamwork producing meaningful results was at Gould, where the total quality management approach was adopted based on cooperation that scrapped traditional methods and management–labor roles. The plant's manager, Kevin Harris, said, "I had to give up my ego and understand how to share decisions." The results have shown up in Gould's improved performance (Sanchez, 1991).

There are many problems that are best solved by team effort. The question arises as to what characteristics of teams facilitate effective problem solving. In general, teams that are cohesive, that interact cooperatively with members possessing compatible personality characteristics, and that are operating under mild to moderate (but not extreme) pressure appear to be most effective. In addition, patterns of communication and the leadership available will also significantly affect performance. A feeling of cohesiveness among members is the most influential determinant of behavior. Cohesive groups experience a high degree of attraction to the group, feel good about their membership, and tend to want to "stick together." Highly cohesive groups work harder than those with low cohesiveness. The fact that they are likely to do so regardless of outside supervision is of particular significance. In addition to feeling a sense of cohesiveness, the members must also be identified with, or feel enthusiastic about, the goals of the group—that is, the problem to be solved. A highly cohesive group is well launched on a successful problem-solving venture if the members feel enthusiastic about the assigned problem, provided the solution is reasonably within reach of the group's capabilities.

Membership in cohesive groups increases the likelihood of member responses that are helpful in problem solving. Cohesiveness generally will increase under the following conditions:

1. When members feel that they are highly valued by the group.
2. When the members are in a cooperative rather than competitive relationship with each other.
3. When they have full opportunity for social interactions.
4. When the group is small.

Group cohesiveness is reduced:

1. When false expectations are raised about the group.
2. When a few members dominate things.
3. When disagreement or failure is experienced too often.

The administrator reading this list may feel overwhelmed by the many things to keep in mind when forming a problem-solving group. Yet each factor, considered by itself, can readily be controlled by relatively simple effort on the part of the group leader or the administrator responsible for the group.

When selecting members for a group, the question of personality compatibility has been raised. It is possible to assess individual personality traits and, thus, to assemble groups whose members are compatible. Such groups should be more productive than groups with incompatible members. Generally, the assessment of personality is a complex process and raises questions about the feasibility of selecting compatible group members in any precise fashion in an organizational setting. Successful groups appear to follow similar patterns. In a series of studies of airplane crews that had to solve the problem of surviving after bailing out over enemy territory, three principal procedures were followed by successful crews. They were able:

1. To make sense of an initially unstructured, unclear situation (a necessary first step in many problem situations).
2. To resume communication among members.
3. To establish a goal to work toward.

The problems of business groups are rarely so critical, or presented in such a challenging setting, yet the procedures for solving problems presumably would be the same.

Margerison and McCann (1985) have developed a team approach that is used for training purposes, development, and more effective problem solving. They have an index called the TMI (team management index) that has been used by a number of companies including Hewlett-Packard, Dupont, Mobil, and Shell. The index covers four basic behaviors that have been observed when people work together in teams and also shows preferences for belonging to or being a member of a team. These include exploring, advising, controlling, and organizing. Their research with over 4,000 managers has shown that the key aspects of work behavior that the TMI measures includes the following:

1. *Advising:* These individuals obtain and disseminate information to others who can use it.
2. *Innovating:* These individuals are very creative and willing to experiment with new ideas and pass these ideas along.
3. *Promoting:* These individuals search for new opportunities and are constantly looking for ways to persuade others to pursue what they have found.
4. *Developing:* These individuals are very good at assessing and testing how well new approaches apply to the particular problems that are being pursued by the team.
5. *Organizing:* These individuals are very good at establishing and implementing the means for making things work, including relationships, assignments, and organization structure.
6. *Producing:* These individuals focus on establishing procedures and practice so that the performance can be done on a more systematic basis and desired results achieved.
7. *Inspecting:* These individuals are the ones who check and audit the performance of the system to ensure that it is meeting its targets and goals.
8. *Maintaining:* These are the people who ensure that processes continue and that standards are met.

There is considerable similarity between the team approach and the approach described that is used in management control systems. The team approach involves planning effectively and facilitates performance appraisal as well as career planning. The TMI is very helpful in training for team building as well as individual development. It provides a tool for managers that allows them to be more effective in carrying out their functions.

# ▲ PROBLEMS IN USING MANAGEMENT CONTROLS FOR IMPLEMENTATION

Why haven't management controls been effective as part of the implementation of decisions? It is partly because of the manner in which the approach to control has been taken. If we look at control simply as a closed-looped feedback system, then obviously all that is needed to correct performance is to take some form of appropriate action. This is reactive and has a negative connotation, whereas generally what is needed is a proactive, positive, and anticipatory approach. Organizations will experience the behavior they reward. Corrective action tells the worker what *not* to do, but not what *to* do. However, this approach does not consider a number of substantive issues such as do we have adequate information to understand the reality of a situation? Also, do measures used indicate true performance? More often than not, what is observed is not what has actually happened.

Perhaps the most important consideration is the fact that there are changing concepts of control. In the past, there has been too much emphasis on the control of individual activities — rather than understanding their interdependencies and the results that might be expected. For example, profitability may not improve performance although it is conceivable that a higher rate of profit might be achieved if different decisions were made.

Another consideration is the problem of cost control. Cost is primarily a result of expenditures and is only incurred after an activity has been carried out. Once cost has been incurred, there is a "Humpty Dumpty" effect; that is, once money has been spent, it is gone and can't be used again. Thus, cost control cannot be viewed in terms of a historical perspective. At best, what managers can do is estimate or anticipate future costs, and then control the activities related to those costs. For example, if an individual bought a piece of equipment and it was nonreturnable, then cost has been incurred. If this cost exceeded the available resources, the situation is out of control. In effect, procuring the equipment should not have been permitted.

In a comparable sense, budgets cannot achieve control. At best, budgets are merely estimates or plans of how to allocate the limited resources of any organization. The budget represents an overall allocation and rarely can deal with the many details that it takes to carry out specific decisions. As such, it provides an overall guideline dealing with the level of resources available and with the question of resource allocation. However, in terms of performance, the budget alone cannot ensure meeting a desired performance goal.

Another misconception concerning control is the issue of cost improvement or cost reduction. When managers focus on a single approach as the basis for taking corrective action, inevitably this will be incorrect. For example, rather than reducing costs, what might be needed is increased expenditures in another area; or if sales are dropping, another option is to reduce the sales force and the production workers to match the new forecast. An approach taken by International Rectifier during the period when transistors flooded the marketplace was to shift their engineering workforce to sales; they actually increased their sales rather than following the downward projection. In any situation, a single factor used as the basis for control will inevitably lead to an incorrect or suboptimal decision.

# ▲ MAKING MANAGEMENT CONTROLS WORK

Making management controls work is an important element of implementation and effective decision making. To make control useful, a number of criteria can be applied, such as:

1. Identification of critical factors using decision criteria as the basis for analysis or comparison between actual and desired performance. In many respects, this is comparable to problem formulation because before controls can be put to work, one must identify what needs correction.

2. Operating on symptoms is an inappropriate control approach. Rather, what is needed is a way of identifying the underlying causes of any problems, and using the symptoms as flags or indicators that there may be a serious situation that needs correction.

3. Before corrective action is taken, the cost and benefit should be examined. Then the appropriate corrective action can be determined. In many respects, this is comparable to problem solving, because the decision maker must understand the constraints limiting what can be done to correct a system.

4. The decision environment is an important concern and the manager must take this into account when attempting to change or correct any aspect of performance.

5. Corrective action is needed when performance is poor or decisions are wrong. Corrective action should lead to improved performance.

6. A management control system must relate the needs of the organization to the needs of the individual. The functions of an organization must be consistent with:
   a. The demands.
   b. Technology.
   c. External environmental forces.
   d. Member personal needs.

Management controls in organizations are different from ones used in technical systems, such as quality control or inventory control. Drucker (1954) has stated this succinctly: "Controls in a social institution are goal setting and value setting, they are not objective, they are of necessity moral. The only way to avoid this is to flood the executive with so many controls that the entire system becomes meaningless, becomes mere noise and this means that the basic question is not how do we control but what do we measure in our control system. That we can quantify something is no reason at all for measuring it. The question that should be asked: is this what the manager should consider important; is this what a manager's attention should be focused on; is this a true statement of the basic realities of the enterprise; and is this the proper focus for control, i.e. effective direction with maximum economy of effort?"

Some work environments require strict and demanding management control systems that assure quality output, as in mass-production manufacturing. In the United States, quality control is often separated from manufacturing and is carried out by sampling methods. Thus, problems are identified after the fact. Parts are scrapped and new parts made, which results in additional costs and time delays. In Japan, the manufacturing and quality control functions are combined with the worker responsible for producing quality parts. This simultaneity produces savings in both cost and time. When a worker is held responsible for the quality of work produced, responsibility is taken more seriously. In this way, the worker—not a checker— examines the product. Making the worker responsible for the quality of the work produced is "control at the point of action."

Diesing (1962) described social systems as an "attempt to change personalities and social relations in the direction of greater harmony and stability. This type of decision may be called an integrative decision. Integrative and maximizing decisions are opposite in several ways. A maximizing decision begins with given ends which it accepts unquestioningly and attempts to achieve. An integrative process treats given ends as clues and symptoms, as hidden beliefs, values, fears, strains, etc., which are not necessarily to be satisfied at all and which may frequently be frustrated in the course of being changed." Still another perspective is offered by Levinson (1978), who discussed the issue of dealing with aberrant behavior where "sometimes in a misguided effort to stimulate the subordinate, the manager offers the possibility of greater responsibility and more active participation in decision making. Such gestures are even more threatening to those who are already immobilized. Sometimes the manager actually promotes such a person in the vain hope that the subordinate will change when he or she has more responsibility or returns from a management development course. If a subordinate is characteristically rigid, dependent or impulsive, he or she is likely to become more so under increasing stress, which is what the pressure of the boss becomes."

Management control systems are not universally accepted. Maerstin, when he was president of Lubrizol (Vanderwicken, 1975), disdained many of the rituals of modern management controls. He learned how to manage the company, he said, from the people in it. "I refuse to go to any management school, because I think that's a waste of time, like for example, long-range planning." He chastised one of his vice-presidents for reading books on management. He insisted on a lean and efficient operation and didn't think it necessary to have a lot of paperwork lying around on an executive's desk. Maerstin pointed out that bureaucracy, the basis used by many companies to "maintain control" over various phases of their business or to assist in decision making, is unnecessary. For example, all pricing decisions at Lubrizol are made by an eight-man committee that can meet at a moment's notice to match any of the competitors' prices. The company has no formal job descriptions and few standard procedures, and employees are simply expected to do their jobs as efficiently as they can. Obviously, this system can be described as a very flexible, adaptive, people-oriented system, rather than one that uses the formal management controls characterized by the typical organization.

Lincoln Electric Company has been considered an efficient company for many years. They expanded over the years as producers of electrical machinery, principally in welding machines and alternating-current motors. The economies realized at Lincoln are based on eliminating the nonessentials, getting by without many of the functions that other companies accept as necessary for doing business. For example, they have simple offices, no elaborate lobby, and no executive dining room, and expendable paperwork is ruthlessly eliminated, as are jobs that consume a considerable amount of time and labor but don't contribute to the final product. Most important, Lincoln employees continuously search for savings by means of a many-faceted program of incentive management (Mrowca, 1983).

## ▲ ▲ ▲ ▲ ▲ CASE: TOP HEAVY MANAGEMENT STIFLES PRODUCTIVITY

Executives comprise only a small portion of any organization and depend on others for carrying out decisions that have been made. Increasingly, it has become obvious that a top-heavy management becomes a "bottleneck" preventing decisions from being made and thereby stifling productivity. Thurow (1985) suggests that participative management can prevent hard-nosed American managers from being driven out by keen foreign competition. He cites as an example the 6.8 percent rise in real output in 1984 while executive employment increased 8 percent and accountant employment increased 12 percent. He concludes there is an overabundance of top-level executives who have not learned how to participate or to form teams, resulting in an overemphasis on control as opposed to operation.

While the executive suite may be overstuffed, the middle managers are being dismantled, according to Flanigan (1984). He equates the corporate ladder to a museum piece that belongs in a museum, not in business. Many white collar workers over age 40 will have to be retrained for second careers, and those who remain will have to be able to adapt to the pervasive change confronting our business system. IBM already has redrawn its reporting structure to realign its top executives and eliminate one layer of management. They hope that this will allow them to respond more quickly to market changes ("IBM Redraws," 1991).

Hewlett-Packard has also had to rethink how it operates because "a suffocating bureaucracy got in the way" (Buell, Hof, and McWilliams, 1991). As an example of the problem confronting Hewlett-Packard, Bob Frankenberg, the general manager, had 38 committees with which he had to interact. They made the decisions on computer features, software, product launching, and similar activities. John Young, HP's president, concluded that this was too much decision overhead and thus needed to be changed. While HP encouraged innovation, abolished rigid chains of command, and created a friendly open organization, the open culture failed to prevent slippage of schedules because of the burdensome bureaucracy. The numerous committees prevented decision making. The result is that Frankenberg now deals with 3 committees instead of the original 38.

In a drastic move to slash bureaucracy, Texaco planned to eliminate 12 layers of operations to streamline its organization (Woutat, 1989). Texaco had the reputation of a company where nobody could make a decision. A major reason for the cutback was to push decision making down to where it was needed by use of participative management and more risk taking. Faced with the dramatic $11 billion court award for the Pennzoil fiasco and with the imminent takeover attempt by Carl Icahn, Texaco had to take drastic action (Vogel and Bremner, 1991). The new CEO, James Kinnear, has shed the company of $7 billion in assets, eliminated 10,965 employees, and reshaped most of the company's operations. Kinnear has transformed Texaco from a rigid company to one that is focused, innovative, and a growing force in the industry.

## ▲ Summary

The material presented in this chapter covers a very critical element of decision making concerned with achieving results. This requires an understanding of motivation, teamwork, quality, and the control process needed to ensure progress and measure performance. The details of implementation can be viewed from a number of perspectives. The one chosen here is to emphasize the operational aspects of control as they impinge on the organization's ability to perform effectively. One of the important issues raised is the distinction between technical control and behavioral considerations. Ultimately, the only real control is a workers's "self-control." That is, by knowing who they are, their personalities and styles, workers can better understand themselves and how best to interact with the organization.

A number of models describing how organizations implement decisions (for example, MBO) were covered to provide guidance in establishing operating control systems. In addition, other models were introduced that describe span of control, loose and tight control, and other concepts felt useful in accomplishing management's ultimate goal of achieving meaningful and sustainable results.

## ▲ Study Questions

1. What are the five basic approaches to control?
2. Why is motivation an important consideration?
3. What determines motivation?
4. How does one achieve a positive self-image?
5. How is the Porter, Lawler, and Hackman model related to expectancy?

6. What kinds of reports can management receive in a behaviorally anchored control system?
7. What is the role of computers in control?
8. What are control styles?
9. What is meant by "span of control"?
10. How is the Pareto Law used?
11. What is the difference between MBO and PMS?
12. Why does teamwork improve performance?
13. What are the major problems in implementation?
14. What is needed to make management control work?

## ▲ References

Argyris, Chris. "How Tomorrow's Executives Will Make Decisions." *Think* (November–December, 1967).

Beer, Mitchell, and Ruh, Robert A. "Employee Growth through Performance Management." *Harvard Business Review* (August 1976).

Buell, Barbara, and Hof, Robert D., with McWilliams, Gary. "Hewlett-Packard Rethinks Itself." *Business Week* (April 1, 1991), pp. 76–79.

Dalton, Gene W., and Lawrence, Paul R. *Motivation and Control in Organizations*. Homewood, IL: Richard D. Irwin, Inc., 1971, p. 6.

Deci, E. L. "The Effects of Externally Directed Mediated Rewards on Intrinsic Motivation." *Journal of Personality and Social Psychology* Vol. 18 (1971).

Diesing, Paul. *Reason in Society*. Westport, CT: Greenwood Press, 1962.

Drucker, Peter F. *The Practice of Management*. New York: Harper Bros., 1954.

Flanigan, James. "Middle Part of the Corporate Ladder Is Being Chopped Away." *Los Angeles Times* (April 22, 1984).

Forrester, Jay. *Industrial Dynamics*. Boston: M.I.T. Press, 1961.

Granick, David. *The Red Manager*. New York: Doubleday, 1960.

Greene, C. N., and Cralt, R. E. "The Satisfaction-Performance Controversy." *Business Horizons* 15 (1972), pp. 31–41.

Hofstede, Geert. "The Cultural Relativity of the Quality of Life Concept." *Academy of Management Review* Vol. 9, No. 3 (1984), pp. 389–398.

"IBM Redraws its Flow Chart of Top Officers." *Los Angeles Times* (August 2, 1991).

Keeley, Michael. "Impartiality and Participant Interest: Theories of Organizational Effectiveness." *Administrative Science Quarterly* (March 1984), p. 1.

Levinson, Harry. "Management by Whose Objectives?" *Harvard Business Review* Vol. 48 (1970).

Levinson, Harry. "The Abrasive Personality." *Harvard Business Review* Vol. 56, No. 3 (1978).

Locke, E. A. "Toward a Theory of Task Motivation and Incentive." *Organizational Behavior & Human Performance* Vol. 3, (1968), pp. 157–189.

Lord, Mary. "How Nabisco Solved its Labor Problem." *U.S. News* (May 20, 1991), p. 60.

Margerison, C. J., and McCann, D. J. "The Team Management Index." New Berlin, WI: National Consulting and Training Institute, 1985.

McGregor, Douglas Murray. "Adventures in Thought and Action: Proceedings of the Fifth Anniversary Convocation of the School of Industrial Management." Cambridge, MA: Technology Press, April 9, 1957.

Mrowca, Maryann. "Ohio Firm Relies on Incentive-Pay System to Motivate Workers and Maintain Profits." *Wall Street Journal* (August 12, 1983), p. 23.

Nord, Walter R. *Concepts and Controversy in Organizational Behavior.* Pacific Palisades, CA: Goodyear Publishing, 1976.

Patz, Alan L., and Rowe, Alan J. *Management Control and Decision Systems.* New York: Wiley, 1977.

Porter, Lyman W., Lawler, Edward E., III, and Hackman, J. Richard. *Behavior in Organizations.* New York: McGraw-Hill, 1975.

Richards, Max D., and Greenlaw, Paul S. *Management Decisions and Behavior.* Homewood, IL: Richard D. Irwin, Inc., 1972.

Ridgway, V. F. "Disfunctional Consequences of Performance Measurement." *Administrative Science Quarterly* No. 2 (September 1956).

Rowe, Alan J. "Competitive Advantage Based Concurrency." USC, December 1990.

Sanchez, Jesus. "Cooperation Forges a Success Story." *Los Angeles Times* (April 26, 1991), p. D1.

Sherwin, Douglas S. "Management of Objectives." *Harvard Business Review* (May–June 1976), p. 149.

Singular, Stephen. "Has MBO Failed?" *MBA* (October 1975), p. 47–48.

Thurow, Lester C. "Top-Heavy Management Stifles Productivity." *Los Angeles Times* (September 15, 1985), Part V, p. 3.

Tosi, Henry L., and Hamner, Clay W. *Organizational Behavior and Management.* Chicago, IL: St. Clair Press, 1974.

Vanderwicken, Peter. "Lubrizol Ignores the Management Manuals." *Fortune* (February 1975), pp. 132–140.

Vogel, Todd, with Bremner, Brian. "Texaco: From Takeover Bait to Dynamo." *Business Week* (July 22, 1991), p. 50–52.

Vroom, V. H. *Work and Motivation.* New York: Wiley, 1964.

Woutat, Donald. "Texaco Plans to Slash Bureaucracy." *Los Angeles Times* (March 8, 1989), Part IV, p. 3.

# Part III

# DECISION-AIDING TOOLS

# 8

# Creative Problem Solving and Decision Making

▲ ▲ ▲  ▲ ▲ ▲ ▲ ▲ ▲ ▲ ▲ ▲ ▲ ▲ ▲ ▲ ▲ ▲

Some managers are more effective at solving problems than others. Some managers are willing to examine a large number of alternatives and often can find good solutions. Or they are willing to take risks in order to come up with good solutions. Other managers tend to avoid solutions involving risk taking. An achievement-oriented manager seeks a challenge and looks at problems as a means of achieving personal goals.

Because managers differ in their decision styles, attitudes, and needs, they use different approaches to solving problems. For example, a high cognitively complex manager will take the time needed to examine many alternatives. He or she will be careful in developing and implementing solutions. On the other hand, a directive style manager typically will focus on results rather than finding the best solution. This manager emphasizes giving answers rather than asking the right questions.

This chapter covers a number of the means used by managers to solve problems. The following indicates some of the questions that are covered:

1. What aptitudes do managers have for finding and solving complex problems?
2. How do they perceive or recognize problems?
3. What approaches do they use to find solutions?
4. How do they gain acceptance for solutions?

## ▲ PROBLEM SOLVING

Successful problem solving is more often a matter of the manager's attitude than a matter of the method or approach used. Consider the case of a student who moved to a new job before completing his MBA degree. He requested permission from the business school's associate dean to take his last two courses at a university in the city where he had moved. The permission was granted and the student completed the two courses. When he applied to the school where he had started his degree, the registrar who reviewed requirements for completion of credits concluded that one of the two courses taken at the other university was the equivalent of an undergraduate course. Because of this, the registrar refused to approve the granting of the MBA degree to the student. Another compounding aspect of the problem was that the associate dean who had originally granted permission was no longer at the business school.

The new associate dean, when confronted with this highly agitated student, looked for a way to help the student graduate. His attitude was that the student had completed the requirements for the degree. The question now was how to deal with the registrar, who had rejected the student's request for the degree. After considerable discussion with the assistant dean, the new associate dean recommended that the student be given retroactive permission to take an undergraduate course. Using an approved undergraduate elective was an allowable procedure for completing the requirements of an MBA degree. Following this recommendation, the student was granted his degree, and what might have been a difficult situation was resolved because of the new associate dean's attitude.

This example illustrates how an effective decision maker is able to find solutions that work and are acceptable. In many cases, the solution per se is not critical, but rather it is the behavior of the people involved. The student who reasonably expected his MBA degree benefited from the associate dean's willingness to find a solution rather than relying strictly on administrative procedures.

Too often we think logically about problems, but what is needed is "lateral or zigzag" thinking. Debono (1969) cites an example of a small hotel whose elevators were very slow. At first, management decided a new, faster elevator was needed to service the guests adequately. Instead, a mirror was installed next to the old elevator. Recognizing people's behavior was the clue: All people look at themselves in a mirror, and thus the guests didn't mind waiting after the mirror was installed. The solution dealt with the problem "laterally" rather than in the ordinary, straightforward, logical manner.

Just as there are many ways to solve problems, there are many considerations that need to be taken into account. For example, the elevator problem involved behavior, cost, service, and the delay to which people objected. The solution also involved behavioral as well as cost considerations. Once the mirrors were installed, the guests didn't mind waiting.

How often has an apparent salary problem been resolved once the manager realized that the solution was to provide more responsibility or greater latitude of work for the subordinate? Because decisions involve humans, there is no way to escape the reality that all decisions made in an organization have behavioral aspects that must be dealt with if the decision is to be accepted and carried out as planned. Acceptance, in turn, depends on people's expectations.

As an example of problem solving in Singapore, housing inspectors were being given lunch by building contractors. The government obviously objected to this practice, but could not prevent it. The government's solution was to make lunch a required practice on the job, thus reducing its possible effect as bribery. Ideally, decision makers would accept challenges, avoid conformity, know how to compromise, create a supportive and trusting environment, and be able to find solutions to problems — solutions that will be accepted.

Japanese companies have emphasized conformity for such a long period of time that they are finding it difficult to break out of the mold and become more creative (Watanabe, 1990). To encourage creativity, Canon has built brainstorming rooms, Fujitsu has built partitions to ensure privacy, Hitachi is whittling away at cumbersome middle management, and Toshiba has recognized the latent creative talent of women workers. The Japanese have found that creativity sometimes is enhanced by privacy, but there are times that interaction increases creativity. The thinking at Canon is that "creativity is rooted in the individual so the individual needs freedom and time to think." At Toshiba, women are given the opportunity to do research and to be creative. Apparently, Japanese women approach research more flexibly and with more patience than men. Females are considered more adventurous and willing to look beyond the books and papers. Matsushita had "Breakthrough" as its slogan for 1990. The company recognizes the need to focus on applying totally new technology for new inventions; however, not a single Japanese researcher is willing to take the risk, so Matsushita is staffing its research lab with foreign scientists.

How does a company compete with the Japanese? Connor Peripherals uses nonstop innovation to keep ahead of competitors. What they found was that the Japanese were their main competitor for personal computer components, including memory chips, displays, transformers, and even floppy disks. Connor succeeded by doing ordinary things extraordinarily well. They use incremental improvements in their products rather than radical departures. They make frequent improvements so that customers know that new products won't be far off. When expanding factory facilities, they keep the processes that have been proven efficient. They work relentlessly against excessive bureaucracy and simplify everything they possibly can. The key to Connor's success while involving continuous innovation is to gear new products to customer wants. Thus, no new product is designed without a firm commitment from a major customer. This translates into the philosophy of "Sell first, then design and then build" (Kupfer, 1990).

## ▲ THE PROBLEM-SOLVING PROCESS

The process shown in Figure 8.1 reveals an important element in problem solving–the role of a manager's perception. The process normally starts with identifying what needs to be done;

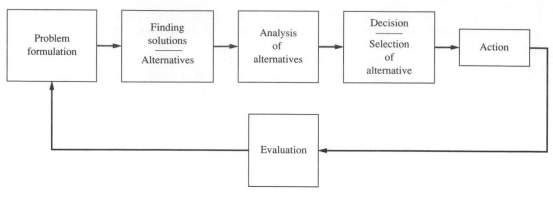

**Figure 8.1   ▲   The Problem-Solving Process**

then the reason for the change is determined; finally, the most likely cause of the problem is identified.

The first step in the problem-solving process is the identification and formulation or description of the problem. This depends upon the perception and understanding of the decision maker who must solve the problem. Once the problem has been identified, there is a search for solutions or alternatives. From the set of alternatives, which may be large in number, judgment based on experience is used to select the most likely alternatives for analysis. The analysis of alternatives leads to the decision to act on one of the alternatives. The final decision to act on a specific alternative may not be based on technical or financial considerations alone. Environmental, social, or behavioral considerations may dictate that a lesser alternative be selected in order to comply with social values.

For example, a high traffic-generating shopping mall might not be put in a residential area because of residents' objections to traffic congestion and pollution, even though the shopping mall would generate high tax increments that would finance much needed community services. The ultimate consideration is not the financial return, but the environmental consideration of the community members. The community members are the ones with the votes, which carries considerable weight in political decision making. We can readily see from this example that business and political decisions are interrelated. Finally, the results of the action taken are evaluated compared with the initial problem to determine whether it has been properly resolved.

What we see depends on how we perceive things and how well we are able to deal with complexity. The analytic and conceptual styles have little difficulty with complex problems; the directive and behavioral styles would be uncomfortable with highly complex problems. There is also a question of what we see. Facts are not always facts. Often we rely on available data that have been reported but not verified or on data that require judgment to determine what they mean. In one case, computer reports showed that costs were almost on budget for a project. When the cost analyst was questioned about the accuracy of the data, the response was, "Well, it's within 30 percent of what it should be." Unfortunately, the project managers were making decisions as though the data were factual and accurate.

In addition to the level of complexity and accuracy of data, what we see depends on our span of attention. For example, the brain operates in three basic modes: the Beta mode at 24 cycles per second, the Alpha mode at 8 cycles, and the Theta mode at 4 cycles. Each of these modes reflects different levels of attention. Beta is the one that is normally used in conversation, Alpha is used when we are relaxed, and Theta when we are about to doze off.

Our level of attention is related to the speed of our brain waves. The Theta mode is our most creative thinking mode. Thomas Edison and Henry Ford were said to frequently function in the Theta mode, and they both were prolific inventors.

## ▲ THE DECISION MAKER AS A PROBLEM SOLVER

Effective managers solve problems rather than make excuses. For example, in Singapore, to protect the environment, burning of refuse is prohibited on building sites. A contractor faced with the problem of disposing of the refuse without spending a huge amount to have it carted away explored his options. He realized that he could put a small amount in with the normal trash collection, thus avoiding a fine for burning the trash or paying for hauling it away in one load. At Hughes Aircraft Company, a computer-driven plotter called ADMA was developed to produce large, inked drawings for the air force. The largest drawing was eight feet long. When the air force requested 16-foot drawings, the department head responsible for the project called a meeting of the programmers. They said the computer program was not designed to handle those large drawings. After almost three hours of discussion, the department head suggested that the computer program act as though it was "pasting" two drawings together. "Impossible," said the programmers. The department head persisted and asked that they at least try the proposed method. They did, and it worked like a charm. The alternative would have been two years of effort to rewrite the computer program. What do these two solutions have in common? They both were in response to a need. In each case, a responsible individual was able to see a way to solve the problem that did not merely pursue a brute-force approach. There was an attitude that "it can be done, so let's try."

People cannot be simply pigeonholed into unique categories such as thinkers, feelers, or doers (Koble, 1990). Unfortunately, many approaches to understanding the decision maker rely on finding unique traits or personality styles. Koble's approach relies on thinking "patterns" that take into account all aspects of the manager's personality. The advantage to this approach is that it recognizes that we all have some potential for making things happen. Koble described this as the instinct to act. Instinct facilitates our ability to probe or find facts, to follow up on those findings, and to do something about what we have found. The creative force in each of us depends on cognition (the power to know), affection (the ability to feel or emote), and conation (the potential to act). Thus, a truly creative person not only finds or knows what needs to be done, but is able to carry out the actions required. This is consistent with the perspective that the attitude to try, as described in the graduate student problem, is more than half the battle to finding creative solutions that work.

The ability to manage intellectuals is an art because these are people with high cognitive complexity who prefer dealing with ideas rather than with tangible problems, who have minds of their own, who demonstrate originality, and who are compulsive about sharing their ideas with others (Donovan, 1989). Managers want some degree of discipline and control, both of which are anathema to highly creative intellectuals. It is almost like presiding over a group bent on anarchy. An example is the attempt by the RAND Corporation to have their intellectuals and Nobel Prize winners clock in when they arrived for work in the morning. The reality was that most of these individuals worked odd hours, often far into the night, to solve a problem on which they were working. Asking them to clock in would be tantamount to telling them they were doing something wrong. Recognizing the potential conflict, RAND management assigned the guards the job of identifying each employee and merely using a recording machine to "in effect" clock in for the individual. This saved a potentially explosive situation.

Unfortunately, highly intellectual people are really never totally committed to the organization. In sociological terms, they are cosmopolitans who associate more with their profession than with the organization. The intellectual rarely agrees with the manager and probably wouldn't be considered as having a fine mind if he or she did. When a critical situation arises, what needs to be done is to be sure that the intellectual is given a fair hearing rather than be "told what to do." Another approach that has been found to work is to ask creative intellectuals to set their own targets. Once having committed to meet a goal, they are ultra high achievers and will do all within their power to succeed. Knowing style gives the manager insight into dealing with these valuable but generally unmanageable employees.

## ▲ PROBLEM FORMULATION

Recognition of a problem, sometimes called problem formulation, is often considered the most important aspect of problem solving. At this phase, the problem solver explores a situation that may or may not be well defined. The manager attempts to structure the problem in a form that can lead to a solution. Unfortunately, because of perceptual biases, the manner in which a problem is stated often determines the possibility of its being solved. The elements of problem formulation are often stated as follows:

1. Criteria are needed to help determine what is important and what to look for.
2. Symptoms are the first indication of a problem and provide the basis for search of information.
3. Deviations from norms signify a problem and help determine what to look for.
4. Patterns or clues are used to provide insight into cause and effect.
5. Questioning, involvement, and participation help find information about the real problem.

As a basis for formulating problems, Elbing (1978) has proposed a number of criteria.

1. Do not accept information at face value, because language alters and distorts.
2. Distinguish facts from opinions.
3. Differentiate facts, inferences, speculation, and assumptions.
4. Determine underlying causes. Avoid fixing blame. Avoid value judgments because of possible emotional bias. Avoid the tendency to evaluate prematurely.
5. Avoid the tendency to search for a single cause.
6. Be explicit and avoid generalizations about human problems.

An approach such as this provides the decision maker some assurance of not missing relevant information and of avoiding errors. Elbing also proposed a framework as the basis for understanding the problem situation as shown in Figure 8.2.

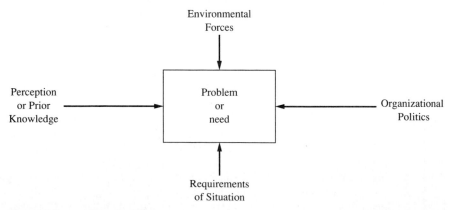

Figure 8.2　▲　Frame of Reference

## ▲ EVALUATION OF ALTERNATIVES

Using the guidelines just cited, how should one analyze alternative solutions, particularly when symptoms or available data are inadequate and do not reflect what has happened? People's motives, drives, aspirations, power struggles, tensions, and anxiety are all factors related to real problems. Thus, data may not represent the real "facts." More often than not, facts represent what an individual would like others to think rather than the true situation.

Decision-aiding tools have helped identify underlying problems even though they are not otherwise obvious. Using appropriate analyses, a manager is better able to recognize patterns that provide clues to the true underlying problem. One of the most successful approaches used to specify the causes of problems was developed by Kepner and Tregoe (1963). Their approach involved recognizing problems by identifying "deviations" to determine possible causes. Once the cause was determined, decisions were made regarding alternative actions, including an assessment of adverse consequences. Plans were developed to take into account future problems, and contingency plans were set to provide control and prevent recurrence of the problem.

Evaluation of solutions depends on a number of considerations, such as urgency, priority of the problem, resources available, and cost–benefit trade-offs. An interesting case was posed by a management club that was having attendance problems and was losing money at dinner meetings. The club president wanted to increase the dues to offset the deficit. However, this approach would tend to further decrease attendance. What was proposed as an alternative was to reduce the dues and encourage greater participation in the club. In addition, reservations would be required for the dinner but not for the meeting. In this way, people could attend the dinner and the meeting, or just the meeting. Thus, the dinner would be scaled proportionately to the number of people making reservations and there would not be any loss. This approach also achieved another important objective, which was to increase attendance. After all, this was the rationale for having a management club in the first place.

Judgment is an important means used to evaluate solutions. Judgment, however, is based on information that is perceived, processed, and transformed by the human mind. Judgment depends on perception, but perception is generally selective because humans have limited memory capacity and rely on simple procedures, rules, or heuristics.

Judgment has been used to develop heuristics based on similarity or resemblance (Tversky, 1977). Similarity can be represented as a collection of features. However, because the human mind can only capture a limited number of features, heuristics may not be able to determine whether an object belongs to a given category, or if several objects belong to the same category. Heuristics also may make poor predictions about causes of a problem based on what has been observed. Individuals also make judgments about frequencies of events and about causal relationships (Tversky and Kahneman, 1975). Of course, everyday judgments could not be made quickly and effectively without heuristics. Nonetheless, these rapid judgments, although reasonable, can be biased and need to be carefully examined.

Another concern is that people's beliefs and values affect the amount of search they are willing to do. People tend to be selective in choosing information that supports their existing beliefs or values. Data that oppose existing beliefs will generally be rejected. Beliefs persist even when there is discrediting of evidence on which the beliefs were based (Hogarth, 1980). Because judgment and heuristics depend on how we think, it is important to recognize and deal with limitations that result from perceptual bias, strongly held beliefs, and values that are not congruent with the goals of the organization and that may lead to possible errors in judgment.

## ▲ CREATIVE PROBLEM SOLVING

Ideas can occur at any time. They are often spontaneous and generally are unexpected. The most fruitful ideas may be based on feedback or may simply stem from being in a situation that provides new ideas. Creativity involves coming up with new patterns, new ideas, and new arrangements that solve a problem. Creative approaches to problem solving can be categorized as follows:

1. *Free association:* approaches such as brainstorming.
2. *Structured relationships:* techniques such as preparing lists.
3. *Analytical:* use of quantitative approaches.
4. *Dialectic approaches:* structured debate and opposite positioning.
5. *Nominal group technique:* facilitates group interaction.

Brainstorming has been used for many years and is a means of bringing a number of individuals together to explore possible solutions. Rules for brainstorming are summarized as:

| | |
|---|---|
| No criticism | Anything goes |
| The wilder the better | Be spontaneous |
| Keep it short | Volume of ideas |
| Don't explain | Positive atmosphere |
| Suspend judgment | Record all ideas |

A novel idea may be interesting, but to be creative it must also be useful.

Structured relationships, including listing and cataloguing, appear to have the potential of stimulating thinking that would not occur if there was no need. Examples of lists include words such as *adapt, modify, minify, substitute, rearrange*, and *reverse*.

Analytical approaches typically are used to examine complex relationships. Individuals who think logically are better able to construct new ideas or associations when information is presented in an analytical format. *Synectics* (Gordon, 1961) is a Greek word meaning the joining together of apparently different or irrelevant elements. The integration of diverse perspectives focuses on the use of psychological mechanisms that enhance creative activity. Synectics reinforces the systematic use of analogical reasoning that helps relate concepts based on some similarity that results in a metaphor. A metaphor assumes equivalence and similarities that consider features that are common among the concepts. A metaphor relates a number of concepts, such as "The sky is blue." The relations can also deal with conditions, such as "Freedom requires responsibility." Analogical reasoning helps the discovery of links between apparently distant terms to provide a new perspective.

Dialectical thinking is another approach that critically examines current assumptions underlying a proposed solution (Veregara, 1977). Dialectics is the process of exploring two opposing solutions to the same problem that might lead to a creative synthesis. Dialectics facilitates creativity by critically examining constraints that are implicit in current thinking. These constraints can be reduced or eliminated by exploring the conflict of possible alternatives or positions that might be overlooked.

The nominal group technique presents ideas without discussion, by the use of written lists. These lists reflect members' feelings and when completed are read to the group. Priorities among the ideas are established by voting. The nominal group process does not rely on verbal interaction and avoids premature evaluation while enhancing risk taking. It also prevents using a single focus that often inhibits performance.

Managers with vision accept the premise that better opportunities exist than they are aware of (Boulgarides, 1970). When accompanied by initiative, this leads to exploratory activities aimed at finding these better opportunities. Exploration, research, investigation, and similar activities all are considered creative. In such activities, steps are taken into the unknown to find new possibilities, which may then be evaluated to determine if they are superior to those that are already known. Such activities consist essentially of prospecting for new opportunities. We can conclude that:

1. Creativity can be significantly increased if people understand the psychological process under which they operate.
2. In the creative process, the emotional component is more important than the intellectual; the irrational more important than the rational.
3. The emotional, irrational elements must be understood to increase the success of problem solving.

Opportunities are not made; they are discovered. The possibility of flight in heavier-than-air machines, for example, has always existed and merely awaited discovery. The steps to follow in the creative process include:

1. *Search for facts and new combinations of facts.* Many successful ideas are merely new combinations of commonly known facts. The highly successful confection widely sold under many names and best described as chocolate-covered ice cream on a stick is the result of combining several simple known facts or ideas.

   In pure research, facts are sought without regard for their specific usefulness, on the premise that a stockpile of knowledge will in some way contribute to society's welfare. Progress rests, without doubt, on facts discovered from efforts to satisfy curiosity.
2. *The economic opening.* This creative step consists essentially of finding an opening through a barrier of economic and physical limitations. When aluminum was discovered, uses had to be found for it that would enable it to be marketed, and means had to be found to improve its physical characteristics and to lower its cost of manufacture.

   Economic limitations are continually changing with the needs and wants of people. Physical limitations are continually being pushed back using science. As a consequence, new openings revealing new opportunities are continually developing.
3. *Circumventing factors limiting success.* The aim of circumventing factors limiting success is related to the search for better means for achieving objectives rather than a search for better objectives.
4. *Solutions result from a search for limiting factors.* This is directly related to the selection of objectives which is without doubt the most important function and the first step toward success in any field of endeavor. Because mental processes are in large measure not illogical, this step must be approached with considerable alertness and curiosity and a willingness to consider new ideas and unconventional patterns of thought.
5. *The creative conference.* This is where a group of persons seek new opportunities or ways to circumvent limitations. In such a conference a problem is posed for solution. Those in attendance are encouraged to let their imagination run free and to suggest solutions to the problem, no matter how fantastic. No criticisms of ideas suggested are permitted on the premise that criticism would inhibit imagination. Ideas produced by the conference then are evaluated elsewhere.

Motamedi (1982) describes the creative process as evolving through seven stages that recognize that experience has a profound effect on creativity. In each stage, relationships change. The seven passages that embody the creative effort consist of:

1. *Framing:* Covers the initial experiences.
2. *Probing:* Further evolution of the initial frame.
3. *Exploration:* Attempts to implement a tentative solution based on new insights.
4. *Revelation:* Leads to discovery.

5. *Affirmation:* Confirms the value of the revelation.
6. *Reframing:* Questions are restated in the light of discovery.
7. *Realization:* The new discovery and its application are made available.

Creativity is not an elusive quality and it can be taught (Smith, 1985). What needs to be done is to break down rigid thinking that blocks new ideas. Thus, to enhance the creative process, a changed way of thinking about creativity is needed. Creativity has been found to involve the logical and intuitive aspects of thinking. Knowledge, imagination, and intuition all contribute to relating ideas and things. Creativity is not a simple process but involves different modes of thinking. Nonetheless, each individual has the propensity of becoming more creative if he or she looks at problems from a more open perspective and doesn't put a limit on imagination.

Unfortunately, individuals and organizaitons often create blocks to creativity. Organizations create environments, politics, or leadership that leads to rigid structures and is authoritarian. This can lead to a perceived threat for nonconformity, especially if there is a lack of goal congruence. Where there is tension, frustration, confusion, or a lack of self-confidence, there is a lower likelihood that creative solutions would be expected. In addition, timing, contradictions, and conflict also block creative problem solving. Inefficient use of time, using wrong facts, or working on low-priority problems limits the creative possibilities.

From a pragmatic perspective, creative solutions are useful if they find workable rather than "best" solutions, and if they involve a search for opportunity rather than merely responding to a problem. Thus, creative approaches extend the boundaries of the problem to find meaningful solutions. They also permit the redefinition of goals when initial objectives cannot readily be achieved.

## ▲  INTUITION IN PROBLEM SOLVING

Intuition has been identified as one of the more important aspects of decision making and problem solving. The intuitive manager is one who can respond quickly because of insights based on experience and judgment. Sometimes, intuition is based on an analysis of symptoms or deviations that permits the decision maker to readily identify what is, in fact, the true situation. For example, intuition was demonstrated in Marseilles, France, when a suspect on board a fishing vessel was thought to be smuggling heroin. Unfortunately, when the naval patrol boarded the vessel, they could not find any drugs. As the naval patrol prepared to depart, one officer noticed that the boat's concrete ballast was located in the front of the ship rather than at its normal position in the center. When the ballast was examined, the patrol discovered that it was hollowed out and contained the largest cache of heroin ever found. The intuition of the naval officer helped solve the problem

Intuition is a key element in decision making because it allows the manager to make rapid and generally good decisions. Intuition is considered the reasoning used that is based on experience, analogy, or instinctive insights. It does not operate at the conscious level and thus does not rely on rational thought processes. For example, under hypnosis, the unconscious recalls many facts that the individual is not aware of having collected (Rowen, 1986). Even though this knowledge resides in our memory, it is not accessed directly, but it does influence the understanding of situations and creates impressions that become the basis for actions that are taken. Intuition is elusive but it guides our mental impressions (often called hunches). It has the ability to sift out irrelevant factors and at the same time to perceive all relevant factors impinging on a situation. Pattern matching that involves unknown reasons for choice often is based on intuition that leads to the uneasy feeling of not really being sure of how the answer came about.

Research done by Mihalasky (1969) strongly suggests that some executives have more "precognitive" ability than others. They are better able to anticipate the future intuitively rather than logically. Thus, when there are few data to support a decision, they rely on intuition. He also found that the higher an executive rises and the more complex the decisions, the more intuition is used. He showed that senior managers typically use intuition when making decisions. However, intuition does not always provide correct answers. Although problem solving often is viewed as a logical process, it generally follows a convoluted sequence.

Intuition is one of the most powerful tools the decision maker can use in terms of rapid response to a situation, especially when dealing with highly ambiguous situations, but it sometimes can lead to erroneous conclusions. Intuition depends on the mind's ability to perceive and process information. Because the human mind has difficulty in dealing with problems having many factors, a wrong or poor solution could result if intuition were the sole basis for problem solving. Facts alone are seldom enough to ensure making the right decision, and this is when instinct and intuition are most valuable (Dreyfact, 1966). Instinct is related to intuition and generally is based on logic, knowledge, and experience. When knowledge of the situation is limited, managers rely on judgment, not facts. Instinct is also useful when human behavior is involved and when timing is critical. However, although intuition is a valuable aspect of decision making, it is not equally applicable to all problems.

## ▲  CHANGE AS A PROBLEM-SOLVING APPROACH

Change is a pervasive aspect of problem solving. The following approach can be used for finding meaningful solutions:

1. Change the problem statement.
2. Change the approach used to formulate the problem.
3. Change the methods used to solve the problem.
4. Change the criteria for evaluating the solution.
5. Change the limits or the size of problem considered.

Each of these is examined next to show how they can be applied to finding solutions.

**Change the problem:** This refers to a revised statement of what one believes the problem to be. Often the only way to solve a problem is to redefine it as a problem that can be solved. Sometimes simplifying the perspective may lead to a solution; sometimes broadening the perspective is needed. An illustration is the case of a programmer who requested a full month off with pay, although his length of service entitled him to only one week's vacation. He contended that he would quit if he could not get a full month off. Defining the problem as an "all-or-nothing" ultimatum, there was no solution, because the company would neither change its vacation benefits nor allow an exception. Redefining the problem required finding a way to give the programmer a month off without changing his benefits. A solution was reached in which the programmer was given the one-week entitlement and was allowed to take one week against his next year's vacation. He also would be allowed to take another two weeks off without pay. The programer accepted this solution.

**Change the approach to formulation:** This refers to looking at the problem from a different perspective. For example, if we look at the problem as requiring a mathematical solution, we might find that none exists. On the other hand, if we look at the problem from, say, a behavioral or qualitative perspective, we might be able to solve it. This differs from changing the problem in that it is not the problem per se that is being considered; rather, it is how we look at or understand the problem. As an example, when Thomas Edison hired a new engineer, he asked him to find the volume of a complicated-shaped bulb on which he had been working. The engineer used calculus to determine that the volume was precisely 24.3 cubic centimeters. Although this approach was satisfactory, it took him all day to complete the assignment. Edison merely filled the bulb with water and then readily measured the volume of the water. The answer was close enough for Edison. His approach was to use the measuring vessel because he wanted only an approximate solution. The young engineer did not know that was what Edison wanted, and so he used mathematics to obtain a very precise result.

**Change the method:** This concerns how the problem is approached. In some instances, this means a change in method, a change in statement of the problem, or simply a different understanding of what the problem really is. Changing the approach can be thought of as considering the best way to look at the problem before attempting to solve it. If one perspective doesn't seem to work, then try another way of looking at or approaching the problem. As was described in the example of the lightbulb, there were at least two methods of solving the problem. If the younger engineer wanted to use a mathematical approach, he could have assumed that the bulb had a simple shape and found the answer in a matter of minutes rather than taking a whole day. At General Electric, the Production Department at Hickory, North Carolina, used a conventional method to schedule the transformer factory. A team of analysts was brought in to study the problem of improving factory performance. They used a computer simulation to demonstrate a potential savings of 50 percent of work-in-process inventory and an 80 percent reduction in the work cycle to produce transformers in the factory. The simulation method required special training, which the analysts brought to the problem. They were able to achieve a significant improvement in operations over conventional methods.

**Change the criteria:** This looks at what the basis is for judging a good solution. It can involve judgment or intuition to determine what is appropriate for a given problem. Often mathematical, financial, or technological criteria are used to determine whether a solution is satisfactory. Based on the judgment of the manager, other criteria such as acceptability or timing might be considered more appropriate in a given situation. A way to change the limits is shown in the case of the Marcona Corporation, which shipped large quantities of iron ore from Los Angeles to Japan. A method for speeding up the handling of the iron ore was proposed that required pumping a mixture of water and ore onto the ship that was to carry it to Japan. When judged on the basis of speed of loading the ore, the method was a complete success. However, nobody had taken into account that during the long voyage the mixture of water and ore would dry and become rock hard and would be difficult to remove from the ship. Faced with this obstacle when the captain arrived in Japan, he knew that a way had to be found to remove the dried ore from the ship. What occurred to him was that the dried material was very weak structurally. He reasoned that if he put a hose in the bottom of the ship, it would create a small pocket and that the dried material above would crumble into the pocket so that it could become a mixture similar to what was first pumped onto the ship. It worked!

By changing the basis for evaluating the desirability of the solution, an excellent method for loading and unloading ore was found. If speed of loading had been the only basis, then the method might have been abandoned. Too often, managers will jump to conclusions and not evaluate results using an overall perspective.

**Change the limits:** This involves looking at the problem by examining the constraints or limits. It is, therefore, a special case of changing the problem. Two simple ways of changing the limits are to consider half of the problem or look beyond the boundaries that are assumed. The case of the reluctant programmer showed how to look at half of the problem by offering him two weeks' vacation rather than the full month he originally desired. Often limits or boundaries are arbitrary and when subjected to questioning they can be changed. At General Electric, the Ceramic Insulator Department in Baltimore had refused to produce a special insulator for the High-Voltage Transformer Department because they would lose money on the order. As an individual profit center, they were accountable for the loss. However, once it was recognized that a loss in insulators would be more than offset by a profit on the transformers, the corporate office changed the limits and they, rather than the Insulator Department, absorbed the loss.

A related way to look at problems is to consider the magic number 3 plus or minus 1. Doing this gives a range of 2 to 4. This way of looking at problems can be useful. In *no* case is looking at one factor a suitable basis to examine problems. The one-factor approach always suboptimizes the solution. On the other hand, the two-factor approach suggests that there are trade-offs or a balance between opposing factors. The four-factor approach assumes a double balance or equilibrium. This is not to suggest that problems are limited to only four factors. Rather, this is merely a way of classifying problems that is useful in examining potential solutions.

## ▲  WAYS OF THINKING ABOUT PROBLEMS

Another approach to finding solutions is changing how we "think" about the problems. These include:

1. Lateral think
2. Logical think
3. Groupthink
4. Opposite think
5. Critical think

**Lateral think:** This approach was developed by Debono (1969) and is sometimes called zigzag think. This is an open-minded or reverse-psychology approach. An example is using oil to flush toilets and recovering the oil to recycle it continuously, providing a solution to the problem of minimizing water waste from flushing toilets.

**Logical think:** This builds on the experimental and analytical ability of the individual. This perhaps has been the most widely recommended approach to problem solving. The solution to finding a location for the new airport at Mexico City involved the use of multi-attribute decision making. This is a quantitative technique that balances the worth of multiple factors to help define a correct solution.

**Groupthink:** This involves some of the approaches previously described including brain-storming and synectics. It is concerned mainly with achieving group involvement. Groupthink, however, suffers from the danger that it can lead to group conformity. John F. Kennedy listened to his staff regarding the Bay of Pigs invasion and committed a far-reaching blunder because his staff were not capable of exploring the drastic consequences of not following through on the invasion.

**Opposite think:** This is perhaps one of the more interesting approaches because it can often solve problems immediately simply by taking the perspective of another person. This is "putting yourself in someone else's shoes." Taking the perspective of another individual often will reveal why a problem exists. This was the case of the reluctant programmer. By understanding his perspective a solution was possible, whereas strictly following company rules would have prevented reaching a compromise solution.

**Critical think:** This identifies those aspects of a problem that are most critical. The Pareto Law, described in Chapter 7, shows how one can approach the question of "which are the critical elements of a problem?" For example, 20 percent of all the decisions a manager makes have significant impact on the organization.

An interesting approach to creative problem solving was described in a book on break-through thinking by Nadler and Hibino (1990). They proposed seven principles for break-through thinking to achieve maximum effectiveness. These are:

1.  Every problem should be thought of as being unique.
2.  Solutions should be directed at achieving a specific purpose.
3.  Ideal solutions should be the target in order to achieve better results.
4.  Problems should be considered as part of a system.
5.  Excessive data can lead to confusion.
6.  Good problem solvers use many sources of information.
7.  Constantly improve solutions rather than relying on past results.

The information and examples contained in their book exemplify the direction needed for more effective managerial decision making. The application of these principles is well documented in the book and helps justify why the Japanese have been able to compete so effectively around the world.

Finding the solution to a problem is hardly the end of the process. Obviously, the more effective the process for finding solutions to problems, the more meaningful will be the results. But beyond this, there is the need for gaining acceptance of solutions. This is not simply a matter of presenting a logical conclusion to those who must carry out the decision. Convincing, influencing, meetings, communication, participation, ownership, and involvement are used so that individuals are committed to the solution. Finally, making the solution work, even after it has been accepted, requires monitoring and performance evaluation.

## ▲ HEURISTICS AS AN AID IN PROBLEM SOLVING

There are many definitions of heuristics, ranging from trial and error to experience or intuitive logic. No matter how one describes heuristics, it involves the way we think, reason, and perceive situations. Polya (1957) was one of the early writers who described heuristics as "the study of methods and rules of discovery and invention. Heuristic reasoning has as its purpose the discovery of a plausible or provisional solution to a problem. If you cannot solve the problem at hand then solve some related problem." In his book on heuristics, Pearl (1984) describes heuristics as a rule of thumb to guide one's actions based on criteria, methods, or principles for deciding which alternative course of action will achieve some goal. He also refers to heuristics as "intelligent search strategies for computer problem solving." Heuristics are increasingly being used as the foundation for developing rules used in artificial intelligence computer programs.

The word *heuristic* is based on the Greek *heuriskein:* to invent or discover through exploring and probing to gain knowledge. As knowledge is gained from success or failure, it is fed back and used to modify the search. It is often necessary to redefine the objectives of the problem before it can be solved. A procedure is then defined using rules that help to find intermediate problems; to discover how to set up these problems for solution; to find the most promising paths in the search for solutions; to find ways to retrieve and interpret information on each experience; and to find the methods that lead to a generalized solution. Thus, heuristic reasoning is not regarded as final. The purpose in using heuristics is to discover an approach that will lead to a generalized solution. Heuristic reasoning facilitates the interpretation of progress toward a solution based on perceiving information in terms of patterns and relationships. An important characteristic of exploring is to see what can be learned. Each probe is guided by the information that has been obtained from previous successful (plausible) or unsuccessful approaches. In addition, variables need to be described, and problems initially perceived may have to be redefined in the light of new information.

A major advantage of the heuristic approach is that it involves managers in the solution to problems. Because managers often use past experience or intuition as the basis for problem solving, the heuristic approach is particularly appropriate. It is based on the experience, insight, understanding, and logic the human mind uses to arrive at solutions to complex problems. Therefore, rather than formal, deductive logic, heuristics allows the decision maker to use informal, inductive logic and thus to be able to solve problems that are otherwise difficult to deal with. Heuristic reasoning is not final and strict. Rather, it is provisional and plausible, and its purpose is to discover a generalized solution. For our purposes, then, the term *heuristic* will be used to describe intuitive logic, ingenuity, insight, or the knowledge of the decision maker.

Although heuristics relies on an analysis of problems, this is not the same as a formal analysis. The heuristic approach uses:

1. A classification that structures the problem.
2. Analysis of the characteristics of the data.
3. A decision rule for finding a solution.
4. An objective test of the adequacy of the solution found.

There are many heuristic problem-solving approaches used by managers, ranging from trial and error to intuitive logic. In one respect, the use of heuristic logic relies on the right brain, whereas analytic logic relies on the left brain. Heuristic reasoning uses the conceptual ability of the manger to innovate by thinking "laterally" rather than deductively. It also reduces the solution to a set of logical rules that can be used in computer applications. The president of a successful company using a heuristic approach remarked when asked what he would do if he did not have sufficient information, "I would take action, recognizing that some of my decisions would not be correct. But, in the process of trying, I would learn how to make the right decision."

There have been many successful applications of heuristics, including:

1. Job shop scheduling
2. Warehouse location
3. Order consolidation for freight savings
4. Truck delivery
5. Traveling salespeople and airline scheduling
6. Scheduling of new-product introduction
7. Media schedules
8. Design of electric motors and transformers
9. Layout of cutting patterns to reduce steel waste

There are many other applications of heuristics. For example, the assignment of jobs to machines typically has relied on using linear programming to find a solution. However, using the computer, several million calculations are required to find the optimum solution. The same problem was solved manually in a little over one minute by applying a heuristic rule. This solution involved organizing the data so that a small percentage of the assignments were seen to be far better than the others. Thus, merely examining the problem in a heuristic manner was sufficient to find the optimum solution (Rowe and Bahr, 1972).

The use of heuristics can have startling results. A plant manager who ran a factory at General Electric was able to achieve only a 65 percent on-time delivery of orders. Applying the heuristics, he was able to achieve a 92 percent on-time delivery of orders, at the same time reducing the average inventory. Using heuristics showed a 42 percent improvement over the intuitive judgment of the manager. The value of heuristics, when applied by persons knowledgeable about the problem, was described by Talbot (1986), who compared a total of 24 heuristic decision rules that had been reported in the literature with the best solution to a line-balancing problem. The results showed the heuristic rule was only 2 percent higher when balancing an assembly line than the best solution that required a computer program and a mathematical approach.

Goeffrian and Van Roy (1979) describe how commonsense methods can lead to failure when using heuristic methods. According to Geoffrian and Van Roy, "Commonsense approaches and heuristics can fail because they are *arbitrary*. They are arbitrary in the choice of a starting point, in the sequence in which assignments or other decision choices are made, in the resolution of ties, in the choice of criteria for specifying the procedure, in the level of effort expended to demonstrate that the final solution is in fact best or very nearly so. The result is erratic and unpredictable behavior—good performance in some specific applications and bad in other." He also expressed concern about a more profound weakness of heuristics in the planning process. It is precisely this kind of problem that requires heuristics that can utilize both the analytic and the intuitive capability of decision makers. He sees a critical need to *solve* planning problems under several alternative sets of assumptions.

Although concerns have been expressed about using heuristics, this is nonetheless the way that managers, who are considered experts, view the world. What the decision maker has to consider is that heuristics typically involve right-brain thinking and that this may not match every manager's style. Heuristic rule development is facilitated when applying appropriate models (for example, use of the Pareto Law to categorize the relative importance of items or use of queuing theory to partition items in a queue into different priority classes without changing the expected delay). Pearl's (1984) approach to computational heuristics as well as Bimson and Burris' (1987) approach to conceptual model based reasoning are part of the class of modeling or methodological bases for developing heuristic rules. Rowe's (1987) heuristic for the traveling salesperson problem illustrates a procedural heuristic that simplifies the computational problem.

A very useful approach to developing heuristic rules is the general Pareto Law. It appears frequently in practical problems and has been applied to inventory control to describe items with high, medium, and low values. It is also used to describe the relative importance of decisions that mangers make. Using the Pareto Law shown in Figure 8.3, it is possible to reduce search to a small number of solutions. When an expert understands the characteristics of the problem being solved, he or she can generally identify the high payoff subset of solutions. In many instances, the payoff is obvious from an examination of the characteristics of the problem itself.

Equal payoff shows that for each new or additional solution, the payoff is the same as for any other solutions. Thus, one solution is as good as another. The Pareto Law, on the other hand, shows that a small portion of the solutions gives the majority of the possible payoff. The Pareto Law describes the general behavior of a number of phenomena and provides a meaningful approach for developing heuristic decision rules. The heuristic approach of separating the problem into more important and less important parts is typically used by managers to find solutions. For example, the manager knows intuitively that a small percentage of the customers contribute to most of the sales. Likewise, a small percentage of workers have most of the accidents, and so on. If we formalize this "intuitive insight," we have a basic building block for a heuristic approach to managerial problems.

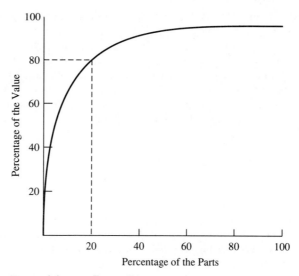

Figure 8.3 ▲ Pareto Distribution

## ▲ ▲ ▲ ▲ ▲ SIMPLOT CASE

An excellent example of problem-solving and decision making is the J. R. Simplot Company. John Richard Simplot started in business in 1924 and by 1990 at age 81 controlled a $1.3 billion a year business empire consisting of food, energy, minerals and mining, fertilizer, high technology, and transportation. The privately held company supplies McDonald's with 80 percent of its golden fries.

Simplot's decision-making style is to use intuition rather than market research. When he was unable to buy fertilizer for his potatoes, he built his own fertilizer factory and now runs four plants producing fertilizer. Later, when he was unable to purchase phosphate for fertilizer, he leased land from an Indian reservation and founded the largest phosphate mine in the West—one of three his company now operates. By converting problems into opportunities Simplot successively built a vertically integrated empire.

Problem solvers such as Simplot are willing to challenge conventional wisdom, which tends to stifle creativity. During World War II, he backed one of his chemists, who thought he could freeze potatoes, going contrary to the accepted belief of farmers that cold weather ruins potatoes. This process, which stabilized the starch in potatoes before freezing, led to the invention of the frozen french fry.

As Simplot expanded his business, one process led to another. Byproducts from food processing were used to feed cattle. A construction group was set up to build his own plants. One of Simplot's most recent ideas was to build a series of coal-fired power plants along the scenic Snake River in Idaho to supply power to the Southwestern states. However, he overlooked the environmental concerns of the public, which is a social issue impacting a business decision.

Simplot is a good example of a visionary decision maker capable of seeing and seizing opportunities even though they might make their first appearance in the form of problems (Brandt, 1990).

▲

## ▲ Summary

In this chapter, problem solving was described as one phase of the decision process. New ways of looking at problems can produce more effective solutions. Both quantitative and behavioral aspects of problems should be considered in finding solutions. Managers have different approaches to problem solving that are reflected in their differing decision styles, attitudes, and needs.

The problem-solving process includes problem formulation and finding solutions. Many approaches are used in problem solving, such as intuition, heuristics, free association, brainstorming, changing the problem, lateral think, changing the approach, and changing the limits. An important aspect of problem solving is being receptive to new ideas. The willingness to search for answers is as critical as the methods used to find solutions.

## ▲ Study Questions

1. Why is intuition important in problem solving?
2. What are the rules for effective brainstorming?
3. What is the Pareto Law?
4. What is the problem-solving process?
5. Why is problem formulation considered critical?
6. What is creative problem solving?
7. In what ways can "change" be used in problem solving?
8. What ways are there to think about problems?
9. Why is heuristics useful in finding solutions?

## ▲ References

Bimson, Kent D., and Burris, Linda B. "Conceptual Model-Based Reasoning for Software Project Management." Lockheed Software Technology Center, 1987.

Boulgarides, James. "The Creative Process." Unpublished paper, 1970.

Brandt, Richard. "J. R. Simplot: Still Hustling After All These Years." *Business Week.* (September 3, 1990), pp. 60–65.

Debono, E. "Virtues of Zig-Zag Thinking." *Think* (June, 1969).

Donovan, Hedley. "Managing Your Intellectuals." *Fortune* (October 23, 1989), pp. 177–178.

Dreyfact, Raymond. "Use that Sixth Sense—Instinct." *Nation's Business* Vol. 54, No. 12, (December 1966), pp. 80–86.

Elbing, Alvar O. *Behavioral Decisions in Organizations.* 2nd ed. Glenview, IL: Scott Foresman, 1978.

Geoffrian, A. M., and Van Roy, T. J. "Caution: Common Sense Methods and Heuristics Can Be Hazardous to Your Corporate Health." *Sloan Management Review.* (Summer 1979).

Gordon, William J. J. "Synectics: The Development of Creative Capacity." Cambridge, MA: Synectics Inc., 1961.

Horgarth, Robin M. *Judgment and Choice.* New York: Wiley, 1980.

Kepner, Charles, and Tregoe, Benjamin S. *The Rational Manager.* New York: McGraw-Hill, 1963.

Koble, Kathy. *The Conative Connection.* Reading, MA: Addison-Wesley, 1990.

Kupfer, Andrew. "America's Fastest Growing Company." *Fortune* (August 13, 1990), pp. 48–54.

Mihalasky, John. "Question: What Do Some Executives Have More of? Answer: Intuition. Maybe." *Think* (November-December 1969).

Motamedi, Kurt. "Extending the Concept of Creativity." Paper, 1982, UCLA.

Nadler, Gerald, and Habino, Shozo. "Breakthrough Thinking." Rocklin, CA: Prima Publishing, 1990.

Pearl, Judea. *Heuristics*. Reading, MA: Addison-Wesley, 1984.

Polya, G. *How to Solve It*. New York: Doubleday, 1957.

Rowe, Alan J. "The Meta Logic of Cognitively Based Heuristics." *Expert Systems Review* Vol. 1, No. 4 (1987).

Rowe, Alan J., and Bahr, Fred R. "A Heuristic Approach to Managerial Problem Solving." *Journal of Economics and Business* (1973).

Rowen, Roy. *The Intuitive Manager*. Boston, MA: Little-Brown, 1986, pp. 11–12.

Simon, Herbert A. "How Managers Express Their Creativity." *The McKinley Quarterly* (Autumn 1986), pp. 67–78.

Smith, Emily T. "Are You Creative?" *Business Week* (September 30, 1985), pp. 80–84.

Talbot, F. B. "A Comparative Evaluation of Heuristic Time Balancing Techniques." *Management Science* (April 1986).

Tversky, Amos. "Elimination by Aspects: A Theory of Choice." *Psychological Review* 79 (1977), pp. 281–299.

Tversky, Amos, and Kahneman, Daniel. "Judgment Under Uncertainty: Heuristics and Biases." In *Utility, Probability and Human Decision Making*. Dirk Wendt and Charles Vlek, eds. Boston, MA: D. Reidel, 1975.

Veregara, Elsa. "Creativity in Planning." Unpublished dissertation, USC, 1977.

Watanabe, Teresa. "Toward Creativity in Japan." *Los Angeles Times* (June 10, 1990), pp. D1–D11.

# 9 Decision-Aiding Tools

▲ ▲ ▲     ▲ ▲ ▲ ▲ ▲ ▲ ▲ ▲ ▲ ▲ ▲ ▲ ▲ ▲ ▲ ▲

In the current era of increasingly complex problems, it is obvious that more powerful methods are needed to aid decision making. The question is how to apply these methods to help improve decision making. As was the case in problem solving, managers first must be willing to use new tools. However, tools need to be explained. To the manager with little or no training, the use of new methods can be overwhelming. Is it any wonder that managers will not stick their necks out to use something unknown? Although the value of applying advanced methods to complex decision problems has been adequately demonstrated, a gap still remains between their application and what the practicing manager uses. Technical specialists are often at fault because they do not adequately explain what they are doing and why it is necessary. Finally, there is the question of whether advanced methods are really useful in solving important problems. As one might suspect, there are two answers to this question. In many instances, using advanced methods is an exercise in futility. They are neither suitable nor cost-effective. On the other hand, there are instances in which the difference between a correct decision and a wrong one depends on using a quantitative approach.

## ▲ APPLICATION OF DECISION-AIDING TOOLS

The most straightforward means of determining how advanced tools can best be applied is by examining the kinds of decisions managers make and how these tools could be applied. For this purpose, problems can be classified as:

1. *Deterministic:* This covers straightforward problems to which quantitative tools can be readily applied.
2. *Complex:* These problems involve many combinations for which computers and quantitative methods can best be used.
3. *Risky:* These problems deal with chance and uncertainty and are solved using decision analysis and statistical methods.

These classifications reflect the technical problems confronting a decision maker and the methodology that could be used. This chapter illustrates how selective techniques from each of the categories can be applied to managerial problems. Any classification of problems is arbitrary. One category is never completely separate from other categories. For example, in the deterministic category, there are very few problems in which every factor is completely known, so it partly overlaps the risky category.

Chapter 1 introduced an approach that can assist the decision maker in identifying a problem—the *linear decision analysis*. Using this technique, all aspects of a problem are viewed as a series of subproblems, each having inputs and outputs. Figure 9.1 is an example of a linear decision analysis. At each level of the diagram, a subproblem is defined that flows into the one below.

Each step is examined in terms of a subproblem that consists of inputs, the subproblem, and the outputs. The inputs represent the data or information used. The subproblem is a way of breaking the main problem into smaller, more manageable units. The outputs represent either the actions taken or the results expected from the subproblem. In most instances, the output of one step or stage becomes the input to the next stage, although this is not required in order to use this method for defining or analyzing a problem.

The linear decision analysis provides a fairly straightforward means to define a problem. Consider a company that is about to introduce a new product. A description of the steps needed to introduce the new product would proceed as shown in Figure 9.1. First, data are required to describe the market served. They can be obtained from forecasts, market surveys, analysis of competition, knowing the customer, and so forth. For purposes of brevity, only a

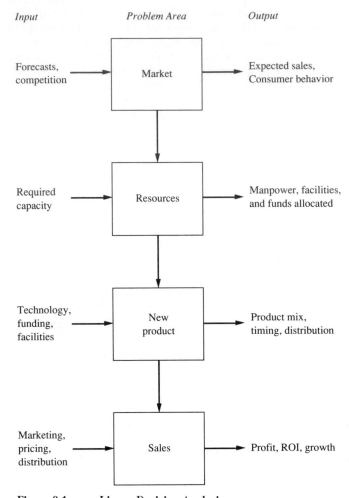

*Input*     *Problem Area*     *Output*

Forecasts, competition → **Market** → Expected sales, Consumer behavior

Required capacity → **Resources** → Manpower, facilities, and funds allocated

Technology, funding, facilities → **New product** → Product mix, timing, distribution

Marketing, pricing, distribution → **Sales** → Profit, ROI, growth

**Figure 9.1** ▲ **Linear Decision Analysis**

limited number of all the factors that have to be considered are shown on the diagram. The market, then, is the problem area under consideration at stage 1. The output of the analysis of the market includes the expected level of sales, what can be expected of consumers, the level of advertising required, and so forth.

Once the market structure, the competition, and the customer are known, the second stage of the analysis examines what the firm has to do in order to meet the requirements defined in stage 1. This is shown by an analysis of existing capacity to produce the new product and to meet expected customer demand, including equipment, capital, and expertise compared with that required for producing existing products. "Resources" then becomes the second problem area under consideration. The result of the analysis of requirements defines the new resources needed, including personnel, facilities, and funds.

Stage 3 combines information from stages 1 and 2 to identify strategies for bringing out the new product. Specifically, the market analysis will specify timing (when the new product should be introduced for most favorable reception) and appropriate distribution channels.

The analysis of resources will show how soon the new product can be introduced, whether the company already has appropriate distribution channels, and whether any changes in the company's overall marketing strategy are necessary.

Stage 4 combines information from the other three stages on cost of development and distribution to estimate the new product's profitability and return on investment and to gauge the product's effect on company growth. Each step represents a problem area that requires information as input and that produces information output. By analyzing problems in terms of a linear decision analysis, the manager is able to introduce structure to the situation, even though the structure is not obvious.

## Decision Tables

Another useful tool for problem analysis is a decision table. The example given in Table 9.1 was used for insurance decisions. In this application, the table shows the relationship between conditions for insurance, decision rules, and actions to be taken for each decision rule.

For example, using the decision table, it is easy to see that a person who drives 15,000 miles per year, is 35 years old, has had two accidents in the past three years, and uses the car for business will pay $2.50 per $1,000 for the insurance. Another 35-year-old who is a better driver and goes only 10,000 miles per year will only pay $1.50 per $1,000.

The decision table, in reality, requires that the decision maker explicitly define all the conditions that apply and what actions or decisions will be made for each set of conditions. Too often, simple rules such as age or number of accidents are used as the basis for a decision. It is clear that simple rules can lead to erroneous decisions; this is why decision tables are useful in helping to identify the relevant factors and how they are combined as the basis for clear-cut decisions.

## Cost–Benefit Analysis

Another important aspect of applying quantitative methods to deterministic problems is that the problems often can be viewed as balancing two competing factors. For example, when trying to evaluate the cost of an investment, the manager typically balances the benefits to be derived from the investment. This balancing of cost with benefit was applied by Kepner and Tregoe (1963) in their approach to finding the best alternative when trying to solve a problem. Many managerial decisions can be treated using this approach, such as:

**Table 9.1 ▲ Decision Table — Insurance Decisions**

| *Factors to Consider* | *Conditions* | | | |
|---|---|---|---|---|
| Miles driven per year | 10,000 | 10,000 | 15,000 | 15,000 |
| Age of driver | 25 | 35 | 25 | 35 |
| Physical defects of driver | None | None | None | None |
| Accidents in past 3 years | 1 | 1 | 2 | 2 |
| Convictions | None | None | None | None |
| Major use | Pleasure | Business | Pleasure | Business |
| *Decision Rules* | | | | |
| Limit ($000s) | 100/300 | 100/200 | 50/100 | 25/50 |
| Rate per $1,000 | 1.12 | 1.50 | 1.75 | 2.50 |
| Type coverage | A | B | C | D |

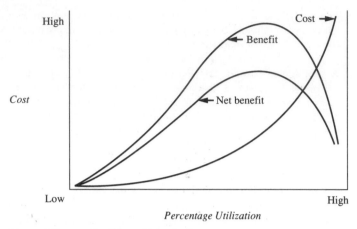

Figure 9.2 ▲ Cost/Benefit Analysis

1. Cost of carrying inventory versus cost of parts shortage.
2. Cost of information versus errors caused by lack of information.
3. Cost of improved quality versus cost of losing customers because of defects.
4. Cost of visiting customers versus the number of sales made.

To illustrate this approach, consider one of the key decisions management must make: What capacity is needed to adequately match customer demand? To answer this, a cost–benefit model is developed, as shown in Figure 9.2. Increased capacity helps reduce lost sales; however, meeting 100 percent of demand may not be the best answer, as is shown by the balance of the cost of lost sales. There is a point of diminishing returns that shows that the benefit or value of reducing lost sales may not be warranted by ever-increasing costs of capacity.

Cost–benefit analysis has been used extensively by the government in its procurement of military hardware. It has also been used by companies such as IBM and GE in evaluating new projects to determine whether the value or benefit achieved was worth the cost expended. Actually, the calculation of the cost–benefit ratio is fairly straightforward and should be less than 1 in order for the project to contribute greater value than its cost. IBM added another feature to the cost–benefit analysis by using both tangible and intangible costs and benefits. They also included in their calculations the urgency of projects, the acceptance of solutions, and the likelihood that the project would succeed. Thus, the result is a useful tool for managers who have to justify large expenditures for projects under their responsibility.

## ▲ HEURISTIC METHODS

The previous chapter provided an introduction to the subject of heuristics and some of its applications. This chapter examines heuristics from a computational perspective. Although deterministic problems are often solved by methods such as linear programming, heuristic methods offer another approach that decision makers can use to solve such problems. Managers faced with the ongoing requirement of satisfying multiple objectives often seek satisfactory rather than optimum solutions to problems. An important consideration is that the manager understand the solution so as to feel comfortable supporting it. Although heuristics is not a sophisticated technique, it requires human judgment and logic to find a workable solution to problems.

Table 9.2 ▲ Setup Costs in a
Sample Job-Assignment Problem (in $)

| Jobs | Machines | | | | |
|---|---|---|---|---|---|
| | 1 | 2 | 3 | 4 | 5 |
| 1 | — | 9 | 6 | ③ | ② |
| 2 | ④ | — | ④ | 7 | 6 |
| 3 | 5 | 9 | — | 8 | 10 |
| 4 | 6 | 7 | ④ | — | ③ |
| 5 | 8 | ④ | 7 | ② | — |

An interesting application of heuristics is the assignment of jobs to machines in a sequence that keeps the cost of setup at a minimum. This is known as the assignment problem. Its solution requires the use of mathematical techniques that are beyond the scope of this book, but we will show how to apply heuristics to solve this problem. This is a difficult problem because there are many ways in which the sequence can be performed, and when the problem is large, involving many jobs and many machines, the number of possible combinations becomes very difficult to solve other than by the use of computers. Heuristics, on the other hand, is simple to apply even to very large problems and does not require the use of computers.

To illustrate how to apply heuristics to the assignment problem, we use the data shown in Table 9.2, which gives the setup costs for all the combinations of sequences in which the machines can be run. Thus, for example, if job 1 is run on machine 2, the setup cost would be $9. On the other hand, if job 1 were run on machine 4, the setup cost would be $3. (Although it is possible to guess a correct solution for a small problem such as the one shown, it becomes increasingly difficult as the size of the problem increases.)

A heuristic rule that could be utilized for this problem is one that uses the logic of the Pareto Law. (See Chapter 8.) This says that a small percentage of the possible answers will be good solutions. Using this approach, we circle the low-cost setups, as in Table 9.2. In Table 9.3 the number of low-cost alternatives is determined by adding the circled costs from Table 9.2 and showing these as counts for the rows and the columns.

The next step is to select the combination of assignments that keeps the costs to a minimum. The heuristic rule used here was:

1. Look at the counts in the rows and the columns.
2. Select an assignment from the lowest counts because this might otherwise be one that would leave you with a high-cost alternative.

Table 9.3 ▲ Identification of the
Minimum-Cost Solutions

| Jobs | Machines | | | | | Count |
|---|---|---|---|---|---|---|
| | 1 | 2 | 3 | 4 | 5 | |
| 1 | — | 9 | 6 | ③ | 2 | 2 |
| 2 | 4 | — | ④ | 7 | 6 | 2 |
| 3 | ⑤ | 9 | — | 8 | 10 | 0 |
| 4 | 6 | 7 | 4 | — | ③ | 2 |
| 5 | 8 | ④ | 7 | 2 | — | 2 |
| Count | 1 | 1 | 2 | 2 | 2 | |

Using the above heuristic rule, we see that row 3 has a zero count, meaning that there are no low-cost setups. Also, columns 1 and 2 have only one low-cost setup. Thus, the rule says first make a choice from the row or column with the lowest choice, which is row 3. We select job 3 to run on machine 1 for a cost of $5. Next, we again look for the lowest count, which is in column 2. We select job 5 to run on machine 2. Because the remaining three jobs have the same count, we select from the remaining three jobs. Jobs 2 and 4 only have one low-cost setup remaining. So, if we choose job 2 to machine 3 and job 4 to machine 5, then job 1 goes to the last open machine, which is 4. This gives us the optimum solution of $19 total setup cost.

# ▲ SOLVING COMPLEX PROBLEMS

The problems that fit this category involve many factors that interact in ways that are difficult to determine ahead of time. The assignment problem just described is an example of this class of problems. These are often called "combinatorial" problems because of the large number of combinations of factors involved. Strategic problems, such as the one described under the linear decision analysis, are also examples of complex problems. Another group of problems that would fit this category involves performance of divisions of a company.

In many instances, the only method for solving such problems is the use of heuristics or intuition. Another approach, computer simulation, has also proven to be useful for dealing with large and very complex problems. The essence of computer simulation is developing a model that describes the problem under consideration in a formal way. This approach forces the manager to clearly identify the problem and to state what a satisfactory solution would be.

To see how modeling can be applied to a management problem, consider International Minerals Corporation (IMC), one of the world's largest producers of fertilizers. IMC was concerned with the problem of determining the maximum level of debt they could sustain for a given investment so that equity capital would be at a desired level of risk. The funds required were in excess of the amount that was available to the company, and thus factors such as the cost of capital, tax savings, interest deductions, and a possible boost in earnings per share all had to be taken into account. A mathematical model was developed including all the factors that affected income (sales volume, prices, and costs); this model took into account estimates of possible levels of profitability or loss covering various debt-to-equity ratios based on IMC's financial structure and an estimate of the chances of each occurrence. The result was that executives based their decision on the value of incurring debt, rather than on an arbitrary approach such as the amount of funds available.

In another case, the Carborundum Company, using the computer for market analysis based on a mathematical model that described operations, was able to determine which district salespeople, distributors, customers, markets, and products were the largest profit producers. The company used the simulation to calculate return on investment from their promotions, determine which were the profitable products, what effect price adjustments would have, the cost for each item on gross margin, and the cost savings.

One of the more interesting approaches was that used by the Borax Corporation. Management considered a quantitative model as the basis for establishing the profits they wanted to achieve for the next five years and was about to do strategic planning based on these profit objectives, including a detailed one-year budget. The objective was to establish an effective management control system. This was accomplished by including operational accounting for the various operating entities of the business, and financial accounting describing the parts of the business that produced the desired level of profitability based on standard costs for products for the year. This model permitted Borax to examine all major lines for the entire budget every week. If manufacturing or marketing conditions changed sufficiently, the company could modify the budget accordingly.

## ▲ APPLICATION OF SIMULATION FOR DECISION MAKING

Scheduling of job shops has long been considered a difficult decision problem. Analytic techniques were not suitable, except in extremely small cases. Simulation models developed to study job shops, however, have been extremely successful in a number of companies, including General Electric, IBM, and Hughes Aircraft. The kinds of decisions this type of simulation included are

1. Determining the capacity needed for equipment, facilities, and labor to meet unpredictable customer demand.
2. Examination of alternative levels of demand and the capability of the system to meet the demand.
3. Examination of the inventory buildup and equipment utilization needed to meet customer demand. (It is generally possible to meet customer demand by maintaining large inventories.)
4. Development of scheduling decision rules to maintain minimal inventory while meeting delivery requirements.
5. Forecasting the scheduling load-level.

In addition to these decisions, the simulation provided information on current shop performance so that management could make decisions on the number of shifts to run, need for additional equipment, or amount of inventory required.

A heuristic approach for scheduling jobs was developed establishing a priority rule for job selection. The time that a job requires in a manufacturing plant consists of three main elements:

1. The actual time to fabricate the part.
2. The time needed to move the part from one location to another.
3. The waiting period for the job at each machine before the work is begun.

It is the waiting time or delay that has been most difficult to determine for the typical machine shop. A heuristic rule was developed based on the delay expected at each machine. A flow allowance was related to the delay at each machine. High-priority jobs could flow through the factory faster than the low-value jobs and still not change the average delay at the machines. A priority rule based on the use of a flow allowance is:

$$\text{Priority} = P = \frac{T - S - F}{n}$$

where

$P$ = priority of the job
$T$ = today's date (sequential day number)
$S$ = scheduled start date
$F$ = flow allowance based on expected delay
$n$ = number of operations remaining

For example, if a job has a scheduled start date of day number 280, a flow allowance of 10 days, and 2 operations remaining as of today (day 250), its priority would be

$$\text{Priority} = P = \frac{250 - 280 - 10}{2} = \frac{-40}{2} = -20$$

The $-20$ priority means that the job is ahead of schedule. A positive priority would mean that the job had used up the flow allowance and was late.

This simulation program was extended to a daily scheduling system at Hughes Aircraft for real-time manufacturing control. The job shop simulator was used to examine alternative scheduling decision rules. These rules, in turn, provided the basis for developing a computer program that was used to generate job order status in the factory on a daily basis. This computer program, by application of the priority decision rules shown, generated new priority lists every day. Thus, the system operated on a daily cycle with all information current and correct as of that point in time.

An important consideration in the application of simulation is the model used to describe the many complexities that exist in an actual problem area. If the problem is readily observed and describable, then the level of confidence regarding how closely the simulation represents the problem can be established. For example, counting the number of cars flowing through a tunnel is easier than estimating the customers' potential response to a new product. Ideally, a model should cover the following aspects of a problem:

1. The structure of the process and the environment.
2. The physical aspects of the process (e.g., change, delays, capacity, etc.).
3. The decisions made.
4. Description of how parts of the process change and affect other parts.

Although simulation has many advantages, the difficulty involved in developing a model, programming it on a computer, and utilizing the results cannot be overlooked. There are many pitfalls that must be avoided, including how to develop a suitable model. The problem of modeling is important because the results of simulation are no better than the data and the model used. Fortunately, a model need not duplicate actual conditions to be useful. Rather, a model is designed to predict behavior resulting from system changes. Thus, because models are used to test new ideas, the simpler the model, the more effective for decision-making purposes. The larger the number of factors included, the more difficult it is to draw meaningful conclusions. Sensitivity analysis can be used to reduce the number of factors. In addition, the range of the variables studied can be limited to the portion of interest to the decision maker.

Another example, called the "traveling salesman problem," has been included here. This has been chosen because of the difficulty in finding a solution, even when computers are applied. The current method for solving the problem involves a procedure known as "branch and bound," which is a reasonably complex heuristic rule. We examine an alternative approach that has proven to be very good for most applications. Before the heuristic is described, see if you can find a solution by examining Table 9.4. The conditions that must be met are:

**Table 9.4 ▲ The Traveling Salesman Problem**

|  |  | From City | | | | |
|---|---|---|---|---|---|---|
|  |  | 1 | 2 | 3 | 4 | 5 |
| To City | 1 | — | 52 | 105 | 50 | 55 |
|  | 2 | 52 | — | 105 | 79 | 49 |
|  | 3 | 105 | 105 | — | 64 | 57 |
|  | 4 | 50 | 79 | 64 | — | 42 |
|  | 5 | 55 | 49 | 57 | 42 | — |

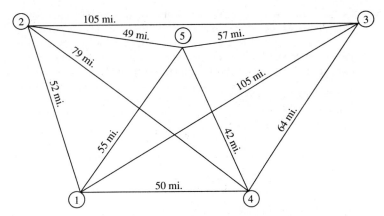

Figure 9.3 ▲ Heuristic Solution to the Traveling Salesman Problem

1. Find the least-cost route that the salesman can follow and still visit all cities at least once.
2. The salesman must return to the city from which he started after he has visited all the other cities.
3. No city may be skipped, especially the home city.

This problem is difficult when there are many cities to visit because of the large number of combinations involved. For example, in the five-city problem used in Table 9.4, there are 120 possible combinations of routes that the salesman can follow. Imagine the number of combinations for a 100-city problem!

After you have tried to guess the answer using Table 9.4, look at Figure 9.3 for the best available solution. The heuristic rule used in this case is fairly straightforward. First, by being able to visualize the problem, you are in a better position to find a solution than by merely examining the data shown in Table 9.4. The heuristic rule is to always travel an exterior route, that is, one that never crosses over another connection. The solution, then, if the salesman started at city 1, is the sequence or combination 1 to 2, 2 to 5, 5 to 3, 3 to 4, and returning home from 4 to 1. Although this may appear to be an obvious answer, try it for a ten-city problem and you will quickly see that without the heuristic rule described, the solution would not be obvious.

As is true with all heuristic solutions, there is no assurance of the absolute best answer. All you can guarantee is always having a very good solution. But, most important, the decision maker readily understands the solution and often can arrive at the answer directly without the need of help.

## ▲ MULTI-ATTRIBUTE DECISION PROBLEMS

When problems have no obvious solutions and when the weighing of criteria is important, one can use an approach called *multi-attribute decision making*. As the name implies, these problems have many factors or attributes that need to be considered when examining alternatives for solving a problem. However, the problems do require that the decision maker explicitly identify alternatives and the criteria that will be used to select the most desirable alternative. Multi-attribute decision making involves a number of considerations, such as how managers establish the value or ranking of criteria and how they take risk into account. We examine a simplified version of the approach next to illustrate its application.

A southern California building contractor had reached a limit to his sales growth. This precluded increased income or opportunities for members of the company. The contractor engaged a consultant, who identified four areas needing improvement:

1. Management back-up
2. Engineering skills
3. Investment capital
4. Nonproductive activities

Four alternatives were proposed for consideration:

1. Continue business as now.
2. Hire a new construction superintendent.
3. Subcontract all construction work.
4. Do contract as well as speculative building.

To evaluate these alternatives, seven criteria were used:

1. Cost of each alternative.
2. Reliability of performance of the organization under each alternative.
3. Flexibility of control for the contractor.
4. Adaptability of the organization in meeting new conditions.
5. Availability of time for the contractor to engage in other activities.
6. Effect of size on the organization.
7. Growth potential for each alternative.

Each of these criteria was given a weight based on confidence in the solution and sensitivity to change. A weighting factor and a rating score were used to indicate the importance of each factor to the individuals in the organization. The weighted scores for the four alternatives were

1. Keep current organization:  123 points
2. Hire a superintendent:  120 points
3. Subcontract:  112 points
4. Enter new markets:  106 points

Table 9.5 summarizes results for alternative 1 (continue business as now) based on interviews in the field and incorporating the contractor's preferences. The recommendation was to maintain the current organization. This was based on rating the importance of each

**Table 9.5 ▲ Sample Weighting for Alternative 1 (Continue Business as Now)**

| Criterion | Rating | Weight | Confidence | Sensitivity | Score |
|-----------|--------|--------|------------|-------------|-------|
| Cost | 10 | 3 | 0.9 | ±0.25 | 30 |
| Reliability | 4 | 4 | 0.7 | ±0.15 | 16 |
| Flexibility | 8 | 3 | 0.9 | ±0.25 | 24 |
| Adaptability | 4 | 2 | 0.7 | ±0.25 | 8 |
| Availability | 4 | 3 | 0.9 | ±0.15 | 12 |
| Size | 9 | 3 | 0.9 | ±0.25 | 27 |
| Growth | 3 | 2 | 0.9 | ±0.25 | 6 |
|  |  |  |  |  | Total 123 |

criterion and weighting how each met the objectives. There was high confidence, indicating that the estimates were considered very good. Obviously, the value of the weighting depends on how valid the estimates were. However, when properly applied, the results justify the effort needed for this kind of analysis. The contractor agreed that in fact this was his preference and that the exercise confirmed his intuitive feeling.

## ▲ COMPUTER-BASED INFORMATION SYSTEMS

Another approach to solving complex problems is the use of computer-based decision support systems. A decision support system is one that uses computer information-processing capability, handles large files of data, is able to access the data via remote terminals, and uses simulation or other models to help interpret information. The job shop simulation program described previously is an example of a decision support system. It had a computer-based production control system that maintained the current data files. These files could be accessed via terminals and the simulation model provided the priorities that aided the supervisors in making scheduling decisions.

Managers use decision support systems as aids in many decision-making problems. IBM forecasts the pricing of new computers to determine the best introductory price for products. International Utilities applies a computer model to determine the future impact of new acquisitions. One of the presidents of Security Pacific Bank used a personal computer to review and examine alternate budget plans. Applications abound and are limited only by the imagination of the decision maker.

To explore how information can help management decision making, it is useful to examine the way in which information systems provide support. For many years ratios or averages were the basis for determining profit, return on investment, and similar ratios. Each ratio provided managers with the information they used for making important decisions. However, with today's ability to track information on a daily, weekly, or monthly basis, managers no longer have to use averages. They can directly examine each of the measures as they change by time period, by profit center, by work group, by product line, or by whatever base is most meaningful.

Information systems can readily provide multiple measures rather than the single measures used in manual systems. For example, in addition to the share of the market, a manager can consider product life cycle, how profit changes over time, number of competitors, product mix, and percentage return on investment. These measures help provide a total evaluation of products and offer a better basis for decision making. Information systems also help achieve more effective control. That is, information provides insights that permit managers to examine the relationship between the actions taken and performance in greater detail, if desired. Rather than looking at control after the fact, it can be looked at ahead of time to prevent variances or problems before they occur. Obviously, there is no way to determine whether a particular activity or function is out of control without measurement and without the basis for knowing what is to be expected. However, variances observed after the fact or based on simplistic ratios or generalizations really do not provide meaningful control information.

Perhaps one of the most significant uses for information systems has been the ability to monitor trends. Information systems can help determine the direction a particular activity is headed, or potential changes in performance, or forecasts of what is likely to happen. It is one of the most powerful tools that management has—that is, to take corrective action ahead of time. Computer-based systems can use trends to provide a meaningful basis for taking corrective action.

To be effective, an information system must be relevant to and understood by the managers who use it. Important decisions require that data are understood. Information systems must adapt to the environment in which they exist; they must be concerned with people and with the way information is used to make decisions. Information systems often are threatening and result in a redistribution of power. Argyris (1967) has indicated that it is not possible to build a system that shows operating departments how they can be fully integrated into a functional whole. Such a system would not succeed because departments that have been locked in conflict have learned combat and survived. Understandably, they would be skeptical about being required to cooperate. A reduction in organizational politics would require that the information system build on valid information that can be used for decision making.

The value of information systems ultimately depends on how managers use information. Computer-produced information is not a substitute for the intuition and judgment needed to assess organizational performance (Greiner, 1970). Qualitative factors provide more sensitive, current clues concerning strength of operating units. They provide clear leads for corrective action and are broader or more general in scope. In a study of what top executives think of using computer information, one said, "I would rather talk to the people who use computers to get their judgment." Another said, "Increasingly concerns are people problems and for information to solve them you go to other people." Still another said, "If I see a computer printout on my desk, I just won't read it." The consensus at the chief executive level is that subjective judgment is still a valuable asset in spite of the availability of computer information (Rowe, 1976).

To be useful as an aid in decision making, information systems must include the following considerations:

1. What information and criteria are needed for effective decision making?
2. Where are the critical control points in a system?
3. What effect do programmed decision rules have on system performance?
4. What are tolerable limits of deviation of system performance?
5. What effect do time lags and priority rules have on system response?
6. How can feedback control and exception reporting be incorporated?
7. What effect will the manager's decision style have on the use of information?

A computer-based information system that can answer questions such as these will provide meaningful support for decisions.

Are such systems economical? The answer is that today's business and government operations would come to a screeching halt without computers. The decision maker increasingly relies on current information as the basis for decision making. With the power and availability of the personal computer, use of computers will become as commonplace as the telephone and the jet. But, most important, computers will aid decision making by being able to handle extremely large and complex problems. To put this statement into perspective, we can examine the cost–benefit analysis of computer usage as shown in Figure 9.4. Adding more and more information merely leads a decision maker to the point of diminishing returns. A decision maker, depending on his or her decision style, can determine the appropriate amount of information, the kind of displays to use, and what decision support systems are most useful as decision aids.

## ▲ DECISION SUPPORT SYSTEMS

To understand the role of information in assisting decision making, it is helpful to look at the kinds of decisions managers make at each level in the organization. At the operating level, transactions occur such as payroll, accounting, inventory, and production. These transactions

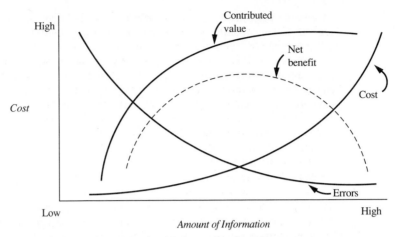

**Figure 9.4  ▲  Cost–Benefit of Information Completeness**

result in regularly scheduled reports used by the operating managers for their day-to-day decisions.

At the middle management level, information often is summarized and used principally for control purposes. Demand reports or summary reports are the ones usually used. In top management, where strategic plans and long-range considerations are critical, the information is summarized even further, and reports are largely in response to special requests by executives.

The fall of many executives has been blamed on their limited use of information. A top executive who relies on authority rather than information is a person headed for trouble, because he or she gives answers rather than asking questions. We live in an information-dominated society, and information is power—yet, as many as one in four corporate executives relies on authority as the basis for decisions. The results show up as unrealistic decisions that are the single most common cause of the removal of chief executives.

Information can be used more effectively in the following areas:

1. *Strategic planning:* To determine how to direct and structure the company to meet uncertainties in the external environment
2. *Adaptive control:* To adjust the organization to new and changing conditions
3. *Organizational congruence:* To facilitate congruence between organizational goals and individual goals.
4. *Decision support:* To provide the information needed to support the actions required in meeting objectives and solving problems.

Each of these factors is examined next to show how it can contribute to supporting more effective managerial decision making.

1. *Strategic planning:* A fixed plan, no matter how well conceived, is not sufficient to deal with a rapidly changing environment. Responsiveness is needed to readjust forecasts as new information and new conditions arise. Information is needed to adjust projections more rapidly and to provide the basis for more effective decisions.
2. *Adaptive control:* As conditions change rapidly and in erratic ways, means are required for organizational adjustment to meet the new conditions. The strategic plan is used to develop the broad, general guidelines and directions that need to be followed, whereas adaptive control is the process that changes the ongoing operation of the organization on a short-term basis to meet new and unanticipated problems.

In the past, management was able to use fixed approaches such as budgets, schedules, and comparable control mechanisms. What is required now is flexibility to change continually as problems arise. The computer can have a major impact on managerial decision making because without rapid and accurate information from appropriate databases, the manager is in no position to assess the current status of the organization. Management can no longer wait for something to go wrong; rather, it must be in a position to anticipate problems and to be able to determine what actions are needed to correct the situation.

3. *Organizational congruence:* This is an attempt to relate the organization's goals more closely to those of the individual. Today's organizations are not rigid, mechanical institutions. Rather, the level of complexity and the amount of judgment required mean that the individual must be involved in the job that is being performed. Information provides a basis for individuals to understand their role and performance requirements.

4. *Decision support:* Decision support systems generally use decision models for strategic plans as well as for adaptive control. At the operating level, the manager needs decision support systems such as simulation programs to respond in a direct and effective manner to current requirements.

An example of a decision support system is one that was used by ARCO. A computer simulation was included in the operation of one of its oil refineries. The computer program was able to define the mix of products to be run. When a major refining unit broke down, it was possible to rebalance the entire operation in 1 day—a process that on a manual basis required 30 days. At today's cost of oil, imagine the value of 29 additional days of operation. This certainly was well worth the cost of a decision simulation model that could be used as the basis for supporting management.

At the strategic level, International Utilities has used a decision model as the basis for evaluating its investments when contemplating new directions or acquisitions. The model provided executives with "information" that they reviewed and used as the basis for identifying the most likely return on investment, the risks involved, and the impact on earnings.

## ▲ ARTIFICIAL INTELLIGENCE FOR DECISION MAKING

A more recent development in the use of computers is the application of artificial intelligence to aid managerial decision making. Artificial intelligence can help augment the reasoning power of executives by incorporating special knowledge that considers the cognitive capability of the decision maker. Although artificial intelligence has been around for a number of years, it now is being used to tackle problems that were not readily solvable by inexperienced managers. It has been successfully applied in areas such as medicine, production scheduling, insurance, and banking. The extension to broader management problems is beginning to occur.

Although artificial intelligence has been defined as "imitating human thinking," we consider artificial intelligence as "the set of computer systems that enhance the decision maker's ability to arrive at a better decision than what could be done without such systems." One might ask how such systems are different from computer-based systems in the past. Artificial intelligence can be structured to include the knowledge of experts. Most computer systems used by management were designed by system analysts. Although there is little doubt that computers can be made to behave in increasingly "intelligent" ways, managerial problem solving is often poorly structured and relies on the intuition of the decision maker. Expert systems, which is a subfield of artificial intelligence, has improved the way problems are formulated. Because we are able to incorporate human "expertise" into computer programs, these systems can specify decision alternatives in a way that is generally superior to that of individuals who have little expertise.

The ultimate potential of artificial intelligence for management is the ability to augment the decision maker's reasoning power. Implicit in expert systems is the ability to capture the "expertise" of persons who have the experience or know-how to perform a complex, ill-defined task. This knowledge is represented in terms of heuristic rules and is incorporated in decision-based systems. Experts have highly developed perceptual ability that allows them to better understand seemingly complex problems. In terms of decision style, experts often fit the analytic or directive category because of their ability to focus on problems and simplify them in heuristic terms. Often, the expert is the key element in system design, even surpassing the importance of the knowledge engineer who is expected to reduce information into terms acceptable by computers.

The integration of expert systems with managerial decision making means that there will have to be a closer matching of the decision maker's decision style and specific decision requirements with the development and use of expert systems. Problems that are extremely complex require problem-solving methodology that is based on issues related to real problems. Successful application of computers to complex problems requires insight, imagination, and a deep understanding of both computers and the problem area. These considerations and the need to better understand the cognitive process help point the way for the development of large-scale, complex expert systems to tackle major decision problems.

Dun & Bradstreet, working with Inference Corporation, a leader in the development of expert systems, developed programs for protecting customers from bad credit risks. The Credit Clearing House (CCH) is a product group within the Dun & Bradstreet Business Credit Services. CCH is dedicated to serving the risk management needs of apparel industry manufacturers, wholesalers, jobbers, and marketers by assigning credit ratings and dollar-specific credit recommendations on their retail customers. In response to its customer needs, D&B sought the help of Information Technology Research (ITR), the data-processing division of the D&B Business Information Group, to develop a business application to provide better credit analysis service to CCH's 4,000 customers. ITR recommended expert system technology as a solution for CCH and outlined the following objectives for the expert system:

1.  Improve product quality.
2.  Improve productivity.
3.  Provide new information as soon as it becomes available.
4.  Improve consistency for the ratings and recommendations to the customer.
5.  Provide a foundation for new and enhanced product development opportunities.

The problem with CCH credit recommendations was that they previously required a staff of trained analysts to review data from several different D&B business information reports, as well as maintaining and updating a database of credit ratings on approximately 200,000 businesses. The quality of this specialized service for apparel industry customers depended not only on the staff's analytical skills, but also on ensuring that recommendations reflected the latest database changes, as well as on the ability to respond quickly to customer requests. Meeting these criteria was extremely time-consuming and affected D&B's ability to meet its customers' growing need for greater speed and accuracy.

Dun & Bradstreet selected the expert system tool ART-IM (Automated Reasoning Tool for Information Management) for development and delivery of the CCH credit recommendations ("Inference," 1990). According to William T. Whitenack, senior vice-president of data resources for D&B, "The ART-IM application has helped us to provide major benefits to our CCH customers. They include increased quality and consistency in ratings, faster recommendations on new apparel business, and expanded coverage of the industry" ("Inference," 1990). The system accesses real-time information stored in CCH's mainframe databases to provide dollar-specific recommendations for its customers within seconds. By dynamically updating available information, the expert system improves CCH's accuracy and response time in handling requests. As a result, CCH's customers can be confident in establishing credit lines for the retail stores they do business with.

ART-IM was chosen because it provided a number of application development benefits, including:

1. It is written in a known programming language.
2. It has an efficient inference engine that enhances application performance.
3. It provides transportability across PCs and DEC computers and has portability to IBM mainframes under MVS.

Before going into full development, ITR developed a prototype of the expert system and on completion demonstrated it to senior management. Conclusions established that many components of the CCH credit analysis were generic and could be reused for a variety of products; and the time needed to develop system requirements for analytical products could be significantly reduced with this knowledge-modeling approach. Initial review of the volume test results showed a 92 percent agreement rate of the experts with the system results. After fine-tuning, the rate was raised to 98.5 percent. In addition, certain "knockout" rules were defined. (A "knockout" is a case for which a system decision cannot be accepted as completely accurate and is instead referred for an analyst's review.)

Two types of decisions are made in the CCH application. One is a decision to offer a recommendation and a dollar guideline. Another is a "no guideline" decision, which results when the system determines that it is unable to offer a dollar guideline. When a case is determined to be a "knockout," two decisions are also produced by the system. The first is based on the analysis completed by the system; the second is a decision that, although not based on a system analysis, reflects the opposing decision. It is then left to the analyst to decide whether to accept the system decision or opt for the opposing decision.

To make a recommendation, the system first receives the request from the CCH customer and accesses information residing in three different segments of the Dun & Bradstreet mainframe database. It then applies a selection of rules from over 800 rules in its knowledge base, makes a decision, and transfers that decision with supporting information back to the user. The time it takes the expert system to make a decision is less than one-half of a second!

How can we tie the elements of artificial intelligence, augmented reasoning, and human decision making together? Augmented reasoning comes from the synergistic integration and support provided by expert systems. This is related to management's need for better "tools." They are being developed and will become an integral aspect of management expertise. We can anticipate expert systems that have a natural language interface, incorporate adaptive learning, have complete and correct knowledge representation, and build on relating the decision maker to the computer. These expert systems will support unstructured decision making and eventually will lead to executive support systems.

## ▲ MODEL-BASED REASONING

Model-based reasoning is an application in expert systems that allows the replacement of heuristic rules by descriptions called models. An example of how this works was described by Fulton and Pepe (1990), who showed that an expert system that had 1,000 rules could be replaced with one that had fewer than a dozen rules using model-based reasoning. As a simple illustration of what this approach entails, the normal distribution in statistics can replace hundreds of data points with only three parameters. A model-based approach also utilizes known models (such as the Pareto Law) to assist management in coping with ever more complex problems and still have them involved in development of the expertise that these systems include.

For the past several years, NASA has been exploring intelligent support systems at the Kennedy Space Center in Florida to diagnose failures and recommend corrective action that could be taken (Fulton and Pepe, 1990). They found that rule-based systems could not provide comprehensive coverage when confronted with a vast amount of data that might be erroneous. Confronted with this situation, NASA built a model of the system. The principal difference between the rule-based system and the model-based system NASA employed was that the latter uses a model that simulates the structure and function of the machinery under observation. The system uses a model of the equipment's internal functioning and processes and thus is better able to determine what are the probable causes of a malfunction and how best to correct it. This is in contrast to rule-based systems that would require an elaborate set of rules relating information received from the sensors to the internal state of the equipment.

In diagnosing a failure, the model-based system determines what could happen in the simulated model that would give the same results as observed with the sensors. The system is not used for actual tracking, but rather provides aggregate-level data to determine what the probable cause of a failure might be. NASA currently is also using the model-based approach for diagnosing faults within the liquid oxygen loading system and for the environmental control unit. A major advantage of the model-based reasoning approach has been the system's ability to detect problems that were not initially considered. Using a rule-based system, the unknown failures could not be diagnosed (Fulton and Pepe, 1990).

Perhaps the most important value of model-based reasoning is its ability to augment the reasoning power of an expert. Managers (who often are the experts) rely on intuition or experience, and they tend to introduce simplistic solutions or in some instances the wrong decision. In addition, experts have different levels of cognitive complexity and therefore reason in different ways. Model-based reasoning can overcome limitations of experts by using appropriate models and intelligent knowledge bases.

Model-based reasoning requires less time to develop a running system, has fewer limits, and ensures consistency from one application to another. Interpretation is often easier because knowledge about the models is more readily available than when hundreds or thousands of explanations are used in a purely rule-based approach.

Another example of model-based reasoning is a causal integrative model developed by Rowe, Somers, and Martin (1988), based on earlier research they had done on disruption theory. This model illustrates how highly integrative elements in a system that have causal relationships can create high levels of uncertainty. The modules that were included in developing the causal model of the program management process are the following:

1. *Environmental uncertainty:* This module includes those variables and factors exogenous to the program that directly affect performance.
2. *Technological uncertainty:* This module deals with the specification of the state of the art and the interdependencies that cause delays or cost overruns.
3. *Contract urgency:* This covers the priority, time compression, stretch out, concurrency, or change in scope of the program needed to be taken into account.
4. *Managerial performance:* This covers the organization's ability to carry out a given program and includes expertise, quality, prior experience, available resources, and manpower.

Although the model was extremely complex, it proved to be a useful means for evaluating the most likely causes of cost overruns and program delays. It was initially tested on development of new hardware. Data from the computer program were used to determine the impact on cost, technical performance, and scheduled delivery. Prior to using the model, the project manager underestimated the cost of labor by 40 percent. The project manager was unable to comprehend the interaction of the many factors involved or their causal relationship. The computer model was able to accurately predict the impact of changes in labor content and availability on all three measures of project performance: cost, schedule, and technical quality. The model now has been applied by the project manager to deal with the complex interactions that otherwise were too difficult to track.

Although still a new field, artificial intelligence is rapidly becoming an essential support tool for helping managers solve problems and provide advice on decisions that previously could be done only by experience or intuition. American Express uses an expert system for all of its credit checking; American Airlines uses it for aircraft scheduling and maintenance; and Ford Motor Company has applied it to inventory control. It obviously works and will continue to grow in usage as more managers become familiar with its capabilities.

## ▲ DECISIONS INVOLVING RISK

Risky decisions overlaps other categories because all decisions that managers make involve future unknowns and thus some degree of uncertainty. Managers may choose to ignore risk, or, in some instances, they are not permitted to take risks because of the organizational climate. But in no case can they make risk disappear. Typically, in their attempt to avoid risk, managers make decisions based on current information. An interesting case is an oil-drilling project in the North Sea. The project manager indicated to his board that the chance of meeting the schedule was only 15 percent and that if the board wanted to increase it to a 50 percent chance, they would have to spend an additional $1 billion. Imagine asking a board to make that kind of decision without a rather thorough and complete analysis. In fact, the risk analysis had clearly identified what the situation was, what the chance of meeting the specific objectives would be, and what actions would be needed to overcome the specific problems.

What is probability and how do managers relate to risk? Decision making under risk and uncertainty requires a basic knowledge of probability. All managers make inferences based on information received. They may do this on a purely judgmental, subjective basis, or they may choose to estimate the chance that something will occur based on past performance. The statement that a customer typically is late in making payments really means that the number of times the payment has been received late, compared with all the bills sent, represents the probability of being late. Thus, probability equals the number of ways some particular event can occur divided by the number of ways all possible events under consideration can occur. It is always a percentage or ratio. Having defined probability as the ratio of specified outcomes to total possible outcomes, we can proceed to examine other aspects of probability and see how they can be used in decision making.

As every loan officer knows, some of the people who are given loans will not repay them. If there were a foolproof way of assigning credit risks, banks would be able to avoid the losses incurred because of those people who default on their loans. Unfortunately, there is no way to avoid the risk. The best that can be done is to understand the problem in terms that help the officer estimate the potential loss (Rowe and Lin, 1982).

Let us examine the problem in the following way. First determine what percentage of people who request loans are considered poor risks. Also estimate what percentage of all the loans that are made will not be repaid. We now have two estimates:

**PR** = poor risks     = the percentage of all people asking for loans who are risks
**DL** = defaults on loans   = the percentage of all loans made that will not be repaid

A problem that arises is that some of the people who are considered poor risks will in fact repay their loans, whereas some who have good credit ratings will not repay their loans. So we have two more percentages to consider:

**PRR** = the percentage of poor risks who repay their loans
**GCD** = the percentage of good credit risks who will default

Now let's put this all together. First we have to determine each of these percentages, which we do by applying the basic definition of probability—the number of ways some particular event can occur divided by the number of ways all possible events under consideration can occur. The general formulas are as follows:

$$PR = \frac{\text{Number of people rated poor risks}}{\text{Total number of people requesting loans}}$$

$$DL = \frac{\text{Number of people who default}}{\text{Total number of people given loans}}$$

$$PRD = \frac{\text{Number of poor risks who default}}{\text{Total number of poor risks}}$$

$$GDC = \frac{\text{Number of good credit risks who default}}{\text{Total number of good credit risks}}$$

Combining these, we can estimate the potential losses to the bank, once we research the bank records. Let's assume we discover that:

**PR** = 4% (If the risk of defaulting is 4%, then good credit risks = GC = 96%.)
**DL** = 8.4%
**PRD** = 90%
**GDC** = 5%

This boils down to the following: Since 90 percent of the poor risks will default, we have 90 percent of the 4 percent rated as poor risks. That results in a default rate of 3.6 percent of loans made to poor risks (90% × 4% = 3.6%). Now, of the remaining 96 percent who are rated as good risks, 5 percent will default. Thus, 4.8 percent of loans will be in default because of loans made to good credit risks (5% × 96% = 4.8%). Adding the two numbers together, 3.6% + 4.8% = 8.4%; 8.4 percent of all loans made end up in default. If we examine the ratios of all loans in default attributed to each kind of risk, we get 3.6 ÷ 8.4 = 43% (poor risks) and 4.8 ÷ 8.4 = 57% (good credit risks). The conclusion that we can draw is that so-called good risks account for a larger percentage of the loans in default. A failure to analyze the losses from good risks would have ignored most of the exposure. For the astute credit manager, it's all a matter of defining probability!

## ▲ RISK ANALYSIS

Risk analysis is another method for providing a systematic approach to decision making. It is particularly useful when making choices between actions that will have complex and uncertain future effects. Risk analysis has been applied to a wide range of business problems including package design, pricing, production, project management, and investments. There have been applications in the areas of engineering, government, and medicine, and risk analysis has been used as the basis for decisions by many companies.

Competitive bidding provides an excellent illustration of where risk analysis makes an important difference in the outcome of the decision. In one case, a risk analysis model was applied to billing in government contracting. It was determined that the chance of the government's paying depended on the type of contract, the time of year, and the agency to whom the bill was submitted. Given this information, when the chance of a bill's being delayed was high, the vice-president would "hand-carry" the bill directly to the appropriate agency and ask them to process it. In one case, this amounted to $5 million that would have been delayed from four to six weeks had the bill not been hand-carried.

Hertz (1988) applied risk analysis to capital investments comparing the conventional "best-estimate" approach with the risks involved. It was a surprise to find that the estimated 25.2 percent return on investment turned out to be only 14.6 percent based on a computer simulation that compared the two alternatives.

In another example, decision analysis was used to determine the best course of action for introducing a major new product at Maxwell House. Faced with considerable uncertainty regarding the technical and commercial feasibility of a new coffee with a dramatic taste advantage and a possible five-year head start over the competition, Maxwell House decided to proceed with a commercial plant to manufacture the new product. However, the firm was concerned with increasing competition from noncoffee beverages, the possible adverse effects of coffee, and a declining rate of growth of instant coffee.

Examining the coffee market, Maxwell House concluded that private brands hurt sales, there was overcapacity in the industry, competition was aggressive, and there was a great similarity in product quality. One of the decisions Maxwell House had to make was whether to increase the price per pound of coffee to offset the introduction of its new approach—the quick-strip can. They used a decision analysis approach to determine which action would be best. It was decided that the best course of action was to increase the price two cents per pound rather than merely trying to offset the cost of introducing the new quick-strip can.

Decision making under uncertainty covers those problems for which the manager does not have any information on the probabilities involving the alternatives under consideration. In these cases, the manager can develop strategies for dealing with the unknown situations by using one of the three following approaches:

1. Based on given objectives or values, determine criteria for selecting one alternative from available courses of action.
2. Using opinions or judgments, develop a conditional estimate of the chance of various events.
3. Use a combination of values and opinions to arrive at choices.

An example of decision making under uncertainty was the location of a new major airport for Mexico City. The decision was based on five criteria:

1. Limit the total construction and maintenance costs.
2. Provide adequate capacity to meet future air traffic demands.
3. Keep the time to drive to the airport to a minimum.
4. Have the highest possible safety.
5. Reduce the effects of noise pollution due to air traffic.

The resulting study and analysis came up with a proposal to locate the airport at Zumpago, some 25 miles away, rather than in Mexico City, and to do it in stages rather than "as soon as possible." The analysis pointed up the "glaring inconsistencies" that were put forth in strongly held positions for a rapid, "all-out" move (de Neufville, 1972).

## ▲ ▲ ▲ ▲ ▲ CRAIG FIELDS CASE

Craig Fields, as director of the Pentagon's advanced research arm, had run-ins with the Bush administration because he wanted the government to support high-definition television. He felt that the government should support the Sematech cooperative in order to improve U.S. computer chip capability. Not agreeing with his superiors, he openly promoted greater government support for high-technology industries. The Pentagon responded to questions about Dr. Fields by saying that he "is not being fired from any position and any such characterization unfairly impugns his years of fine service to the nation." Here was a case of conflict between a strong executive and persons to whom he reported who felt differently about the decisions he made. What is the probability that this story will be repeated where capable, hard-driving executives run counter to their organization (Redburn, 1990)?                                                              ▲

## ▲ Summary

The value of decision-aiding tools is to provide support to the decision maker in coping with increasingly difficult problems. Without such tools, the decision maker "muddles through" the maze of complexity and uncertainty. It is not the methodology that is important. Rather, it is the recognition that there are appropriate ways that can augment the decision maker's basic decision-making ability. In doing this, it is important to recognize the decision maker's preference when designing information systems.

This chapter presented a number of decision-aiding approaches that can be used by managers seeking to improve their decision-making skills. First, the linear decision analysis showed that adding structure to a problem can facilitate the understanding of relevant factors. Decision tables provided another method that helps formalize the factors and decision rules used in arriving at conclusions. Heuristic decision rules and computer simulation were described and examples given to illustrate their application. Three basic decision problems were defined as deterministic, complex, and risky. Each was explained by showing selected methods that could be applied to finding solutions to problems that fit each category. Information systems and computer applications were described as having significant potential for decision support systems—artificial intelligence and expert systems. Decision making under risk and uncertainty was described along with examples of how managers could use the concepts. Finally, it was pointed out that managers have no choice when it comes to risk-taking decisions. The effective manager recognizes these risks and attempts to deal with them in an appropriate manner.

## ▲ Study Questions

1. Why are decision aids needed?
2. What kinds of problems do decision makers typically face?
3. What is a linear decision analysis?
4. Why are decision tables useful?
5. What does the concept of balancing factors mean?
6. What is an example of a multi-attribute decision problem?
7. How can computers aid decision making?
8. Explain how heuristics are used to solve problems.
9. Why should risk be taken into account in decision making?

## ▲ References

Argyris, Chris. "How Tomorrow's Executives Will Make Decisions." *Think* (November-December 1967).

de Neufville, R. L. "Use of Decision Analysis in Airport Development for Mexico City." In *Analysis of Public Systems*. Drake, A. W., Keeney, R. L., and Morse, P. M. eds. Cambridge, MA: M.I.T. Press, 1972.

Fulton, Steven P., and Pepe, Charles O. "An Introduction to Model-Based Reasoning." *A.I. Expert* (January 1990), pp. 45–56.

Greiner, Larry. "What Managers Think of Participant Leadership." *Harvard Business Review* (1973).

Henry, Harold W. *Long-Range Planning Practices in 45 Industrial Companies*. Englewood Cliffs, NJ: Prentice-Hall, Inc., 1967, pp. 85–105.

Hertz, David Bendel. *The Expert Executive*. New York: Wiley, 1988.

"Inference and the Art of Building Expert Systems." El Segundo, CA: Inference Corporation, 1990.

Kepner, Charles, and Tregoe, Benjamin S. *The Rational Manager*. New York: McGraw-Hill, 1963.

Redburn, Tom. "Pentagon's High-Tech Promoter Transferred." *Los Angeles Times* (April 21, 1990), p. D1.

Rowe, Alan J. "How Executives Make Decisions," from *Modern Business Reports*. New York: Alexander Hamilton Institute, 1976.

Rowe, Alan J., and Bahr, Fred R. "A Heuristic Approach to Managerial Problem Solving." *Journal of Economics and Business* (1972), pp. 159–163.

Rowe, Alan J., and Lin, C. Y. "Decision Making." In *Encyclopedia of Chemical Processing And Design*. John J. McKetta, ed. New York: Marcel Dekker, Inc., 1982.

Rowe, Alan J., Somers, Ivan A., and Martin, M. Dean. "Critical Issues in the Application of Artificial Intelligence to Acquisition Management." From *Proceedings* of Forum on Artificial Intelligence for Management, Dayton, OH (May 1988).

# Part IV

# The Decision Environment

# *10* Global Decisions

▲ ▲ ▲  ▲ ▲ ▲ ▲ ▲ ▲ ▲ ▲ ▲ ▲ ▲ ▲ ▲ ▲ ▲ ▲ ▲ ▲

This chapter explores the way in which globalization of business will affect decision making. The increasing dependency and interrelationship of the economies of nations places demands on managers to deal more effectively with complex, long-term, and risky decisions. The evidence shows the importance of global decision making to assure a stronger competitive position. To compete on a global basis, quality, pricing, service, and design (including technology) will have to be incorporated into products so that they can match or exceed foreign-made products. Many organizations insist that their executives have overseas experience before being promoted to higher positions.

An example of a company that is moving toward a global strategy is General Electric, which sold its consumer electronics business and then bought Thompson's medical equipment business. Understanding Japanese management is increasingly important to American managers who want to become more competitive in the shrinking global environment. Interestingly, many management practices that are followed by the Japanese were invented in the United States. The problem for American managers and organizations is that the good management practices that have been implemented so effectively by the Japanese have not taken hold on a broad basis in the United States. As a result, American business has not been able to compete effectively on price or quality with the Japanese, Koreans, Taiwanese, and Singaporeans in the areas of automobiles and electronics. This is a dilemma confronting American decision makers who are concerned with long-term, potentially devastating effects on the economic health of the United States.

## ▲ SUCCEEDING IN A GLOBAL ENVIRONMENT

How will American managers and executives deal with the issue of the globalization of the economy? Will they view globalization as a threat or an opportunity? A new and broader thought process is needed to deal effectively with the issue of globalization. Leaders are needed with the vision to see beyond the immediate situation and with the ability to identify future possibilities.

In order to succeed in a global environment, there is need for an overarching culture that focuses on strategic thrust and intent. This is the focus that has made some companies winners in the global environment. Focused organizations are more effective and have the competitive advantage needed to match their global rivals. In this sense, regaining competitive advantage will mean thinking about strategy differently rather than simply in terms applied to the United States alone. The strategic-fit concept that matches resources and opportunities, or the generic strategies of low costs have only led to a reduction in competitive advantage for many companies in the United States. To attain a new competitive position, strategies will have to be quite different from what has been utilized in the past. It is not sufficient to have minor adjustments to current thinking; revitalization will require an entirely new rethinking rather than accepting small incremental improvements. For example, merely having the facts about what competitors are doing does not provide any insight into their inventiveness or ways in which we can become more competitive. The companies that have succeeded in the global environment, regardless of their resources and capability, seem to have an obsession with becoming leaders that exists at all levels of the organization and over a long period of time. This is termed "strategic intent" (Hamel and Prahalad, 1990).

Strategic intent becomes meaningful in an organization when top management engages in

1. Creating a sense of urgency so that all individuals become part of the challenge to create the competitive advantage.

2. Developing a competitor focus at every level throughout the organization by use of competitive intelligence so that workers understand what their competitors are doing.
3. Finding employees who have the skills for the work that needs to be done.
4. Doing a thorough job and being sure that it is completed effectively before moving into still another challenging area.
5. Having very clear targets, milestones, and review mechanisms to ensure that progress is being made.

Using strategic intent, successful companies have to take on competitors that tend to be larger and have more resources. What that implies is that management must be able to utilize scarce resources more effectively and must be able to do things significantly better than their competitors. It is in effect competitive warfare, not simply imitation, but it means taking the risks that need to be taken by innovating and being more effective. The four approaches identified are

1. Building advantage.
2. Searching for opportunities.
3. Changing what happens.
4. Competing through collaboration.

Companies that have a strategic advantage tend to have a wide product portfolio so that in any competitive situation, they have less risk because there are alternative ways of meeting problems.

Exploring opportunities and the use of surprise are important and effective means for gaining competitive advantage. Changing the ways things are done provides still another means for achieving competitive advantage through innovation. For example, Canon was able to change the competitive environment in Japan by standardizing machines and components in order to reduce cost and to distribute those components through office product dealers rather than to compete head-on with Xerox or Kodak. Collaboration can be achieved through licensing, joint ventures, and strategic alliances. Many significant ventures have benefited from this approach to achieving competitive advantage in the global environment. The most important area that needs to be avoided is an extremely conservative approach in contrast to truly creative strategy. If top management is overly cautious, it typically reflects a lack of confidence in their ability to achieve revitalization as their strategic intent, which is needed to fully and effectively compete in a global economy.

A good example of the benefits of cooperation is the case of IBM and Apple Computer. Apple President John Sculley said that Apple had no choice but to abandon its loner approach and join a strong partner if it intended to be a force in the computer industry in the 1990s. According to the arrangement between IBM and Apple, in exchange for Apple's proprietary software, Apple received the right to use an important IBM microprocessor. This could lead to the interchangeability and linking of Apple and IBM workstations by 1993 (Hof et al., 1991). John Sculley explained the alliance between IBM and Apple as a radical strategy shift at Apple away from its "go-it-alone" approach. Sculley predicted that the two cultures at IBM and Apple would work well together (Weber, 1991).

## ▲ JAPANESE MANAGEMENT

Participation in the United States appears to be limited in terms of real influence on the decision maker. Decisions still tend to be made primarily by the manager; however, pseudo-participation seems to play an important role in the way in which American managers attempt to influence the behavior of subordinates.

A somewhat different style of management has been practiced by the Japanese. Johnson and Ouchi (1974) indicated that there were five important aspects of the managerial approach used by Japanese in the United States. These include

1. Emphasis on a flow of information and initiative from the bottom up.
2. Making top management the facilitator of decisions rather than the issuer of edicts.
3. Using middle management as the means for shaping solutions to problems.
4. Stressing consensus as the way of making decisions.
5. Paying close attention to the personal well-being of employees.

This approach has produced significant results. For example, *Fortune* describes the productivity level of Japan as beginning to exceed that of the United States. The Japanese also rely heavily on automation and on the use of the learning curve as the basis for reduced cost per unit. Their management style must be credited with achieving considerable improvement. Johnson and Ouchi indicate that the typical Japanese approach to personnel relations is exemplified by the way Sony employees are treated as "whole persons." Productivity at Sony is high, and absenteeism and turnover are low. At Sony's San Diego operation, these figures are below those of other electronics companies. Also in California, a Japanese bank has grown twice as fast as most small banks in the state. "Americans working for this bank repeatedly refer to the aggressiveness and esprit de corps that the Japanese staff instills in fellow managers and workers" (Johnson and Ouchi, 1974, pp. 61–69).

The typical American manager uses much stronger personal leadership, which makes it difficult to arrive at innovative decisions such as in Japan. Because achieving consensus is very exhausting, American management funnels tasks to a number of committees assigned to a particular problem. They define the tasks and build on the expertise of the directors and the committees. Although consensus implies a cumbersome process, in reality it means knowing the people and getting problems solved within the company.

When examining a number of instances of how Japanese managers operate (for example, in a metal zipper company in Macon, Georgia), the management methods were found to be similar to those used in Japan, where employees are invited to take initiative. At the subsidiary's meetings, the president sits at the center of the conference table, but it's up to his subordinates to tell him how they would like to solve problems (Kraar, 1989). The motto of the company implies a sharing of benefits among the company and its suppliers, customers, and employees. In another instance, Sony indicates that employees who play together work better together, so the company not only sponsors a softball team in San Diego, but also throws frequent parties for workers. Japanese managers strive for what they call an informal family atmosphere and even provide billiard tables in their factory so that employees can relax together during breaks. Such consideration of employees makes a company "worker friendly," so that there is a closer identification of the worker with the company. Employees are then more willing to work hard to help meet the goals of the company. If companies take care of their workers, the workers will take care of the company.

The accessibility of top Japanese executives particularly impresses Americans. It makes a lot of difference when you can walk into the president's office anytime without going through five secretaries. Many American executives are surprised and often dismayed by the fact that the chairman will sometimes go directly to an area to encourage workers or appear on an assembly line and talk directly to the individuals involved. This vitality and excellence of communication helps the whole company move toward its objective; in American companies, more is expected of management rather than of the workers.

In the article "How We See Each Other" (1981), it is indicated that although decision making is slow and nobody is in charge of anything, the secret may be something called *wa*.

As a chairman of Hitachi emphasized, the meaning of *wa* is harmony, which leads to strength. This is very difficult to explain to American executives and employees. Harmony, consensus, and concern for the individual all reflect differences between American management and that used by Japanese businesses. Although *wa* is a fundamental principle of Japanese thought, the Japanese have a different sense of responsibility. Americans tend to think of themselves as individuals distinct from the group and are quick to take defensive action to protect themselves, whereas the Japanese consider themselves as primarily responsible for the group or company and think of the best interests of the group. This, along with lifetime employment, comes under the *wa* spirit and good relations with the unions. However, *wa* does have its problems, and the Japanese are currently concerned with ways in which to deal with the issue of lifetime employment.

The reaction from individuals who have worked for Japanese companies is that consensus really is communication. By providing information, Japanese managers attain cooperation rather than consensus or participative decision making. However, the final decision is made by either the president or the chairman of the board. This is not obvious because so much information filters up and is discussed and reviewed, and so many meetings are held, that workers feel there really is consensus. The reaction to consensus decision making is that it leads to more highly committed workers rather than the conflict that exists in many American organizations. American managers have to deal with unions that are less cooperative than in Japan, where the workforce is basically supportive.

Japanese and American management practices differ in the areas of permanent employment, job rotation, specialization, benefits, tradition of overtime, bonuses, starting at the bottom, promotion, harmony and open communication, seniority, and compensation. The importance of the employee, however, is illustrated by the statement made by Akio Morita, co-founder and chairman of The Sony Corporation, that "the workers and the management are in the same boat. Harmony is the most important element in an organization. You can't just lay off people because of a recession. Because a recession is not the fault of the worker, management must sacrifice profit and share the pain caused by the recession. In Japan, management does not treat labor as a tool but as a partner. We share a common face" (Range, 1982). Salary and wage differentials in Japan are relatively narrow by a ratio of about 17 times. In the United States, the average big-company CEO made about 150 times the average worker. The management of a large Japanese textile firm that faced a long-term decline in the market took five years to lay off unneeded workers. One of the first steps taken was to reduce management salaries (Teisin, 1981). In contrast, at the time in 1991 when General Dynamics was planning to reduce at least one-third of its 90,000-member workforce over a span of four years, William A. Anders, chairman and chief executive officer, received an annual salary of $800,000. He received an additional $1.6 million in May based on the price of company stock in an executive compensation plan adopted at the February 1991 stockholders' meeting (Martin, 1991). We see a stark contrast between the treatment of workers and executives in the United States and in Japan. This must certainly have a major impact on the attitudes and commitment of workers to the organization.

## ▲ CONSENSUS MANAGEMENT

In Japan, a general attitude of consensus and cooperation prevails, called "consensus management." Although there certainly is much discussion over a long period of time, and a great deal of input is received from all levels, ultimately the top executive makes and is held responsible for decisions. These decisions are generally accepted without question and are supported at all levels. There are other approaches, however, such as that of Hisao Tsubouchi, who is a Japanese boss whose "consensus" is an iron fist. Tsubouchi's tough autocratic style has earned him a reputation for breaking unions, firing employees, and instilling fear in subordinates. Is he successful? He is the sole owner of Kurushimadork Group, which had revenues of $3.3 billion in 1983. Is Tsubouchi the exception? According to *Nihon Keizai Shimbum,* Japan's leading business newspaper, in its list of excellent companies, numbers 1 and 2 were like military dictatorships. ("List," 1984). Ichiro Isoda, chairman of Sumitomo Bank, says, "You need someone at the top who can change gears fast." The one-man shows are running the most aggressive companies, and they are the pace setters in their industries (Smith, 1985).

The Japanese describe decision by consensus as a difficult and slow process. In reality it is not participative management as we know it here in the United States (Tsurumi, 1984). Rather, it is a policy of having superiors and subordinates cooperate and, in the process of communication, arrive at a consensus. Also, the individuals in each functional area are aware of what is required to carry out the decision. It does not involve the interminable meetings, squabbling, and indecision that characterize management consensus practiced in the United States. The method requires considerable patience and directors do not always take part in decisions. Also more emphasis is put on a person's merit than on seniority, and they prefer to recruit personnel from the outside rather than hire from within the firm.

In the United States, employees are less willing to follow the top man blindly, and they tend to be more adversarial. Furthermore, culture varies greatly from one company to another and often within the same company. Thus, executives in America must have broader skills because they cannot rely on shared cultural value systems for legitimacy and support (Lawrence, 1985).

The Japanese approach to power also evokes support and commitment. True power, according to the Japanese, is achieved through consensus decision making, which is a group process. Authoritarian power, or positional power, generally is not considered as effective as the power of persuasion. Voluntary agreement can be gained through true understanding, even though it may take longer to generate power through consensus.

## ▲ STRATEGIC DECISION MAKING

Strategic decision making is often described as "the destiny decisions" of the organization. This is because the survivability and often the level of profitability are closely tied to the key strategic decisions made by organizations. The decision by Lockheed to use the Rolls Royce engine for its L-1011 aircraft seemed like the right thing to do. When making this decision, Lockheed was aware of the fact that Rolls Royce had never built the size engine desired, nor did they have experience with the technology for an engine using three different motor spools. Most importantly, no one had ever built an engine using hifil blades, which would be lighter than the normal titanium blades. The result was well over a year's delay in introducing the L-1011 to compete with other wide-bodied aircraft. This was a high-risk decision that did not pay off.

The L-1011 performed quite well, although it now appears that it might have been a better decision to use the General Electric engine, which had been tested and was available a year earlier. The time lost waiting for the Rolls Royce engine resulted in lost market share. Compounding their problems, the Airbus A300 appeared to be a formidable competitor. Concessions were made to airlines in order to induce them to substitute the two-engine wide-bodied A300 for the three-engine Lockheed L-1011. Efficiency, fuel consumption, and other advantages were claimed. Using the Rolls Royce engine in the Lockheed L-1011 appears to have been a decision that may have been instrumental in Lockheed's leaving the wide-bodied commercial jet market.

Another example is the Bulova Watch Company which introduced the Accutron watch in the mid-1960s. When Harry Henshel took control of Bulova, he indicated that he did not want to be a "me, too" president and embarked on a strategy to make Bulova a prestigious watch company. He started with the introduction of the Accutron even though he was opposed by not only his technical staff but his entire board. Another company had already spent $1 million in the unsuccessful development of a similar type of tuning fork for watches and had abandoned the project. Henshel, with perseverance and foresight, insisted that the Accutron project be continued, and this turned out to be highly successful. On the basis of this success, Henshel decided to introduce a mid-priced watch, the Caravelle, in direct competition with the Swiss watch companies that supplied many of the components for Bulova. Again there was immediate success. Given this situation, Henshel decided to reduce the number of distributors and use only those that would exclusively handle Bulova watches. Again, instant success. Thus, the decision to pursue a very unlikely and problematical course made the difference in Bulova's achieving an extraordinary level of growth and profitability.

In the early 1970s, when digital watches were introduced, Bulova was approached about entering that field. They claimed it was a passing fad and that people would not give up their normal watch in exchange for reading numbers. The result was that the decision not to enter the digital watch field took away all the advantage that Bulova had gained with the introduction of the novel Accutron watch. By 1975, Bulova's stock and profits had reached a point where they were forced to sell the company and thus give up the position that had been obtained through the developments, the perspective, the insight, and the risk taking that only ten years previously had made it one of the dominant watch makers in the field. Thus, one decision to enter a risky market brought success; another decision to avoid a risky market brought the sellout of Bulova to Stellex.

It is obvious that the decisions being described are extraordinarily complex and rarely can be made by a single individual. More typically, they require not only the perspective and understanding of key executives, but the support and execution of the entire organization in order to meet desired objectives. Still, in the critical "destiny decisions," the special insight needed to be correct in order to survive cannot be guaranteed by consensus decision making. In the first case of the Bulova Watch Company, Harry Henshel was opposed by both his technical staff and his entire board, but he was right. If he had followed consensus decision making, he probably would not have proceeded with the Accutron project that proved so successful. The question remains, Was the Bulova decision not to introduce digital watches a consensus decision?

There are three major assumptions used as the basis for strategy. First is the assumption that strategies will provide guidelines for the decisions made at all levels of the organization. However, the way in which strategic decisions filter down is a function of the manager's decision style and leadership. The second assumption is that all levels of management in the organization are aware of and willing to support the overall strategy espoused at the corporate level. The third assumption is that there is an overall framework used to carry out the corporate objectives. Possibly the most difficult aspect of strategic decision making is the heavy interdependency of the many decisions that have to be made. Although Lockheed chose Rolls Royce to produce its engines, the ramifications of that decision were enormous, not only on survivability but on the ability to implement and effectively carry out the decision.

What are the strategic alternatives available? Which are controllable by management? What range of choice do they have? Successful executives employ a number of approaches, depending on the environment. In a complex environment, successful firms utilize intelligence, specialists, and market innovation. Unsuccessful firms drift and enter new markets or acquisitions without requisite analysis.

Today's economic climate and old assumptions no longer hold true, and what is needed are new tools to help management make more accurate strategic decisions concerning the future (Clifford, Bridgewater, and Hardy, 1975). The president of a large corporation stated that the biggest poker pot he ever won was with a pair of nines. The president then paused for the effect to take hold before continuing. "I'm trying to make a point," he said. There has to be a sense of relative values, timing, or waiting it out, when the chips are flying and signals are confusing. Extreme interest rate fluctuations, unprecedented sales drop, inventory build-up, and stock decline are all symptoms of the environment. What should a company do? Does it wait or just throw in the towel? Or cut the dividend, reduce research, or spin off products? These are the awesome decisions confronting executives who live in a topsy-turvy world (Rowe, 1983).

If management could make better strategic decisions, would these ensure the survivability, growth, and profitability of the organization? Gerstner (1975) claimed, "However valuable it may be as a concept, in many companies, strategic planning amounts to little more than an academic exercise with no real bottom-line impact." The fundamental weakness, said Gerstner, is that most corporate planning efforts do not lead to major current decisions that have to be made. Salveson (1974), commenting on how strategic decisions are made, observed, "Hanging heavy in the balance and outweighing all other factors in the effectiveness of the management of strategy is one fact, the mind of the chief executive." In the process this involves conscious and unconscious motivations, aspirations, needs, fears, and frustrations. The strategies chosen will be defensive, conservative, expansive, or entrepreneurial—all depending on the personality of the executive. Strategies are rational only within the chief executive's personality.

## ▲ TOOLS FOR STRATEGIC DECISIONS

We should distinguish the kinds of tools needed for strategic decision making from those used in future forecasting, futures research, delphi technique, or long-range planning. Each of these has a direct bearing on the strategic decisions management must make. Assessment of the future is not in and of itself making strategic decisions. The development of any strategic decision must start with a clear idea of the basic objectives, goals, and directions the organization is considering. These in turn must be related to the capabilities, unique strengths, and achievable goals rather than wishful thinking. Obviously, these are dependent on alternatives that are available and require tools of analysis in order to determine which are the feasible and realistic goals for an organization to consider. Having these, there are then decisions concerning organization design, individual commitment, utilization of resources, timing, and direction.

An example of a highly successful application of tools for strategic decisions was developed by International Utilities. A simulation model was used based on a number of assumptions relevant to the environment of the business. The political economy, economic demand, productive capability, organization and planning, control reporting, evaluation of risk and return for alternatives, and allocation of capital were all included. The major advantage of the simulation approach was the ability to examine many alternatives in order to determine the financial impact and the potential risks involved (Rowe, 1970).

The application of scenarios that describe various potential occurrences, their likelihood, and what the consequences might be has become increasingly useful in today's turbulent world. Of the 20 items that were forecast to occur in the period of 1960–2030, such as desalinization of water, oral contraceptives, ultralight construction, organ transplants, reliable weather forecasts, information retrieval, artificial organs, and nonnarcotic drugs, *all* have been achieved already (Kahn and Briggs, 1972).

Strategic decisions, although far more complex than many of the routine decisions managers make because of the potential impact of such decisions, are still only part of decision making. The basic underlying decision process still requires the inputs of decision makers, the risk propensity and decision styles of the manager, and the need for the organization to carry out any decision that is reached.

## ▲ STRATEGIC VISION

Strategic vision covers the a, b, c's of strategy. It is concerned with the underlying assumptions (a) that the executive makes based on his or her beliefs and (b) an understanding of the potential outcome or (c) consequences. It is not simply the visionary who out of the blue conceives of new concepts or new ideas (Rowe et al., 1989). Embodied in the concept of vision is the ability to foresee possibilities and how that vision really affects strategy. When asked if television would replace movies, Darryl F. Zanuck, who was the founder of Twentieth Century Fox, said it would not, but that both would continue to survive together. He envisioned the time when there would be worldwide distribution of entertainment, and that is, of course, what has promoted the large number of movies that are seen abroad. This also led to high-definition television, which is what Sony saw as the possibility of competing directly with the big screens in movie theaters. Rupert Murdoch put together the Fox movie studio to use a satellite television service called Sky Channel. And so it goes. These are individuals who have vision and understand what might be possible in the future (Flanigan, 1989).

In 1899, Japan decided to open its doors to foreign trade and teamed up with Western Electric to form the U.S.-backed venture there. It imported Western's telephones and then decided to make its own. Since that time, Nippon Electric (NEC) has become the world's largest seller of computer chips, it is fifth in size in telecommunications equipment and fourth in size in computers built. But for the future, NEC has a vision that is all consuming and is driven by technology as specified by Koji Kobayashi, the one who transformed the telephone company into an electronics powerhouse. Kobayashi is credited with the vision for building a powerful information network and is the one who sees the future in computing and communications. It takes this kind of vision and dedication to make things really happen (Ness et al., 1990).

## ▲ A GLOBAL PERSPECTIVE

American managers will have to develop a global perspective in order to effectively compete in the newly expanding global economy. Everything is changing. The Eastern bloc of communist nations is no longer a monolithic whole. Competition and privatization will create tremendous opportunities for American firms. At the same time, the reverse is also occurring, with foreign firms increasingly penetrating the American market. Honewen Inc. has transformed itself from an ailing conglomerate to a streamlined world leader in automated controls. Chairman James J. Renier expresses his vision as, "We can bid something in the U.S., spec it in France, buy a part in Kuwait, and deliver it anywhere in the world" (Therrien, 1991).

In a deal with rival Mitsubishi, IBM has agreed to have its Japanese subsidiary build mainframe computers for Mitsubishi Electric Corp. This will be the first time IBM has manufactured machines for others from its most advanced family of products. This underscores IBM's aggressive push to improve sluggish international sales. IBM feels that as the number-2 mainframe supplier in Japan, by joining with number 5, it can increase its penetration with potential sales to Japanese companies that have not been IBM customers. Historically, IBM and Mitsubishi have collaborated in business dealings since the 1970s (Lazzareschi, 1991).

We see some important factors involved in global relations: new, innovative methods, reciprocal gains, and long-term relationships. Eastern Europe is moving toward a market economy (Schares et al., 1991). Europe proper is emerging as an integrated economy. With the unification of Germany, that nation may emerge as the colossus of the realigned Eastern Europe. Old business contacts may prove to be the key to this possibility (Marshall, 1991).

IBM is under assault in Europe from its competitors in the United States and its Japanese rivals. Europe generates half of IBM's total profits. IBM Europe Chairman David E. McKinney is initiating a sweeping reorganization to protect the $28 billion business. With Europe becoming one big market, "McKinney wants his local managers to think big, too." In an effort to keep dealer loyalty, IBM has invested $100 million in nearly 200 joint ventures and partnerships. Change is the order of the day. According to McKinney, "No organization is permanent" (Levine and Schares, 1991). American companies will have to be innovative in dealing in the global economy. Companies will also have to be flexible in terms of responding to the actions of the competition as well as the needs of the customer. Japanese car manufacturers have been building plants in the United States in order to avoid quota restrictions. In 1984, direct Japanese investment in the United States reached $1.7 billion and was expected to top $2.5 billion in 1985 ("How Germany Sells Cars," 1985).

Japanese firms reached an agreement with Boeing Company to take their largest role ever in the development and production of the Boeing 777 jetliner, scheduled for completion in 1995. Under the agreement, Mitsubishi Heavy Industries, Kawasaki Heavy Industries, and Fuji Heavy Industries will jointly develop and manufacture components valued at 21 percent of the cost of the airframe of the 777. Japanese firms are also supplying parts worth 15 percent of the value. The Japanese firms are not full partners with Boeing, but they are program partners. These firms are supplying a major portion of the airframe, such as fuselage panels and other items. The great benefit for the Japanese is that for the first time their engineers will be involved with Boeing in some of the design work. Japanese engineers will learn how to design some aircraft parts from scratch. This is a step toward Japan's goal of developing an aircraft industry (Helms, 1990).

## ▲ GLOBAL COMPETITION

Global competition can be expected to be fierce in the years to come. However, there will also be major efforts at cooperative ventures. The value of the dollar, the trade gap, deficit spending, the national debt, and energy costs are all major factors that may have disruptive impacts on the environment in which the decision maker operates. The decision maker must be cognizant of these environmental forces and account for them during the decision-making process. Change will be the constant.

How will American firms stack up to foreign competition in the global market? There is evidence that in some situations American firms can be very competitive. As an example, Timken Roller Bearing, a Canton, Ohio company known for its quality, innovation, and low-cost products, is poised to penetrate the Japanese market. Timken has done the right things to be a successful and competitive company. Founded in 1899, Timken has consistently invested heavily in technology, new plants, and equipment. It has refined and improved its products, concentrated on its core business and avoided diversification, globalized, exported, and taken the long view. Manufacturer of the tapered roller bearing, Timken is barred from entering the lucrative Japanese auto market because of Japan's trade barriers, even though the firm provides a superior product. The ability to provide quality products is the result of a $500 million investment in 1981 in a new steel plant to control the quality of the metal used in its bearings (Woutat, 1991).

Another competitive firm is Motorola, Inc. Motorola's strengths are a strong R&D, built-in quality, and an emphasis on service. As a result of its efforts, Motorola is first in semiconductors in the United States and fourth in the world. Motorola's position in the world market is the result of a far-reaching technology exchange agreement with Toshiba Corp. of Japan. Toshiba put Motorola back in the business of making DRAMs and in return received Motorola's microprocessors. This represented a good exchange of value in both directions (Therrien, 1989).

Other notable American firms that consistently have been able to hold their own against foreign competition are steelmaker Nucor and arc welding equipment manufacturer Lincoln Electric. Such firms follow employment practices that are similar to those of the Japanese in terms of employee security, responsibility, and rewards. As an illustration, when business was down, the president of Nucor took a reduction in his salary. Nucor employees are rewarded on the basis of team performance, which encourages cooperation and improves productivity. It can be done in the United States, but it takes visionary leadership with integrity and the right human values to make it happen.

## ▲ CULTURAL DIFFERENCES

As we move farther along the continuum from nationalism to the globalization of our economy, we are presented with new challenges regarding the issue of cultural differences. To be accepted by other cultures, Americans must understand those cultures and behave appropriately when dealing with them. We must overcome the old image of the "ugly American" who was insensitive to other cultures and projected an image of arrogance. Although our own culture in the United States is changing, other cultures are also changing. We must recognize these phenomena. In terms of the thematic approach of this book with respect to the decision maker, it is appropriate to consider data regarding decision makers in different cultures. We previously considered data on decision style, values, organization culture, and communication for Americans. In this section we deal with such data and compare them for Americans with those for foreign nationals. Our purpose is to determine whether there are differences and what they are.

### Decision Style Comparison

Managers' decision-making styles, as discussed in Chapters 3 and 4, usually include multiple styles. For example, senior executives typically have a combination of analytic and conceptual decision styles (Rowe and Mason, 1987). In a study comparing American managers, with managers from other countries, combinations of styles was also observed (Boulgarides and Oh, 1985). The data covered eight different groups of managers, including Japanese, Korean, American, American executives, Hong Kong, Singaporean, northern Irish, and southern Irish. The Japanese and Korean managers are more behavioral, or people-oriented. Hong Kong managers are more directive or results-oriented, followed by Singaporean, northern Irish, American, southern Irish, and Korean managers. The American executives are the most analytic, followed closely by Singaporean and then American, northern Irish, and Hong Kong managers. The American executives are the most conceptual, followed by the southern Irish and Japanese managers. (Boulgarides and Oh, 1985; Murray, Moran, and Bougarides, 1988).

Table 10.1 ▲ Decision Style Data for Eight Samples—Managers

| | Japanese | Korean | American | American Executives | Hong Kong | Singaporean | N. Irish | S. Irish |
|---|---|---|---|---|---|---|---|---|
| Sample size | 16 | 14 | 71 | 80 | 17 | 25 | 17 | 12 |
| Age | — | 37 | 39 | 55 | — | 34 | 44 | 42 |
| Directive | 71 | 75 | 78 | 70 | 86 | 81 | 80 | 77 |
| Analytic | 76 | 80 | 86 | 90 | 84 | 88 | 86 | 81 |
| Conceptual | 85 | 80 | 75 | 93 | 69 | 78 | 80 | 87 |
| Behavioral | 68 | 65 | 61 | 47 | 61 | 53 | 54 | 55 |

The data shown in Table 10.1 cover the eight sample groups described above. The table gives the decision style scores for each group. It provides one basis for comparing differences in decision-making approaches in each country. For example, Americans and Singaporeans are the most analytic and Americans are significantly more conceptual than any other of the groups (Boulgarides and Oh, 1985).

Three samples of police were compared—from mainland America, Maui, and Singapore. The decision style comparison is shown, in Table 10.2. The mainland Americans were more directive. On Maui, they were more behavioral, followed by those in Singapore. Mainland Americans were more analytic, followed by the Maui and Singapore police. The Singapore police were more conceptual, followed by those on Maui. Overall, mainland Americans were left-brain, whereas the Singapore and Maui police were both right-brain. This would indicate that the latter would approach their jobs with more of a people orientation. The Singapore and Maui police were very similar to each other in overall characteristics.

## Values Comparison

Values comparisons were made for the three police departments. The police on mainland America were the most pragmatic. They were the same as the Maui police in the theoretic category. Singapore police were the most idealistic and humanistic. Overall, the Maui were between mainland America and Singapore in values.

## Organization Culture Comparison

Organization culture comparisons were made for the three police departments. An overall observation is that all three see their organization cultures in about the same way. This seems reasonable because we are looking at essentially the same function even though in different locations. The anomaly here is that although the organization cultures

Table 10.2 ▲ Decision Style Comparison—Police

| | Mainland America | Maui | Singapore |
|---|---|---|---|
| Sample size | 65 | 15 | 27 |
| Age | 33 | 33 | 33 |
| Directive | 80 | 70 | 73 |
| Analytic | 95 | 91 | 89 |
| Conceptual | 71 | 74 | 76 |
| Behavioral | 54 | 65 | 62 |

Table 10.3 ▲ Values Comparison—Police

|  | Mainland America | Maui | Singapore |
|---|---|---|---|
| Sample size | 65 | 15 | 27 |
| Age | 33 | 33 | 33 |
| Pragmatist | 89 | 80 | 77 |
| Theorist | 82 | 82 | 76 |
| Idealist | 74 | 78 | 80 |
| Humanist | 55 | 60 | 67 |

are perceived to be essentially the same by the three groups, their decision styles and values are different. A statistical analysis has shown that the mainland American sample had the highest level of internal consistency. The overall assessment, based on personal contact and objective measures, indicates that it is also the best performing of the three organizations in terms of effectiveness.

These data are shown to demonstrate how comparisons can be made among different ethnic populations. This provides an idea of what differences in operational behavior could be expected from different cultural groups. Such knowledge should give us a starting point for understanding how and why behaviors might be different in other countries. The data also provide information that can be used to determine organizational effectiveness once standards of effectiveness have been defined.

Table 10.4 ▲ Organization Culture Comparison—Police

|  | Mainland America | Maui | Singapore |
|---|---|---|---|
| Sample size | 65 | 15 | 27 |
| Age | 33 | 33 | 33 |
| Productivity | 93 | 92 | 94 |
| Quality | 86 | 87 | 83 |
| Creativity | 66 | 64 | 63 |
| Cooperation | 55 | 57 | 60 |

## ▲ ▲ ▲ ▲ ▲ ▲ GM SATURN CASE

The General Motors Saturn program represents an example of a major American corporation's response to global competition. The impact of Japanese small car sales in the United States has had a devastating effect on American small car manufacturers. The complexity of the GM Saturn decision was almost total in terms of the factors involved in automobile manufacture. When the GM Saturn was announced publicly in January 1985, the concept was for a totally new GM company named Saturn Corporation with the sole mission to produce inexpensive subcompact cars to compete successfully against the lowest priced Japanese imports. GM also hoped that the new concepts developed at Saturn would serve as a prototype for other parts of the General Motors organization. Planned to be capitalized at $5 billion, the GM Saturn was certainly a mega-decision (Nicholson et al., 1985).

The Saturn program was described as being "counterculture" by C. Reid Rundell, who was executive vice president of the venture and one of its early leaders (Lawrence, 1985). Key among the many changes at Saturn was the agreement by the United Auto

Workers to cooperate closely with management to make the project a success. Saturn workers were to be full partners with representatives of the UAW sitting in on planning and operating committees. Work teams would operate without foremen, old titles would be changed, and blue-collar workers would receive salaries just like managers (Edid, 1985). The Saturn commitment to workers includes five days of awareness training for new arrivals, with continuing training for workers of 5 percent of their time.

The GM Saturn plant, located in Spring Hill, Tennessee, was the largest single construction project in GM's history. The facility is highly integrated, including power-train, engine assemble, and plastic molding plants so that materials and parts flow smoothly from one plant to the next. This is in sharp contrast to the other GM car assembly plants where key components are supplied by factories hundreds of miles away. New production methods were expected to reduce spending for tools and machinery by 30 percent by casting methods which produce more intricate parts that require less machining. Even the paperwork has been streamlined with the use of an all-electronic financial system that consists of a single data base for all its financial operations such as purchasing, dealer billing, and payroll (Treece, 1990). The use of just-in-time production as a result of the integration of manufacturing reduces transportation and warehousing (inventory) costs. Robots play a much greater role in automated assembly (Whiteside, 1985).

The long-term commitment in a decision such as the GM Saturn is made clear by the fact that while the announcement was made in 1985, the effort was initiated in 1982, with cars expected to be shipped in 1990. Major decisions such as the GM Saturn involve massive commitments in resources and time to come to fruition. The GM Saturn represents a total shift in a company culture away from the traditional auto manufacturing methods as applied for decades in the United States. The Saturn operation was given its own autonomy and introduced both technical manufacturing and personnel practices that were totally foreign to other car manufacturing plants of GM. In October 1990, eight years after launching the Saturn division, Saturn cars were put on sale in selected markets (Treece, 1991).

Problems surfaced that had to be corrected. As of March, 1991 production was at 300 units a week, with preparations for a second shift in April or May of 1991. As of September 1991, it is still too early to tell whether the GM Saturn program has been a success. The Saturn represents a major step in terms of remaking the American workplace in an industry that had at one time been dominated by the United States and one in which foreign competition has made significant impact. The GM Saturn experiment may be as significant for American industry in the 1990s as the Hawthorne experiments were in the 1930s. The global challenges continue. While the Saturn is moving forward to production, new competing innovations must be faced, such as the lean-burn engine developed by Honda, which was introduced in September 1991 (Miller and Armstrong, 1991).

There is a parallel between giant IBM with its 360,000 employees and GM with its 800,000 employees. Both companies face the challenge of more nimble competitors who are technologically ahead and are not encumbered by archaic organizational structures and culture. How do companies such as IBM and GM review themselves? IBM Chairman John F. Akers' frustration that the "tension level" is not high enough at IBM may not be as productive as the bold GM Saturn experiment. The IBM approach of forming alliances with Mitsubishi, GO, Metaphor, Novell, Borland, Wang, Lotus, and Apple may, on the other hand, be an ingenious response to the technological market forces impacting the computer giant (Depke, 1991). If you can't beat 'em, join 'em.   ▲

## ▲ Summary

In this chapter we have dealt with decision making in the global environment. Our concern about decision making in a global environment is a result of the changes that impact on the American economy and the quality of life in our society. It would be foolhardy for decision makers to ignore or to unrealistically assess global forces. Responsible decision makers must make sound decisions for the well-being of their companies as well as American society in general. If we are unable to compete in the global economy, we will slip into a second-class status with a reduced role of influence in global affairs. The knowledge is available for Americans to be successful. The issue is whether we have the desire and will to succeed. We also in this chapter presented some hard data for comparison among cultures to show how to predict expected behavior. These examples provide food for thought and raise provocative questions. Global conditions present us with excitement and challenge.

## ▲ Study Questions

1. What is needed to succeed in the global environment?
2. What factors are necessary for a meaningful strategic intent?
3. What is the difference in decision making between Japanese and American organizations?
4. Explain the meaning of *wa*.
5. Describe consensus decision making.
6. Describe the weakness in the Lockheed choice of the Rolls Royce engine for the L1011.

## ▲ References

Boulgarides, James, and Oh, M. David. "Comparison of Japanese, Korean and American Managers." *Learning and Organization Development Journal* Vol. 6, No. 8 (1985).

Clifford, D. K., Bridgewater, B. A., and Hardy, T. "The Game Has Changed." *The McKinsey Quarterly* (Autumn 1975).

Depke, D. A. "IBM's New Allies." *Business Week* (July 22, 1991), p. 25.

Edid, Marilyn. "How Power Will Be Balanced on Saturn's Shop Floor." *Business Week* (August 5, 1985), pp. 65–66.

Flanigan, James. "Time Warner Mixes Vision and Power." *Los Angeles Times* (March 8, 1989).

Gerstner, L. V. "Does Strategic Decision Making Pay Off?" *McKinsey Quarterly* (Winter 1975).

Groves, Martha. "Iowa and Hong Kong Weave an Unusual Alliance." *Los Angeles Times* (May 9, 1988), Part IV, p. 3.

Hamel, Gary, and Prahalad, C. K. "Strategic Intent." *McKinsey Quarterly* (Spring 1990), pp. 36–61.

Helms, Leslie. "Japanese Firms to Do 21 Percent of Work on the Boeing 777." *Los Angeles Times* (December 10, 1990).

Henshel, H. "The President Stands Alone." *Harvard Business Review* (September 1971).

Hof, Robert D., Depke, Deidre A., and Levine, Jonathan B. "An Alliance Made in PC Heaven." *Business Week* (June 24, 1991), pp. 40–42.

"How Germany Sells Cars Where Detroit Can't." *Business Week* (September 9, 1985), p. 45.

"How We See Each Other." In Focus: Special Japan Section. *Fortune* (September 1981).

Johnson, Richard T., and Ouchi, William S. "Made in America (Under Japanese Management)." *Harvard Business Review* (September-October 1974), pp. 61–69.

Kahn, Herman, and Briggs, Bruce B. *Things to Come*. New York: Macmillan Company, 1972.

Kraar, Louis. "Japan's Gung-ho U.S. Car Plants." *Fortune* (January 30, 1989), p. 98.

Lawrence, John F. "A Company's Culture Shapes Performance." *Los Angeles Times* (January 27, 1985).

Lawrence, John F. "Saturn Project Bets on Togetherness." *Los Angeles Times* (November 10, 1985).

Lazzareschi, Carla. "IBM Will Build Mainframes for Rival Mitsubishi." *Los Angeles Times* (June 2, 1991), Business Section.

Levine, Jonathan B., and Schares, Gail E. "IBM Europe Starts Swinging Back." *Business Week* (May 6, 1991).

"List of Excellent Japanese Companies from Nihon Keizai Shimbum." *Business Week* (July 23, 1984), p. 176.

Marshall, Tyler. "Germany Certain to Emerge as Colossus of a Realigned East Europe," *Los Angeles Times* (June 19, 1990), World Report, Part H., p. 4.

Martin, Kim S. "General Dynamics to Cut Force." *Santa Monica Outlook* (May 2, 1991).

Meehan, John, and Friedman, Jon, with Leah J. Nathans. "American Express: The Failed Vision." *Business Week* (March 19, 1990), pp. 108–113.

Miller, K. M., and Armstrong, L. "55 Miles Per Gallon: How Honda Did It." *Business Week* (September 23, 1991), pp. 82–83.

Murray, Maurice, Moran, Bernard, and Boulgarides, James D. "Management Decision Styles: A Cross-Cultural Pilot Study." *Irish Business and Administration Research* Vol. 9, 1988.

Ness, Robert, McWilliams, Gary, Hoff, Rob, Therrien, Lois, and Coy, Peter. "Why NEC Has U.S. Companies Shaking in Their Boots?" *Business Week* (March 26, 1990), pp. 90–92.

Nicholson, Tom, Manning, Richard, Cook, William, and Leslie, Connie. "GM's 'Saturn' Satellite." *Business Week* (January 21, 1985), pp. 56–67.

Range, Peter R. "The Playboy Interview." *Playboy* (July 1982).

Rowe, Alan J. "Computer Simulation—A Solution Technique for Management," in *Information For Decision Making* by Alfred Rappaport, ed. Englewood Cliffs, NJ: Prentice-Hall, 1970.

Rowe, Alan J. "Interviews with Senior Executives." Unpublished paper, U.S.C., Los Angeles, 1983.

Rowe, Alan J., and Mason, Richard O. *Managing with Style*. San Francisco, CA: Jossey-Bass, 1987.

Rowe, Alan J., Mason, Richard O., Dickel, Karl E., and Snyder, Neil H. *Strategic Management*. Reading, MA: Addison-Wesley, 1989.

Salveson, Melvin E. "The Management of Strategy." *Long Range Planning* (February 1974).

Schares, Gail E., Olsen, Ken, Reaves, Lynne, and Weiner, Elizabeth. "Reawakening: A Market Economy Takes Root in Eastern Europe." *Business Week* (April 15, 1991), pp. 46–50.

Smith, Lee. "Japan's Autocratic Managers." *Fortune* (January 7, 1985), pp. 56–64.

"Teisin Reduces its Work Force." Teisin Limited executives case, Tokyo, 1981.

Therrien, Lois. "Honeywell is Finally Tasting the Sweet Life." *Business Week* (June 3, 1991), p. 34.

Therrien, Lois. "The Rival Japan Respects." *Business Week* (November 13, 1989), pp. 108–118.

Treece, James B. "Here Comes GM's Saturn." *Business Week* (April 9, 1990), pp. 56–62.

Treece, James B. "Are the Planets Lining Up at Last for Saturn?" *Business Week* (April 8, 1991), pp. 32–34.

Tsurumi, Yoshi. *Multinational Management*. Cambridge, MA: Ballinger Publishing Company, 1984.

Weber, Jonathan. "Apple's Chairman Has Great Expectations for Alliance with IBM." *Los Angeles Times* (August 2, 1991), p. D11.

Whiteside, David. "GM's Bold Bid to Reinvent the Wheel." *Business Week* (January 21, 1985), pp. 34–35.

Whiteside, David, Brandt, R., Schiller, Z., and Gabor, A. "How GM's Saturn Could Run Rings Around Old-Style Carmakers." *Business Week* (January 28, 1985).

Woutat, Donald. "U.S. Bearing Maker on a Roll in Bid to Open Japan Market." *Los Angeles Times* (April 21, 1991).

# 11 The Future of Decision Making

▲ ▲ ▲   ▲ ▲ ▲ ▲ ▲ ▲ ▲ ▲ ▲ ▲ ▲ ▲ ▲ ▲ ▲ ▲ ▲ ▲

Assessing future changes in managerial decision making is indeed a challenge. At the very best, one can only approximate what the future holds. Nonetheless, it is important to address future possibilities and to be prepared for the changes they portend. A key perspective is provided by Argyris (1967), who maintained that there will be a blizzard of data generated by the information explosion. This will make one-person operations obsolete, and groups will be necessary for effective decision making. Directive, controlling executives will become strong and subordinates will become weak. To protect themselves from strong superiors, subordinates will censor information or the timing when it is sent. This will tend to make organizations increasingly rigid and unable to effectively cope with the explosion of information.

One can hardly question that the information explosion will have a significant impact on both organizations and decision makers. As greater use is made of forecasting models, simulation approaches, on-line decision support systems, and expert systems, the impact of the computer on decision making will obviously increase and will thus affect the way managers make decisions.

Future organizations will depend more on competence and will narrow the use of power. These new organizations will be more adaptive and able to change rapidly.

## ▲ CHANGES IN DECISION MAKING

How should one explore the potential changes confronting future managerial decision making? Perhaps the recognition of decision making as an integral aspect of management is the most important change. Although decision making has been a significant area of study, it has only recently become a focus of academicians and persons concerned with improved organizational effectiveness.

A number of changes have taken place in decision making. On the one hand is finding the optimum technical solutions including computer applications and management science, balanced on the other with an emerging recognition that effective decisions are contingent on leadership, organizational structure, environmental uncertainty, and the needs of individuals.

One can argue that decision making is or is not becoming increasingly complex, or that the environment is or is not becoming less structured, or that there is or is not greater turbulence and uncertainty. Regardless, it would be difficult to say that knowledge of business systems and an understanding of the behavior of individuals and organizations is not increasing. The ability to predict possible consequences of actions and decisions can lead management to move from the "art of decision making" to something closer to a "skill of decision making."

What changes in strategic decisions will the decision maker face in the future? If we consider the 25-year period 1965–1990, we can identify a number of unexpected events that have significantly impacted American society and the way American firms as well as American society have had to adjust. The oil crisis of 1974 was a great financial drain on the resources of the United States. Energy costs affected every segment of American society as well as causing great inconvenience to individuals as a result of gasoline rationing. The social and economic impacts in one region of the world can literally reach around the globe. The response to such events can involve major social costs, as in the cases of oil explorations in the North Sea and the Alaskan pipeline. The battle for markets in basic products (for example, steel) and consumer products (for example, automobiles and electronics) has been fierce and promises to be even more so in the future. No area appears to be safe from competition in the future, and no firm can afford to rest on its laurels or the successes of the past. Technology can quickly render products and facilities obsolete. What actions must organizations take to cope with the fast-paced changes of the future? At a very minimum, organizations will have to develop the ability to change at a rapid pace, to adapt, to anticipate the future or face the consequences of becoming obsolete.

In the year 1991, Asia was identified as the emerging center of world commerce (Jameson, 1991). The Pacific Rim, consisting of the nations of Japan, South Korea, Taiwan, Hong Kong, Singapore, Thailand, Indonesia, and Malaysia, is expected to emerge as a new megamarket by the year 2000. By that year, the six-country Association of Southeast Asian Nations (ASEAN) will be a bigger market for Japan than for the United States. ASEAN is made up of the countries of Malaysia, Indonesia, the Philippines, Thailand, Singapore, and Brunei. Between 1951 and 1989, Japan had invested over $40 billion in ASEAN nations. Japanese investments in these countries ensure that Japan will have an advantage in exploiting their booming growth. American firms would appear to be losing the opportunity to gain economic benefits.

According to Bob Martin, managing director of Colgate-Palmolive (Thailand) and former president of the American Chamber of Commerce in Bangkok, "Japan's strategy is economic-driven. . . . The United States hasn't articulated a strategy. . . . The United States has to develop a vision if it wants to compete." As an indication of the magnitude of change, he stated, "Southeast Asia has taken over from Northeast Asia as the world's fastest-growing region—the home of the newest of the newly industrialized countries that are expected to challenge such European countries as England and France in the size of their economies by the turn of the century." Economists predict an entirely new world power center. How can American business firms compete with this new situation? There is no assurance that under the changing circumstances, Pacific Rim markets will be as accessible to American firms as they are at the present time (Jameson, 1991).

The upshot is a major expansion of Asia's industrial base that promises to bring the region through the Persian Gulf War less scathed than the rest of the world. The wave of investment is also giving the leader—Japan—still more clout and creating influence for new investors, especially Taiwan. The old top investor—the United States—is in retreat. American diplomats and executives warn that U.S. businesses are failing to take advantage of new growth in one Asian nation after another. A new "megamarket" for consumer and industrial products will emerge in the coming ten years in South Korea, Taiwan, Hong Kong, Singapore, Thailand, Indonesia, and Malaysia, Kenneth S. Courtis, senior economist for Deutsche Bank Capital Markets, predicted recently in Tokyo. According to Courtis, Japanese investments in these countries ensure that Japan will be in the best position to take advantage of their booming growth (Jameson, 1991). Donald Gregg, U.S. ambassador to South Korea, said in an interview in Seoul that he fears that the United States will let the opportunities slip by and fail to gain economic benefits in Asia commensurate with the cost of providing security to the region.

A number of topics appear increasingly relevant as future prospects for changes in decision making.

1. Increased participation and power sharing to obtain commitment and resolve organizational conflict.
2. Improved communication of decisions with subordinates to increase consensus.
3. Shift toward leadership in contrast to autocratic management.
4. Greater emphasis on ethics, social responsibility, and ecological awareness.
5. Use of decision styles, culture, and values in the design of organizational structures, hiring, promotions, and transfers.
6. Use of more flexible, adaptive decision strategies that can deal rapidly with changing situations.
7. Identification of objectives and priorities by both management and employees to ensure empowerment.

8.  Greater use of decision models to assist the manager in predicting and understanding the potential consequences of decisions.
9.  Use of simulation models that incorporate expert systems that are highly realistic and utilize real-time data to provide current status and prediction of system performance.
10.  Greater emphasis on entrepreneurial management and creative problem solving.
11.  Globalization of the decision environment.
12.  Increased emphasis on strategic decision making in contrast to emphasis on operational control.
13.  Greater understanding of drives, motives, and personal preferences that influence decisions.
14.  Use of multiple measures of effectiveness in addition to financial ones as criteria for decision making.
15.  Increased recognition of the importance of risk taking as part of decision making.
16.  More flexible organizational structures.

In terms of commitment, only one out of four job holders claims that he or she is working to full potential, and half said that if they were required they could put more effort into their job. The overwhelming majority claimed that they could be far more effective than now, and that they do not work as hard as they used to. There appears to be a significant gap between what individuals are doing and what they are getting paid for. This can be attributed to a decline in the work ethic or to leaders who have failed to provide commitment, vision, meaning, and trust by empowering the workers so that they could become an effective part of the organization.

## ▲  HOW TO APPROACH THE FUTURE OF DECISION MAKING

If one were to examine the classic approach to decision making in the past, flaws, errors, and misconceptions could be found in almost every area. Issues such as the one best way to manage have now given way to the situational approach to management, and adaptive, strategic decisions are used in contrast to merely responding to changes. Forecasting and predictive models are used to identify the consequences and the impact of decisions ahead of time rather than trying to take corrective action after the fact. More definitive knowledge and techniques are now employed to facilitate understanding the role and impact of behavior and its effect on decision making. Motivation and work satisfaction through job redesign rather than manipulation are used.

There is hardly an instance in which newer concepts are not increasingly replacing approaches previously used as the basis for decision making. The fact is that for a long time decision making was construed primarily as a choice from among alternatives without any recognition of how the decision was being made or how it would be carried out. This has given way to recognizing that it is a decision process that helps predict the consequences of choices made. Decision styles and leadership approaches have begun to deal with the questions of how to recognize problems and how motivation helps in carrying out solutions. By using the entire decision process, decision making can become more effective.

Today's economic climate makes old assumptions invalid, and what is needed are new tools to help management make more accurate strategic decisions concerning the future (Clifford, Bridgewater, and Hardy, 1975). There has to be a sense of relative values and timing when the chips are flying and signals are confusing. Extreme interest rate fluctuations, unprecedented sales drop, inventory build-up, and stock decline are all symptoms of the environment. What should a company do? Does it wait or just throw in the towel? Should it cut the dividend, reduce research, or spin off products? These are the awesome decisions confronting executives who live in our topsy-turvy world.

Complexity presents still another important aspect of the world in which leaders have to function. The number of bankruptcies has been increasing, as well as mergers leading to larger and larger organizations. Savings and loans and other banks are unsafe or unsound and many have failed already; furthermore, there are almost 50 nations that as borrowers will probably fail to repay loans. These are just indicators of the signs of our times, and perhaps what may happen in the future. This increasing complexity results in situations that are more complicated and less well understood than in the past. In many cases, a manager or executive without previous experience is confronted with an intolerable level of ambiguity as well as a credibility gap between what people say and what in fact exists. A credibility gap stems in part from the questioning and challenging of authority as well as the new information age, where the public has access to information that was not previously available. In many instances, people are experiencing a sense of insecurity and loss of belief in the systems that they once trusted. Specific changes confronting the manager are a society that will be increasingly reliant on information technology and one in which technology itself will become increasingly important. The global economy will be more important than the national economy and will persist in the long term.

## ▲ IMPROVING DECISION MAKING

At this point in time, education is a major weakness in the United States. While more people are being educated, according to Peter Drucker (1988), "We have one and only one basic weakness: our schools. The first signs of a turnaround are beginning to be seen. . . . Now, you're up against an entrenched ideology" (Gergen, 1990). A Kidder Peabody report by economist Sam Nakagama observed: "Japan has become the greatest commercial nation of the East by developing a highly effective educational system." A New York Stock Exchange study concluded that Japan's economic miracle is "a product of the effectiveness of Japanese primary and secondary schooling and the unique way the Japanese companies train and prepare their managers" (Doyle and Hartle, 1985).

Companies will have to take the responsibility for training their managers if they are to grow. In Asia, businesses are facing the problem of fast growth outstripping the supply of people to lead them. According to Ng Pock Too, the lack of qualified managers is "the greatest restraint I face." As chief executive of the Sembawang Group, what he seeks are "not just any managers, but flexible, creative professionals at home in an increasingly competitive and sophisticated market." Companies are being forced to "devote even more attention to training young managers and to devising new incentives to keep them from leaving once they have been developed" (Worthy, 1991).

How does one know when a good decision has been made or how to improve decision making? The technique of multiple measures proposed by Mott (1972) and other authors provides an increasingly meaningful basis for dealing with future decisions. Managers are becoming more aware of the differentiated nature of the world in which we live. However, what has been missing are the techniques, approaches, and frames of reference within which to examine and understand our complex environment. Unfortunately, examining the various facets of an organization and individuals and the manner in which individuals interact leads to increasingly complex decision making. Not only must the manager of the future be a veritable leviathan capable of dealing with a multitude of technologies, computers, and social problems, but he or she must also be a psychologist, sociologist, and political scientist who can understand the vagaries and problems inherent in any organization.

Is it realistic to hope that one individual, no matter how well schooled, can in fact deal with the order of complexity described? The answer is rather obvious—it would be difficult to find any one individual who could become the universal manager capable of handling all situations. Rather, what appears to be a more meaningful approach is recognizing that there are many facets and aspects to the decision process and that teams will be more effective than any individual. If each facet is understood and dealt with in a more cooperative fashion, then the total process has a greater likelihood of being effective.

If one looks at the new breed of executives entering on the scene, it is quite obvious that top executives who will be running corporate America in the future are bound to be quite different from the people who are at the helm today. The new executives will tend to be younger—in the range of 52 years old—whereas current top executives on the average are 61 years old. Younger executives are not aware of World War II or the Great Depression of the 1930s. They have grown up with television, and many have spent their entire careers in a single corporation. Examples of the new executives are Irving Shapiro of Dupont and Reginald Jones of General Electric, both of whom have a reputation of speaking out on corporate and economic issues. Both are considered "business statesmen" (Taylor, 1988).

Decentralization, ownership, and empowerment become increasingly important through the participatory involvement of workers. The networking among individuals through joint ventures, strategic alliances, and cooperative efforts will become increasingly important, as will the number of options available to the manager in the future. To achieve success, leaders of the future will have to embody some basic strategies to ensure focus and attention through positive vision, to achieve and attain meaning through effective communication, to obtain trust by understanding and positioning themselves with regard to workers, and finally to have a positive self-image as leaders. They can achieve change in direction of the organization through the following methods.

1. Use a network of information.
2. Extend horizons.
3. Make vigorous communications.
4. Teach managers about the future intuitively.
5. Create an attitude of comfort with the future.
6. Focus on long-term strategic decisions.

Allan Cohen, professor of management at Babson College, Wellesley, MA, describes expectations of the modern day work force: "There's a whole new kind of work force that has high expectations of being listened to. It's a new model of leadership both on shared responsibility and teams (Skrzycki, 1989). Teamwork in organizations is the message of the future. Communication is a vital element in developing and maintaining teamwork. Without a script or any rehearsal, Mike Walsh, CEO of Union Pacific Railroad since 1986, holds the stage for 5½ hours as employees from 24 sites across the country fire questions at him via satellite. With disarming candor, Walsh answers queries on everything from job security to workplace safety. "As a result of his efforts at open communication, Union Pacific has been transformed from a fat, sluggish hierarchical company to a lean, progressive one." In the past, employees addressed each other on a formal basis and teamwork between departments did not exist. "Now, first names prevail, cross-functional work teams are common among the 29,000 employees, and morale is high, despite the fact that about 6,000 workers lost their jobs after Walsh took over." Walsh held town meetings and asked employees to pitch in with their ideas after explaining company strategy and recent industry changes describing their effects on workers (Rice, 1991).

Approaches to decision making have progressed to the point where there is a recognition that behavioral considerations can have a greater impact on decision making and decision implementation than the technical soundness alone. Scot Paltrow (1991) described how Colt changed a difficult situation in his article "Buyout Hits the Bull's-Eye at Colt's." For decades, the strife between management and unionized workers at the two Colt firearms plants was so bitter that exploding dynamite all but leveled the company president's home during a strike in 1935. After that, strikes, walkouts, and job actions punctuated periods of uneasy coexistence. During 1990, however, this ugly relationship underwent a remarkable transformation. In December of that year, management and workers held the first joint Christmas party that anyone could remember. A joint picnic was planned for June. Workers wrote to the chief executive saying how much they enjoyed going to work. The company now solicits advice from workers on design changes and is modifying products and production techniques at employees' suggestions. Management has begun taking assembly workers along to trade shows. And Lester Harding, the taciturn United Auto Workers shop chairman who stubbornly led the years-long strike, now spends much of his time exhorting workers to work harder and sitting in as a trusted adviser in the chief executive's office. He has a seat on the board. The outbreak of good feelings was triggered by an experiment in management and employee co-ownership. The long strike ended when plant managers and striking workers got together and agreed to buy the gun-making subsidiary from its corporate parent, Colt Industries, renamed Coltec.

# ▲  THE IMPORTANCE OF LEADERSHIP

"Leaders can provide the proper setting for innovative learning by designing open organizations in which participation and teamwork together can expand the time horizon of decision makers, broaden their perspectives, allow for the sharing of assumptions and values, and facilitate the development and use of new approaches" (Bennis and Nanus, 1985). To understand future leadership, one has to recognize three major areas:

1. Commitment
2. Complexity
3. Credibility

Leadership has been characterized as the function of management that is able to create an environment that fosters commitment on the part of workers and that evokes performance beyond normal expectations. This has been called "transformational leadership." True leadership involves a complex transaction between leaders and followers. The distinction between managers and leaders has been described by Zaleznick (1977) as having fundamentally different world views. Leaders think about goals in a way that creates images and expectations about the direction a business should take. Leaders influence changes in the way people think about what is desirable, possible, or necessary. Managers, on the other hand, tend to view work as a means for achieving goals based on the actions taken by workers. Thus, leaders make decisions that are systematic and pragmatic in marshalling resources, designing organizations, motivating workers, solving problems, and controlling activities.

In his book, *Mind of a Manager, Soul of a Leader* (1990), Hickman describes how managers and leaders differ. The manager is a person who typically is analytic and who prefers structure and control, is deliberate and orderly. At the other end of the spectrum, the leader (who is conceptual) typically is a visionary who is willing to experiment and be flexible, uncontrolled, and creative. Managers and leaders deal with organizational problems in a different manner because of their differences in style and perspective. Hickman claimed that it is important that both are respected and work for the benefit of the organization. A leader tends to make a poor manager, and vice versa.

In the article "Wanted: Leaders Who Can Make a Difference," Jeremy Main (1987) described a situation confronting U.S. companies. Mere management may no longer be enough. Rather, he contended that executives must be able to transform organizations and create the future. Drucker (1988) also believes that a true leader makes demands of himself, not demands on others.

The importance of participatory management has been universally recognized. At Lucky-Goldstar, Chairman Koo Cha-Kyung's "hierarchical decision-making style" was partly to blame for the slip in quality and innovation (Nakarmi, 1991). According to one senior executive, "Nobody had the guts to tell him to get out of daily management and let the professionals run the business." Koo is now giving more decision-making authority to his frontline managers. The difficulty in changing the organization culture, however, was illustrated by the firing of three top executives in the summer of 1990 for not allowing authority to be moved downward.

At Daewoo, the once hands-off Chairman Kim took control and slashed executive ranks (Nakarmi, 1991). Kim, in early January 1991, warned 5,000 of the company's top managers "that Daewoo needed to transform itself dramatically—and quickly—or its very survival would be at stake." Founded in 1967 as a maker of shirts for Sears, Roebuck & Company, Daewoo had grown to annual revenues of about $15 billion in 1990. Kim's most pressing problem was the restructuring of Daewoo's management. As a hands-off manager, Kim had ceded day-to-day control to the presidents of the 19 companies in the Daewoo Group. When losses piled up in 1990, Kim undertook a revolution at his own group. This is comparable to many of the changes that Ross Perot had prescribed for GM in Chapter 6 (Perot, 1988).

A basic assumption is that effective leaders impact subordinates' motivation, performance, and satisfaction by influencing the subordinates' perceptions of their work and personal goals, and the path to their attainment. Subordinate characteristics and environmental factors are used as the basis for explaining the relationship between leader behavior and subordinate satisfaction and acceptance (House and Mitchell, 1974). Dessler's (1978) review of the House and Mitchell path-goal approach cites evidence that role ambiguity and dissatisfaction are related to stress, tension, anxiety, and dissatisfaction, and that ambiguous or uncertain situations are conducive to task-oriented or structured leaders.

Many executives now recognize that employees have achieved higher levels of education, are more mobile, and expect greater opportunity and satisfaction in their work. They no longer are robots that can be ordered to perform—they need to be led. This reflects the single most significant change confronting managers and undoubtedly accounts for the explosive attention being given to leadership. Control and action are giving way to empowerment and vision. Warren Bennis (1984), whose name is synonymous with leadership, claims it is probably the most studied subject and the least understood of any topic. Between enthusiasm over the Japanese model and the acceptance of *In Search of Excellence* (Peters and Waterman, 1982) the quest goes on for the holy grail of leadership. Can it be achieved? Can it be identified? Can it be taught? All are thought-provoking questions that we attempt to answer. Bennis and Nanus (1985) described information obtained by observing effective leaders that can be used as guidelines for forward-looking managers.

1. *Vision:* Create a new focus and agenda.
2. *Communication:* Share meaning, interpret reality, facilitate coordination, capture imagination.
3. *Trust:* Engender feelings that lubricate and make the organization work.
4. *Positioning:* Actions needed to implement vision.
5. *Constancy:* Willingness to stay the course.
6. *Innovation:* Take risks, face challenges.

7. *Positive self-regard:* Recognize strengths and deal with weaknesses.
8. *Nurture:* Build skills using discipline, create self-confidence in others.
9. *Deployment of self:* Use failure as a springboard for hope.
10. *Empowerment:* Create an open environment by translating intention into reality and building confidence on the job.

One of the principal concerns of leaders is expected performance and employee satisfaction. The "willingness" of a subordinate to accept a decision does not depend solely on the leadership style of the manager. It also depends on co-workers, peer pressures, personal needs, environmental factors, legitimacy, and values. Thus, when viewed from a broader perspective, a leader's decision style may be considered effective if results are achieved within the constraints of a given situation.

## ▲ HOW LEADERSHIP AFFECTS PERFORMANCE

A number of authors have examined the relationship between leadership and effective performance. For example, Mott (1972) reported that in a number of studies of the branches in NASA using multifactor theories, effectiveness could not be predicted. He found that leadership is important when tasks are independent of one another and require coordinating activities. At the operating level, where the task structure was high, technical skills, not leadership, was associated with effectiveness. This finding is supported by Stogdill (1974), who examined and found that leadership is "a working relationship among members of a group, in which the leader acquires status through active participation and demonstration of his/her capacity for carrying cooperative tasks through to completion" (1974, p. 386). Porter, Lawler, and Hackman (1975) conclude that "effective leadership represents interaction between the characteristics of the leader and the situation, including the kinds of people to be led (1975, p. 433).

Zaleznick (1990) characterized the leader as the one who induces change and often is a disruptive force in an organization. Leadership inevitably requires using power to influence thoughts and actions of other people and to develop fresh approaches and open new options. To be effective, the leader must be able to project his or her ideas into images that excite people in their work. Leaders who are concerned with ideas relate in intuitive and empathetic ways and attract strong feelings of identity, difference, love, or hate. Warren Bennis warned that leadership may be a beleaguered species. He felt that to lead others, the leader must first know himself or herself. Further, he stated that "the leader must be a social architect who studies and shapes what is called the culture of work—those intangibles that are so hard to discern but are so terribly important in governing the way people act, the values and norms that are subtly transmitted to individuals and the group and that tend to create binding and bonding" (1976, p. 3).

One of the early approaches to leadership was the continuum of leadership behavior developed by Tannenbaum and Schmidt (1973). They described the authoritarian manager as one who makes decisions alone whereas a democratic manager provides the maximum freedom for subordinates to function in. This is a useful way to examine leaders' behavior; however, the effectiveness of leaders requires a perspective that includes the individuals' personality and cognitive complexity.

Tannenbaum and Schmidt did recognize the importance of situational variables, and they described the successful manager as "one who maintains a high batting average in accurately assessing the forces that determine what his most appropriate behavior at any given time should be and in actually being able to behave accordingly. Being both insightful and flexible, he is less likely to see the problems of leadership as a dilemma" (1973, p. 165). The question of attitude change appears to be related to cognitive structures. Although most leaders strive for consistent attitudes, can they adapt their attitudes, beliefs, and personality to a given situation? Flexibility, adaptiveness, and ability to cope with change can be considered inherent characteristics of effective leaders. Inconsistent behavior on the part of the leader can result in cognitive conflict where expectations of subordinates are misunderstood. Too often change is not viewed as adaptive, but as lack of consistency that creates uneasiness on the part of the subordinate.

Early research on leadership focused on factors such as those provided by Halpin and Winer (1957):

1. *Consideration:* Friendship, mutual trust, respect, and warmth.
2. *Initiating structure:* Organizing of communication, work facilitation.
3. *Production emphasis:* The manner of motivating the group to achieve greater productivity through goal of missions emphasis.
4. *Sensitivity:* Leader's awareness of and sensitivity to social interrelationships and pressures either inside or outside of the group.

Bower and Seashore (1966) derived four basic structural elements related to leadership effectiveness:

1. *Support:* Enhancing an individual's feeling of personal worth and importance.
2. *Interaction facilitation:* Encouraging group members to develop close and mutually satisfying relationships.
3. *Goal emphasis:* Stimulating enthusiasm for meeting the group's goal of excellent performance.
4. *Work facilitation:* Activities that help achieve goal attainment, such as scheduling, coordination, planning, and material and technical knowledge.

The research they conducted identified the elements required for leadership. What emerged were two independent dimensions labeled *consideration* and *initiating structure*.

Blake and Mouton (1985) extended the application of leadership to a grid in which they could identify extreme positions such as the 9,9 or 1,1 leader. The categories included:

9,1   Produce or perish.
1,9   Kid-glove permissiveness
1,1   Neutrality
5,5   Accommodation and compromise
9,9   Solution-seeking

An extension of the two basic dimensions of task and people orientation was introduced by Reddin in his three-dimensional managerial styles. Reddin's approach to management styles is situationally dependent, and he concluded that "no one style is always effective. Their style effectiveness depends on the situation in which they are used." Reddin also contended that an effective manager must have situational sensitivity skill, style flexibility skill, and situational management skill. He maintained that the situation has five elements: organization, technology, manager, co-workers, and subordinates (1970, p. 12–13).

A life cycle theory of leadership has been proposed by Hersey and Blanchard (1972), which is an outgrowth of Reddin's 3-D model. It is based on the relationship between leadership style and level of maturity of followers. According to the life cycle theory, as followers mature, appropriate leader behavior requires less task structure with increasing consideration but lower relationship support. Maturity is defined in terms of achievement motivation and the ability or capability for assuming responsibility and task experience. The model is related to the Maslow–Hertzberg motivators and to Argyris' maturity continuum. As with the Vroom model, the life cycle theory is a normative basis for managerial style. The managerial styles approaches deal with the performance aspect of the leader's job and the acceptance and commitment of subordinates.

In many companies, the leader's style is important for effective implementation of strategic change. Johnson & Johnson, under the leadership of James Burke, is subtly bringing about a change in corporate culture that will shift the company from band aids and medication to sophisticated, high-tech medical products ("Changing," 1984). Burke has been able to inculcate a culture that recognizes that to be able to fail in high tech may be a necessary part of the job. American managers are faced with much more diversity in corporate culture, whereas Japanese firms are more monolithic in their culture, structure, and value systems. Although decisions take a long time in Japanese firms, there is considerable input from all levels, and everyone knows what is going to happen beforehand. This generally leads to more loyalty and acceptance.

Can American managers manage as well as the Japanese? When dealing with American workers, who are a very heterogeneous group with a low sense of company loyalty compared to Japanese workers, can American managers achieve the same level of output in terms of quality and cost as their Japanese counterparts?

A case example is seen in two General Motors plants: one in Fremont, California and the other in Van Nuys, California. The Fremont plant is a joint venture between Toyota and GM. The Fremont plant had been closed by GM in 1982. There had been a high level of unrest in that plant and there were 800 unresolved grievances at the time of the plant closing. In 1983 Toyota, GM, and the United Auto Workers embarked on a historic effort to fuse the dramatically different American and Japanese labor–management traditions. A form of Japanese management applying the idea of quality circles was introduced as a way of improving performance.

During the same period, the GM plant in Van Nuys was experiencing difficulties and faced the threat of being closed. While the Fremont plant was managed by the Japanese, the Van Nuys plant was managed by Americans. In 1990, the Fremont plant was highly successful whereas the Van Nuys plant was experiencing major problems (Stavro, 1990).

Some new employees of the New United Motor Manufacturing, Inc., the GM–Toyota joint venture, were flown to Japan for training. One American commented that "while there is more work per man, they make it easier for the worker. They listen to suggestions from the worker on how to improve his job" (Jameson, 1984). In 1991, workers at the GM Van Nuys plant suffered the traumatic experience of being laid off when the plant was finally closed.

## ▲ SITUATIONAL LEADERSHIP

It is becoming increasingly evident that both the internal and external environments have a significant impact on leader effectiveness. With a limited range of external opportunities, management is constrained by competition, legislation, technology, changing markets, and limited resources when making strategic decisions. Morse and Lorsch also described the need to match the organization's characteristics with the needs of the individuals and demands of the task.

Fiedler (1967), who conducted extensive research on the situational aspects of leadership effectiveness, identified three factors that determine what style of leader performed best.

He examined correlations between test scores of leaders and their performance related to situational factors. The relations-motivated leader performs best where the leader position is not strong. Task-motivated leaders perform best when the leader-member relations are good and the leader power position is strong. This last category represents poor member relations and a weak leader who is attempting to deal with a poor situation. Because that situation is unfavorable, Fiedler's model would require a task-oriented leader to keep the situation from falling apart. An obvious alternative would be to replace the leader.

To deal with the issue of matching style to the situation, Vroom and Yetton (1973) developed an approach that deals with leader-subordinate interaction. Their model explicitly recognizes that an effective style depends on situational variables such as the leader's expertise, the task structure, and the employees' willingness to accept a solution. The key elements in sharing of leader power are the maximization of technical effectiveness and subordinate motivation or acceptance. If technical effectiveness is not crucial and motivation and acceptance are not important, the decisions are made by the leader alone. On the other hand, if the technical difficulties are important but motivation is low, the leader attempts to obtain more information. When technical effectiveness is unimportant but motivation and acceptance are high, delegation becomes a useful approach. Finally, if the problem is high on the technical level and there is a need for acceptance, then the decision is shared with the group.

The situational determinants of leadership show that there is consistency in the behavior of a leader when he or she performs in different situations. Patterns of interpersonal behavior can be transferred even when work performances change to meet new requirements (Stogdill, 1974). Leaders also change in response to differing group task demands. Leaders who facilitate work accomplishment are accepted most easily. When viewed in terms of decision styles, the flexible manager adapts to new situations, whereas the rigid, task-oriented manager maintains consistent patterns of behavior in most situations. This suggests that the task-oriented manager does not react well to situational changes.

Another perspective that relates leader style to the situation is described by Filley et al. (1975), who concluded that there are four situational factors that influence leader style. These are:

1. *Intrinsic job pressure:* Acceptance of structure by subordinates.
2. *Intrinsic job satisfaction:* Satisfaction leads to less impact of leader consideration.
3. *Leader's consideration:* Leader's job structure does not cause dissatisfaction.
4. *Subordinates' need for information:* Personality and ambiguity lead to tolerance of structure.

# ▲ INFORMATION AND TECHNOLOGY

In describing information and decision technology in the 1990s, Forgionne (1990) indicated that new information systems will be required to support all phases of decision making. Included are problem recognition, formulation, analysis, solution, interpretation, and implementation. These new systems will be required to provide all the technology needed by management to provide an integrated system so that individuals or group decision makers will have the best possible information to support their decisions. This complete technology for management will include all the various approaches and decision-aiding tools (such as simulation models, expert systems, forecasting, and various kinds of economic and accounting models), as well as the needed system hardware that will network computers. Everybody will have access to the same data in addition to receiving the kinds of displays that will make information more meaningful.

The application of expert knowledge in expert systems will introduce an important consideration into such future systems. Using the decision maker's knowledge makes him or her a part of the system. They have ownership. Ownership is an important aspect of introducing motivation, and managers who are unfamiliar with systems will tend to disregard them. On the other hand, if such information systems provide data, trends, analysis, forecasts, tables, graphs, or whatever the decision maker wants, then he or she is more likely to use that system. The projection is that because the computer will become interactive and enable managers to incorporate many more insights and judgments into evaluating problems, the technology that involves a computer will change from decision support to augmenting the manager's ability to make better decisions. This will also tap into the creativity and intelligence that managers have and will allow them to enhance that creativity through their ability to use available information in databases or knowledge bases.

The decision technology of the future can be considered in the following subcategories:

1. *Management information systems* will be used to analyze data developed as a result of actual operations in a company. Models, trends, forecasts, or other analytic tools will be applied. Reports more likely will be on demand, often in graphic form on terminals rather than via the myriad written reports that currently are provided to managers.
2. *Decision support systems* will allow for continuous interaction with the computer, with greater application of the decision maker's judgment and insight to formulate and structure problems as well as to tap into statistical, economic, or accounting data or models to help analyze and produce specific kinds of output needed by the decision maker.
3. *Expert systems* will provide the manager with an ability to store knowledge in a form that is readily available and can be retrieved in order to exercise judgment or use rules that have been applied previously. In this area, approaches to reasoning and judgment will become increasingly important, as well as understanding the cognitive complexity of the decision maker so as to better match the new systems to the requirements of the decision maker.
4. *Executive information systems* provide a continuous evaluation and monitoring of the decision environment. They will be able to provide warnings, timely information, and analysis so that top-level managers who are not concerned with ongoing daily operations and the myriad details that exist in every organization can be alerted to important events and requirements for their decisions.
5. *The automated office of the future* will provide all kinds of written, oral, group interaction, teleconferencing, and teleprocessing, as well as the ability to obtain information from knowledge-based systems the way we do today in database systems. This will help support more creative linking and application of judgment to problems confronting decision makers.

Fortunately, much of the required support for the new decision technology of the 1990s exists today in terms of both hardware and software or computer programs. It is a matter of better organization of the information in a form that is readily accessible and useful to the decision maker to avoid problems of redundancy, to increase accuracy and timeliness, to provide information in an intelligible way so as to become a useful tool rather than an obstacle.

The division director of a large organization was given the monthly payroll output which consisted of several hundred pages approximately eight inches thick. When the director asked the manager of personnel why he was receiving this information, he was told, "Well, of course, you need to know everything that is in those reports." Convinced, the director continued to receive the monster report which he occasionally glanced at. Each month it was thrown into the wastebasket as the new report arrived. One day he decided that he would like to know what the president's salary was. The print-out said this information is confidential and is not available to the management of the company. Totally discouraged, the division director called the manager of personnel and asked to be taken off the distribution list because this monster report not only provided no information but even on an innocent inquiry indicated that the information was not available (Forgionne, 1990).

In order to take advantage of new technology, the importance of people cannot be overlooked. Shenandoah Life Insurance Co. installed a $2 million computer system to process claims at its headquarters. The results were disappointing. Processing time was 27 working days and handling applications required 32 clerks in three departments. Shenandoah's bureaucratic maze was the problem. A radical reorganization was needed in order to realize the benefits of automation. Teams of clerks were organized into five- to seven-member "semiautonomous" groups. Each group performed tasks that had previously been spread over three departments. The result was job enrichment for the workers as they learned new tasks. Case handling time dropped to two days and complaints practically disappeared. Finally, 50 percent more applications were processed with 10 percent fewer employees in 1986 as compared to 1980. "American managers are finally learning what the Japanese discovered years ago. In order to realize the full potential of automation, people and technology must be integrated as a 'sociotechnical' system that revolutionizes the way work is organized and managed." This is a significant departure from the old bureaucratic way of organizing and managing work (Hoerr, 1986).

A look far into the future indicates some startling possibilities in the application of information to support decision making. Neural networks provide a frontier that perhaps may change the way managers look at decision making and at support systems. Neural networks in a sense are crude but powerful simulations of the nervous system that try to mimic the way the brain works. Although this is not crucial, the important aspect of neural networks is that, in fact, they are a hybrid analogue/digital computer with speeds about 1,000 times faster than current systems. They are able to process information 1 billion times faster than current conventional digital computers. Applications include a variety of tasks from machine vision and robotics to speech recognition, tests, and hand-writing recognition. They have been able to solve very complex problems that involve patterns, such as interpretation or evaluation of military vehicles and analysis of integrated computer circuitry. In banking, neural networks have helped Chase Manhattan detect credit card fraud. Security Pacific Bank uses the system to analyze commercial and automobile loan risks. In addition to such applications, neural networks have been applied in medicine, to detect abnormal heart sounds and interpret electrocardiograms. At Roarck University in England, an electronic nose that recognizes smells has been developed. A similar system is used in Japan to test the freshness of sushi. Ford Motor Company is developing a computer, which is actually on the automobile, that simultaneously monitors all aspects of the automotive operation—the engine, the power train, suspension, electronic steering, brakes, climate control, and so forth (Moore, 1990).

In addition to the capabilities mentioned, neural networks have been used in Japan for a variety of applications that try to simulate human behavior. They incorporate a concept of "fuzzy logic." This logic does not deal with precise values but on the concepts, such as a very bright finish; however, *bright* can have a range of values, which is why this logic is called "fuzzy." On the other hand, the Japanese have applied it to washing machines where the water can be determined as being dirty or not dirty. Again, a fuzzy concept. We will also see a drastic change in the way computers are built and the kind of software they will use. In particular, parallel architecture that allows the program to process over a large number of electronic routes provides an ability to do things that we cannot do very efficiently with digital computers. This will enhance the processing speed but will also introduce some interesting new and yet untested capabilities. The impact on decision makers and management is yet to be determined; however, its potential is that because it tries to mimic the mind, perhaps it can be more human-like and help make more effective decisions.

## ▲ FUTURE ORGANIZATIONS

To be successful in the future, companies will have to change the way they respond to new requirements and will have to be extremely fast. They will have to find new ways of rewarding workers who have higher expectations and consumers who are increasingly quality- and service-conscious. One reason for the rapid changes that require organizations to respond quickly is the introduction of more technology in almost every product. A second is that the designs are being simplified so that, in fact, companies can produce things more quickly and still have improved products (Main, 1988).

Information also is changing the way organizations will have to respond to customers and competitors. Legal and physical aspects of companies will have to be modified, as will access to information that suppliers may require when they want to reorder. Everyone in the organization from the chief executive on down will be influenced and impacted by the information that will be required in the next decade. Organizations will also change from the purely hierarchical model that has been used in business for many years to one that will allow more people to report to a single manager because of available information. Following the Peters and Waterman (1982) recommendation, corporate staff will be "lean and mean" and, in some cases, will almost disappear. This will mean fewer layers of supervision between the chief executive and the front-line supervisor. Instead of building large staffs, they will tend to work with temporary task forces that respond to specific problems. In addition, to be more competitive, organizations will form strategic alliances and partnerships with a goal of penetrating more markets than they can do on their own. An example is the Sematech Corporation, which gets half of its funding from Congress and the remainder from the U. S. semiconductor business that is trying to remain competitive.

In some cases, partnerships may be necessary for companies to survive and extend their capability (Edid, 1985). The union between Zenith and Lucky-Goldstar provides benefits to both companies. Korea's Lucky-Goldstar agreed to pay $15 million for the just under 5 percent of Zenith, the last major U. S. TV manufacturer. While Goldstar has the global reach with $25 billion in sales, "Zenith can offer technology and marketing expertise in the U.S."

Business managers in the 1990s and beyond must have a broader global perspective than in the past as there are opportunities in all parts of the world. Japanese companies now build plants in the United States. In 1984 Japanese investment in the U.S. reached $1.7 billion and it was expected to be $2.5 billion in 1985. The Mazda plant in Flat Rock, Michigan was expected to generate in excess of 10,000 supplier and service jobs in that depressed area.

One can hardly question that the information explosion will have a significant impact on both the organization and the decision makers. As greater use is made of forecasting models, simulation approaches, on-line decision support systems, and expert systems, the impact of computers on decision making will obviously increase and thus affect the way in which managers make decisions. In light of available computer technology, managers need to be computer literate in order to capitalize on the power of this tool.

Once these systems are installed and once data are available, it is obvious that decision makers will increasingly rely on that information to provide a better picture of performance as a way to make predictions concerning output, productivity, and schedules. Does all this portend a radical change in decision making? Possibly, but most important is the recognition that there are many environmental factors impinging on the organization that are perhaps far more significant than any internal changes. Consider for a moment what changes are taking place in the environment. There are crises in the cities, expansion of multinational corporations, and increased involvement of the government in management decision making. Given all of these influences, there is little doubt that the way managers will make decisions will change.

Estimates from the U.S. Department of Labor are that the number of jobs will grow faster than the size of the labor force. Thus, to attract workers—and especially to attract women, who it is estimated will make up two-thirds of new workers—companies will have to have new approaches. It will not be sufficient merely to attract workers; companies will have to find ways to keep them. This will not simply be higher pay, but meeting the expectations and requirements for satisfaction of workers. Employee motivation, which is identified with commitment, ownership, and participation leading to higher employee involvement, is the basis for maintaining an effective and productive workforce. By providing ownership, companies also help to engender an entrepreneurial spirit in employees. For example, Xerox, 3M, and Honeywell have had a number of new divisions started by employees who had ideas that they wanted to exploit. Finally, successful companies of the future will have to have more elaborate accounting systems than have been available in the past. Accounting information will need to be much more managerially oriented rather than merely providing the information needed for income tax or stockholder purposes. Typical of this requirement is being able to differentiate costs among products and to spread general costs in a more proportionate manner than in the past.

One of the major strengths of the U.S. economy is the ability to attract brilliant new scientists because of the advanced laboratory facilities and stimulation that they can achieve in the United States that is not possible elsewhere. Approximately one-quarter of all new scientists come from other lands. The U.S. science and engineering community is almost 1 million strong, which is twice the size of Germany's or Japan's comparable scientific storehouse. It is this trend that can keep the United States competitive in the future environment where markets and resources become increasingly difficult to achieve. It will, however, also require managers who understand and can deal with the requirements of these scientists, who do not think in the same manner as a factory worker (Bylinsky, 1990).

Strategic awareness has strikingly hit Americans in terms of U.S. economic losses on a global basis since the 1970s. The oil embargo in the early 1970s can be used as a benchmark that signifies the awakening of other nations to the power that they possessed in terms of their natural resources and their productive potential. On the average, U.S. productivity has only increased 1 percent per year since 1973 (Berger, 1987). By comparison, Korea has increased output per worker by 6 percent. Only Italy is lower than the United States in productivity.

The negative impact on the American people was double-digit inflation in addition to loss of the competitive edge in basic industries such as steel and automobiles. This in turn resulted in loss of jobs, a large negative balance of payments with other nations, and a major shift from the world's major producer nation to the leading consumer nation. For example, in 1986 imports of autos was 30 percent and was predicted to rise to 37 percent by 1990 (Port and Wilson, 1987).

At this point in time in the 1990s, the technological edge that was held by the United States is also shifting to other nations. The question has been raised whether the United States is going the way Great Britain has gone, with only a 1 percent average rise in GNP (Pennar, 1987). The question that emerges from this recent history is, Can America remake itself, can the United States reinvent its past? There is an urgency to this question that demands rapid, bold rethinking and action by American business if the balance of payments is to be brought closer to equilibrium. If such balance is not achieved, America may continue on its present course, drifting into second-class world status.

While these questions might seem out of place in a text on decision making for American business managers, they are at the core of the issue of how American business, and hence American society, will fare in the changing global economy. Just by traveling overseas, one sees the immediate impact on prices of the devalued dollar. Foreign travel by Americans is no longer a bargain.

Will American products be able to compete in the global economy on the basis of price and quality? For the first time in the late 1980s and the start of the 1990s, based on the devalued dollar, Japanese auto firms are manufacturing cars in the United States and are able to ship them from the United States to Japan.

## ▲ OVERVIEW OF THE BOOK

This book started with the discussion of the endangered spotted owl and the battle with the logging industry, which has to deal with the irreplaceable ancient forests. Unfortunately, this controversy threatens a way of life for the business of logging. The timber industry estimates that somewhere between 25,000 and 30,000 loggers will lose their jobs out of a total workforce of 170,000. However, the spotted owl does have friends. One of these is Harry Merlo from Louisiana Pacific. He espouses the use of a new product that is stronger than sheetrock, is more fire- and moisture-resistant, and can be made from gypsum and wood fiber reclaimed from recycled paper. This would mean there are no trees to be cut down or any spotted owls that will lose their homes (Beauchamp, 1990). Not only is the new product a savior of the environment, but it turns out to be 25 percent cheaper. At the same time, it has properties that are far more effective than conventional wood products currently used in structural paneling. Another approach to avoiding the problem of how to maintain the spotted owl and avoid cutting back the 100-year-old douglas firs is the approach specified by an article in *The Economist* titled "Messy Loggers Welcome" (1990). The foresters are attempting something different, which they call "new forestry." Instead of taking out all the undergrowth and leaving the ground bare for easier planting, they leave behind old standing trees, trunks, snags, debris, undergrowth, and fallen timber. Interestingly, this encourages genetic diversity at the same time that it fertilizes through decomposition the area from which the trees were cut down. New trees grow more readily and, most importantly, the spotted owl has been found to nest in the foliage and, thus, is no longer so endangered by the logging industry.

Perhaps the most significant change that the future portends is the shift away from the purely intuitive, heuristic, emotionally based decisions to a more rationalistic, behaviorally considered, well-understood decision process. The goal is not to substitute computers for the decision maker; the human being shows a creativity that still confounds us. Nonetheless, when we recognize that only 10 to 20 percent of an individual's capability is utilized in his or her work, we can see the potential for not only increased commitment to work, but also increased mental productivity when the decision maker is aided by appropriate tools. Decision making is complex. Any attempt to change this obvious truism will in most instances lead to poor results. Nonetheless, the mind cannot deal with unlimited complexity, so approaches are needed that can bring decision making into an appropriate focus—into a perspective that can be dealt with.

There is hardly an instance in which newer concepts are not increasingly replacing approaches previously used as the basis for decision making. The fact is that for a long time decision making was construed primarily as a choice from among alternatives without any recognition of how the decision was being made or how it would be carried out. This has given way to a decision process that helps predict the consequences of the choices.

Much of the material presented here has been concerned with looking at decision making as a central theme of effectiveness in an organization, with all the ramifications this premise entails. By providing an appropriate perspective, the manager of the future can have a basis for determining how to make better decisions. These problem-solving illustrations are designed to help combat difficult situations and make decisions more effective. Managers who avoid or simply ignore problems cannot be considered effective. Effective managers deal directly with the problem and use intuition and innovation to come up with solutions that can be implemented. It is to this end that this book has been written.

## ▲ ▲ ▲ ▲ ▲ IBM CASE

IBM has always been recognized as a forward-looking company. In 1991, IBM chairman John F. Akers, after six years as head of the world's largest computer maker, shows increasing signs of frustration at sagging revenues, declining profits, and customer defections and is described as being "mad as hell about it" (Lazzareschi, 1991). Part of the problem has been identified as the failure of managers who have risen through the ranks of large companies to perceive the need for change. Their inability to take the drastic steps necessary to maintain a competitive edge is another part of the problem.

Prior to the 1980s, it was inconceivable that IBM would ever face such a crisis. Increasing competition from the Japanese electronics giants and U.S. entrepreneurial ventures combined with a multitude of technological advances have fragmented the computer industry and gradually broken the control of IBM over the industry. According to Robert Reich, professor of government at Harvard University, "The single largest impediment to change in times of challenge is prior success." With a revenue growth from $23 billion in 1979 to $46 billion in 1984, the company may have developed a "can-do-no-wrong" attitude. IBM based its decisions on projections during the 1970s that sales would reach $100 billion by 1990 and it started to build its staff and operations to support those levels. However, revenues during 1990 were only $69 billion, far short of the projected $100 billion.

Akers long ago recognized that these projections, which he helped make as a member of the executive team in the 1970s, were far off target. But he has been unable to scale the company back and alter its comfortable, employee centered culture fast enough to avoid being repeatedly tripped up. At the same time, IBM's overall worldwide computer market share has slipped to about 23 percent in 1990 from 37 percent in 1983. Reshaping a huge corporation of 360,000 employees with a deeply ingrained culture is a difficult task. According to Harvard's Reich, "It's hard going from a big company managed from the top down to a group of entrepreneurial groups bound by lateral ties. A large culture resists that kind of reverse engineering. But that is what it's going to take to be as nimble as companies need to be to succeed in today's global economy."

Akers acknowledges responsibility of leadership. "It's not the people's fault, not the shareholders' fault. The problem belongs to those who manage the business."

Akers' frustration underscores the difficulty of managers who have risen from within the ranks of a huge company to change its course once they arrive at the top, management experts say. By the time they have climbed the ladder, these career managers are so much a part of their environment that they either fail to perceive the need for change or are unwilling to impose the drastic medicine required.

The question therefore remains, Can John Akers restore IBM to its prior luster? Although he says the company is at last facing up to the realities of the marketplace, one must still ask if IBM really learned what the customer wants, if it learned how to bring new products more quickly to the marketplace, and perhaps most importantly, if it learned how to deal with Japanese competition. ▲

## ▲ Study Questions

1. What factors can you see that will add to complexity for decision makers in the future?
2. What are some of the assumptions held by decision makers in the past that are no longer valid?
3. What are the three major areas that future leadership must recognize?
4. What did Ross Perot attempt to do at GM, and why did he fail?
5. What should be the focus of attention for the executive decision maker, according to Zaleznick?
6. Where is the new megamarket expected to emerge?
7. What decision technologies can be expected in the future?

## ▲ References

Argyris, Chris. "How Tomorrow's Executives Will Make Decisions." *Think* (November–December 1967).

Beauchamp, Marc. "Friend of the Spotted Owl." *Forbes* (April 30, 1990), pp. 144–148.

Bennis, Warren. "Leadership: A Beleaguered Species." *Organizational Dynamics* Vol. 5, No. 1 (1976), pp. 3–16.

Bennis, Warren, and Nanus, Burt. *Leaders*. New York: Harper & Row, 1985, pp. 6–15, 212–213.

Berger, John. "Productivity: Why it's the No. 1 Underachiever." *Business Week* (April 20, 1987), pp. 54–55.

Blake, R. P., and Mouton, J. S. *The Managerial Grid*. Houston, TX: Gulf Publications, 1985.

Bowers, David G., and Seashore, Stanley L. "Predicting Organizational Effectiveness with a Four Factor Theory of Leadership." *Administrative Science Quarterly* (September 1966), pp. 238–63.

Bylinsky, Gene. "American's Hot Young Scientists." *Fortune* (October 8, 1990), pp. 56–69.

"Changing a Corporate Culture." *Business Week* (May 14, 1984), pp. 130–138.

Clifford, D. K., Bridgewater, B. A., and Hardy, T. "The Game Has Changed." *The McKinsey Quarterly* (Autumn 1975).

Dessler, Gary. *Organization and Management*. Englewood Cliffs, NJ: Prentice-Hall, 1978, pp. 172–173.

Doyle, Denis P., and Hartle, Terry W. "Superior Education Gives Japan the World Trade Edge." *Los Angeles Times* (October 7, 1985).

Drucker, Peter. "The Coming of the New Organization." *Harvard Business Review* (January–February 1988), p. 45.

Edid, Maralyn, Treece, James B., and Weiner, Elizabeth. "Why Mazda Is Settling in the Heart of Union Territory." *Business Week* (September 9, 1985), pp. 94–95.

Fiedler, Fred E. *A Theory of Leadership Effectiveness*. New York: McGraw-Hill, 1967.

Filley, Alan C., House, Robert J., and Kerr, Steven. *Managerial Process and Organizational Behavior*. Glenview, IL: Scott Foresman & Co., 1975.

Forgionne, Guisseppi A. "OR/MS and Decision Technology in the 1990s." *OR/MS Today* (June 1990), pp. 20–21.

Gergen, David. "People Are Everybody's Business." *U. S. News & World Report* (May 21, 1990), p. 54.

Halpin, A. W., and Winer, B. J. "A Factorial Study of Leader Behavior Descriptions." In Stogdill, R. M., and Coons, A. E., "Leader Behavior: Its Descriptions and Measurements." Columbus, OH: Ohio State University, Bureau of Business Research, 1957.

Hersey, Paul, and Blanchard, Kenneth H. *Management of Organizational Behavior.* Englewood Cliffs, NJ: Prentice Hall, 1972.

Hickman, Craig R. *Mind of a Manager, Soul of a Leader.* New York: Wiley, 1990.

Hoerr, John, Pollock, Michael and Whiteside, David. "Management Discovers the Human Side of Automation." *Business Week* (September 29, 1986), pp. 70–79.

House, Robert J., and Mitchell, Terence R. "Path-Goal Theory of Leadership." *Journal of Contemporary Business* (Autumn 1974), p. 86.

Jameson, Sam. "Asia an Emerging Center of World Commerce." *Los Angeles Times* (February 17, 1991).

Jameson, Sam. "U. S. Trainees Praise Toyota System." *Los Angles Times* (June 19, 1984), p. B1.

Lazzareschi, Carla. "Chairman Faces Immense Task in Reshaping IBM." *Los Angeles Times* (February 12, 1991).

Main, Jeremy. "Wanted: Leaders Who Can Make a Difference." *Fortune* (September 28, 1987).

Main, Jeremy. "The Winning Organization." *Fortune* (September 26, 1988), pp. 50–60.

"Messy Loggers Welcome." *Economist* (September 1, 1990), p. 25.

Moore, Peter D. "Networks that Mimic Thinking." *Los Angeles Times* (August 29, 1990).

Mott, P. E. *The Characteristics of Effective Organizations.* New York: Harper & Row, 1972.

Nakarmi, Laxmi. "At Daewoo, a 'Revolution' at the Top." *Business Week* (February 18, 1991), pp. 68–69.

Nakarmi, Laxmi. "At Lucky-Goldstar, the Koos Loosen the Reins." *Business Week* (February 18, 1991), pp. 72–73.

Paltrow, Scot. "Buyout Hits the Bull's-Eye at Colt's." *Los Angeles Times* (April 14, 1991).

Pennar, Karen. "Is the U. S. Going the Way of Britain?" *Business Week* (April 20, 1987), pp. 64–66.

Perot, Ross. "How I Would Turn Around G. M." *Fortune* (February 15, 1988), pp. 44–49.

Peters, Tom J., and Waterman, Robert H., Jr. *In Search of Excellence.* New York: Harper & Row, 1982.

Port, Otis, and Wilson, John W. "Making Brawn Work with Brains." *Business Week* (April 20, 1987), pp. 56–60.

Porter, L. W., Lawler, E. E., and Hackman, R. *Behaviors in Organizations.* New York: McGraw-Hill, 1975, p. 433.

Reddin, William J. *Managerial Effectiveness.* New York: McGraw-Hill, 1970, p. 12–13.

Rice, Faye. "Champions of Communication." *Fortune* (June 3, 1991), pp. 111–120.

Skrzycki, Cindy. "Corporate America Learns to Listen to Workers." *Los Angeles Times* (August 10, 1989).

Stavro, Barry. "State's Two Car Plants—Study in Sharp Contrasts." *Los Angeles Times* (January 28, 1990), p. D1.

Stogdill, Ralph. *Handbook of Leadership.* New York: Free Press, 1974, p. 386.

Tannenbaum, R., and Schmidt. W. H. "How to Choose a Leadership Pattern." *Harvard Business Review* (May–June 1973), pp. 162–180.

Taylor, Alex III. "Tomorrow's Chief Executives." *Fortune* (May 9, 1988), pp. 30–40.

Vogel, Todd. "Where 1990s Style Management Is Already Hard at Work." *Business Week* (October 23, 1989), pp. 92–100.

Vroom, V. H., and Yetton, P. *Leadership and Decision-Making*. Pittsburgh, PA: University of Pittsburgh Press, 1973.

Worthy, Ford S. "You Can't Grow If You Can't Manage." *Fortune* (June 3, 1991), pp. 83–88.

Zaleznick, A. "Managers and Leaders: Are They Different." *Harvard Business Review* (1977).

Zaleznick, Abraham. "Power and Politics in Organizational Life." *Harvard Business Review* (May–June 1970).

# NAME INDEX

▲ ▲ ▲ ▲ ▲ ▲ ▲ ▲ ▲ ▲ ▲ ▲ ▲ ▲ ▲ ▲ ▲ ▲ ▲ ▲ ▲ ▲ ▲

# SUBJECT INDEX

▲ ▲ ▲ ▲ ▲ ▲ ▲ ▲ ▲ ▲ ▲ ▲ ▲ ▲ ▲ ▲ ▲ ▲ ▲ ▲ ▲ ▲ ▲ ▲

**249**